THE Graduate student's COMPLETE SCHOLARSHIP BOOK

Student Services, L.L.C.

 Sourcebooks, Inc.

Naperville, IL

Published by: **Sourcebooks, Inc.**
P.O. Box 372, Naperville, Illinois 60566
(630) 961-3900
FAX: 630-961-2168

This publication is designed to provide accurate and authoritative information in regard to the subject matter covered. It is sold with the understanding that the publisher is not engaged in rendering legal, accounting, or other professional service. If legal advice or other expert assistance is required, the services of a competent professional person should be sought.

From a Declaration of Principles Jointly Adopted by a Committee of the American Bar Association and a Committee of Publishers and Associations

Every effort has been made to provide you with the best, most up-to-date information on private sector financial aid. However, if you discover an award in this book is listed incorrectly, please contact our research department by mail at: Research Department, Student Services, L.L.C., 2550 Commonwealth Avenue, North Chicago, IL 60064.

Disclaimer

Care has been taken in collecting and presenting the material contained in this book; however, Student Services, L.L.C., and Sourcebooks, Inc., do not guarantee its accuracy.

Student Services, L.L.C., and Sourcebooks, Inc., are private corporations and are not affiliated in any way with the U.S. Department of Education or any other government agency.

Library of Congress Cataloging-in-Publication Data
The graduate student's complete scholarship book/ Student Services, L.L.C.
        p.   cm.
   Includes index.
   ISBN 1-57071-195-X
   1. Scholarships—United States—Directories.   2. Graduate students—Scholarships, fellowships, etc.—United States—Directories.   3. Student Aid—United States.   I. Student Services, L.L.C.
LB2338.G685   1998
378.3'4—dc21   97-32077
                                                                         CIP

Printed and bound in the United States of America.

Paperback — 10 9 8 7 6 5 4 3 2 1

Read This First

Congratulations! You hold in your hands one of the most thoroughly researched publications ever produced on the subject of non-government financial aid for graduate and professional students. Financial aid from non-government organizations is provided by philanthropic foundations, corporations, employers, professional societies and associations, clubs, religious organizations, and civic service groups. This book lists more than eleven hundred sources of college financial aid, representing over twenty-seven thousand college scholarships, fellowships, grants, and low-interest loans from private organizations.

That range of financial aid possibilities is important to students because graduate school can be expensive, with annual fees running anywhere from $4,000 at a public university to $20,000 or more at a private institution. Those figures may sound intimidating, but remember that you are making an investment in your future—and that a careful, thorough search can turn up sources of aid that will go a long way in helping you make that investment.

Eligibility Requirements

Many students think that college financial aid is for someone else—that they are not "poor enough" or "smart enough" to receive aid. In reality, however, financial aid for graduate school is awarded for many different reasons, to many different kinds of people. In fact, eligibility for private aid can be based on a variety of criteria, including:

➤ career objectives;
➤ gender;
➤ disabilities;
➤ financial need;
➤ academic performance;
➤ participation in the military;
➤ race and heritage;
➤ religious affiliation;
➤ the state in which you are a resident;
➤ membership in clubs and associations;
➤ upcoming school year (graduate, doctorate, post-doctorate);
➤ work experience.

Many graduate students rely on awards given to support research in certain areas. For example, you can find money that is designed to help graduate students explore everything from healthcare, psychology, and economics to history, aviation, numismatics, orchids, and large game animals.

In short, financial aid for graduate school encompasses a wide range of students and subjects. It is up to you to understand your own needs, interests, and strengths, and then to match them with the right sources of financial aid.

Types of Assistance

Financial aid for graduate school and professional degrees is offered in three basic forms:

➤ grants and scholarships (grants are usually given to a student in order to fund graduate research)
➤ assistantships and internships, in which the student performs a service in return for aid;
➤ loans designed especially for students.

Grants and scholarships, sometimes referred to as gift assistance, do not have to be repaid.

Assistantships and other service-related awards are paid to the student in return for research or work performed according to the guidelines set forth by the sponsor of the award.

Student loans must be repaid. Generally, these loans feature favorable rates of interest and/or deferred payment options.

Where the Money Comes From

Much of the money that's available to graduate students comes from the federal government. The government provides this aid through a number of agencies, including the Department of Education, NASA, and the Department of Energy. Some aid is channeled directly through a government agency, and some through Financial Aid Offices.

Most federal aid to graduate students is offered in the form of loans, although some grants and other service-related funding is available. Although graduate students are not eligible for the well-known undergraduate Federal Pell Grants or Federal Supplemental Educational Opportunity Grants, they are eligible for:

➤ specialized scholarships and grants, such as the Patricia Roberts Harris and National Science Foundation fellowships;
➤ Federal Work-Study aid, which provides employment opportunities for students;
➤ loan programs, such as Federal Stafford Loans, Federal Direct Loans, and Federal Perkins Loans.

The first step in applying for federal programs is usually to submit a Free Application for Federal Student Aid (FAFSA) form (or a Renewal FAFSA, if applicable).

Millions of dollars in aid are also provided through many (but not all) state governments. The programs vary from state to state; many are targeted at minorities, women, or special fields of study, such as medicine or education. To qualify, you usually have to be a resident of the state and attend a college in the state.

Another source of money is the college or university itself. Schools typically offer aid in the form of departmental fellowships and grants and teaching and research assistantships.

Finally, there are the private-sector sources of aid—the foundations, religious organizations, employers, clubs, local governments, individuals, and corporations that offer millions of dollars a year in service-related awards, loan programs, and grants to graduate students. Most of the sources of such private sector funding are listed in this book. However, do not rely just on the opportunities listed here. It is always wise to pursue several options, including federal and state-sponsored programs.

How to Request Applications for College Financial Aid from Private Donors

To save time and effort, we suggest that you use a standard form letter when requesting applications and additional information from private donors. Here is a standard form letter that works well:

<Date>

<Contact Name at Donor Organization>
<Name of Donor Organization>
<Donor's Street Address>
<Donor's City, State Zip>

Dear Sir or Madam:

Please forward an application and any additional information concerning your financial aid program for post-secondary education.

Sincerely,

<Your Name>
<Your Address>
<Your City, State Zip>

Be sure to enclose a self-addressed, stamped envelope with your form letter.

How to Use This Book

This book lists over eleven hundred different sources of financial aid from private organizations for graduate, professional, and post-graduate studies. Many donors target their money toward specific fields and areas of study, often based on skills, research, and personal background.

To help you quickly and easily find the awards that are most appropriate to you, *The Graduate Student's Complete Scholarship Book* provides you with two ways to find your most likely private sector donors:

➤ Extensive indexes at the end of the book, identifying awards available by school, major, or career objective, ethnic background, gender, religion, marital status, military background of you or your parents, disability, and intercollegiate athletics.

➤ An icon system that allows you to scan the sources quickly.

The Icon System

The icons in this book will allow you to visually identify scholarships that may be appropriate for you based on majors and special criteria.

Majors/Career Objective

College majors have been grouped into nine categories to guide you to general fields of study. The following list includes the most common majors within each category and the icon that will identify them.

Business
Accounting
Advertising/Public Relations
Banking/Finance/Insurance
Business Administration
Economics
Human Resources
Management
Marketing
Sales
Transportation

Education

Childhood Development
Early Childhood Education
Education (General)
Education Administration
Elementary Education
Middle-Level Education
Post-Secondary Education

Engineering

Aerospace Engineering
Architecture
Aviation
Civil Engineering/Construction
Computer Science
Engineering (General)
Material Science
Surveying/Cartography
Telecommunications

Fine Arts

Art
Filmmaking
Fine Arts (General)
Graphic Design
Music (General)
Performing Arts
Photography

Humanities

Broadcasting/Communications
Classical Studies
English/Literature
Foreign Languages
Humanities (General)
Journalism
Library/Information Sciences
Philosophy
Religion

Medicine

Dentistry
Healthcare Management
Medicine/Medical (General)
Nursing
Pharmacy/Pharmacology/Pharmaceutical
Public Health
Therapy (General)
Veterinary Medicine

Science

Agriculture
Animal Science
Biology
Chemistry
Ecology/Environmental Science
Energy-Related Studies
Geology
Land Management/Design
Marine Sciences
Mathematics
Meteorology
Physics
Science (General)

Social Sciences

Anthropology
Archaeology
Ethnic Studies
Foreign Studies
Geography
Government
History
International Relations
Law
Military Science
Political Science
Psychology
Social Sciences (General)
Sociology
Women's Studies

Vocational

Automotive
Court Reporting
Data Processing
Food Services
Funeral Services
Heating/Plumbing/Cooling Industry
Hotel/Motel Management/Administration
Manufacturing
Real Estate
Textiles
Travel and Tourism
Vocational (General)

Special Criteria

The following categories are the most common criteria on which private sector scholarship awards are based. Look for these icons to help find awards for which you may qualify.

Athletics

Almost all athletic scholarships are talent-based. Primarily, these scholarships will only be appropriate for you if you plan to compete at the intercollegiate level or major in physical education.

Disability

Many scholarships are available to individuals who are challenged with a mental or physical disability. Awards marked with this icon include those for the blind, hearing impaired, learning disabled, and physically challenged, in addition to several other disabilities.

Ethnic

This category includes scholarships awarded based on race and heritage. The most common are for African-American, Asian-American, Hispanic, and Native American students, but the range of available awards is truly global and can get very specific. Consider your family background, and be sure to check with the scholarship provider if you are not sure whether you fit its requirements.

Grade Point Average (GPA)

Three cutoffs have been established for the GPA icons—at 2.5+, 3.0+, and 3.5+. Some scholarships' actual requirements may be somewhere between these numbers, so be sure to read the complete listing for the exact GPA criteria.

Military

Scholarships marked with this icon most often require that either you or one of your parents serve or served in the armed forces. Many of these awards are available to veterans or children of veterans of particular military actions or branches of the service. Also, many scholarships are for students whose parents were disabled or killed in military action. Items marked with this icon may also denote a major in military science or a related field.

Religion

Religious groups and organizations offer scholarships to students who are involved in religious or church-related activities, attending or coming from a religious school, or are interested in professional religious study.

Women

This icon identifies scholarships that are available to women only. Please note that many other scholarships are not for women only, but will often give preference to women.

Reading the Listings

Each scholarship listing includes the following information:

- ➤ Scholarship name
- ➤ Dollar amount of the available award or awards
- ➤ Deadline for submission of application materials
- ➤ Fields/Majors of intended study
- ➤ Further information you may need in order to apply
- ➤ The award sponsor's address to write for application forms and additional information

Identifying the Icons

Major/Career Objective

Business

Education

Engineering

Fine Arts

Humanities

Medicine

Science

Social Sciences

Vocational

Special Criteria

Athletics

Disability

Ethnic

Military

Religion

Women

GPA 2.5+

GPA 3.0+

GPA 3.5+

Powerful Cash-for-College Tips That You Should Know

Tip 1. Learn All You Can about the College Financial Aid Process

Graduate school represents a significant investment, but many students stumble confused through the financial aid process—and therefore miss key opportunities. Don't be one of those students; you can gain a tremendous advantage by taking time to learn thoroughly about college financial aid. Such knowledge can help you to understand and weigh all your options; avoid missing deadlines; and, ultimately, position yourself to get a better financial aid package. Good sources of information include:

➤ the financial aid office at your college;
➤ financial planners, if they are reputable and specialize in college financing;
➤ the Federal Student Aid Information Center at 1-800-4-FED-AID, for information on eligibility for federal aid, the process used to determine award amounts, and which schools participate in federal aid programs;
➤ Web sites. However, be aware that the accuracy and timeliness of web-based information varies widely. An especially good Internet site is Fastweb, at http://www.fastweb.com, which contains up-to-date information on private and government sources of financial aid, as well as pointers to other helpful financial aid sites.

Tip 2. Submit a FAFSA[1], Even if You Do Not Think You Will Be Eligible for Federal Financial Aid

To be considered for federal financial aid, you must submit a FAFSA form. Even if you think you will not be eligible for federal assistance, submit a FAFSA anyway. This is important for four reasons:

1. You might be pleasantly surprised by the results; many middle-class students are eligible for federal financial aid (typically, loans with favorable interest rates and payment-deferment options).
2. Even if you do not qualify for federal loans with deferred-payment options, you might still qualify for loans with favorable interest rates.

3. Submitting a FAFSA is often a prerequisite for many non-federal financial aid programs.
4. Being rejected for financial aid from the government is sometimes a pre-condition for private sector awards.

Tip 3. To Pursue Research Grants and Fellowships, Find Out What Worked Before

Research grants usually require you to write a proposal, and fellowships usually require an essay. Try to find samples of previous winning proposals and essays. Often, graduate students are willing to share their accepted proposals with others.

Tip 4. Don't Be Intimidated by Writing Grant Proposals

Writing a research grant proposal can seem like a frightening proposition. But if you find a potential grant that fits your interests, it is worth the effort to apply, for two reasons. First, if you do not try, you will certainly not be awarded the grant. Second, if you try and your grant proposal is rejected, you might learn something. That is because research grant rejections often include specific feedback about why the proposal was turned down—and that feedback can help you polish your proposal for your next effort.

Tip 5. Exploit Your Age

If you are not going directly from undergraduate to graduate school, look for programs that target "returning" students. For example, the Association for Women Geoscientists Foundation awards $750 Chrysalis Scholarships to women who are candidates for an advanced degree in a geoscience field and have had their education interrupted for at least one year. Or, the Business and Professional Women's Foundation awards Wyeth-Ayerst Scholarships to women twenty-five years old or older who are within twenty-four months of completing an accredited course of study that will lead to entry or advancement in the workforce.

Also, some graduate programs provide credit for the older student's "life experience"—that is, learning that has taken place outside of school.

---

[1] A 'FAFSA' is a 'Free Application for Federal Student Aid'

Tip 6. Consider Working for a Year or Two Between Undergraduate and Graduate School

Working full-time for a year or two after earning an undergraduate degree gives you a chance to pay off loans and save up for graduate school. If the job is in a field related to your intended area of graduate study, the experience may help you get into the program you want and open the door to additional aid. However, in the sciences and some other fields, such a delay may make you less desirable, because your undergraduate knowledge may be regarded as somewhat outdated. So before you decide to take some time off from school, check with the program you are interested in and with school counselors to make sure you are making the right move.

Tip 7. Investigate Financial Aid from Your Company

If you are already employed, your employer may subsidize the cost of graduate school. In some cases, the employer will grant a leave of absence so you can attend college full-time. More often, however, employers prefer participants to attend part-time while maintaining a full-time schedule at work. As long as you like the employer and the job, this company-sponsored aid can be a great deal. You get financial help and 'guaranteed' employment upon graduation, and you open up opportunities for career advancement with your higher degree.

Tip 8. Find Out Whether Your Parents' Employer(s) Offer College Scholarships

Many big corporations offer scholarships and tuition reimbursement programs to children of employees. Refer questions about availability and eligibility requirements to the human resources department at your parents' employer(s).

Tip 9. Consider Attending Graduate School Part-Time

Many people attend graduate school on a part-time basis. The advantage, of course, is that you may be able to finance your education by maintaining a well-paying job while you are in school. The downside is that it will take you longer to complete your studies when you attend only part-time. Therefore, if your degree will be one that will increase your salary potential, you will be delaying those increased earnings. Weigh lost future earnings against the extension of tuition payments involved in going part-time.

Tip 10. If Applicable, Use Your Heritage and Background to Your Advantage

Many college scholarships provided by the private sector are based to some degree on race, heritage, religion, or gender. In fact, women and minorities have an advantage in the search for financial aid, because they can apply for all general scholarships, as well as the scholarships designed for people within specific groups.

Even if just one of your parents or grandparents was a member of a 'minority' group, this might improve your financial aid package.

In terms of scholarships, most of us belong to a minority group in some way. There are, of course, awards for African-Americans, Hispanics, and Native Americans. But there are also awards for Pacific Islanders, Presbyterians, people with hearing problems, etc.

Tip 11. Consider Staying Home

A growing number of schools allow you to earn academic credit through "distance learning"—that is, via computer network, television, and video tapes. In addition, many offer evening classes at satellite facilities that may be located near your home. These approaches can allow you to keep working while earning credit, avoid the expense of moving to another locale, and often, learn at your own pace.

Tip 12. Satisfy Prerequisites at Less Expensive Community Colleges

Some graduate programs and certifications may require prerequisites that were not completed during undergraduate studies. For instance, if a drama student with a B.A. is interested in pursuing a graduate degree in education, he or she may not have taken enough undergraduate math and science courses to receive a state teaching certificate. Often, these prerequisites can be satisfied by taking equivalent courses at an accredited two-year college. This is often a more economical option than taking the course at the more expensive graduate degree school.

Tip 13. Do Not Absorb More Debt Than You Can Handle

To put debt in perspective, suppose that after finishing graduate school you could afford to pay a maximum of $250 a month towards a total of $20,000 in loans with an average interest rate of 10 percent. Paying off that debt would take more than ten years!

A high debt burden can take a staggering toll on the quality of your life. During the time that every cent is diverted to paying back college loans, you may have to forgo: buying a car, saving for a house, going on vacation, and perhaps even starting a family. Be especially wary of building up too much debt on high-interest credit cards.

Tip 14. Do Not Be *Unduly* Afraid of Debt

Recent government statistics show that more than two-thirds of graduate school students end up carrying some debt—on average, about $8,000 for public university students. Think of the money you spend on graduate school as an investment in future higher earnings, and invest an amount that is justified by the eventual payoff.

Tip 15. Create a Financial Plan

Often, students head into graduate school with only a sketchy game plan: Get accepted, beg or borrow to pay for your education, and when you're finished, do whatever you have to do to pay off debts. Instead of "flying by the seat of your pants," create a financial plan. That means mapping out your approximate financial picture for the next ten or fifteen years—projecting graduate school costs and aid, future income, inflation, payments, and so on. This will help you to:

➤ avoid taking on too much debt;
➤ determine if earning a graduate degree will be worth the sacrifices;
➤ make any necessary adjustments to your lifestyle early on, when these adjustments will have a greater effect and not impact future dependents, if any.

Creating a financial plan may also help you realize that you can actually afford to do more than you thought.

Tip 16. Try to Establish Residency in the State Where You Will Attend College

Publicly-funded colleges charge in-state students substantially less tuition than they charge out-of-state students for identical educational programs.

If you plan to attend a public graduate school, an easy way to save several thousand dollars is to attend a public college that is located in the state where you have already satisfied residency requirements.

Alternatively, if you have strong reasons to attend an out-of-state graduate school, you can try to establish new state residency, wherever the college you attend happens to be located.

Guidelines for establishing residency vary, so check with each of the schools that interest you. Generally, some of the factors considered include:

➤ Do you and/or your parents own property in the state?
➤ Have you and/or your parents lived primarily in that state during the previous two years?
➤ Do you possess a driver's license in the state?
➤ Did you earn a significant portion of your income in the state in the year prior to attending college?
➤ Did you file an income tax return for that state?

Tip 17. Be on Time and Accurate

Deadlines for applying for graduate school aid are usually very strict. Generally, an application that is even one day late won't be considered. The race for graduate school money is very competitive, and these deadlines provide a first cut at narrowing the field.

Tip 18. Ensure that 'Cost of Attendance' Calculations Accurately Reflect Your Circumstances

The federal government and universities consider 'Cost of Attendance' as a component in determining your financial need. Cost of Attendance includes not only tuition and fees, but also other costs associated with going to school. Ensure that your Financial Aid Administrator(s) includes all reasonable costs in your Cost of Attendance calculation and that he or she knows about any unusual costs you may incur. For instance:

➤ If you have to travel far from your residence to the school, you may be able to include those costs.

➤ If you have a disability, you may be able to include costs for necessities such as Telecommunications Devices for the Deaf (TDDs) or reading services.

➤ If you have children, you may be able to include childcare expenses.

Tip 19. Encourage Your Professor(s) to Convert Poor Grades into an Assessment Marked 'Incomplete'

Some grants and scholarships require certain minimum grade point averages. A poor grade will lower your GPA. An 'incomplete' grade, however, will not be factored into your GPA, and thus will have the effect of artificially 'raising' your average. Therefore, if your GPA is dangerously close to disqualifying you from an award, then try to encourage your professor to change your worst grade into an assessment marked 'incomplete'.

'Incomplete' means that you will receive a final grade at some point in the future, after you have had an opportunity to submit additional material to your professor(s) for evaluation.

Tip 20. Consider Joining the Military

Ignore this idea if you dislike hierarchy, rebel against authority, or conscientiously object to the activities of the military. However, if you would consider it an honor to serve your country as a member of the armed services, the military can be a tremendous source of college financial aid.

The U.S. armed forces provide several options that help students defray or eliminate their college costs. While you are in the military, the government may forgive portions of your undergraduate student loans, pay for off-duty courses you take at a civilian college, and even pay up to your entire tuition in return for subsequent service upon graduation.

When you are honorably discharged, you are eligible for Veterans Education Benefits, such as the Montgomery GI Bill and the Post Vietnam Era Veterans Educational Assistance Program. In both of these programs, you accept a monthly deduction in your military pay, and then later get a substantially higher monthly payment while you are in school.

These veterans' programs apply to graduate school, and they are not needs-based; they are based on the fact that you earned the aid.

Tip 21. Stay in Touch

Keep in close contact with your Financial Aid Office. The financial aid picture changes from time to time—especially federal and state aid, which is subject to congressional action and shifts in the political climate.

It is also important to let the Financial Aid Office know about changes in your personal situation that may effect your financial status—changes such as increased medical costs or the birth of a child. If the office is aware of such changes, they may be able to make adjustments or find other sources of aid. Also, for short-term problems, many universities maintain an emergency financial aid fund.

In Summary...

Many students have the erroneous belief that they are not eligible for financial aid for graduate school. In reality, however, the only students who are disqualified from the start are those who do nothing about finding aid. It sounds simple, but many students forget that you cannot receive financial aid for any of the awards in this book if you do not apply. A great number of students dip into the financial aid process without following up. Perhaps they feel overwhelmed by the process or simply lose interest. Whatever the reason, their loss can be your gain.

Admittedly, seeking financial aid can be daunting and time-consuming, but it is not impossible. Every year, thousands of students much like you search for and win financial awards to help them through graduate school. Be an informed, educated, and assertive consumer of higher education services and resources. Do not leave your financial aid eligibility to chance. Conduct research on as many resources as possible. Read and understand your rights, responsibilities, and opportunities. Be persistent in talking to all the people who could either help you or direct you to the right resources for help—counselors, professors, members of local, civic, women's, and minority organizations—and, of course, your Financial Aid Administrator.

In short, it will take some work—but the effort will be worth it. The money that you find for graduate school will lighten your financial burden and help you increase your earning potential. But more importantly, it will also open doors to experiences and knowledge that can enrich your life intellectually and socially for decades to come.

Awards

1

A. David Nichols Memorial Scholarship

AMOUNT: None Specified **DEADLINE:** February 1
FIELDS/MAJORS: Law

Awards for upper-class law students. Must demonstrate financial need and academic merit. Contact the Assistant Dean, Chase College of Law, for further information.

Northern Kentucky University
Chase College of Law
Office of Admissions
Highland Heights, KY   41099

2

A.E. Clark Memorial Graduate Scholarship

AMOUNT: $500 **DEADLINE:** None Specified
FIELDS/MAJORS: Education

Scholarships are available at the University of Oklahoma, Norman for full-time Ph.D. candidates in education at the dissertation stage. Must demonstrate financial need and academic promise. One award offered annually. Write to the address below for information.

University of Oklahoma, Norman
College of Education
Room 105, ECH
Norman, OK   73019

3

A.F.U.D. Research Scholar Program, Medical Student Fellowship

AMOUNT: None Specified **DEADLINE:** September 1
FIELDS/MAJORS: Urology, Medical Research

Fellowships, awards, and research grants for medical students, researchers, and clinicians in urology and urologic diseases. Renewable. Write to the A.F.U.D. at the address below for details.

American Foundation for Urologic Disease, Inc.
Research Scholar Program
300 West Pratt Street, Suite 401
Baltimore, MD   21201

4

AAAS Fellowships

AMOUNT: None Specified
DEADLINE: January 15
FIELDS/MAJORS: Science, Engineering, Arms Control, International Security

Fellowships are available for outstanding scientists and engineers to support work on critical arms control or national security issues with an appropriate federal agency, congressional committee, or nonprofit agency in Washington, D.C. Must be a U.S. citizen and have a Ph.D. Write to the address below for information.

American Association for the Advancement of Science
Fellowship Program
1333 H Street NW
Washington, DC   20005

5

AACP-AFPE First Year Graduate Scholarship Program

AMOUNT: $5000 **DEADLINE:** May 1
FIELDS/MAJORS: Pharmacy, Pharmacology

Scholarships for students in a pharmacy college. Created to encourage students to pursue Ph.D. degree after undergraduate studies. Must be a participant in the AACP undergraduate research participation program for minorities or the Merck Undergraduate Research Scholar Program. For U.S. citizens or permanent residents. Information may be available in your school or department of pharmacy. If not, write to the address below.

American Foundation for Pharmaceutical Education
One Church Street
Suite 202
Rockville, MD   20850

6

AAS Short-Term Fellowships

AMOUNT: $950–$2850
DEADLINE: None Specified
FIELDS/MAJORS: American History, History of Publishing, 18th Century Studies, Etc.

One- to three-month fellowships in support of research utilizing the collections of the American Antiquarian Society. The AAS has extensive holdings of published materials (books, pamphlets, almanacs, etc.) from Antebellum America. Joint application with the Newberry Library (in Chicago) is encouraged. Write to the society at the address below for further information. Please specify the award name when writing.

American Antiquarian Society
Director of Research and Publication
185 Salisbury Street, Room 100
Worcester, MA   01609

7

AASA-Convention Exhibitors Scholarship

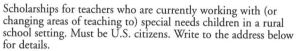

AMOUNT: $2000   DEADLINE: September 1
FIELDS/MAJORS: School Administration

Scholarships to encourage graduate students to prepare for careers in school administration. For graduate students enrolled in a school administration program at an accredited institution. Six awards per year. To express your interest to be considered as a candidate, check with the office of the dean of education at your school.

American Association of School Administrators
1801 N. Moore Street
Arlington, VA   22209

8

AAUW Grants

AMOUNT: $1000   DEADLINE: May 15
FIELDS/MAJORS: All Areas of Study

Scholarships for female graduate students from the Norwalk-Westport area or for women (in the same area) who are furthering their education or who are changing careers. Must be a resident of Norwalk, Westport, Wilton, Weston, or Darien. One award is offered annually. Please enclose a legal-sized SASE with your request for an application. Write to Willadean Hart, Chair, at the address below.

American Association of University Women,
   Norwalk-Westport Branch
Chair, Student Grant Committee
36 Colony Road
Westport, CT   06880

9

Abel Wolman Doctoral Fellowship

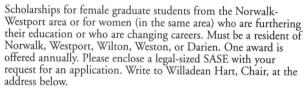

AMOUNT: $20000   DEADLINE: January 15
FIELDS/MAJORS: Water Supply and Treatment

Fellowships are available to encourage promising students to pursue advanced training and research in the field of water supply and treatment. Applicants must anticipate completing the requirements for a Ph.D. within two years of the award and be a citizen or permanent resident of the U.S., Canada, or Mexico. Write to the address below for more information.

American Water Works Association
Fellowship Coordinator
6666 W. Quincy Avenue
Denver, CO   80235

10

Abigail Associates Research Grants

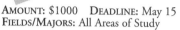

AMOUNT: $1000–$3000   DEADLINE: April 17
FIELDS/MAJORS: Women's Studies

Awards are available at from the College of St. Catherine for preparation and presentation of publishable quality research in women's studies.Grants are awarded in two categories: contribution of women from the Catholic tradition to public policy and/or services, and self-esteem among women and girls.
For female researchers. Does not require residency at the center. Write to Sharon Doherty at the address below for information.

College of St. Catherine
Abigail Quigley McCarthy Center
2004 Randolph Avenue
St. Paul, MN   55105

11

Acres Scholarships

AMOUNT: $500   DEADLINE: December 10
FIELDS/MAJORS: Special Education

Scholarships for teachers who are currently working with (or changing areas of teaching to) special needs children in a rural school setting. Must be U.S. citizens. Write to the address below for details.

American Council on Rural Special Education
Department of Special Education
221 Milton Bennion Hall, Univ. of Utah
Salt Lake City, UT   84112

12

Adelaide Fortune Holderness Fellowship

AMOUNT: $5000
DEADLINE: None Specified
FIELDS/MAJORS: Art, Musical Arts, Human Development

Award for master's candidate in art and doctoral candidate in musical arts or human development and family studies. Contact the address below for further information.

University of North Carolina, Greensboro
Financial Aid Office
723 Kenilworth Street
Greensboro, NC   27412

13

Adeline Fortune Holderness Fellowship

AMOUNT: $5000
DEADLINE: None Specified
FIELDS/MAJORS: Art, Music, Child Development, Family Studies

Award open to master's candidates in art and doctoral candidates in musical arts or human development/family studies. Contact the address below for further information.

University of North Carolina, Greensboro
Financial Aid Office
723 Kenilworth Street
Greensboro, NC   27412

14

Adelle and Erwin Tomash Fellowship in History of Information Processing

AMOUNT: Maximum: $12000   DEADLINE: January 15
FIELDS/MAJORS: Computer Science, History of Technology

Fellowships, to be carried out at any appropriate research facility, into the history of computers and information processing. Research may be into the technical, social, legal, or business aspects of information processing. Preference is given for dissertation research, but all doctoral students are invited to apply. Two one-year continuations are permitted. Write to the Institute at the address below for details.

Charles Babbage Institute, University of Minnesota
103 Walter Library
117 Pleasant Street, SE
Minneapolis, MN   55455

15

Adrian Berryhill Family Agricultural Scholarship

AMOUNT: $1000   DEADLINE: March 1
FIELDS/MAJORS: Animal Science and Range Science

Two $1000 scholarships awarded annually to upperclassmen, one in animal science and one in range science. Must be New Mexico residents (preferably from New Mexico ranching families). Write to the address below for details.

New Mexico State University
College of Agriculture and Home Economics
Box 30001, Box 3AG
Las Cruces, NM   88003

16
Advanced Nursing Practice Scholarship

AMOUNT: Maximum: $2500   DEADLINE: September 1
FIELDS/MAJORS: Nursing

Open to nurses pursuing an advanced clinical practice degree to become a nurse practitioner or clinical nurse specialist. Write to the address below for more information.

Emergency Nurses Association (ENA) Foundation Funding
   Program
216 Higgins Road
Park Ridge, IL   60068

17
Advanced Opportunity Fellowships

AMOUNT: Maximum: $17500   DEADLINE: January 15
FIELDS/MAJORS: All Areas of Study

Fellowships available for qualified minority students enrolled at any level in a graduate program. Applicants must be U.S. citizens or permanent residents. See your department and the AOF Fact Sheet at the Office of Fellowships and Minority Programs for specific eligibility requirements and application procedures. Contact your department office for details.

University of Wisconsin, Madison
Graduate School Fellowships Office
217 Bascom Hall, 500 Lincoln Drive
Madison, WI   53706

18

AERA/Spencer Doctoral Research Fellowship Programs

AMOUNT: $4000–$16000   DEADLINE: April 21
FIELDS/MAJORS: Educational Research

Applicants must be full-time doctoral candidates in the U.S. who are at least midway through their program but have not begun their dissertation. The one-year program awards up to $16000 plus travel funds for professional development activities. The Travel Fellowship awards $4000 to students who wish to take part in professional development activities at their home institutions. Students at institutions that receive research training grants directly from the Spencer Foundation are not eligible but should inquire at their institution about support. Contact the address listed for further information.

American Educational Research Association/Spencer Foundation
AERA/Spencer Fellowship
1230 17th Street, NW
Washington, DC   20036-3078

19
AESF Graduate Scholarships

AMOUNT: $1000   DEADLINE: April 15
FIELDS/MAJORS: Finishing Technologies, Chemical/Environmental Engineering, Materials Science

Awards for graduate students in the above fields. Based on achievement, scholarship potential, and interest in the finishing technologies. For full-time study. Write to the address below for more information.

American Electroplaters and Surface Finishers Society
Central Florida Research Park
12644 Research Parkway
Orlando, FL   32826

20
AFPE First Year Graduate Scholarship Program

AMOUNT: $7500   DEADLINE: January 15
FIELDS/MAJORS: Pharmacy, Pharmacology

Scholarships for members of either Rho Chi or Phi Lambda Sigma who are in their first year of graduate studies toward the Ph.D. in pharmacy. Must be a U.S. citizen or permanent resident. Details on how to apply may be obtained at your school of pharmacy, from your chapter of Rho Chi/Phi Lambda Sigma, or from the AFPE at the address below.

American Foundation for Pharmaceutical Education
One Church Street
Suite 202
Rockville, MD   20850

21
African Dissertation Internship Awards

AMOUNT: $20000   DEADLINE: March 2
FIELDS/MAJORS: Agriculture, Education, Health, Humanities, Population

Doctoral dissertation internships are available for African doctoral candidates currently enrolled in U.S. or Canadian institutions to travel to Africa for twelve to eighteen months of supervised doctoral research. U.S. citizens, permanent residents, and Canadian landed immigrants are not eligible. Please write to the address listed for complete information.

Rockefeller Foundation
Fellowship Office
420 Fifth Avenue
New York, NY   10018

22 Afro-American and African Studies Fellowships

AMOUNT: $12500–$25000 DEADLINE: December 2
FIELDS/MAJORS: African-American and African Studies

Post-doctoral and predoctoral residential fellowships at the University of Virginia Carter G. Woodson Institute. Supports projects in the disciplines of the humanities concerning Afro-American and African studies. Predoctoral candidates should have completed all requirements except the dissertation. Current University of Virginia employees are not eligible (until at least one year of separation). Contact the address below for further information.

University of Virginia, Carter G. Woodson Institute
Afro-American and African Studies
102 Minor Hall
Charlottesville, VA   22903

23 AFUD Research Scholars, Practicing Urologist's Research Award

AMOUNT: Maximum: $5500 DEADLINE: None Specified
FIELDS/MAJORS: Urology, Nephrology

Research support for postdoctoral, post-residency, and practicing scientists and medical doctors concentrating in the area of urologic diseases and dysfunctions. Peer review is available, if desired, for research proposals. Write to the AFUD at the address below for details.

American Foundation for Urologic Disease, Inc.
Research Program Division
300 West Pratt Street, Suite 401
Baltimore, MD   21201

24 AGBU Education Loan Program

AMOUNT: $5000–$7500
DEADLINE: May 15
FIELDS/MAJORS: Communication, Education, or Public Administration, Armenian Studies, International Relations

Loans for students of Armenian heritage pursuing master's degrees in the fields listed above, doctoral degrees in Armenian studies, or professional degrees in law or medicine. Applicants must have an undergraduate GPA of at least 3.5. Loan repayments begin after graduation at an interest rate of 3%. Write to the address below for more information.

Armenian General Benevolent Union
Education Department
31 West 52nd Street
New York, NY   10019

25 Ahmanson and Getty Postdoctoral Fellowships

AMOUNT: $18400 DEADLINE: March 15
FIELDS/MAJORS: 17th, 18th Century Studies

Residential fellowships for scholars who hold a doctorate and would benefit from the interdisciplinary, cross-cultural programs at the Clark Library Center for 17th and 18th Century Studies at UCLA. Topics of study include western Americana, British studies, history of science, literature, law, philosophy, and musicology. The $18400 stipend is for two quarters. Write to the fellowship coordinator at the address below for details.

UCLA Center for 17th and 18th Century Studies
395 Dodd Hall, UCLA
405 Hilgard Avenue
Los Angeles, CA   90024

26 AIAA Technical Committee Graduate Scholarship Awards

AMOUNT: $1000 DEADLINE: January 31
FIELDS/MAJORS: Astronautics, Aeronautical Engineering, Aerospace Engineering

Awards for master's or doctoral students in specific areas of interest to the AIAA. Must have a GPA of at least 3.0, have completed at least one year of graduate studies, and be a U.S. citizen. Applicants need not be AIAA members to apply, but must become members before receiving an award. Write to "Technical Committee Graduate Scholarships" at the address below for details. Deadline to request applications is January 15.

American Institute of Aeronautics and Astronautics
Scholarship Program
370 L'enfant Promenade, SW
Washington, DC   20024

27 AICPA Doctoral Fellowships

AMOUNT: Maximum: $5000
DEADLINE: April 1
FIELDS/MAJORS: Accounting

Doctoral fellowships for students who hold CPA certificates and are applying to or accepted into doctoral programs in accounting. Preference given to students with outstanding academic performance or significant professional experience. Must be a U.S. citizen. Renewable for up to two years. Write to the address below for details. At least a 3.3 GPA is required

American Institute of Certified Public Accountants
AICPA Doctoral Fellowships Program
1211 Avenue of the Americas
New York, NY   10036

28

Air and Waste Management Association Graduate Study Scholarships

AMOUNT: None Specified   DEADLINE: December 4
FIELDS/MAJORS: Waste Management, Air Quality Management

Scholarships are available to assist graduate students working toward and training for careers in areas of air pollution control or waste management. Write to the address below for information.

Air and Waste Management Association
One Gateway Center, Third Floor
Pittsburgh, PA   15222

29

AIA/AHA Fellowship in Health Facility Planning and Design

AMOUNT: $22000   DEADLINE: January 15
FIELDS/MAJORS: Architecture

Sponsored jointly by the Institute and the American Hospital Association, this fellowship has several options for graduate students to design or study the health facilities field. Write to the address below for details.

American Institute of Architects/American Hospital Association
Fellowship Coordinator
1 North Franklin
Chicago, IL   60611

30

Albert J. Beveridge Grant for Research

AMOUNT: $1000   DEADLINE: February 1
FIELDS/MAJORS: Western Hemisphere History

Applicants must be American Historian Association members who are doing doctoral or postdoctoral research in the history of the western hemisphere. Write to the address below for details.

American Historical Association
Award Administrator
400 A Street, SE
Washington, DC   20003

31

Albert W. Dent Scholarship

AMOUNT: $3000   DEADLINE: March 31
FIELDS/MAJORS: Hospital/Healthcare Management

Varying number of scholarships for students in an accredited graduate program in healthcare management. Must be student associate of the American College of Healthcare Executives. Financial need is considered. Must be U.S. or Canadian citizen. Previous scholarship recipients ineligible. Goal of scholarship is to increase enrollment of minority students. Write to address below for details.

Foundation of the American College of Healthcare Executives
1 North Franklin Street, Suite 1700
Chicago, IL   60606

32

Alexander and Geraldine Wanek Graduate Scholarship

AMOUNT: None Specified   DEADLINE: March 1
FIELDS/MAJORS: Geological Resources

Awards are available at the University of New Mexico for graduate students studying geological resources with preference given to those concentrating in the area of leasable minerals. Write to the address below for more information.

University of New Mexico, Albuquerque
Office of Financial Aid
Albuquerque, NM   87131

33

Alice E. Smith Fellowship

AMOUNT: Maximum: $2000
DEADLINE: July 15
FIELDS/MAJORS: American History

An outright grant for any woman doing research in American History. Preference given to graduate research on the history of the Middle-West or Wisconsin. Applicants should submit four copies of a two-page, single-spaced letter of application describing her training in historical research and summarizing her current project. Write to the address below for details.

State Historical Society of Wisconsin
State Historian
816 State Street
Madison, WI   53706

34

Alice Freeman Palmer Fellowship

AMOUNT: Maximum: $4000   DEADLINE: December 16
FIELDS/MAJORS: All Areas of Study

Fellowships are available at Wellesley for study or research abroad and in the United States. The holder must be no more than twenty-six years of age at the time of her appointment and unmarried throughout the whole of her tenure. Write to the address below for information.

Wellesley College
Committee on Graduate Fellowships
106 Central Street, Career Center
Wellesley, MA   02181

35

Alice Koenecke Fellowship

AMOUNT: $2000   DEADLINE: January 15
FIELDS/MAJORS: Home Economics/Related Fields

Applicants must be members of Kappa Omicron Nu and enrolled in a Ph.D. program in home economics. Awards announced April 1. Write to the address below for details.

Kappa Omicron Nu Honor Society
4990 Northwind Drive, Suite 140
East Lansing, MI   48823

36
Alice McGuffey Laughlin Fellowship

AMOUNT: None Specified
DEADLINE: January 2
FIELDS/MAJORS: Literature, Art

Awards open to graduate students in either of the above fields. Contact the address below for further information.

Bryn Mawr Graduate School of Arts and Sciences
101 N. Merion Avenue
Bryn Mawr, PA 19010

37
Allen & Hanburys and Devilbiss Health Care Literary Awards

AMOUNT: $2000–$3500 DEADLINE: None Specified
FIELDS/MAJORS: Respiratory Care

Awards for practitioners and physicians who submit the best papers involving scientific investigations, evaluation on case reports, or new or current technologies in respiratory care. Papers to be published in "Respiratory Care". Contact the address below for further information about both awards.

American Respiratory Care Foundation
11030 Ables Lane
Dallas, TX 75229

38
Allied Health Student Loan-for-Service

AMOUNT: Maximum: $12000 DEADLINE: July 1
FIELDS/MAJORS: See Below

Loans for students who are studying the following areas of health: physical therapy, occupational therapy, speech-language pathology, audiology, pharmacy, nutrition, respiratory care practice, laboratory technology, radiologic technology, mental health services, or emergency medical services. Applicants must be New Mexico residents doing post-graduate study in New Mexico. Write to the address below for more information. Loans will be forgiven if the student works in a shortage area upon graduation.

New Mexico Commission on Higher Education
Financial Aid and Student Services
PO Box 15910
Santa Fe, NM 87506

39
Alpha Lambda Delta Fellowship

AMOUNT: $3000 DEADLINE: December 31
FIELDS/MAJORS: All Areas of Study

Applicants must be Alpha Lambda Delta members who have graduated with a 3.5 GPA or higher. Award is for graduate and professional study only. Write to the address below for details.

Alpha Lambda Delta
Executive Director
PO Box 4403
Macon, GA 31208

40
ALTA Endowment Fund Travel Fellowships

AMOUNT: None Specified DEADLINE: June 30
FIELDS/MAJORS: Translation

Awards are available for outstanding students or beginning translators who would be interested in attending the ALTA conference in Richardson, TX. Write to the address below for more information.

American Literary Translators Association
UTD, MC35
PO Box 830688
Richardson, TX 75083

41
Alumni Chapter-at-Large Grant

AMOUNT: $500 DEADLINE: February 15
FIELDS/MAJORS: Home Economics/Related Fields

Applicants must be Kappa Omicron Nu members. Awarded annually as a project of the Alumni Chapter-at-Large. Awards announced April 15. Write to the address below for details.

Kappa Omicron Nu Honor Society
4990 Northwind Drive, Suite 140
East Lansing, MI 48823

42
Alumni Society of Christopher Newport University Graduate Scholarship

AMOUNT: $1000 DEADLINE: April 1
FIELDS/MAJORS: All Areas of Study

Awarded to all students enrolled in graduate studies at the university. Write to the address below for more information.

Christopher Newport University
Office of Financial Aid
50 Shoe Lane
Newport News, VA 23606

43
Ambrose H. Lindhorst Scholarship

AMOUNT: $2500 DEADLINE: February 1
FIELDS/MAJORS: Law

Awards for law students who demonstrate a high level of academic promise. Preference will be given to a part-time student who intends to practice in Cincinnati. Renewable for four academic years for part-time students and three academic years for full-time students. Contact the Assistant Dean, Chase College of Law, for further information.

Northern Kentucky University
Chase College of Law
Office of Admissions
Highland Heights, KY 41099

44 Amelia Earhart Fellowship Awards

AMOUNT: $6000   DEADLINE: November 1
FIELDS/MAJORS: Aerospace Engineering and Related Sciences

Graduate fellowships for women. Must have a bachelor's degree in science as preparation for graduate work in aerospace sciences. Must be women of exceptional ability and character. Approximately thirty fellowships per year. Renewable once (or twice in exceptional cases). Completion of one year of graduate school or well-defined research on a specific project is required. Write to the address below for details.

Zonta International Foundation
Amelia Earhart Fellowships
557 W Randolph Street
Chicago, IL   60661

45 American Accounting Association Fellowship Program in Accounting

AMOUNT: $2500   DEADLINE: June 1
FIELDS/MAJORS: Accounting

Fellowships for students entering doctoral programs in accounting with career plans to teach accounting in colleges or universities in the U.S. or Canada. Must be a U.S. or Canadian resident. Foreign students may apply if enrolled in or have a degree from a U.S. or Canadian graduate program. Four or five awards offered annually. Write to Mary Cole, Office Manager, at the address below for details.

American Accounting Association
5717 Bessie Drive
Sarasota, FL   34233

46 American Antiquarian Society—Newberry Library Fellowships

AMOUNT: None Specified   DEADLINE: January 20
FIELDS/MAJORS: American and European History, Literature, Humanities, Cartography

Fellowships for scholars who could benefit from access to the Newberry's collections or the American Antiquarian Society. Applicants must possess Ph.D. or have completed all requirements except the dissertation. Award amount is paid monthly. Write to the committee at the address below for details.

Newberry Library
Committee on Awards
60 W. Walton Street
Chicago, IL   60610

47 American Art Therapy Association, Inc., Anniversary Scholarship

AMOUNT: None Specified   DEADLINE: June 15
FIELDS/MAJORS: Art Therapy

Scholarships for graduate students who have demonstrated academic excellence and are in an AATA approved art therapy program. Applicants must demonstrate financial need and have a minimum undergraduate GPA of 3.25. Write to the address below for complete details.

American Art Therapy Association, Inc.
Scholarship Committee
1202 Allanson Road
Mundelein, IL   60060

48 American Association for Geodetic Surveying Fellowship

AMOUNT: Maximum: $2000   DEADLINE: November 10
FIELDS/MAJORS: Geodetic Surveying, Geodesy

Open to graduate students in a program with a significant focus on geodetic surveying or geodesy at a school of the recipient's choice. Contact the address below for further information.

American Cartographic Association
Lilly Matheson, ACSM Awards Program
5410 Grosvenor Lane, #100
Bethesda, MD   20814-2144

49 American Cartographic Association Scholarship Award

AMOUNT: None Specified   DEADLINE: November 10
FIELDS/MAJORS: Cartography

Fellowships are available to recognize outstanding cartography and mapping sciences students and to encourage the pursuit of graduate studies. Write to the address below for information.

American Cartographic Association
Lilly Matheson, ACSM Awards Program
5410 Grosvenor Lane, #100
Bethesda, MD   20814-2144

50 American Concrete Institute Scholarships

AMOUNT: $3000   DEADLINE: February 1
FIELDS/MAJORS: Engineering, Construction, Material Science, Etc.

Graduate fellowships for first- or second-year students in engineering, architectural, and/or material science programs in the area of concrete where design, materials, construction, or combination of these are studied. Membership in the American Concrete Institute is not required. Write to the address below for details. Awards offered are the Katharine and Bryant Mather Fellowship (one award), ACI-W.R. Grace Fellowship (one award), the ACI Fellowships (two awards), and the V. Mohan Malhotra Fellowship (one award). Only one application is required to apply for all of the above awards.

American Concrete Institute
Director of Education
PO Box 19150
Detroit, MI   48219

51
American Dietetic Association Programs

AMOUNT: None Specified
DEADLINE: February 15
FIELDS/MAJORS: Dietetics/Nutrition

Applicants must be enrolled in an advanced degree program. Must be a U.S. citizen. Some scholarships require specific areas of study. Includes the Graduate Scholarships, Dietetic Internships, and Preprofessional Practice Program. Information is published annually in the Journal of the American Dietetic Association. Alternately, write to the address below for details.

American Dietetic Association Foundation
Education and Accreditation Team
216 W. Jackson Street, #800
Chicago, IL   60606

52
American Fellowships— Postdoctoral or Dissertation

AMOUNT: $5000–$25000   DEADLINE: November 15
FIELDS/MAJORS: All Areas of Study

Fellowships for postdoctoral or dissertation research for female scholars. Must be a citizen or permanent resident of the United States. Available for the summer as well as the school year. One-year fellowships and summer programs start June 1. Write to the address below for complete details.

American Association of University Women Educational
    Foundation
2201 N. Dodge Street
Iowa City, IA   52243

53
American Indian Graduate Program

AMOUNT: None Specified
DEADLINE: None Specified
FIELDS/MAJORS: Public Health

American Indian or Alaskan native graduate students in public health. Consideration is given to past experience and academics and also to goals of working with Indian communities. Write for complete details.

University of California, Berkeley
School of Public Health
American Indian Graduate Program
Berkeley, CA   94720

54
American Indian M.B.A. Scholarship

AMOUNT: None Specified
DEADLINE: March 1
FIELDS/MAJORS: Business

Scholarships are available at the University of New Mexico for full-time American Indian graduate students in an M.B.A. program. Write to the address below for information.

University of New Mexico, Albuquerque
Department of Student Financial Aid
Mesa Vista Hall North
Albuquerque, NM   87131

55
American Medical Women's Association Medical Education Loans

AMOUNT: $2000   DEADLINE: April 30
FIELDS/MAJORS: Medicine (Medical and Osteopathic)

Loans for women who are members of the American Medical Women's Association. Must be a U.S. citizen or permanent resident enrolled in an accredited U.S. medical or osteopathic medicine school. Additional loans may be made to a maximum of $4000. Payment and interest deferred until graduation. Write to the address below (or call 703-838-0500) for details.

American Medical Women's Association Foundation
Student Loan Fund
801 N. Fairfax Street, Suite 400
Alexandria, VA   22314

56
American Meteorological Society Industry Graduate Fellowships

AMOUNT: $15000   DEADLINE: February 17
FIELDS/MAJORS: See Listing of Fields Below

Fellowships for graduate students in their first year of study who wish to pursue advanced degrees in meteorology, hydrology, atmospheric science, ocean science, or those planning a career in one of the above fields who are currently studying chemistry, computer science, engineering, environmental science, mathematics, or physics. Application forms and further information may be obtained through the AMS headquarters at the address below.

American Meteorological Society
45 Beacon Street
Boston, MA   02108

57
American Paralysis Association Research Grants

AMOUNT: Maximum: $50000   DEADLINE: June 1
FIELDS/MAJORS: Paralysis Research

Awards are available for research related to spinal cord injuries and paralysis. Grants are intended for new research projects and are allocated based on scientific merit and adherence to the APA's priorities. Write to the address below for more information.

American Paralysis Association
Ms. Susan P. Howley, Research Director
500 Morris Avenue
Springfield, NJ   07081

58
American Research Institute in Turkey

AMOUNT: Maximum: $30000
DEADLINE: November 15
FIELDS/MAJORS: Humanities, Social Sciences

Scholarships are available for graduate students engaged in research in ancient, medieval, or modern times in Turkey, in any field of the humanities and social sciences. Applicants must be of Czech, Hungarian, Polish, or Slovak heritage. Two to three awards offered annually. Write to the address below for more information.

University of Pennsylvania Museum
33rd and Spruce Streets
Philadelphia, PA   19104

59
American Society for Eighteenth-Century Studies Fellowships

AMOUNT: $800–$2400   DEADLINE: March 1
FIELDS/MAJORS: 18th Century Studies (1660–1815)

Postdoctoral residential fellowships lasting one to three months for scholars of 18th century studies. All fellowship offers are residential. Write to the committee on awards at the address below.

Newberry Library
Committee on Awards
60 W. Walton Street
Chicago, IL   60610

60
Amgen, Sandoz, Smithkline, Upjohn First-Year Graduate Programs

AMOUNT: $5000   DEADLINE: May 1
FIELDS/MAJORS: Pharmacy

Awards to encourage undergraduates or college graduates in pharmacy to pursue an advanced degree providing a valuable background for a career in the pharmaceutical industry. Must be in the final year of an undergraduate degree program or a recent graduate. For U.S. citizens or permanent residents. Write to the address below for more information.

American Foundation for Pharmaceutical Education
One Church Street
Suite 202
Rockville, MD   20850

61
Amy Reiss Blind Student Scholarship

AMOUNT: None Specified
DEADLINE: February 1
FIELDS/MAJORS: Law

Scholarship for a blind student admitted or matriculated in the Fordham University School of Law (studying toward J.D.). Award is based on financial need. Write to the address below for details.

Morrison, Cohen, Singer & Weinstein
Amy Reiss
750 Lexington Avenue
New York, NY   10022

62
Anderson Publishing Company Minority Scholarship

AMOUNT: $2500   DEADLINE: February 1
FIELDS/MAJORS: Law

Awards for minority law students who are residents of the greater Cincinnati area. Contact the Assistant Dean, Chase College of Law, for further information.

Northern Kentucky University
Chase College of Law
Office of Admissions
Highland Heights, KY   41099

63
Andrew M. Longley Jr., D.O., Scholarship

AMOUNT: $1000   DEADLINE: May 1
FIELDS/MAJORS: Osteopathic Medicine

Award for an entering or continuing student enrolled at the University of New England College of Osteopathic Medicine who is a Maine resident and has demonstrated interest in practicing primary care medicine in Maine. Write to the address below for more information.

Maine Osteopathic Association
Executive Director
RR 2 Box 1920
Manchester, ME   04351

64
Andrew W. Mellon Fellowships in the Humanities

AMOUNT: $32000   DEADLINE: October 15
FIELDS/MAJORS: Humanities

Fellowship applicants must have held the Ph.D. for a period of no fewer than three and no more then eight years. Applicants must address themselves to an interdisciplinary humanities research project. Duration of award is one year in residence. Three or four awards offered annually. Write for complete details.

University of Pennsylvania
16 College Hall
Chairman, Humanities Coordinating Comm.
Philadelphia, PA   19104

65
Andrew W. Mellon Postdoctoral Fellowship in the Humanities

AMOUNT: Maximum: $30000   DEADLINE: January 15
FIELDS/MAJORS: Humanities

Postdoctoral fellowships at Bryn Mawr are available for scholars in the humanities, with preference given to those specializing in multi-cultural areas. Applicants must have obtained the Ph.D. within the past five years. Write to the address below for information.

Bryn Mawr College
Dean James C. Wright
Graduate School of Arts and Sciences
Bryn Mawr, PA   19010

66
Ann Laurie Granstaff Memorial Scholarship

AMOUNT: None Specified   DEADLINE: February 15
FIELDS/MAJORS: Communication Disorders

Scholarships are awarded to a graduate student in the field of communication disorders at Murray State University. Write to the address below for more information.

Murray State University
Office of University Scholarships
Ordway Hall, PO Box 9
Murray, KY   42071

67
Ann Olson Memorial Doctoral Scholarship

AMOUNT: $3000   DEADLINE: December 1
FIELDS/MAJORS: Oncology Nursing

Scholarships available to doctoral students in the field of oncology nursing. All applicants must be currently licensed registered nurses. Write to the address below for more information.

Oncology Nursing Foundation
501 Holiday Drive
Pittsburgh, PA   15220

68
Anna C. and Oliver C. Colburn Fellowship

AMOUNT: $11000   DEADLINE: February 1
FIELDS/MAJORS: All Areas of Study

One fellowship will be awarded to an applicant contingent upon his or her acceptance as an incoming associate member or student associate member of the American School of Classical Studies at Athens. Competition is open to U.S. or Canadian citizens or permanent residents who are at the predoctoral stage or who have received the Ph.D. degree within the last five years. Write to the address below for details.

Archaeological Institute of America
Boston University
656 Beacon Street, 4th Floor
Boston, MA   02215

69
Anna C. Klune Memorial Scholarship

AMOUNT: None Specified
DEADLINE: November 1
FIELDS/MAJORS: Marketing

Open to second-year M.B.A. students who are Connecticut residents. Selection based on academics and financial need. At least 3.0 GPA required.

American Marketing Association—Connecticut Chapter
Ms. Cathy Dangona, Executive Director
1260 New Britain Avenue
West Hartford, CT   06110

70
Anne Louise Barrett Fellowship

AMOUNT: $3000   DEADLINE: December 16
FIELDS/MAJORS: Music

Fellowships for graduates of Wellesley College studying or performing research in music, especially music theory, composition, or in the history of music. For study in the U.S. or abroad. Contact the address below for further information.

Wellesley College
Sec'y, Committee on Graduate Fellowships
106 Central Street, Career Center
Wellesley, MA   02181

71
Antonio Cirino Memorial Fund

AMOUNT: $2000–$10000
DEADLINE: April 15
FIELDS/MAJORS: Art Education

Scholarships available for residents (of at least five years) of Rhode Island who are at the graduate level in art education programs. Ten awards offered annually. Write to the address below for information.

Rhode Island Foundation
70 Elm Street
Providence, RI   02903

72
APA Fellowships

AMOUNT: $2000–$4000
DEADLINE: May 15
FIELDS/MAJORS: Urban Planning

Applicants must be minority graduate students enrolled in an accredited planning program. Must be able to document need for financial assistance. Must be a United States citizen. Minority groups eligible for this program are African-American, Hispanic, and Native Americans. Contact your department, or write to "APA Planning Fellowships" at the address below for further information and application forms.

American Planning Association
Attn: Asst. for Div. and Student Services
1776 Massachusetts Avenue, NW
Washington, DC   20036

73 Architectural Study Tour Scholarship

AMOUNT: None Specified
DEADLINE: None Specified
FIELDS/MAJORS: Architecture, Architectural History, City Planning, Landscape Arch.

Awards are available for graduate students in any of the fields listed above to participate in the SAH tour of Tidewater, Virginia. All tour expenses are paid for by the society. Applicants must be members of the SAH to apply. Write to the address below for more information.

Society of Architectural Historians
1365 North Astor Street
Chicago, IL   60610

74 Arnold and Bess Ungerman Charitable Trust Scholarship

AMOUNT: None Specified   **DEADLINE:** None Specified
FIELDS/MAJORS: Medicine

Scholarships are available at the University of Oklahoma for medical students who are of African-American or Native American heritage. Four awards offered annually. Write to the address below for information.

University of Oklahoma, Norman
Director, Office of Financial Aid
OUHSC, PO Box 73190
Oklahoma City, OK   73190

75 Arnold W. Brunner Grant

AMOUNT: $15000   **DEADLINE:** November 4
FIELDS/MAJORS: Architecture (Research)

Grants for research at the graduate level or beyond into areas of use and interest to the practice, teaching, or the corpus of knowledge of architecture. Must be a professional architect for at least five years and a U.S. citizen. Write to the address below for details.

American Institute of Architects, New York Chapter
Arnold W. Brunner Grant
200 Lexington Avenue
New York, NY   10016

76 Arnzen, Parry and Wentz, P.S.C. Scholarship

AMOUNT: $1000   **DEADLINE:** February 1
FIELDS/MAJORS: Law

Awards for law students who are Kentucky residents. Contact the Assistant Dean, Chase College of Law, for further information.

Northern Kentucky University
Chase College of Law
Office of Admissions
Highland Heights, KY   41099

77 Arthur Holstein '34 Scholarship

AMOUNT: Maximum: $1000
DEADLINE: March 1
FIELDS/MAJORS: Medicine

Open to a graduating senior athlete who will be attending medical school. Contact the address listed for further information.

Brooklyn College
Office of the V.P. for Student Life
2113 Boylan Hall
Brooklyn, NY   11210

78 Arthur N. Wilson, M.D. Scholarship

AMOUNT: $3000   **DEADLINE:** May 1
FIELDS/MAJORS: Medicine

Award for medical students who graduated from high schools in southeast Alaska. Award is not automatically renewable, but recipients may reapply. Write to the address below for more information.

American Medical Association Education and Research Foundation
Ms. Rita Palulonis
515 N. State Street
Chicago, IL   60610

79 Arthur S. Tuttle Memorial National Scholarship

AMOUNT: $3000–$5000   **DEADLINE:** February 20
FIELDS/MAJORS: Civil Engineering

Applicant must be a national ASCE member in good standing academically. Financial need and academic performance will be considered in selection. Award is to be used to finance first year of graduate school in a civil engineering program. Write to the address below for complete details.

American Society of Civil Engineers
Student Services Department
1801 Alexander Bell Drive
Reston, NY   20191

80 Arthur Weinberg Fellowships for Independent Scholars

AMOUNT: $800   **DEADLINE:** March 1
FIELDS/MAJORS: History (American and European), Humanities, Literature

Fellowships are available for scholars doing research or working outside the academic setting who need to use the library's collections. Applicants need not have a Ph.D., but must have demonstrated, through their publications, particular expertise in a field appropriate to the Newberry. Write to the address below for more details.

Newberry Library
Committee on Awards
60 W. Walton Street
Chicago, IL   60610

81 ASA Minority Fellowship Program

AMOUNT: $10000   DEADLINE: December 31
FIELDS/MAJORS: Sociology, Mental Health

Applicants must be minority graduate students who have an interest and can express a commitment to the sociological aspects of mental health issues relevant to ethnic and racial minorities. Write to the address below for details.

American Sociological Association
Minority Fellowship Program
1722 N Street, NW
Washington, DC   20036

82 ASM Faculty Fellowship Program

AMOUNT: $4000   DEADLINE: February 1
FIELDS/MAJORS: Microbiological Sciences

One- to two-month fellowship for full-time minority undergraduates in the field of microbiological sciences. Applicants must be ASM members and U.S. citizens or permanent residents. This is a joint application with an ASM member faculty mentor. Write to the address below for additional information.

American Society for Microbiology
Office of Education and Training
1325 Massachusetts Avenue, NW
Washington, DC   20005

83 Assistance for Graduate Students

AMOUNT: Maximum: $7350   DEADLINE: February 15
FIELDS/MAJORS: All Areas of Study

Scholarships for graduate students at Western Michigan enrolled in master's or doctoral programs. Programs include graduate college fellows, doctoral associateships, Thurgood Marshall assistantships/grants, and teaching and research assistantships. Contact the address below for further information.

Western Michigan University
Student Financial Aid
3306 Faunce Student Services Building
Kalamazoo, MI   49008

84 Assistantships for Minority and Women Graduate Students

AMOUNT: $2005   DEADLINE: None Specified
FIELDS/MAJORS: All Areas of Study

Scholarships are available to graduate minority students in all fields and to women who are pursuing doctorate degrees in academic fields. Must be U.S. citizens or permanent residents. Write to the address below for more information.

University of Wyoming
Office Specialist
Graduate School Room 109; Knight Hall
Laramie, WY   82071

85 Associated Industries of Massachusetts Award

AMOUNT: None Specified   DEADLINE: None Specified
FIELDS/MAJORS: Management

Scholarships are awarded to Massachusetts residents who have done outstanding graduate work in the school of management and who plan to work in a Massachusetts enterprise upon graduation. Applications for School of Management scholarships will be available in the SOM Development Office, Room 206.

University of Massachusetts, Amherst
School of Management
SOM Development Office, Room 206
Amherst, MA   01003

86 Association for the Advancement of Health Education

AMOUNT: $500   DEADLINE: December 30
FIELDS/MAJORS: Health Education

Award is open to master's level students who are currently enrolled in a health education program with a GPA of 3.0 or better. Write to the address below for more information.

Association for the Advancement of Health Education
AAHE Scholarship Committee
1900 Association Drive
Reston, VA   22091

87 Association for Women Veterinarians Scholarship

AMOUNT: $1500   DEADLINE: February 18
FIELDS/MAJORS: Veterinary Medicine

Awarded to current second- or third-year veterinary medical students who are attending a college or school of veterinary medicine in the U.S. or Canada. Four awards offered annually. Write to the address below for more information.

Association for Women Veterinarians
Sherrilyn Wainwright, D.V.M.
3201 Henderson Mill Road, #27C
Atlanta, GA   30341

88 Astra Merck Advanced Research Training Awards

AMOUNT: $36000   DEADLINE: September 10
FIELDS/MAJORS: Gastroenterology

Applicants must be MD's currently in a gastroenterology-related field. Awards to help prepare physicians for independent research careers in digestive diseases. Contact the address below for further information or websites: http://www.gastro.org; http://www.asge.org; or http://hepar-sfgh.ucsf.edu.

American Digestive Health Foundation
Ms. Irene Kuo
7910 Woodmont Avenue, 7th Floor
Bethesda, MD   20814

89 Astrophysics and Cosmology Centennial Fellowships

AMOUNT: Maximum: $1000000   DEADLINE: December 15
FIELDS/MAJORS: Astrophysics, Cosmology

The intent of the Centennial Fellowships is to support and encourage exceptional scientists and scholars in the early stages of their careers. Candidates should be able to demonstrate great scholarly promise, but have not yet achieved full academic maturity and/or professional recognition. Applicants must be actively engaged in research and have a commitment to teaching and demonstrate a superior ability to communicate their work to broad audiences. Candidates should be less than forty years of age at time of application or not more than twelve years from the completion of their academic training (receipt of Ph.D.). Fellowships awarded in this category will support research expected to contribute fundamentally to our understanding of the large scale evolution of the universe or that will change our understanding of physical processes under extreme astrophysical conditions. Applications must be submitted by the sponsoring institution. The institution must agree to accept the award. Contact the address below for further information and instructions.

James S. McDonnell Foundation
1034 S. Brentwood Boulevard, Suite 1850
St. Louis, MO   63117

90 Audio Engineering Society Educational Foundation Grants

AMOUNT: Maximum: $3000   DEADLINE: May 15
FIELDS/MAJORS: Audio Engineering

Grants for graduate students in audio engineering, based on interest and accomplishments in the field and on faculty recommendations. Renewable for one additional year. Awards usually made in August. Write to the address below for details.

Audio Engineering Society Educational Foundation
60 East 42nd Street
New York, NY   10165

91 Audrey Lumsden-Kouvel Fellowship

AMOUNT: Maximum: $3000
DEADLINE: January 20
FIELDS/MAJORS: Late Medieval or Renaissance Studies

Fellowships are available for postdoctoral scholars wishing to pursue extended research in late medieval or renaissance studies. Must anticipate being in continuous residence at the library for at least three months. Write to the address below for more details.

Newberry Library
Committee on Awards—Renaissance Studies
60 W. Walton Street
Chicago, IL   60610

92 Aura E. Severinghaus Award

AMOUNT: $2000   DEADLINE: August 31
FIELDS/MAJORS: Medicine

For senior minority medical students attending Columbia University, College of Physicians and Surgeons. Must be U.S. citizen. Minorities are defined as African-American, Mexican-American, mainland Puerto Rican, and American Indian. Based on academics and leadership. One award is presented annually. Send a SASE to the address below for additional information.

National Medical Fellowships, Inc.
110 West 32nd Street, 8th Floor
New York, NY   10001

93 Austrian Cultural Institute Grants

AMOUNT: $740–$810   DEADLINE: January 31
FIELDS/MAJORS: Music, Art

Grants are for foreign students for studies at academies of music and dramatic art or at art academies in Austria. Applicants for the program must be advanced students and between twenty and thirty-five years old. Write to the address below for more information.

Austrian Cultural Institute
950 Third Avenue, 20th Floor
New York, NY   10022

94 Awards for Study in Scandinavia

AMOUNT: None Specified   DEADLINE: November 1
FIELDS/MAJORS: Scandinavian Studies

Awards for graduate students who have a well-defined research or study project that makes a stay in Scandinavia essential. Applicants must be U.S. citizens or permanent residents and have completed their undergraduate degree by the start of their project in Scandinavia. Write to the address below for more information.

American-Scandinavian Foundation
725 Park Avenue
New York, NY   10021

95 AWIS Predoctoral Awards

AMOUNT: $500
DEADLINE: January 15
FIELDS/MAJORS: Engineering, Mathematics, Physical, Life, and Behavioral Sciences

Scholarship aid and incentive awards for women who are working actively toward a Ph.D. degree in the above fields. For U.S. citizens who are studying in the U.S. or abroad, or for foreign citizens studying in the U.S. Usually awarded to a student at dissertation level. Four awards per year. (AWIS also publishes a directory of financial aid.) Write to the address below for details.

Association for Women in Science Educational Foundation
AWIS National Headquarters
1200 New York Avenue, NW, #650
Washington, DC   20005

96 B.C. Scholarship, Marcella H. Brown Medical Scholarship

AMOUNT: None Specified   **DEADLINE:** None Specified
FIELDS/MAJORS: Medicine

Scholarships are available at the University of Oklahoma for female medical students. Write to the address below for information.

University of Oklahoma, Norman
Director, Office of Financial Aid
OUHSC, PO Box 73190
Oklahoma City, OK   73190

97 B.G. Taylor Graduate Award in Mechanical Engineering

AMOUNT: None Specified   **DEADLINE:** March 1
FIELDS/MAJORS: Mechanical Engineering

Awards are available for full-time graduate students who received their BSME degree from UNM during the previous year. Must have a minimum GPA of 3.2 or better during the last two years of undergraduate study. Write to the address below for more information.

University of New Mexico, Albuquerque
Office of Financial Aid
Albuquerque, NM   87131

98 B.H. Taylor Scholarship

AMOUNT: None Specified
DEADLINE: February 7
FIELDS/MAJORS: Early Childhood Education

Scholarships are available at the University of Oklahoma, Norman for full-time graduate students in early childhood education, with GPAs of at least 3.0, who reside in Oklahoma. One award offered annually. Write to the address below for information.

University of Oklahoma, Norman
School of Human Development
610 Elm
Norman, OK   73019

99 Bainbridge Bunting Fellowship

AMOUNT: None Specified
DEADLINE: March 1
FIELDS/MAJORS: Art History, History of Architecture

Scholarships are available at the University of New Mexico for full-time graduate art history or architecture history majors. Applicants must have at least one semester of study completed at UNM. Write to the address below for information.

University of New Mexico, Albuquerque
College of Fine Arts
Office of Graduate Studies
Albuquerque, NM   87131

100 Barbara Goldwin Garland Award

AMOUNT: None Specified   **DEADLINE:** March 1
FIELDS/MAJORS: Psychology

Awards are available at the University of New Mexico for graduate students in psychology involved in treatment with teenagers. Write to the address below for more information.

University of New Mexico, Albuquerque
Office of Financial Aid
Albuquerque, NM   87131

101 Beale Family Memorial Scholarship

AMOUNT: $1000   **DEADLINE:** May 1
FIELDS/MAJORS: Osteopathic Medicine

Award for a continuing student who is a Maine resident, presents proof of enrollment at an approved college of osteopathic medicine, and demonstrates interest in practicing primary care medicine. Preference given to applicant from the Bangor, Maine, area. Write to the address below for more information.

Maine Osteopathic Association
Executive Director
RR 2 Box 1920
Manchester, ME   04351

102 Behavioral Sciences Research Training Fellowships

AMOUNT: $30000   **DEADLINE:** April 1
FIELDS/MAJORS: Epilepsy Research

Open to behavioral scientists to develop expertise in techniques used in working with people with epilepsy. Applicants must have doctoral degrees in a field of the social sciences. Contact the address below for further information.

Epilepsy Foundation of America
Behavioral Sciences Fellowship Program
4351 Garden City Drive
Landover, MD   20785

103 Behavioral Sciences Student Fellowship, Mary Litty Memorial Fellowship

AMOUNT: Maximum: $2000   DEADLINE: March 1
FIELDS/MAJORS: Behavioral, Social Sciences, Counseling

For students in the behavioral sciences for work on an epilepsy study project. The fellowship is awarded to a student of vocational rehabilitation counseling. An advisor/preceptor must accept responsibility for the study and its supervision. Write to the address below for further information.

Epilepsy Foundation of America
Fellowship Program
4351 Garden City Drive
Landover, MD   20785

104 Behavioral/Psychosocial Research Grants

AMOUNT: Maximum: $35000   DEADLINE: March 1
FIELDS/MAJORS: Behavioral/Psychosocial Research

Grants for younger faculty or scientists beginning new projects at Massachusetts institutions. Contact the address below for further information.

American Cancer Society
30 Speen Street
Framingham, MA   01701

105 Ben Barnett M.B.A., Ph.D., Scholars Awards

AMOUNT: $1000–$5000   DEADLINE: February 8
FIELDS/MAJORS: Business Administration

Scholarships are available at the University of Oklahoma, Norman for full-time M.B.A. or Ph.D. candidates in business administration. Four awards offered annually. Write to the address below for information.

University of Oklahoma, Norman
College of Business Administration
307 W. Brooks
Norman, OK   73019

106 Benjamin Franklin Haught Scholarship in Psychology

AMOUNT: None Specified   DEADLINE: March 1
FIELDS/MAJORS: Psychology

Awards are available at the University of New Mexico for doctoral students in psychology with demonstrated excellence in research. Write to the address below for more information.

University of New Mexico, Albuquerque
Office of Financial Aid
Albuquerque, NM   87131

107 Berkshire District Medical Society Scholarship Loan Program

AMOUNT: $2500   DEADLINE: April 1
FIELDS/MAJORS: Medicine

Must be resident of Berkshire County, Massachusetts, and be accepted into an accredited American or Canadian medical school. Write to the address below for details.

Berkshire District Medical Society
741 North Street
Pittsfield, MA   01201

108 Bernard J. Gilday Sr. Scholarship

AMOUNT: $1200   DEADLINE: February 1
FIELDS/MAJORS: Law

Awards for law students who demonstrate financial need and academic merit. Renewable for three academic years for full-time students and four academic years for part-time students. Contact the Assistant Dean, Chase College of Law, for further information.

Northern Kentucky University
Chase College of Law
Office of Admissions
Highland Heights, KY   41099

109 Bertha Margaret Diaz Health Services Scholarship Fund

AMOUNT: $1500   DEADLINE: March 5
FIELDS/MAJORS: Health Service Administration

Scholarship is available to a deserving health services administration graduate student who maintains a 3.1 GPA or better and is of Hispanic descent. Write to the address below for more information.

Florida International University
College of Urban and Public Affairs
Office of the Dean—AC1 200
North Miami, FL   33181

110 Bess Zeldich Ungerman Scholarship

AMOUNT: $1500   DEADLINE: September 1
FIELDS/MAJORS: Law

Scholarships are available at the University of Oklahoma, Norman for full-time, third-year minority law students. Write to the address below for information.

University of Oklahoma, Norman
Admissions and Records, Law Center
Room 22, 300 Timberdell Road
Norman, OK   73019

111 Beta Delta Chapter, Sigma Theta Tau, International Scholarship

AMOUNT: None Specified   DEADLINE: July 1
FIELDS/MAJORS: Nursing

Scholarships are available for graduate nursing students at the University of Oklahoma who are members of Sigma Theta Tau. Write to the address below for information.

University of Oklahoma, Norman
Director, Office of Financial Aid
OUCON, PO Box 26901
Oklahoma City, OK   73190

112 Betty Lea Stone Research Fellowship

AMOUNT: $3000   DEADLINE: March 1
FIELDS/MAJORS: Cancer Research

Fellowship for a ten-week summer research project. Applicant must be enrolled in a Massachusetts medical school. Contact the address below for further information.

American Cancer Society
30 Speen Street
Framingham, MA   01701

113 Beverly Myers Award

AMOUNT: $200–$500   DEADLINE: April 1
FIELDS/MAJORS: Optometry

Candidates must be senior students currently enrolled in an opticianry program accredited by the Commission on Opticianry Accreditation. Write to the address below for more information.

National Academy of Opticianry
10111 M.L. King Jr. Hwy., #112
Bowie, MD   20720

114 Bezanson Graduate Voice Scholarship

AMOUNT: None Specified   DEADLINE: March 1
FIELDS/MAJORS: Vocal Music

Awards for graduate students studying in the music department for outstanding vocal performance. Contact the Director of Scholarships, Department of Music, at the address below for more information.

University of Massachusetts, Amherst
Director of Scholarships, Department of Music
Amherst, MA   01003

115 Billy M.C. Shibley Scholarship

AMOUNT: None Specified   DEADLINE: None Specified
FIELDS/MAJORS: Medicine

Scholarships are available at the University of Oklahoma for medical students who are married and planning a career in rural medicine. Write to the address below for information.

University of Oklahoma, Norman
Director, Office of Financial Aid
OUHSC, PO Box 73190
Oklahoma City, OK   73190

116 Bishop Greco Graduate Fellowship Program

AMOUNT: Maximum: $2000
DEADLINE: May 1
FIELDS/MAJORS: Special Education

Fellowship for graduate students in a full-time program for the preparation of classroom teachers of mentally retarded children. Applicants also must be a member of the Knights in good standing or the wife, son, or daughter of a member and have a good academic record. Special consideration will be given to students who attend a Catholic graduate school. Write to the secretary of the committee on fellowships at the address below for details.

Knights of Columbus
Secretary of the Committee on Fellowship
PO Box 1670
New Haven, CT   06507

117 Blanch Wiley Shafer Memorial Fund

AMOUNT: None Specified   DEADLINE: February 1
FIELDS/MAJORS: Law

Awards for law students who show outstanding academic achievement. Must demonstrate financial need. Contact the Assistant Dean, Chase College of Law, for further information.

Northern Kentucky University
Chase College of Law
Office of Admissions
Highland Heights, KY   41099

118 Bliss Prize Fellowship in Byzantine Studies

AMOUNT: None Specified
DEADLINE: November 1
FIELDS/MAJORS: Byzantine Studies

Fellowships for students who are (or are soon to be) graduated with a bachelor of arts degree and intend to enter the field of Byzantine studies. Must have studied at least one year of ancient or medieval Greek. Fellows are usually offered a Junior Fellowship at Dumbarton Oaks after completing two years of the Bliss Fellowship. These awards cover graduate school tuition and living expenses for two years. Write to the address below for details.

Dumbarton Oaks
Office of the Director
1703 32nd Street, NW
Washington, DC   20007

119
Bluebird Society Research Grants—Bluebird Research Grants

AMOUNT: $1000   DEADLINE: December 1
FIELDS/MAJORS: Ornithology: Avian Research and Study—Bluebirds

Research grants available to student, professional, and individual researchers for a research project focused on any of the three species of bluebird from the genus "Sialia." Proposal required. Supported on a one-year basis. Interested persons should write to the address below for further information.

North American Bluebird Society, Inc.
Kevin Berner, Research Comm. Chairman
State University of New York
Cobleskill, NY   12043

120
Bluebird Society Research Grants—Student Research Grant

AMOUNT: $1000   DEADLINE: December 1
FIELDS/MAJORS: Ornithology: Avian Research and Study—Bluebirds

Student research grant (one) available to a full-time college or university student, for a research project focused on any North American avian cavity-nesting species (genus "Sialia" and cavity-nesting species native to North America). Proposal required. Supported on a one-year basis. Interested students should write to the address below for further information.

North American Bluebird Society, Inc.
Kevin Berner, Research Comm. Chairman
State University of New York
Cobleskill, NY   12043

121
Board of Governors Dental Scholarship Program

AMOUNT: $5000   DEADLINE: None Specified
FIELDS/MAJORS: Dentistry

Program for students accepted for admission to the UNC School of Dentistry. Applicants must be a resident of North Carolina, have financial need, and express an intent to practice dentistry in North Carolina. Scholarship provides an annual stipend of $5000 plus tuition, mandatory fees and approved cost for certain instruments and supplies. The program encourages minorities to enroll in dental education. Write to the address below for details.

North Carolina State Education Assistance Authority
PO Box 2688
Chapel Hill, NC   27515

122
Board of Governors Medical Scholarship Program

AMOUNT: $5000   DEADLINE: None Specified
FIELDS/MAJORS: Medical

Scholarships for students accepted to one of four medical schools in North Carolina: Bowman Gray School of Medicine of Wake Forest University, Duke University School of Medicine, East Carolina University School of Medicine, and the University of North Carolina at Chapel Hill School of Medicine. Applicants must be residents of North Carolina and have financial need. Students must express the intent to practice medicine in North Carolina. The program encourages minorities to pursue a medical education. Write to the address below for details.

North Carolina State Education Assistance Authority
PO Box 2688
Chapel Hill, NC   27515

123
Bob and Audrey Conner Fund Scholarship

AMOUNT: None Specified   DEADLINE: January 2
FIELDS/MAJORS: Biology

Award open for summer support to graduate students in biology. Contact the address below for further information.

Bryn Mawr Graduate School of Arts and Sciences
101 N. Merion Avenue
Bryn Mawr, PA   19010

124
Bound-to-Stay-Bound Books Scholarship

AMOUNT: $6000   DEADLINE: March 1
FIELDS/MAJORS: Library Science, Children's

Applicants must be entering or enrolled in an ALA-accredited program for the master's or beyond the master's with a concentration in children's library services. Must be U.S. or Canadian citizen. Recipients are required to work in a children's library for a minimum of one year after graduation. Write to the address shown below for details.

American Library Association
Assn. for Library Service to Children
50 E. Huron Street
Chicago, IL   60611

125
BPW/Sears-Roebuck Loan Fund for Women in Graduate Business Studies

AMOUNT: Maximum: $2500   DEADLINE: April 15
FIELDS/MAJORS: Business Administration

Loans to encourage women to enter programs in business administration. Must demonstrate financial need. May apply annually for additional loans totaling $2500. Must be a U.S. citizen and enrolled in accredited M.B.A. program. BPW Foundation and Sears-Roebuck Foundation employees are not eligible. Write to address below for details.

Business and Professional Women's Foundation
Loan Programs
2012 Massachusetts Avenue, NW
Washington, DC   20036

126

Bristol Bar Association Scholarships

AMOUNT: None Specified   **DEADLINE:** April 12
FIELDS/MAJORS: Law

Scholarships for students entering law school who are residents of the city of Bristol (CT) or the surrounding towns of Burlington, Plainville, Terryville, and Plymouth. Based also on need, achievement, and extracurricular activities. Number and amount of awards varies. Contact Attorney Margaret M. Hayes, Chairperson of the Bristol Bar Association Scholarship Committee, for details.

Bristol Bar Association
Anderson, Alden, Hayes & Ziogas, L.L.C.
PO Box 1197
Bristol, CT   06011

127

British Marshall Scholarships

AMOUNT: Maximum: $24000   **DEADLINE:** October 15
FIELDS/MAJORS: All Areas of Study

Scholarships for American graduate students to study in a university in the United Kingdom. The primary purpose of the program is to allow young Americans, who will one day become leaders, opinion formers, and decision makers in their own country, to study in Great Britain and understand and appreciate British culture. Must be U.S. citizens, under age twenty-six, and have a minimum 3.7 GPA. Write to the address below for complete details.

British Information Services
845 Third Avenue
New York, NY   10022

128

Broome County Medical Society Auxiliary Loan Program

AMOUNT: None Specified   **DEADLINE:** May 1
FIELDS/MAJORS: Medical

Financial assistance is given to students attending medical school in Broome County, or to Broome County residents attending an accredited medical school in the United States or Canada. Assistance is given in the form of a no-interest loan, which students are required to repay within five years of completion of residency training. Write to the address below for further details.

Broome County Medical Society Auxiliary
4513 Old Vestal Road
Vestal, NY   13850

129

Brown, Todd and Heyburn Scholarship

AMOUNT: None Specified   **DEADLINE:** February 1
FIELDS/MAJORS: Law

Awards for first-year, full-time law students who are Kentucky residents. Undergraduate school achievement, including academic merit and leadership will be considered. Contact the Assistant Dean, Chase College of Law, for further information.

Northern Kentucky University
Chase College of Law
Office of Admissions
Highland Heights, KY   41099

130

Bryan Advisory Board Award and Bryan Fellowship

AMOUNT: None Specified   **DEADLINE:** February 1
FIELDS/MAJORS: Business, Economics

Awards open to graduate students in business or economics. Contact the address below for further information about both awards.

University of North Carolina, Greensboro
Financial Aid Office
723 Kenilworth Street
Greensboro, NC   27412

131

Buchanan/Arms Award

AMOUNT: None Specified   **DEADLINE:** March 1
FIELDS/MAJORS: British Literature

Awards are available at the University of New Mexico for graduate students in the fields of British literature. Write to the address below for more information.

University of New Mexico, Albuquerque
Office of Financial Aid
Albuquerque, NM   87131

132

Burton H. and Carmelita B. Bell Scholarship Fund

AMOUNT: None Specified   **DEADLINE:** March 1
FIELDS/MAJORS: Family Medicine

Awards are available at the University of New Mexico for fourth-year medical students who demonstrate excellence in their third-year clinical clerkships. Applicants must be planning to pursue family medicine. Write to the address below for more information.

University of New Mexico, Albuquerque
Office of Financial Aid
Albuquerque, NM   87131

133
Business Education Alumni Award

AMOUNT: None Specified
DEADLINE: None Specified
FIELDS/MAJORS: Business Education

Award made annually to an alumnus who has completed bachelor's degree requirements in business education at Central Connecticut State University. Write to the address below for more information.

Central Connecticut State University
CCSU Foundation, Inc.
PO Box 612
New Britain, CT   06050

134
Buzzard Scholarship, Gamma Theta Upsilon

AMOUNT: None Specified
DEADLINE: August 1
FIELDS/MAJORS: Geography/Geophysics

Scholarship for students entering graduate school. Based on GPA, activities in GTU chapters, service to Geography Department, and recommendations. Awarded after first term of enrollment in graduate school. One may apply for only one GTU scholarship. Write to Mr. Lawrence R. Handley, First Vice President, at the U.S. Fish and Wildlife Service, National Wetlands Research Center, at the address below. Info may be available from your local chapter or the current issue of "The Geographical Bulletin." GPA must be at least 3.0.

Gamma Theta Upsilon—International Geographical Honor Society
Office of the Dean
Eisenhower Hall, Kansas State University
Manhattan, KS   66506-0801

135
Byron Hanke Fellowships

AMOUNT: Maximum: $2500
DEADLINE: None Specified
FIELDS/MAJORS: Related to Community Associations

Fellowships are available for students enrolled in an accredited master's doctoral or law program. Topics must be related to the community associations (cooperative, condominium, and homeowners) research project. Write to the address below for information.

Community Associations Institute Research Foundation
1630 Duke Street
Alexandria, VA   22314

136
C. Maxwell Dieffenbach Scholarship

AMOUNT: None Specified   **DEADLINE:** February 1
FIELDS/MAJORS: Law

Awards for part-time law students who demonstrate academic promise and financial need. Contact the Assistant Dean, Chase College of Law, for further information.

Northern Kentucky University
Chase College of Law
Office of Admissions
Highland Heights, KY   41099

137
Cal Grant and Graduate Fellowship Program

AMOUNT: None Specified   **DEADLINE:** March 2
FIELDS/MAJORS: All Areas of Study

Graduate awards are available to California residents who wish to pursue a doctoral degree at an accredited California college or university, and plan to follow a career as a college or university faculty member. Write to the address below for information.

California Student Aid Commission
Customer Service Division
PO Box 510845
Sacramento, CA   94245

138
California Executive Fellows Program

AMOUNT: None Specified   **DEADLINE:** February 19
FIELDS/MAJORS: Public Policy, Government and Related

Fellowships are available at Cal State, Sacramento to provide an opportunity for individuals to participate in the development and implementation of public policy in the executive branch. Applicants must have graduated with a four-year degree. Fifteen fellowships are awarded yearly. Contact the financial aid office at the address below for details.

California State University, Sacramento
California Executive Fellows Program
6000 J Street, Center for California Studies
Sacramento, CA   95819

139
California Graduate Fellowship

AMOUNT: Maximum: $6490   **DEADLINE:** March 2
FIELDS/MAJORS: All Areas of Study

For California graduate students who intend to become college or university faculty members. Must be U.S. citizens, permanent U.S. residents, or eligible non-citizens. This award provides tuition and fee assistance. Selections based on parent information, income, educational level, and financial need. Write to the address below for more information.

United States International University
Financial Aid Office
10455 Pomerado Road
San Diego, CA   92131

140
California Senate Associates Program Internships

AMOUNT: $1638   DEADLINE: February 19
FIELDS/MAJORS: All Areas of Study

Applicants must have graduated from a four-year college. Recipients must register as graduate students at CSU, Sacramento. Awards include a stipend and twelve graduate units. Recipients will be placed in Capitol offices and perform a variety of tasks in different areas. Write to the address below for information.

California Senate Associates Program
Senate Rules Committee
State Capitol, Room 500A
Sacramento, CA   95814

141
CAMFT—Clinton E. Phillips Scholarship

AMOUNT: $1000   DEADLINE: February 26
FIELDS/MAJORS: Marriage/Family Counseling

Scholarship providing assistance for students pursuing an advanced degree in marriage and family therapy. Based on academics, financial need, community activities, and commitment to the profession of marriage and family therapy. Write to the address below for further information.

California Association of Marriage and Family Therapists
Educational Foundation
7901 Raytheon Road
San Diego, CA   92111

142
CAMFT—Educational Foundation Scholarships

AMOUNT: $1000   DEADLINE: None Specified
FIELDS/MAJORS: Marriage/Family Therapy

Scholarship or research grant for members of CAMFT who are pursuing a doctorate in the field of marriage and family therapy. Applicants may also be conducting research, participating in advanced training, education, or an internship. Contact the foundation at the address below for details.

California Association of Marriage and Family Therapists
Educational Foundation
7901 Raytheon Road
San Diego, CA   92111

143
CAMFT—Ronald D. Lunceford Scholarship

AMOUNT: $1000   DEADLINE: February 26
FIELDS/MAJORS: Counseling (Marriage, Family, Child Counseling)

Scholarship for a member of an underrepresented minority group studying toward a M.A., M.S., or Ph.D. and qualifying for licensure as a marriage, family, and child counselor. Write to the address below for details.

California Association of Marriage and Family Therapists
Educational Foundation
7901 Raytheon Road
San Diego, CA   92111

144
Career Development Grants

AMOUNT: $1000–$5000
DEADLINE: January 3
FIELDS/MAJORS: All Areas of Study

Grants to prepare for re-entry into work force or training for a career change. Special consideration is given to qualified AAUW members, minorities, women pursuing their first terminal degrees, and women pursuing degrees in nontraditional fields. Must be a U.S. citizen or permanent resident and have earned last degree at least five years previously. Write to the address below for details.

American Association of University Women Educational Foundation
2201 N. Dodge Street
Iowa City, IA   52243

145
Carl E. Green Graduate Fellowship

AMOUNT: None Specified
DEADLINE: None Specified
FIELDS/MAJORS: Environmental/Geotechnical Engineering, Environmental Geology

Awards are available to graduate students specializing in the fields of study listed above. Based on scholarship, potential for success, and financial need. Write to the address below for more information.

Portland State University
Engineering and Applied Sciences
118 Science Building 2
Portland, OR   92707

146
Carlsbad Foundation Scholarship

AMOUNT: None Specified   DEADLINE: March 1
FIELDS/MAJORS: Physics

Awards are available at the University of New Mexico for doctoral students in physics. Write to the address below for more information.

University of New Mexico, Albuquerque
Office of Financial Aid
Albuquerque, NM   87131

147
Carolyn Harper Fellowship

AMOUNT: None Specified   DEADLINE: None Specified
FIELDS/MAJORS: Resource Economics

Fellowship is awarded to a graduate student studying resource economics. Contact the Department Head, Resource Economics for more information.

University of Massachusetts, Amherst
Department Head
Resource Economics
Amherst, MA   01003

148 Carolyn M. Flora Memorial Scholarship

AMOUNT: None Specified
DEADLINE: March 1
FIELDS/MAJORS: Music Education

Awards are available at the University of New Mexico for a full-time graduate student in the field of music education. Write to the address below for more information.

University of New Mexico, Albuquerque
Office of Financial Aid
Albuquerque, NM   87131

149 CASW—Nate Haseltine Fellowships in Science Writing

AMOUNT: Maximum: $2000   **DEADLINE:** June 15
FIELDS/MAJORS: Science Writing

Fellowships for students who hold an undergraduate degree in science or journalism. Preference is given to journalists with at least two years of experience. Based on resume, transcript, recommendations, writing samples, and application. Write to the address below for full details. Not for pursuit of careers in public relations or public information work.

Council for the Advancement of Science Writing, Inc.
Ben Patrusky, Executive Director
PO Box 404
Greenlawn, NY   11740

150 Catherine Beattie Fellowship

AMOUNT: Maximum: $4000   **DEADLINE:** December 31
FIELDS/MAJORS: Botany or Related Fields

Fellowships are available for graduate students at a botanical garden jointly serving the Center for Plant Conservation and the student's academic research. Open to students with academic qualifications and an interest in rare plant conservation. Preference given to those with an interest in and whose projects focus on the endangered flora of the Carolinas and southeastern U.S. Write to the address below for information.

Garden Club of America—Center for Plant Conservation
Anukriti Sud, Missouri Botanical Garden
PO Box 299
St. Louis, MO   63166

151 Cathy Lynne Richardson Endowed Doctoral Scholarship

AMOUNT: Maximum: $4000   **DEADLINE:** April 1
FIELDS/MAJORS: Special Education

Applicants must be enrolled or accepted as full-time doctoral students in the Department of Special Education. Must have and maintain a minimum GPA of 3.0. Contact the following address for further information.

University of South Florida—College of Education
Chairperson, Dept. of Special Education
Hms 421
Tampa, FL   33620

152 Cay Drachnik Minorities Fund

AMOUNT: None Specified
DEADLINE: June 15
FIELDS/MAJORS: Art Therapy

Scholarships for minority students who are enrolled in an AATA approved art therapy program. Applicants must demonstrate financial need. This award is designed primarily for the purchase of books. Write to the address below for complete details.

American Art Therapy Association, Inc.
Scholarship Committee
1202 Allanson Road
Mundelein, IL   60060

153 Celine Davis Raff Endowed Scholarship

AMOUNT: None Specified
DEADLINE: March 1
FIELDS/MAJORS: Latin American Studies

Awards are available at the University of New Mexico for graduate students in a Latin American studies program. Applicant must exhibit financial need and academic achievement. Must be a female resident of New Mexico. Write to the address below for more information.

University of New Mexico, Albuquerque
Office of Financial Aid
Albuquerque, NM   87131

154 Center for Advanced Study in the Visual Arts Fellowships

AMOUNT: None Specified   **DEADLINE:** November 15
FIELDS/MAJORS: Visual Arts and Related Areas

Fellowships for Ph.D. candidates who have completed all coursework except the dissertation. Requires knowledge of two foreign languages related to topic of dissertation. Applicants must be U.S. citizens or legal residents. Application must be made through graduate departments of art history (or other appropriate departments). Direct inquiries to the address below.

National Gallery of Art
Center for Advanced Study in Visual Arts
Fellowship Programs
Washington, DC   20565

155 Center for Renaissance Studies Fellowships

AMOUNT: None Specified
DEADLINE: None Specified
FIELDS/MAJORS: Renaissance Studies

Fellowships are available for graduate students and faculty members of the Center's thirty-two member institutions, to participate in a broad range of archival or interdisciplinary programs. Write to the address below for details.

Newberry Library/Center for Renaissance Studies
Committee on Awards
60 W. Walton Street
Chicago, IL   60610

156 Central Institute for the Deaf Scholarships and Awards

AMOUNT: None Specified   DEADLINE: None Specified
FIELDS/MAJORS: Communication Disorders, Speech/Hearing

Scholarships for graduate students at the Central Institute for the Deaf at Washington University of St. Louis. The institute also administers several self-help programs. Write to the address below for details.

Washington University
Central Institute for the Deaf
818 S. Euclid Avenue
St. Louis, MO   63110

157 Chancellor's Graduate Fellowship Program

AMOUNT: $19291   DEADLINE: January 15
FIELDS/MAJORS: College or University Education

Fellowships for African-American graduate students at Washington University in St. Louis who plan to pursue a career teaching on the college level. Contact Mrs. Joyce Edwards at the address below for further information.

Washington University
Graduate School of Arts and Sciences
Campus Box 1187, One Brookings Drive
St. Louis, MO   63130

158 Charles A. Eastman Dissertation Fellowship for Native American Scholar

AMOUNT: $25000   DEADLINE: March 15
FIELDS/MAJORS: Arts and Sciences

Fellowships are available for U.S. citizens of Native American descent who plan careers in college or university teaching. Write to the address below for information.

Dartmouth College
Office of Graduate Studies
6062 Clement, Room 305
Hanover, NH   03755

159 Charles Abrams Scholarship Program

AMOUNT: $2000   DEADLINE: April 30
FIELDS/MAJORS: Urban Planning

Scholarships for master's students enrolled in a planning program at one of the following schools: Columbia University, Harvard University, Massachusetts Institute of Technology, New School for Social Research, or University of Pennsylvania. Nomination by department, financial need, and U.S. citizenship required. Contact your department head, or write to "Charles Abrams Scholarship Program" at the address below if further information is required.

American Planning Association
Fellowships and Scholarships in Planning
1776 Massachusetts Avenue, NW
Washington, DC   20036

160 Charles G. Coulson Jr. Scholarship

AMOUNT: None Specified   DEADLINE: February 1
FIELDS/MAJORS: Law

Applicants must be law students who are academically qualified. Contact the Assistant Dean, Chase College of Law, for further information.

Northern Kentucky University
Chase College of Law
Office of Admissions
Highland Heights, KY   41099

161 Charles Legeyt Fortescue Fellowship

AMOUNT: $24000   DEADLINE: January 15
FIELDS/MAJORS: Electrical Engineering

The fellowship is for one year of full-time graduate work in electrical engineering at an engineering school of recognized standing located in the U.S. or Canada. Must have bachelor's degree from an engineering school of recognized standing. For beginning graduate students only. Write to the address below for details.

Institute of Electrical and Electronics Engineers, Awards Board
Secretary of the Fellowship Committee
445 Hoes Lane, PO Box 1331
Piscataway, NJ   08855

162
Charles M. Ross Trust

AMOUNT: $500–$1200
DEADLINE: August 1
FIELDS/MAJORS: Religion, Sociology, Medicine, Teaching

Candidate should be an active member of a local church and should have earned grades in their undergraduate education, which are within the first 10% of their class. Must have courses in the fields listed above. Scholarships are available at Lexington Theological Seminary, Marquette University, University of Chicago, Texas Christian University, Centenary College, and Vanderbilt University. Write to the address below for more information. At least 3.5 GPA required.

Charles M. Ross Trust
Paul G. Mason, Executive Director
113 W. Walnut
Fairbury, IL   61739

163
Charles River District Medical Society Scholarships

AMOUNT: None Specified   DEADLINE: April 1
FIELDS/MAJORS: Medicine

Open to first-year medical students enrolled at an approved medical school who is a resident of the following towns in the Charles River District: Needham, Newton, Waltham, Wellesley, or Weston. Applications must be received before April 1 of the freshman year, as the scholarship is awarded for the sophomore year. May be renewable for junior year at the discretion of the committee on medical education. Write to the Society at the address below for details.

Charles River District Medical Society
Attn: Scholarship Program
1440 Main Street
Waltham, MA   02154

164
Chase Minority Educational Opportunity Tuition Award

AMOUNT: $1410   DEADLINE: February 1
FIELDS/MAJORS: Law

Awards for minority students who have been admitted to Chase College of Law. Contact the Assistant Dean, Chase College of Law, for further information.

Northern Kentucky University
Chase College of Law
Office of Admissions
Highland Heights, KY   41099

165
Chester Dale Fellowship

AMOUNT: Maximum: $16000
DEADLINE: November 15
FIELDS/MAJORS: Western Art, Visual Art, and Other Related Areas

One-year fellowship for doctoral student doing dissertation research in the fields of study above. The Dale Fellows may use the grant to study in the U.S. or abroad. Applicants must know two foreign languages related to topic of their dissertation and be U.S. citizens or legal residents. Contact the chairperson of the graduate department of art history at your school (or other appropriate department) or write to the address below for more information.

National Gallery of Art
Center for Study in the Visual Arts
Predoctoral Fellowship Program
Washington, DC   20565

166
Children's Literature Association Grants

AMOUNT: Maximum: $1000   DEADLINE: February 1
FIELDS/MAJORS: Literature

Funds are available for graduate students who wish to pursue scholarly investigation or publication in the field of children's literature. Access to facilities and resources of Weston Woods also possible. Includes the CHLA Research Fellowships and the Margaret P. Esmonde Memorial Scholarship. Contact Dr. Wilson at the address below for details.

Children's Literature Association
Dr. Anita Wilson, Dept. of English
Miami University
Oxford, OH   45056

167
China Area Studies Fellowships

AMOUNT: Maximum: $25000
DEADLINE: October 15
FIELDS/MAJORS: Foreign Studies—China

Fellowship for Ph.D. candidates requiring dissertation research abroad (except the People's Republic of China). While there are no citizenship restrictions, foreign nationals must have resided in the United States for at least two consecutive years at the time of application. Postdoctoral fellowships are also available. Write to the address below or visit the website http://www.acls.org for details.

American Council of Learned Societies
Office of Fellowships and Grants
228 E. 45th Street
New York, NY   10017

168 Chinese Association of Greater Toledo Memorial Scholarships

AMOUNT: None Specified   DEADLINE: None Specified
FIELDS/MAJORS: Political Science

Awards open to full-time international graduate students with an ethnic Chinese background. Contact the address below for further information.

University of Toledo
Dr. Harold H. Lee, Dept. of Biology
1025 Bowman-Oddy
Toldeo, OH   43606

169 Chinese-American Medical Society Scholarships

AMOUNT: $1500   DEADLINE: March 31
FIELDS/MAJORS: Medicine, Dentistry

Awards for medical and dental students of Chinese heritage for completion of their studies in the U.S. Must be able to demonstrate financial need. One award offered annually. Contact the address below for further information.

Chinese-American Medical Society
Dr. H.H. Wang, Executive Director
281 Edgewood Avenue
Teaneck, NJ   07666

170 Chiron Therapeutics/ H.M. Roussel, Inc./Ortho Biotech Research Fellows

AMOUNT: Maximum: $10000   DEADLINE: June 1
FIELDS/MAJORS: Oncology Research

Awards for post-doctorate, short-term research training that is relevant to oncology nursing. Applicants must be registered nurses who have completed advanced research preparation and have a doctorate in nursing or related discipline. Contact the address listed for information about all three awards.

Oncology Nursing Foundation
501 Holiday Drive
Pittsburgh, PA   15220

171 Chiropractic Education Assistance Program

AMOUNT: $3000   DEADLINE: None Specified
FIELDS/MAJORS: Chiropractic Medicine

Awards for Oklahoma residents who are students at out-of-state accredited institutions of chiropractic medicine. Write to the address below for more information.

Oklahoma State Regents for Higher Education
State Capitol Complex
500 Education Building
Oklahoma City, OK   73105

172 Chiyoko and Thomas Tomotsu Shimazaki Memorial Scholarship

AMOUNT: None Specified   DEADLINE: April 1
FIELDS/MAJORS: Oncological Research, Medicine

Applicants must be graduate students of Japanese ancestry who are pursuing cancer research. Must be a member of the JACL to apply. Applications and information may be obtained from local JACL chapters, district offices, and the national headquarters at the address below. Please indicate your level of study and be certain to include a legal-sized SASE.

Japanese American Citizens League
National Scholarship and Award Program
1765 Sutter Street
San Francisco, CA   94115

173 Christa McAuliffe Award for Excellence

AMOUNT: None Specified   DEADLINE: January 1
FIELDS/MAJORS: Education

Scholarship program for current teachers, principals, or administrators who wish to continue their education in a Washington State college or university. It is in recognition of their leadership, contributions, and commitment to education. Selections are made in March. Write to the address below for information.

Washington Higher Education Coordinating Board
917 Lakeridge Way
PO Box 43430
Olympia, WA   98504

174 Christie School Scholarship

AMOUNT: $3000   DEADLINE: March 1
FIELDS/MAJORS: Social Work

Award for a graduate student who agrees to fulfill a three-term, two-day a week field instruction assignment at the Christie school. One award offered annually. Contact the Graduate School of Social Work for more information.

Portland State University
Graduate School of Social Work
300 University Center Building
Portland, OR   97207

175 Chrysalis Scholarship

AMOUNT: $750   DEADLINE: March 1
FIELDS/MAJORS: Geoscience Fields

Scholarships available to women who are candidates for an advanced degree in a geoscience field. Applicants must have had their education interrupted for at least one year. Applicant must be completing her thesis during the current academic year. Awards will be made by March 31. Write to the address below for further details.

Association for Women Geoscientists Foundation
G & H Production Company
518 17th Street #930
Denver, CO   80202

176 CIAR Postdoctoral Fellowships

AMOUNT: Maximum: $30000   **DEADLINE:** October 31
FIELDS/MAJORS: Indoor Air Research

Fellowship grants are awarded to individuals for the purpose of providing stipends in support of postdoctoral candidates engaged in research of indoor air. Applicants must hold the Ph.D. or the M.D. at the time of the award. Write to the address below for more information.

Center for Indoor Air Research
1099 Winterson Road
Suite 280
Linthicum, MD   21090

177 Cires Visiting Fellowship

AMOUNT: None Specified   **DEADLINE:** December 10
FIELDS/MAJORS: Environmental Sciences, Atmospheric Chemistry, Remote Sensing

One-year visiting fellowship for senior scientists and recent Ph.D. recipients in the fields of study above. Preference is given to candidates with research experience at institutions outside the Boulder scientific community. Write to Dr. Howard P. Hanson at the address below for more details.

Cooperative Institute for Research in Environmental Sciences
Cires Visiting Fellows Program
University of Colorado
Boulder, CO   80309

178 Clarence M. Mills Scholarship

AMOUNT: $1500   **DEADLINE:** September 1
FIELDS/MAJORS: Law

Scholarships are available at the University of Oklahoma, Norman for full-time, first-year law students, with a parent who is a district or associate district judge. Based on need and merit. Write to the address below for information.

University of Oklahoma, Norman
Admissions and Records, Law Center
Room 22, 300 Timberdell Road
Norman, OK   73019

179 Clark Short-Term Fellowships

AMOUNT: $2000–$6000
DEADLINE: March 15
FIELDS/MAJORS: 17th, 18th Century Studies

Residential predoctoral and post-doctoral fellowships at the center for 17th and 18th century studies at UCLA. Supports research, restoration, or dissertation concerns. Terms of fellowships are one to three months. Award amount is $2000 per month. Research topics include history of printing, western Americana, British studies, and literature. Write to the fellowship coordinator at the address below for details.

UCLA Center for 17th and 18th Century Studies
William Andrews Clark Memorial Library
2520 Cimmarron Street
Los Angeles, CA   90018

180 Clifford W. Oliver Memorial Scholarship in Cardiology

AMOUNT: None Specified   **DEADLINE:** March 1
FIELDS/MAJORS: Cardiology Medicine

Awards are available at the University of New Mexico for fourth-year students in medical school who plan to enter the cardiology profession. Applicants must be New Mexico residents with an acceptable GPA. Write to the address below for more information.

University of New Mexico, Albuquerque
Office of Financial Aid
Albuquerque, NM   87131

181 Clinical Fellowships and Internships

AMOUNT: Maximum: $6000   **DEADLINE:** March 30
FIELDS/MAJORS: Psychology

Fellowships and internships in cognitive behavior therapy for graduates only. Applicants must have a Ph.D. in psychology; or an M.D., R.N., or M.S.W. and be eligible for state certification. Nine awards are given annually. The fellowship program is an eleven-month, two-year program, and the internship is an eleven-month, one-year program. Write to address below for details.

Institute for Rational-Emotive Therapy
Director of Training
45 E. 65th Street
New York, NY   10021

182 Clinical Fellowships

AMOUNT: Maximum: $36000   **DEADLINE:** October 1
FIELDS/MAJORS: Medical Research—Cystic Fibrosis

Fellowships for early career M.D.s and Ph.D.s interested in preparing for a career in academic medicine. Applicants must be eligible for board certification in pediatrics or internal medicine by the time the fellowship begins. Awards are $36000 (first year) and $37500 (second year). Training must encompass diagnostic and therapeutic procedures, comprehensive care and CF related research. Applicants must be U.S. citizens or permanent residents. Write to the address below for more information.

Cystic Fibrosis Foundation
Office of Grants Management
6931 Arlington Road
Bethesda, MD   20814

183
Clinical Pharmacology and Postdoctoral Research Fellowships

AMOUNT: $25000   DEADLINE: October 1
FIELDS/MAJORS: Pharmacology, Clinical Pharmacology

Fellowships for Ph.D. candidates and recent recipients of doctorates in pharmacology or a related area to gain and expand research skills through formal training. Tenure is for two years. One careers award and three postdoctoral awards. Must be U.S. citizen or permanent resident. Write to the address below for details.

Pharmaceutical Manufacturers Association Foundation, Inc.
1100 15th Street, NW
Washington, DC   20005

184
Clinical Training Fellowship

AMOUNT: Maximum: $8340
DEADLINE: January 15
FIELDS/MAJORS: Psychology, Clinical

Fellowships for minority doctoral students of psychology who are specializing in clinical training. Must be a U.S. citizen or permanent resident enrolled in a full-time academic program. Fellowships are usually awarded for ten months with a monthly stipend of $834. Write to the address below for more information.

American Psychological Association
750 First Street, NE
Washington, DC   20002

185
Clyde Farrar Fellowship

AMOUNT: $5000   DEADLINE: March 1
FIELDS/MAJORS: Electrical Engineering

Scholarships are available at the University of Oklahoma, Norman for full-time graduate students in electrical engineering. One award offered annually. Write to the address below for information.

University of Oklahoma, Norman
College of Engineering
Room 107, CEC
Norman, OK   73019

186
College of Education Awards

AMOUNT: None Specified
DEADLINE: February 21
FIELDS/MAJORS: Education

Scholarships for graduate students enrolled in the college of education who have a minimum cumulative GPA of 3.0. Write to the address below for further details.

Wayne State University
Dean's Office
Room 441 Education Building
Detroit, MI   48202

187
College of Education Graduate Scholarship

AMOUNT: $500   DEADLINE: None Specified
FIELDS/MAJORS: Education

Scholarships are available at the University of Oklahoma, Norman for full-time doctoral level graduate students, with preference given to those at the dissertation stage. Must demonstrate financial need and academic promise. Write to the address below for information. At least 3.0 GPA required.

University of Oklahoma, Norman
College of Education
Room 105, ECH
Norman, OK   73019

188
College of Law First-Year Minority Scholarships

AMOUNT: $1000–$4000   DEADLINE: September 1
FIELDS/MAJORS: Law

Scholarships are available at the University of Oklahoma, Norman for full-time, first-year minority law students. Includes the Sequoyah Scholarship, the ADA Lois Sipuel Fisher Scholarship, and the Oklahoma State Regents Professional Study grants. Six to seven awards offered annually. Write to the address below for information.

University of Oklahoma, Norman
Admissions and Records, Law Center
Room 22, 300 Timberdell Road
Norman, OK   73019

189
College of Law First-Year Scholarships

AMOUNT: $500–$4000   DEADLINE: September 1
FIELDS/MAJORS: Law

Scholarships are available at the University of Oklahoma, Norman for full-time, first-year law students. Includes the George B. Fraser, Judge John D. Brett and Robert D. Hudson, Justice Harry L.S. Halley Memorial, Kerr-McGee, Lee B. Thompson, McKinney, Stringer & Webster, and Tannell A. and Madelyn Shadid Memorial scholarships. Individual award requirements will vary. Write to the address below for information.

University of Oklahoma, Norman
Admissions and Records, Law Center
Room 22, 300 Timberdell Road
Norman, OK   73019

190
College of Nursing Graduate Scholarships

AMOUNT: None Specified   DEADLINE: July 1
FIELDS/MAJORS: Nursing

Scholarships are available for graduate nursing students at OU. Includes the Ada T. Hawkins, Alice Sowers Scholarship Fund, DHHS Traineeship, and the Parry Scholarship. Individual award requirements may vary. Write to the address below for information.

University of Oklahoma, Norman
Director, Office of Financial Aid
OUHSC, PO Box 73190
Oklahoma City, OK   73190

191
Columbus State University Presidential Scholarship

AMOUNT: None Specified   DEADLINE: None Specified
FIELDS/MAJORS: All Areas of Study

Scholarships are available to the top five graduates of
Chattahoochee Valley Community State University. Contact the
address listed for further information.

Columbus State University
Financial Aid Office
4225 University Avenue
Columbus, GA   31907

192
Commonwealth Scholarship for Legal Studies

AMOUNT: $1410   DEADLINE: February 1
FIELDS/MAJORS: Law

Applicant must be a Kentucky resident admitted to Chase College
of Law. Contact the Assistant Dean, Chase College of Law, for
further information.

Northern Kentucky University
Chase College of Law
Office of Admissions
Highland Heights, KY   41099

193
Communication Disorder Scholarship

AMOUNT: $500   DEADLINE: March 1
FIELDS/MAJORS: Communication Disorders

Applicants must be maintaining legal residence in Massachusetts
and present a letter of endorsement from a sponsoring Women's
Club in your community. For graduate study in communication
disorders. Write to the address below for details, be sure to
include a SASE.

General Federation of Women's Clubs of Massachusetts
Scholarship Chairman, 245 Dutton Road
PO Box 679
Sudbury, MA   01776

194
Communicative Disorders Scholarship

AMOUNT: Maximum: $1000
DEADLINE: April 1
FIELDS/MAJORS: Speech Language Pathology and/or Audiology

Awards for master's students in the fields above who are from the
tri-district Pennsylvania area (Lancaster, York, Dauphin, Lebanon,
or Chester Counties). Applicants must be U.S. citizens or permanent residents and have a GPA of at least 3.2 coming out of college.
Must be enrolled in an ASHA accredited program. One award is
offered annually. Write to the address below for more information.

Hear/Say Fund, Inc.
321 Bareview Drive
Leola, PA   17540

195
Computational Science Fellowship Program

AMOUNT: None Specified
DEADLINE: January 24
FIELDS/MAJORS: Life or Physical Science, Engineering,
Mathematics

Fellowships are available at Iowa State for graduate students in
their second year of graduate studies (or above). For science or
engineering students with career objectives in computational science. Must be a U.S. citizen or permanent resident. The awards
are $1500 per month, and the deadline date to apply is the third
Wednesday of every January. Write to the address below for information.

Iowa State University
Ames Laboratory
125 S. Third Street, Sherman Place
Ames, IA   50010

196
Congressional Science and Engineering Fellows Program

AMOUNT: None Specified   DEADLINE: January 15
FIELDS/MAJORS: Engineering, Science

Two fellowships are offered in the White House
Office of Science and Technology: one a senior
industrial scientist or engineer with at least fifteen
years professional experience; the other, for those
with at least five years. Fellows will be expected to
apply technical knowledge to formulating public
policy. Must be U.S. citizens. Write to "science and technology
programs" at the address below for details.

American Association for the Advancement of Science
1200 New York Avenue, NW
Washington, DC   20005

197
Conoco Fellowship

AMOUNT: $8800   DEADLINE: March 1
FIELDS/MAJORS: Chemical Engineering,
Materials Science

Scholarships are available at the University of Oklahoma, Norman
for full-time graduate students in chemical engineering or materials science. Must be U.S. citizens to apply. One award offered
annually. Write to the address below for information.

University of Oklahoma, Norman
Chemical Engineering and Materials Science
100 East Boyd Street, Energy Center
Norman, OK   73019

198
Consortium for Graduate Study in Management

AMOUNT: None Specified   DEADLINE: February 1
FIELDS/MAJORS: Business, Economics

Graduate fellowships for minorities. U.S. citizenship required.
Must have received bachelor's degree from accredited institution
and must submit GMAT scores. Each fellow undertakes the regular M.B.A. curriculum at one of the eleven consortium graduate
schools of business. Must be a member of one of the following
minority groups: Native American, African-American, or
Hispanic. Write to the address below for details.

Consortium for Graduate Study in Management
200 S. Hanley Road, Suite 1102
St. Louis, MO   63105

199
Constance Jordan Award

AMOUNT: $4000   DEADLINE: May 1
FIELDS/MAJORS: Gay and Lesbian Studies

Award for city university of New York doctoral students working
on a topic in "gay and lesbian literary studies with historical con-
tent." Write to the address below for more information.

Center for Lesbian and Gay Studies
City University of New York
33 West 42nd Street, Room 404N
New York, NY   10036

200
Construction Science Graduate Student Service Award

AMOUNT: $500   DEADLINE: April 15
FIELDS/MAJORS: Construction Science

Scholarships are available at the University of Oklahoma, Norman
for graduate students in construction science. Awarded on the
basis of service to the department and college. Write to the
address below for information.

University of Oklahoma, Norman
Dean, College of Architecture
OMS, Room 252
Norman, OK   73019

201
Continuing Education Grants

AMOUNT: $100–$500
DEADLINE: December 1
FIELDS/MAJORS: Medical Library Science

Grants for Medical Library Association members to develop
knowledge of the theoretical, administrative, technical aspects, or
a combination of the above, in library sciences. Write to the
address below for details.

Medical Library Association
Program Services
6 N. Michigan Avenue, Suite 300
Chicago, IL   60602

202
Continuing Education Scholarships

AMOUNT: Maximum: $300
DEADLINE: November 30
FIELDS/MAJORS: Teaching, Nursing

Open to credentialed classroom teachers and school nurses for
continuing education courses. For use at accredited colleges and
universities in California. Applications available after August 1.
Send a legal-sized SASE to the address listed for an application.

California Congress of Parents, Teachers, and Students, Inc.
930 Georgia Street, PO Box 15015
Los Angeles, CA   90015

203
Cora Smith King Scholarship Endowment

AMOUNT: None Specified   DEADLINE: April 15
FIELDS/MAJORS: Medicine

Awards for female students enrolled in the School of Medicine.
Contact the address below for further information or the financial
aid office at your school's location.

University of North Dakota—School of Medicine
Sandra Elshaug, Financial Aid Office
PO Box 9037—501 N. Columbia Road
Grand Forks, ND   58202

204
Corning Scholarship

AMOUNT: $2000–$3000   DEADLINE: May 7
FIELDS/MAJORS: Optometry

Two awards are available for fourth-year optometry students who
submit the best papers of 600–1000 words on any one of a given
list of topics decided each year by Corning. Write to the address
below or contact your department of optometry for information.

American Optometric Foundation
4330 East West Highway, Suite 1117
Bethesda, MD   20814

205
CPCU—Harry Loman Foundation Graduate Grants

AMOUNT: Maximum: $1000
DEADLINE: None Specified
FIELDS/MAJORS: Insurance

Grants are available for graduate students studying full-time or
doing research in the property/casualty insurance field. Academics
will be considered. This is a matching scholarship that will match,
up to $1000, the award granted by local chapters. There are 152
chapters in the U.S. working with local colleges and universities.
Write to the address below for information.

CPCU—Harry Loman Foundation
Joyce Natalie, Administrator
720 Providence Road, PO Box 3009
Malvern, PA   19355

206 Crane-Rogers Foundation Fellowship

AMOUNT: None Specified   **DEADLINE:** April 1
FIELDS/MAJORS: Foreign Studies—East-Central Europe, Middle East

Fellowships are available to postdoctoral scholars to support research in an area of interest to the foundation, including those areas mentioned above. Tenure is two years. Applicants must be age thirty-six or less. Write to the address below for information.

Institute of Current World Affairs
Gary L. Hansen, Program Administrator
4 West Wheelock Street
Hanover, NH   03755

207 Critical Teacher Shortage Tuition Reimbursement Program

AMOUNT: None Specified   **DEADLINE:** None Specified
FIELDS/MAJORS: Education

Incentive program to encourage Florida public school district employees certified to teach to become certified in or gain a graduate degree in a critical teacher shortage area. Must complete courses with a minimum GPA of 3.0. Get further information from district school board offices or the office of student financial assistance.

Florida Department of Education
Office of Student Financial Assistance
1344 Florida Education Center
Tallahassee, FL   32399

208 Cuyahoga County Medical Foundation

AMOUNT: $500–$1500   **DEADLINE:** June 1
FIELDS/MAJORS: Medicine, Dentistry, Pharmacy, Nursing, Osteopathy

Student must be a bonafide resident of Cuyahoga County. Students must be attending school for doctor of medicine, osteopathic medicine, dentistry, pharmacy, or nursing. Ten to fifteen awards are offered annually. Write to the address below for more information.

Cuyahoga County Medical Foundation
6000 Rockside Woods Boulevard, Suite 150
Cleveland, OH   44131

209 D. Elizabeth Williams International Fellowship

AMOUNT: None Specified
DEADLINE: January 1
FIELDS/MAJORS: Human Environmental Sciences

Award open to international graduate students in human environmental sciences. Contact the address below for further information.

University of North Carolina, Greensboro
Financial Aid Office
723 Kenilworth Street
Greensboro, NC   27412

210 Daad Fellowships in German-Jewish History and Culture

AMOUNT: $2000   **DEADLINE:** November 1
FIELDS/MAJORS: Jewish Studies

Research fellowships available at the Leo Baeck Institute for postdoctoral scholars who are studying the social, communal, and intellectual history of German-speaking Jewry. Applicants must be less than thirty-six years of age and citizens of the U.S. Write to the address below for information.

Leo Baeck Institute
Fellowship Programs
129 East 73rd Street
New York, NY   10021

211 Daad Fulbright Grants

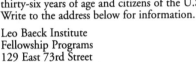

AMOUNT: None Specified
DEADLINE: October 31
FIELDS/MAJORS: German Studies

Grants for graduate study/research in Germany for one academic year. Applicants must be U.S. citizens between eighteen and thirty-two years of age and be fluent in German. Contact your campus Fulbright program advisor, write to the address below for further details, or see website; http://www.daad.org.

Daad German Academic Exchange Service
Institute of International Education
809 United Nations Plaza
New York, NY   10017

212 Daad-Center for Contemporary German Literature Grant

AMOUNT: Maximum: $3000   **DEADLINE:** January 1
FIELDS/MAJORS: German Literature

Grants for scholars/faculty planning to work in the field of German literature at the Center for Contemporary German Literature at Washington University in St. Louis, Missouri. Contact Prof. Paul Michael Luetzeler, Director, at the address below for more information or see website: http://www.daad.org.

Daad German Academic Exchange Service
Center for Contemp. German Literature
Washington Univ., Campus Box 1104
St. Louis, MO   63130

213
Dale and Coral Courtney Scholarship

AMOUNT: $2000   DEADLINE: None Specified
FIELDS/MAJORS: Geography

Awards are available at Portland State University for graduate students studying geography. Application consists of an essay and recommendations. Contact the geography department office for more details.

Portland State University
Geography Department Office
424 Cramer Hall
Portland, OR   97207

214
Daniel B. Goldberg Scholarship

AMOUNT: $3500   DEADLINE: February 14
FIELDS/MAJORS: Business and Finance

Scholarship for graduate students preparing for a career in state and local government finance. For full-time study. Must have a superior academic record. One award per year. Must be a legal resident of the U.S. or Canada. Information may be available from the head of your accounting department. If not, write to the address below. Applications are available in November for awards in the following spring. GPA of at least 2.8 required.

Government Finance Officers Association
Scholarship Committee
180 N. Michigan Avenue, Suite 800
Chicago, IL   60601

215
Daniel E. Cordova Scholarship Fund

AMOUNT: None Specified   DEADLINE: March 1
FIELDS/MAJORS: Medicine

Awards are available at the University of New Mexico for medical students from New Mexico who have financial need. Write to the address below for more information.

University of New Mexico, Albuquerque
Office of Financial Aid
Albuquerque, NM   87131

216
Daniel G. McNamara Memorial Scholarship

AMOUNT: $500   DEADLINE: None Specified
FIELDS/MAJORS: Public Administration

Awards open to full-time graduate students in public administration. Contact the address below for further information.

University of Toledo
Chair, Dept. of Political Science
1032 Scott Hall
Toldeo, OH   43606

217
Daughters of Penelope National Scholarship Awards (Graduate)

AMOUNT: $750–$1500   DEADLINE: June 20
FIELDS/MAJORS: All Areas of Study

Scholarships for women who are currently enrolled in a post-graduate degree program (M.A., Ph.D., M.D., etc.) who are immediate family members (or members themselves) of Daughters of Penelope, Order of AHEPA, or Maids of Athena. Must be enrolled for 9 credits/year minimum. Not renewable. Nine award programs are offered each year. Write to the address below for details.

Daughters of Penelope National Headquarters
National Scholarship Awards
1909 Q Street, NW, Suite 500
Washington, DC   20009

218
David Baumgardt Memorial Fellowships

AMOUNT: $3000   DEADLINE: November 1
FIELDS/MAJORS: Jewish Studies

Fellowships are available for research at the Leo Baeck Institute for current predoctoral scholars who are studying the social, communal, and intellectual history of German-speaking Jewry. Applicants must be U.S. citizens. Write to the address below for information.

Leo Baeck Institute
Fellowship Programs
129 East 73rd Street
New York, NY   10021

219
David E. Finley Fellowship, Paul Mellon Fellowship

AMOUNT: $16000   DEADLINE: November 15
FIELDS/MAJORS: Western Art, Visual Arts, and Related Areas

Three-year fellowships are available for doctoral scholars researching for the dissertation. Two years will be spent in Europe in research, and one year will be spent at the National Gallery of Art. Applicants must be U.S. citizens or legal residents. One fellowship is given annually. Write to the address below for information.

National Gallery of Art
Center for Advanced Study in Visual Arts
Predoctoral Fellowship Program
Washington, DC   20565

220
David Glass Outstanding Graduate Student Award

AMOUNT: $250   DEADLINE: February 7
FIELDS/MAJORS: Business

Applicants must be an outstanding graduate students of COBA. Contact the COBA office for more information.

Southwest Missouri State University
Office of Financial Aid
901 South National Avenue
Springfield, MO 65804

221

David H. Clift Scholarship

AMOUNT: $3000   DEADLINE: April 1
FIELDS/MAJORS: Library Science

Applicants must be graduate students who are entering or
enrolled in an ALA-accredited master's program and be U.S. or
Canadian citizens. Based on academic accomplishment, leadership
potential, and desire to pursue a career in Librarianship. For students who have completed fewer than 12 semester hours toward
master's (by June of preceding year). Write to the address below
for details.

American Library Association
Staff Liaison, ALA Scholarship Juries
50 E. Huron Street
Chicago, IL 60611

222

David Hall Scholarship

AMOUNT: $200   DEADLINE: September 1
FIELDS/MAJORS: Law

Scholarships are available at the University of
Oklahoma, Norman for full-time, first-year African-
American law students, who earned at least a B+
in contracts. Write to the address below for
information. At least 2.9 GPA required.

University of Oklahoma, Norman
Admissions and Records, Law Center
Room 22, 300 Timberdell Road
Norman, OK 73019

223

David L. Owens Scholarship

AMOUNT: $10000   DEADLINE: April 1
FIELDS/MAJORS: Water Utility Industry

Scholarship for graduating seniors or master's level students pursuing a degree in the water utility industry. Must be a U.S. citizen.
Write to the address below for more information.

National Association of Water Companies
Scholarship Committee
1725 K Street, NW, Suite 1212
Washington, DC 20006

224

David Rozkuszka Scholarship

AMOUNT: None Specified   DEADLINE: December 1
FIELDS/MAJORS: Library Science

Awards for ALA-accredited master's degree candidate currently
working in a library with government documents, with a commitment to government documents librarianship. Write to the
address below for additional information.

American Library Association
Susan Tulis, Law Library
University of Virginia, 580 Massie Road
Charlottesville, VA 22901

225

David Tamotsu Kagiwada Memorial Scholarship

AMOUNT: None Specified   DEADLINE: March 15
FIELDS/MAJORS: Theology

Applicants must be Asian-American members of the Christian
Church (Disciples of Christ) who are preparing for the ordained
ministry. For full-time study. Financial need is considered. Must
have at least a "C+" grade average. Write to the address below for
details. GPA of at least 2.3 required.

Christian Church (Disciples of Christ)
Attn: Scholarships
PO Box 1986
Indianapolis, IN 46206

226

Day Dugan Scholarship

AMOUNT: $2566   DEADLINE: None Specified
FIELDS/MAJORS: Business Administration

Open to full-time M.B.A. students in good standing. Preference
for unsupported students. Contact the address below for further
information.

University of Northern Iowa
Geofrey Mills, College of Business Admin
325 Business
Cedar Falls, IA 50614

227

DC Commission on the Arts and Humanities Grants

AMOUNT: $2500–$20000   DEADLINE: March 17
FIELDS/MAJORS: Arts

Applicants must be artists and reside in Washington, D.C. Awards
are intended to generate arts endeavors within the Washington,
D.C., community. Write for further details.

District of Columbia Commission on the Arts and Humanities
Stables Art Center
410 Eighth Street, NW, Fifth Floor
Washington, DC 20004

228

Dean C. Fletcher Graduate Fellowship in Clinical Dietetics

AMOUNT: None Specified   DEADLINE: February 1
FIELDS/MAJORS: Clinical, Community Nutrition

Award for graduate student with a minimum GPA of 3.5 to conduct research in clinical or community nutrition. Contact the
address below for further information.

Washington State University—Scholarship Committee
College of Agriculture and Home Economics
423 Hulbert Hall
Pullman, WA 99164

229 Dean John A. Knauss Marine Policy Fellowship

AMOUNT: $30000 DEADLINE: September 2
FIELDS/MAJORS: Marine Related Fields

This program matches highly qualified graduate students with hosts in the legislative or executive branch, or appropriate associations/institutions in the Washington, D.C., area for one year. Write to the address below for information.

SUNY at Stony Brook—New York Sea Grant Institute
Ms. Ruth Tompkins
115 Nassau Hall
Stony Brook, NY   11794

230 Deborah Slosberg Fund

AMOUNT: None Specified DEADLINE: None Specified
FIELDS/MAJORS: Poetry or Prose Writing

Awards for students at UMass pursuing in an MFA in one of the areas above. Based on substantial and worthy achievement over the entire career in the program. Contact the Director, Master of Fine Arts Program, at the address below for more information.

University of Massachusetts, Amherst
Director, Master of Fine Arts Program
Amherst, MA   01003

231 Delaney MFA Fellowship Fund Scholarship

AMOUNT: None Specified DEADLINE: None Specified
FIELDS/MAJORS: Fiction Writing

Awards for nontraditional students at UMass pursuing a MFA in fiction. Preference is given to women thirty years of age or above. Contact the Chair, English Department at the address below for more information.

University of Massachusetts, Amherst
Chair of the English Department
Amherst, MA   01003

232 Delores Auzenne Fellowship

AMOUNT: $5000 DEADLINE: February 1
FIELDS/MAJORS: All Areas of Study

Fellowships available for African-American graduate students attending school full-time. Must have a minimum GPA of 3.0 and be U.S. citizens or permanent residents. Write to the address below for more information.

Florida International University
Equal Opportunity Program, PC 215
University Park
Miami, FL   33199

233 Dental Scholarship Program, Continuing Dental Scholarship Program

AMOUNT: $3000–$5000 DEADLINE: March 1
FIELDS/MAJORS: Dentistry

Scholarships are available to incoming as well as continuing students in the School of Dentistry at Marquette. Most based primarily on merit, others consider financial need. Dental scholarship program application/recommendation forms will be required. Contact the School of Dentistry for further information and forms. At least 2.9 GPA required.

Marquette University, School of Dentistry
Office of Admissions
604 N. Sixteenth Street
Milwaukee, WI   53233

234 Dental Scholarships

AMOUNT: $1000–$4000 DEADLINE: March 1
FIELDS/MAJORS: Dentistry

Open to full-time dental students. These three awards are annual competitions: Dr. John E. and Lucille O. Koss Memorial; Dr. Raymond and Marcella Schweiger Endowed, and the David and Roseann Tolan Family Academic Scholarship. Some criteria varies, but most is standard in looking at academics, extracurricular activities, and financial need. Contact the address below for further information. At least 2.8 GPA required.

Marquette University
Office of Admissions
1217 W. Wisconsin Avenue
Milwaukee, WI   53233

235 Dental Student Scholarship

AMOUNT: $2500 DEADLINE: June 15
FIELDS/MAJORS: Dentistry

Applicant must be a U.S. citizen enrolled full-time entering their second year in a dentistry program accredited by the Commission on Accreditation of the American Dental Association. Students must have a GPA of 3.0 or above and demonstrate financial need. Students receiving a full scholarship from any other source are ineligible for this scholarship. Contact the address below for further information.

ADA Endowment and Assistance Fund, Inc.
211 East Chicago Avenue
Chicago, IL   60611

236 Department Awards and Graduate Assistantships

AMOUNT: None Specified DEADLINE: March 1
FIELDS/MAJORS: All Areas of Study

Tuition remissions for a specific number of semester hours for graduate assistants. Must be nominated by department heads for departmental awards. Contact the financial aid office and your department for further information.

Alaska Pacific University
APU Scholarships
4101 University Drive
Anchorage, AK   99508

237 Departmental Awards

AMOUNT: None Specified   **DEADLINE:** None Specified
FIELDS/MAJORS: All Areas of Study

Many departments in the graduate school award teaching and research assistantships to graduate students. The awards provide a stipend, 6 to 10 credits of graduate tuition per term, and subsidized health insurance. Write to the chairperson of your department for further details.

Wayne State University
Graduate School
Office of the Dean
Detroit, MI   48202

238 Departmental Financial Aid for Graduate Students at BYU

GPA 3.0+

AMOUNT: None Specified   **DEADLINE:** None Specified
FIELDS/MAJORS: All Areas of Study

Teaching/research assistantships, internships, and supplementary awards for graduate students at BYU. These are administered by the individual departments. Applicants must be admitted into a graduate program and have a minimum GPA of 3.0. You must contact your department at least several weeks in advance of the start of graduate studies to be considered for financial aid.

Brigham Young University
Graduate School
B-336, ASB
Provo, UT   84602

239 Disciple Chaplains' Scholarship

AMOUNT: None Specified   **DEADLINE:** March 15
FIELDS/MAJORS: Theology

Applicants must be members of the Christian Church (Disciples of Christ) who are entering first year in seminary. For full-time study. Financial need is considered. Must have better than a "C+" (2.3) grade average. Write to the address below for details.

Christian Church (Disciples of Christ)
Attn: Scholarships
PO Box 1986
Indianapolis, IN   46206

240 Discovery Research Proposal

AMOUNT: Maximum: $25000   **DEADLINE:** May 15
FIELDS/MAJORS: Meat Science, Swine Studies

Awards are available for scientists in the areas of pork production. Graduate students as well as postdoctoral scholars are eligible for this award. Requires applicant to submit a research proposal to the council. Write to the address below for more details.

National Pork Producers Council
PO Box 10383
Des Moines, IA   50306

241 Dissertation and Postdoctoral Research Fellowships

AMOUNT: $1000–$2000   **DEADLINE:** April 1
FIELDS/MAJORS: Jewish Studies

Six fellowships are available for postdoctoral candidates or persons at the doctoral dissertation stage for up to three months of active research or writing at the American Jewish Archives. Contact address below for complete information.

American Jewish Archives
Administrative Director
3101 Clifton Avenue
Cincinnati, OH   45220

242 Dissertation Awards

AMOUNT: $1000   **DEADLINE:** None Specified
FIELDS/MAJORS: All Areas of Study

Cash awards are available at the University of Oklahoma, Norman for the four best dissertations by graduate students in the preceding year. Write to the address below for information.

University of Oklahoma, Norman
Graduate College
1000 Asp Avenue, Room 313
Norman, OK   73019

243 Dissertation Fellowship

AMOUNT: $7500   **DEADLINE:** May 1
FIELDS/MAJORS: U.S. Military and Naval History

A fellowship is available for doctoral candidates performing dissertation research in an area of history relevant to the Marine Corps. Applicants must be U.S. citizens and have all requirements for the doctoral degree completed by the time of application, except the dissertation. Some portion of the work is expected to be done at the Marine Corps Historical Center in Washington, D.C. Write to the address below for information

Marine Corps Historical Center
Building 58
Washington Navy Yard
Washington, DC   20374

244 Dissertation Fellowships

AMOUNT: $8000   DEADLINE: February 1
FIELDS/MAJORS: American Military History

Doctoral dissertation fellowships for civilian Ph.D. candidates at recognized graduate schools. All requirements for Ph.D. (except dissertation) should be completed by September of award year. Must be a U.S. citizen or legal resident. Write to the address below for complete details.

U.S. Army Center of Military History
Dissertation Fellowship Committee
1099 14th Street, NW
Washington, DC   20005

245 Dissertation Fellowships

AMOUNT: Maximum: $14500
DEADLINE: November 15
FIELDS/MAJORS: All Areas of Study

Fellowships for women in their final year of writing their dissertations. Applicants must have completed all course work, passed all preliminary exams, and have their dissertation research proposal (or plan) approved by November 15. Must be a United States citizen or permanent resident. Awards are for one year beginning July 1. The fellow is expected to devote full time to the project for the fellowship year. Scholars may apply up to two times for a dissertation fellowship on the same topic. Write for complete details.

American Association of University Women
2401 Virginia Avenue, NW
Washington, DC   20037

246 Dissertation Fellowships

AMOUNT: Maximum: $6000
DEADLINE: September 15
FIELDS/MAJORS: History, Business, Technology, Industry, Economic, Science

Residential fellowships for Ph.D. candidates who have completed all course work and are starting the dissertation process. The dissertation must be within the center's research fields and collecting interests. Programs for postdoctoral scholarly work are also available. Write to address listed for more details.

Hagley Museum and Library
PO Box 3630
Wilmington, DE   19807

247 Dissertation Fellowships

AMOUNT: None Specified   DEADLINE: November 1
FIELDS/MAJORS: Music, Drama, Playwriting

Fellowships are available to Ph.D. candidates for dissertation research that is directly related to the musical works of Kurt Weill and to the perpetuation of his artistic legacy. Write to the address below for information.

Kurt Weill Foundation for Music, Inc.
Joanna C. Lee, Associate Director
7 East 20th Street
New York, NY   10003

248 Diversity Tuition Waiver Program

AMOUNT: None Specified   DEADLINE: April 15
FIELDS/MAJORS: Medicine

Awards for Native Americans and Alaskans and economically disadvantaged students. Emphasis is given to American Indian medical students from the twenty-four tribes of North Dakota, Montana, Nebraska, South Dakota, and Wyoming. Contact the address below for further information or the financial aid office at your school's location.

University of North Dakota—School of Medicine
Sandra Elshaug, Financial Aid Office
PO Box 9037—501 N. Columbia Road
Grand Forks, ND   58202

249 Doctoral and Postdoctoral Fellowship

AMOUNT: $3700–$4300
DEADLINE: November 1
FIELDS/MAJORS: Japanese Studies

Fifteen fellowships available to doctoral or postdoctoral students in field of Japanese studies who have completed all the academic requirements except the dissertation. Applicants must be able to speak Japanese in order to successfully continue their research in Japan. Write to the address listed for additional information.

Japan Foundation
New York Office
152 West 57th Street
New York, NY   10019

250 Doctoral Dissertation Fellowships in Jewish Studies

AMOUNT: $6000–$8500   DEADLINE: January 3
FIELDS/MAJORS: Jewish Studies

Awards are available for students who have completed all academic requirements for the doctoral degree except the dissertation in the field of Jewish studies. Must be a U.S. citizen or permanent resident and give evidence of a proficiency in a Jewish language. Write to the address below for more information.

National Foundation for Jewish Culture
330 Seventh Avenue
21st Floor
New York, NY   10001

251 Doctoral Dissertation Fellowships in Law and Social Science

AMOUNT: $15000   **DEADLINE:** February 3
FIELDS/MAJORS: Law, Social Science

Fellowships are available for Ph.D. candidates who have completed all doctoral requirements except the dissertation. Proposed research must be in the areas of sociolegal studies, social scientific approaches to law, the legal profession, or legal institutions. Fellowships are held in residence at the ABF. All fellows are provided with personal computers and access to the libraries of Northwestern University and the University of Chicago. Minority students are encouraged to apply. Write to the address below for information.

American Bar Foundation
Ann Tatalovich, Assistant Director
750 N. Lake Shore Drive
Chicago, IL   60611

252 Doctoral Dissertation Grant Program

AMOUNT: $10000   **DEADLINE:** January 31
FIELDS/MAJORS: Purchasing, Business, Management, Logistics, Economics, Industrial Engineering

Doctoral dissertation research grants are available for research that can be applied to the management of the purchasing and materials management functions and to help develop high-potential academicians who will teach and conduct research in the field. For doctoral candidates in an accredited U.S. college or university. Must be U.S. citizens or permanent residents. Write to the address below for information.

National Association of Purchasing Management
Doctoral Research Grant Committee
PO Box 22160
Tempe, AZ   85285

253 Doctoral Dissertation Research in Chinese Studies Scholarships

AMOUNT: $10000   **DEADLINE:** August 15
FIELDS/MAJORS: Humanities, Social Science

Applicants must be doctoral candidates, in humanities or social sciences, with an approved dissertation prospectus. Enrollment in a university in the U.S. or Canada required. Write to the address below for more information.

China Times Cultural Foundation
136-39 41 Avenue, #1A
Flushing, NY   11355

254 Doctoral Fellowship Program in Biomedical Engineering

AMOUNT: None Specified   **DEADLINE:** December 11
FIELDS/MAJORS: Biomedical Engineering

Doctoral fellowships are available to support graduate students of outstanding scholarship, ability, and aptitude for future achievements in biomedical engineering research. Write to the address below for information.

Whitaker Foundation
Fellowship Programs
1700 North Moore Street, Suite 2200
Rosslyn, VA   22209

255 Doctoral Fellowships

AMOUNT: $14000   **DEADLINE:** February 21
FIELDS/MAJORS: Environmental Studies, Restoration, Hydrology

Fellowships are available to master and Ph.D. students seeking to fund thesis work conducted on the Hudson River. Projects may reflect disturbed coastal environments, dredging and filling activities, hydrological restrictions to tidal wetlands, and minimum habitat requirements for maintaining resource species. Write to the address below for information.

Hudson River National Estuarine Research Reserve
NYS Dept. of Environmental Conservation
c/o Bard College Field Station
Annandale, NY   12504

256 Doctoral Fellowships in Art Education

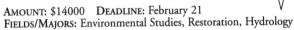

AMOUNT: Maximum: $12500
DEADLINE: November 1
FIELDS/MAJORS: Art Education

Open to doctoral students for the final research and writing stages of their doctoral studies. Must have completed an approved dissertation proposal that is significantly related to discipline-based art education at an accredited university in the U.S. or Canada. Awards will be announced by April 15. Contact the address listed for further information.

Getty Education Institute for the Arts
Dr. Jeffrey H. Patchen
1200 Getty Center Drive, #600
Los Angeles, CA   90049-1683

257 Doctoral Scholarships

AMOUNT: $3000   **DEADLINE:** February 1
FIELDS/MAJORS: Oncology Nursing

Scholarships available to doctoral students in the field of oncology nursing. All applicants must be currently licensed registered nurses. Three awards offered annually. Write to the address listed for more information.

Oncology Nursing Foundation
501 Holiday Drive
Pittsburgh, PA   15220

258 Donald E. and Phyllis J. Kuhn Graduate Fellowship

AMOUNT: None Specified   DEADLINE: March 1
FIELDS/MAJORS: Chemistry

Awards for doctoral students in the department of chemistry. Must be U.S. citizens. Preference given to students who demonstrate outstanding performance in research or teaching and have financial need. Contact the chemistry department for more information.

University of Massachusetts, Amherst
Chemistry Department
Amherst, MA   01003

259 Dorothy I. Cline Fellowship

AMOUNT: None Specified   DEADLINE: March 1
FIELDS/MAJORS: American Politics and Government, Public Policy, Political Theory

Awards are available at the University of New Mexico for Ph.D. students in the areas listed above who have completed their comprehensive exams. Write to the address below for more information.

University of New Mexico, Albuquerque
Office of Financial Aid
Albuquerque, NM   87131

260 Dorothy I. Mitstifer Fellowship

AMOUNT: $2000   DEADLINE: January 15
FIELDS/MAJORS: Home Economics/Related Fields

Applicants must be chapter advisers of Kappa Omicron Nu and wish to pursue graduate or post-graduate study. Awards will be announced April 1. Write to the address below for details.

Kappa Omicron Nu Honor Society
4990 Northwind Drive, Suite 140
East Lansing, MI   48823

261 Dorothy Ornest Graduate Fellowship

AMOUNT: None Specified   DEADLINE: March 1
FIELDS/MAJORS: Music

Awards for graduate music students based on outstanding performance. Contact the Director of Scholarships, Department of Music, for more information.

University of Massachusetts, Amherst
Director of Scholarships
Department of Music
Amherst, MA   01003

262 Dorothy Woodward Memorial Scholarship

AMOUNT: None Specified
DEADLINE: March 1
FIELDS/MAJORS: Southwest/Borderlands History

Awards are available at the University of New Mexico for advanced graduate study in southwest/Borderlands history. Award primarily for dissertation project. Write to the address below for more information.

University of New Mexico, Albuquerque
Office of Financial Aid
Albuquerque, NM   87131

263 Dow Elanco Graduate Scholarship

AMOUNT: $1000   DEADLINE: February 1
FIELDS/MAJORS: Plant Science, Plant Pathology, Forestry, Wildlife, Fisheries

Open to graduate students who have been at Purdue for at least one year. Must be U.S. citizens. Preference for doctoral students. Two awards offered annually. Write to the address below for more information.

Purdue University—School of Agriculture
Thomas W. Atkinson
1140 Agricultural Admin. Building, #121
West Lafayette, IN   47907

264 Dr. A.F. Zimmerman Award

AMOUNT: $750–$1250   DEADLINE: March 15
FIELDS/MAJORS: History

Applicants must be a student member of Phi Alpha Theta entering a graduate program leading to a master's degree in history. Three awards offered annually. Write to address below for details. Please indicate the name of your chapter. Information may be available from your chapter officers.

Phi Alpha Theta—International Honor Society in History
Headquarters Office
50 College Drive
Allentown, PA   18104

265 Dr. A.K. Saiki Memorial Scholarship

AMOUNT: None Specified   DEADLINE: April 15
FIELDS/MAJORS: Medicine

Awards for students who have completed the first- or second-year of medical school. Must have a strong dedication to medicine, strong work ethic, and positive attitude. Contact the address below for further information or the financial aid office at your school's location.

University of North Dakota—School of Medicine
Sandra Elshaug, Financial Aid Office
PO Box 9037—501 N. Columbia Road
Grand Forks, ND   58202

266 Dr. Alonzo Atencio Medical Scholarship

AMOUNT: None Specified
DEADLINE: March 1
FIELDS/MAJORS: Medicine

Awards are available at the University of New Mexico for minority medical students who demonstrate financial need and academic achievement. Must be enrolled full-time and be a resident of New Mexico. Write to the address below for more information.

University of New Mexico, Albuquerque
Office of Financial Aid
Albuquerque, NM   87131

267 Dr. and Mrs. C.L. Gardner Memorial and Walter A. Sperry Scholarships

AMOUNT: $1000   **DEADLINE:** February 28
FIELDS/MAJORS: Medicine, Nursing, Dentistry, Engineering

Scholarships for students pursuing graduate or professional degrees in medicine, nursing, dentistry, or engineering. Applicants must be residents of Aurora and have graduated from an Aurora high school. Write to the address below for details about both awards.

Aurora Foundation
111 W. Downer Place, Suite 312
Aurora, IL   60506

268 Dr. and Mrs. Emil Amberg Memorial Scholarship

AMOUNT: None Specified   **DEADLINE:** March 1
FIELDS/MAJORS: Medicine

Awards are available at the University of New Mexico for medical students who demonstrate academic ability and financial need. Write to the address below for more information.

University of New Mexico, Albuquerque
Office of Financial Aid
Albuquerque, NM   87131

269 Dr. Donald J. Reichert Endowment Scholarship Fund

AMOUNT: None Specified   **DEADLINE:** April 15
FIELDS/MAJORS: Medicine

Awards for upperclassmen in the School of Medicine with good academic records. Contact the address below for further information or the financial aid office at your school's location.

University of North Dakota—School of Medicine
Sandra Elshaug, Financial Aid Office
PO Box 9037—501 N. Columbia Road
Grand Forks, ND   58202

270 Dr. E.M. Gullat Memorial Scholarship

AMOUNT: None Specified   **DEADLINE:** None Specified
FIELDS/MAJORS: Medicine

Scholarships are available at the University of Oklahoma for medical students who plan to establish a practice in a smaller Oklahoma town (e.g., Ada, OK). Two awards offered annually. Write to the address below for information.

University of Oklahoma, Norman
Director, Office of Financial Aid
OUHSC, PO Box 73190
Oklahoma City, OK   73190

271 Dr. Floyd and Ann Marshall Medical Scholarship Fund

AMOUNT: None Specified   **DEADLINE:** April 15
FIELDS/MAJORS: Medicine

Awards for medical students who are North Dakota residents. Contact the address below for further information or the financial aid office at your school's location.

University of North Dakota—School of Medicine
Sandra Elshaug, Financial Aid Office
PO Box 9037—501 N. Columbia Road
Grand Forks, ND   58202

272 Dr. G. Layton Grier Scholarship Fund

AMOUNT: $1000   **DEADLINE:** February 1
FIELDS/MAJORS: Dentistry

Open to full-time dental students entering their second year of study at an accredited dental school, who are residents of Delaware. Based on grades, test scores, recommendations, and interview. Write to the address below for details.

Delaware State Dental Society
1925 Lovering Avenue
Wilmington, DE   19806

273 Dr. Irvin E. Hendryson Scholarship Fund

AMOUNT: None Specified
DEADLINE: March 1
FIELDS/MAJORS: Medicine

Awards are available at the University of New Mexico for Native American medical students. Write to the address below for more information.

University of New Mexico, Albuquerque
Office of Financial Aid
Albuquerque, NM   87131

274 Dr. J.R. Van Atta Memorial Scholarship

AMOUNT: None Specified   DEADLINE: March 1
FIELDS/MAJORS: Medicine

Awards are available at the University of New Mexico for third-year medical students. Write to the address below for more information.

University of New Mexico, Albuquerque
Office of Financial Aid
Albuquerque, NM 87131

275 Dr. James L. Gutman Family Scholarship

AMOUNT: None Specified
DEADLINE: None Specified
FIELDS/MAJORS: Dentistry

Open to full-time dental students of Native American descent. Amounts vary depending upon fund availability. Contact the address below for further information.

Marquette University
Office of Admissions
1217 W. Wisconsin Avenue
Milwaukee, WI 53233

276 Dr. John Pine Memorial Award

AMOUNT: $750–$1000   DEADLINE: March 15
FIELDS/MAJORS: History

Applicants must be members of Phi Alpha Theta who are advanced graduate students in history. Three awards offered annually. Write to address below for details. Please indicate the name of your chapter. Information may be available from your chapter officers.

Phi Alpha Theta—International Honor Society in History
Headquarters Office
50 College Drive
Allentown, PA 18104

277 Dr. Kiyoshi Sonoda Memorial Scholarship

AMOUNT: None Specified   DEADLINE: April 1
FIELDS/MAJORS: Dentistry

Applicants must be of Japanese ancestry, majoring in dentistry, and be a member of the JACL. Applications and information may be obtained from local JACL chapters, district offices, and the national headquarters at the address below. Please indicate your level of study and be certain to include a legal-sized SASE.

Japanese American Citizens League
National Scholarship and Award Program
1765 Sutter Street
San Francisco, CA 94115

278 Dr. Lloyd Ralston Memorial Medical Scholarship Endowment

AMOUNT: None Specified   DEADLINE: April 15
FIELDS/MAJORS: Medicine

Awards for fourth-year medical students or UND School of Medicine graduates who are in North Dakota residency programs. Contact the address below for further information or the financial aid office of your school's location.

University of North Dakota—School of Medicine
Sandra Elshaug, Financial Aid Office
PO Box 9037—501 N. Columbia Road
Grand Forks, ND 58202

279 Dr. Louis B. Silverman Memorial Medical Scholarship Endowment

AMOUNT: None Specified   DEADLINE: April 15
FIELDS/MAJORS: Medicine

Awards for students beginning their third or fourth year of medical school. Based on dedication, integrity, leadership, community service, and financial need. Contact the address below for further information or the financial aid office of your school's location.

University of North Dakota—School of Medicine
Sandra Elshaug, Financial Aid Office
PO Box 9037—501 N. Columbia Road
Grand Forks, ND 58202

280 Dr. Mae Davidow Memorial Scholarship

AMOUNT: $1000   DEADLINE: March 1
FIELDS/MAJORS: All Areas of Study

Applicants must be legally blind graduate students who demonstrate outstanding academic achievement. Write to the address below for details.

American Council of the Blind
Scholarship Coordinator
1155 15th Street, NW, Suite 720
Washington, DC 20005

281 Dr. Paul and Mary Bender Scholarship

AMOUNT: $2800   DEADLINE: April 20
FIELDS/MAJORS: Languages

Open to full-time graduate students who have completed a bachelor's degree in the UNI Department of Modern Languages. Must have a minimum GPA of 3.3, not hold a graduate assistantship during current year, and be a U.S. citizen or permanent resident. Contact the address below for further information.

University of Northern Iowa
Flavia Vernescu
Department of Modern Languages
Cedar Falls, IA 50614

282
Dr. Paul Quistgard Scholarship Endowment

AMOUNT: None Specified   DEADLINE: April 15
FIELDS/MAJORS: Medicine

Awards for students enrolled in the School of Medicine, based on achievement, industry, and need. Must be able to demonstrate satisfactory scholarship. Contact the address below for further information or the financial aid office at your school's location.

University of North Dakota—School of Medicine
Sandra Elshaug, Financial Aid Office
PO Box 9037—501 N. Columbia Road
Grand Forks, ND   58202

283
Dr. Philip Woutat Memorial Medical Scholarship Fund

AMOUNT: None Specified   DEADLINE: April 15
FIELDS/MAJORS: Medicine

Awards for medical students who have completed their first year and show proficiency in radiological anatomy. Must also demonstrate a dedication to the improvement of the image of the medical profession. Contact the address below for further information or the financial aid office at your school's location.

University of North Dakota—School of Medicine
Sandra Elshaug, Financial Aid Office
PO Box 9037—501 N. Columbia Road
Grand Forks, ND   58202

284
Dr. Richard Klemer Memorial Fellowship

AMOUNT: None Specified   DEADLINE: January 1
FIELDS/MAJORS: Human Development, Family Studies

Award open to graduates in the above areas. Contact the address below for further information.

University of North Carolina, Greensboro
Financial Aid Office
723 Kenilworth Street
Greensboro, NC   27412

285
Dr. Robert W. and Sarah H. Allen Memorial Medical Scholarship

AMOUNT: None Specified   DEADLINE: April 15
FIELDS/MAJORS: Medicine, Diabetes Research

Awards only for students who are interested in pursuing a summer elective in public health with preference given to those interested in diabetes research. Contact the address below for further information or the financial aid office of your school's location.

University of North Dakota—School of Medicine
Sandra Elshaug, Financial Aid Office
PO Box 9037—501 N. Columbia Road
Grand Forks, ND   58202

286
Dr. Ruby Gilbert Barnes Scholarship

AMOUNT: None Specified   DEADLINE: March 1
FIELDS/MAJORS: Nursing

Award open to graduate students in nursing. Contact the address below for further information.

University of North Carolina, Greensboro
Financial Aid Office
723 Kenilworth Street
Greensboro, NC   27412

287
Dr. Sherman A. Wengerd and Florence Mather Wengerd Fellowship

AMOUNT: None Specified   DEADLINE: March 1
FIELDS/MAJORS: Earth and Planetary Sciences

Awards are available at the University of New Mexico for graduates in the areas above to support field work and other travel related to thesis or dissertation work. Write to the address below for more information.

University of New Mexico, Albuquerque
Office of Financial Aid
Albuquerque, NM   87131

288
Dr. Theodore Von Karman Graduate Scholarship Program

AMOUNT: $5000   DEADLINE: None Specified
FIELDS/MAJORS: Engineering, Mathematics, Sciences

Scholarships for graduating ROTC cadets who plan to pursue a graduate degree in engineering, mathematics, or science. Write to the address below for details.

Aerospace Education Foundation
Financial Information Department
1501 Lee Highway
Arlington, VA   22209

289
Draper-Gullander-Largent Graduate Fellowship in History

AMOUNT: None Specified   DEADLINE: None Specified
FIELDS/MAJORS: History, Education

Award open to graduates majoring in history and pursuing a career in teaching. Contact the address below for further information.

University of North Carolina, Greensboro
Financial Aid Office
723 Kenilworth Street
Greensboro, NC   27412

290

Du Bois-Mandela-Rodney Residential Postdoctoral Scholarship Program

AMOUNT: $30000   DEADLINE: January 16
FIELDS/MAJORS: Identity Research

Residential fellowships for post-graduates engaged in postdoctoral work on the Afro-American and Caribbean experiences of men and women of color. Candidates must have gained their Ph.D.s within the last ten years. Contact the address below for details.

University of Michigan
Center for Afro-American and African Study
200 West Hall Building
Ann Arbor, MI   48109

291

E.B. Fred Competition

AMOUNT: Maximum: $17500   DEADLINE: February 1
FIELDS/MAJORS: All Areas of Study

For graduate students who have had an interruption in their formal education for at least five years. Must be in a Ph.D. program. Departments nominate their most academically competitive candidates to a divisional fellowship committee in early February. Write to the address listed for further information.

University of Wisconsin, Madison
Graduate School Fellowships Office
217 Bascom Hall, 500 Lincoln Drive
Madison, WI   53706-1380

292

E.J. Sierleja Memorial Fellowship

AMOUNT: $500   DEADLINE: November 15
FIELDS/MAJORS: Transportation

Scholarships are available for graduate industrial engineering majors who are enrolled on a full-time basis, members of the institute, with a GPA of at least 3.4. Preference is given to students with a career interest in the rail transportation industry. Students must be nominated by their department heads. Contact your school's industrial engineering department head for information.

Institute of Industrial Engineers
Scholarship Program
25 Technology Park/Atlanta
Norcross, GA   30092

293

E.K. Wise Loan Program

AMOUNT: None Specified
DEADLINE: None Specified
FIELDS/MAJORS: Occupational Therapy

Applicants must be female students who already hold a bachelor's degree and are members of AOTA. Must be U.S. citizen or permanent resident. Write to the address below for details.

American Occupational Therapy Association
1383 Piccard Drive, Suite 300
Rockville, MD   20850

294

Earl Warren Legal Training Program General Scholarships

AMOUNT: $3000–$4500   DEADLINE: March 15
FIELDS/MAJORS: Law

Scholarships for entering African-American law students. Preference is given to applicants who express an interest in Civil Rights or in Public Interest Litigation. Must be a U.S. citizen. Applications are available after November 15. Twenty to twenty-five awards are offered annually. Write to the address below for further information.

Earl Warren Legal Training Program, Inc.
99 Hudson Street, Suite 1600
New York, NY   10013

295

East European Area Studies Fellowships and Grants

AMOUNT: Maximum: $15000   DEADLINE: November 1
FIELDS/MAJORS: East European Studies

Fellowships for advanced graduate training and dissertation work and grants for language training and travel (for fieldwork). For U.S. citizens or permanent residents. Write to the address below for details.

American Council of Learned Societies
Office of Fellowships and Grants
228 E. 45th Street
New York, NY   10017

296

Eastern Star Religious Scholarships

AMOUNT: $500   DEADLINE: May 1
FIELDS/MAJORS: Theology, Seminary Studies

Scholarships are available for college graduates desiring to enter or continue in a theological school or seminary in California. Applicant must demonstrate financial need and have a GPA of at least 3.5. Write to the address below for additional information.

Order of the Eastern Star, Grand Chapter of California
Scholarship Committee Chairman
870 Market Street, Suite 722
San Francisco, CA   94102

297

EBSCO/NMRT Scholarship

AMOUNT: $1000   DEADLINE: December 1
FIELDS/MAJORS: Library and Information Science

Applicants must be ALA/NMRT members who are entering an ALA-accredited master's program or beyond. Must be U.S. or Canadian citizens. Write to NMRT Scholarship Committee Chair, at the address below for details.

California Institute of Technology Library
Pamela Padley, CA Tech. Library System
Mail Code 1-32.
Pasadena, CA   91125

298
Ecole Des Chartes Exchange Fellowship

AMOUNT: None Specified
DEADLINE: January 3
FIELDS/MAJORS: Archival Paleography, Bibliography, History of the Book

Awards provide a monthly stipend and tuition for a graduate student who is a U.S. citizen at the Ecole Nationale Des Chartes, in Paris. Applicant must be a doctoral candidate at any of the consortium schools. Contact the address below for further information.

Newberry Library
Committee on Awards—Renaissance Studies
60 W. Walton Street
Chicago, IL   60610

299
Ed Shipp Memorial Scholarship

AMOUNT: $1000   DEADLINE: September 1
FIELDS/MAJORS: Law

Scholarship available at the University of Oklahoma, Norman for full-time law students who reside in Pushmataha, McCurtain, or Choctaw County in Oklahoma. One award offered annually. Write to the address below for information.

University of Oklahoma, Norman
Admissions and Records, Law Center
Room 22, 300 Timberdell Road
Norman, OK   73019

300
Edilia De Montequin Fellowship

AMOUNT: $1000   DEADLINE: None Specified
FIELDS/MAJORS: Spanish, Portuguese, or Ibero-American Architectural History

Awards available are intended to support junior scholars, including graduate students, but senior scholars may apply. Research proposal must focus on any of the areas listed above. Applicants must have been a member of the Society of Architectural Historians for at least one year before applying. Write to the address below for more information.

Society of Architectural Historians
1365 North Astor Street
Chicago, IL   60610

301
Edna V. Moffett Fellowship

AMOUNT: Maximum: $2500
DEADLINE: December 16
FIELDS/MAJORS: History

Fellowships for a young Wellesley alumna. Preferably for a first year of graduate study in history. Contact the address below for further information.

Wellesley College, Fellowships for Wellesley Alumnae
Sec'y, Committee on Graduate Fellowships
106 Central Street, Career Center
Wellesley, MA   02181

302
Edna Yelland Memorial Scholarship

AMOUNT: $2000   DEADLINE: May 31
FIELDS/MAJORS: Library Science

Applicants must be a member of ethnic minority group who is pursuing a graduate library degree in library or information sciences. Must be U.S. citizen or permanent resident and California resident. For study in a master's program at a California library school. Must be able to demonstrate financial need. Request an application form and further information from the address below.

California Library Association
Scholarship Committee
717 K Street, Suite 300
Sacramento, CA   95814

303
Educational Grants for Specialized Training in Guidance and Counseling

AMOUNT: None Specified   DEADLINE: December 10
FIELDS/MAJORS: Guidance and Counseling

Grants are available to graduate students enrolled in a master's or Ph.D. level guidance or counseling program. Based on scholastic achievement, financial need, and personal qualifications. Write to the address below for information.

Delta Theta Tau Sorority, Inc.
Chairman, Philanthropy Committee
R.R. 4, Box 812
Bloomfield, IN   47424

304
Edward Henderson Student Award

AMOUNT: $500   DEADLINE: December 8
FIELDS/MAJORS: Geriatrics

Award available for a student who has demonstrated a commitment to the field of geriatrics through: leadership in areas pertinent to geriatrics, initiation of new information or programs in geriatrics, or scholarship in geriatrics through original research or reviews. Applicants must be nominated by one faculty member with at least two supporting letters from other faculty. Write to the address listed for more information.

American Geriatrics Society
770 Lexington Avenue, Suite 300
New York, NY   10021

305
Edward N. Reynolds Graduate Diversity Scholarship

AMOUNT: None Specified DEADLINE: March 2
FIELDS/MAJORS: All Areas of Study

For first-time and continuing full-time domestic traditionally underrepresented ethnic minority graduate students. Must demonstrate academic achievement and/or promise, and financial need. Awarded on a competitive basis. Priority consideration given to those filing their university admissions application by May 1. Write to the address below for more information. At least 2.9 GPA required.

United States International University
Financial Aid Office
10455 Pomerado Road
San Diego, CA   92131

306
Edwin O. Stene Scholarship Program

AMOUNT: $1000 DEADLINE: April 25
FIELDS/MAJORS: Public Administration

Scholarships are available for public administration graduate students specializing in local government. Write to the address below for more information.

International City/County Management Association (ICMA)
   Monica Bowman
777 North Capitol Street, NE, Suite 500
Washington, DC   20002

307
Eileen C. Maddex Fellowship

AMOUNT: $2000 DEADLINE: April 1
FIELDS/MAJORS: Home Economics/Related Fields

Applicants must be members of Kappa Omicron Nu and a master's candidate. Awards will be announced May 15. Write to the address below for details.

Kappa Omicron Nu Honor Society
4990 Northwind Drive, Suite 140
East Lansing, MI   48823

308
El Paso Natural Gas M.B.A. Fellowship

AMOUNT: None Specified
DEADLINE: March 1
FIELDS/MAJORS: Business

Open to minority students pursuing an M.B.A.. Based on academics and financial need. Contact the address below for further information. At least 2.7 GPA required.

New Mexico State University
College of Business Admin. and Economics
Box 30001 Dept. 3AD
Las Cruces, NM   88003-8001

309
Elaine J. Hudson Memorial Medical Scholarship

AMOUNT: None Specified DEADLINE: March 1
FIELDS/MAJORS: Medicine

Awards are available at the University of New Mexico for female students enrolled in the UNM School of Medicine. Write to the address below for more information.

University of New Mexico, Albuquerque
Office of Financial Aid
Albuquerque, NM   87131

310
Eldred L. Jenne Research Scholarship

AMOUNT: None Specified
DEADLINE: February 1
FIELDS/MAJORS: Horticulture

Award open to graduate students with a minimum GPA of 3.5. Must be able to demonstrate financial need. Contact the address below for further information.

Washington State University—Scholarship Committee
College of Agriculture and Home Economics
423 Hulbert Hall
Pullman, WA   99164

311
Elinor C. Morris Scholarship Fund

AMOUNT: None Specified DEADLINE: March 1
FIELDS/MAJORS: Geology

Scholarships are available at the University of Oklahoma, Norman for full-time graduate geology majors, who reside in Guthrie, Oklahoma. Write to the address below for information.

University of Oklahoma, Norman
Director, School of Geology and Geophysics
100 East Boyd Street, Room G-810
Norman, OK   73019

312
Elisabeth M. and Winchell M. Parsons Scholarship

AMOUNT: $1500 DEADLINE: February 15
FIELDS/MAJORS: Mechanical Engineering

Applicants must be studying toward a doctorate in mechanical engineering. Must be ASME members and U.S. citizens. Write to the address below for details. Please be certain to enclose a SASE with your request.

American Society of Mechanical Engineers Auxiliary, Inc.
Mrs. Kenneth O. Cartwright
910 Rasic Ridge Road
Glendale, CA   91207

313 Elizabeth Duffy Fellowship

AMOUNT: None Specified   DEADLINE: None Specified
FIELDS/MAJORS: Psychology

Award open to graduate students in the field of psychology. Contact the address below for further information.

University of North Carolina, Greensboro
Financial Aid Office
723 Kenilworth Street
Greensboro, NC   27412

314 Elizabeth Monroe Drews Scholarships

AMOUNT: $500   DEADLINE: None Specified
FIELDS/MAJORS: Education

Award for outstanding graduate students in education who meet admission requirements. Based on letters of recommendation, an essay, and possibly an interview. Contact the Dean's office in the School of Education.

Portland State University
Student Services
412 School of Education Building
Portland, OR   97207

315 Ellen Setterfield Memorial Scholarship

AMOUNT: $3000–$10000
DEADLINE: March 31
FIELDS/MAJORS: Social Sciences

Open to legally blind students studying any of the social sciences on the graduate level. Write to the address below for complete details.

National Federation of the Blind
Mrs. Peggy Elliott, Chairman
814 Fifth Avenue, Suite 200
Grinnell, IA   50112

316 Elsa Jorgenson Awards

AMOUNT: $6000   DEADLINE: April 15
FIELDS/MAJORS: Foreign Language, English, Science

Awards are available at Portland State University for full-time graduate students in the areas of study above. Selection is based on merit and need. Every applicant must also receive a full tuition remission from another source for the award year. Two awards offered annually. Write to the address below for more information. Applications are not available until March 1.

Portland State University
Office of Graduate Studies and Research
105 Neuberger Hall
Portland, OR   97207

317 Elsevier Research Initiative Awards

AMOUNT: $25000   DEADLINE: January 9
FIELDS/MAJORS: Gastroenterology Research, Related Fields

Awards for investigators who possess an M.D. or Ph.D. (or equivalent) and hold faculty positions at universities or institutions. Applicants must also be members of any of the ADHF organizations. Women and minorities are encouraged to apply. Awards to assist reaching career goal of research. Contact the address below for further information or websites: http://www.gastro.org; http://asge.org; or http://hepar-sfgh.ucsf.edu.

American Digestive Health Foundation
Ms. Irene Kuo
7910 Woodmont Avenue, 7th Floor
Bethesda, MD   20814

318 Emma and Fritz Guggenbuhl Fund in Mathematics

AMOUNT: None Specified   DEADLINE: January 2
FIELDS/MAJORS: Mathematics

Awards open to graduate students in mathematics. Contact the address below for further information.

Bryn Mawr Graduate School of Arts and Sciences
101 N. Merion Avenue
Bryn Mawr, PA   19010

319 ENA Foundation Doctoral Scholarship

AMOUNT: Maximum: $4500   DEADLINE: April 1
FIELDS/MAJORS: Nursing

Scholarship is for a nurse pursuing a doctoral degree. Write to the address below for more information.

Emergency Nurses Association (ENA) Foundation Funding Program
216 Higgins Road
Park Ridge, IL   60068

320 ENA Foundation Research Grant

AMOUNT: Maximum: $10000   DEADLINE: June 1
FIELDS/MAJORS: Nursing

Scholarship is for nurses to advance their specialized practice of emergency nursing. Write to the address below for more information.

Emergency Nurses Association (ENA) Foundation Funding Program
216 Higgins Road
Park Ridge, IL   60068

321 ENA Foundation Special Project/Program Development Grants

AMOUNT: Maximum: $2000   DEADLINE: June 1
FIELDS/MAJORS: Nursing

Scholarship is for nurses to enhance the care of emergency patients. Write to the address below for more information.

Emergency Nurses Association (ENA) Foundation Funding Program
216 Higgins Road
Park Ridge, IL   60068

322 ENA Foundation/Emergency Medicine Foundation Team Research Grant

AMOUNT: Maximum: $10000   DEADLINE: February 20
FIELDS/MAJORS: Medicine, Nursing

Scholarship is for physicians and nurses to improve clinical research in emergency care. Contact Emergency Medicine Foundation, PO Box 619911, Dallas, TX 75261-9911 for more information.

Emergency Nurses Association (ENA) Foundation Funding
    Program
216 Higgins Road
Park Ridge, IL   60068

323 ENA Foundation/Sigma Theta Tau Joint Research Grant

AMOUNT: Maximum: $6000   DEADLINE: March 1
FIELDS/MAJORS: Nursing

Scholarship is for emergency nurses advancing their specialized practice. Write to the address below for more information.

Emergency Nurses Association (ENA) Foundation Funding
    Program
216 Higgins Road
Park Ridge, IL   60068

324 Endoscopic Research Awards

AMOUNT: $25000   DEADLINE: September 3
FIELDS/MAJORS: Endoscopic Research

Candidates must be M.D.s currently in a gastroenterology-related and endoscopic practice in institutions or private practice. Awards will be made to individual members or to trainees sponsored by an individual member of the ADHF partner societies. Contact the address below for further information or websites: http://www.gastro.org; http://asge.org; or http://hepar-sfgh.uscf.edu.

American Digestive Health Foundation
Ms. Irene Kuo
7910 Woodmont Avenue, 7th Floor
Bethesda, MD   20814

325 Endowed Law Scholarships

AMOUNT: $100–$3000   DEADLINE: September 1
FIELDS/MAJORS: Law

Twenty-two to twenty-four scholarships offered annually to full-time law students. Includes the Gretchen A. Harris, Leon J. York Jr., May M. Walker, Mineral Lawyers Society of Oklahoma, Moyers, Martin, Santee, Imel & Tetrick, Oklahoma Bar Foundation, Oklahoma City Title Attorneys, Rayburn L. Foster, Steve Sack Memorial, and the William R. Bandy scholarships. Individual award requirements will vary. Write to the address below for information.

University of Oklahoma, Norman
Admissions and Records, Law Center
Room 22, 300 Timberdell Road
Norman, OK   73019

326 Energy Research Summer Fellowships

AMOUNT: $3000   DEADLINE: January 1
FIELDS/MAJORS: Electrochemistry and Related Fields

Awards are available for graduate students enrolled in a college or university in the U.S. or Canada. Applicants must be studying a field related to the objectives of the Electrochemical Society. Renewable. This program is supported by the U.S. Department of Energy. Five awards offered annually. Write to the address below for more information.

Electrochemical Society, Inc.
10 South Main Street
Pennington, NJ   08534

327 Engineering Dissertation Fellowships

AMOUNT: $14500   DEADLINE: November 15
FIELDS/MAJORS: Engineering

Fellowships are available to those women who have successfully completed all required course work and exams by November 15. Awards are to be used for the final year of doctoral work. Fellowships cannot cover tuition for additional course work. Degree should be received at the end of the award year. Fellow is expected to devote full time to the project during the award year. Write for details.

American Association of University Women Educational
    Foundation
2201 N. Dodge Street
Iowa City, IA   52243

328 Environmental Fellows Program

AMOUNT: None Specified   DEADLINE: January 15
FIELDS/MAJORS: Environmental Sciences

Applicants must be at least postdoctoral scholars. Ten awards for the ten-week program. Must demonstrate exceptional competence in their fields and have a broad scientific/technical background. Fellows are placed in the EPA. Must be U.S. citizens or permanent residents. Write to the address below for details.

American Association for the Advancement of Science
1200 New York Avenue, NW
Washington, DC 20005

329 Environmental Toxicology and Chemistry (SETAC) Fellowship

AMOUNT: $15000 DEADLINE: September 1
FIELDS/MAJORS: Environmental Chemistry and Toxicology

Awards are available for predoctoral students pursuing dissertation research in the areas of environmental chemistry or toxicology. Write to the address below for more information.

Society of Environmental Toxicology and Chemistry
Mr. Rodney Parrish, Executive Director
1010 North 12th Avenue
Pensacola, FL 32501

330 Established Investigator Grant

AMOUNT: $75000 DEADLINE: None Specified
FIELDS/MAJORS: Medical Research (Cardiovascular and Other Related Areas)

Grants for investigators beyond four to nine years of their first faculty appointment in the fields of cardiovascular research. Based on demonstrated outstanding progress in leading an independent research program and the scientific merit and originality of the proposed project. Write to the address below for more information.

American Heart Association
National Center
7272 Greenville Avenue
Dallas, TX 75231

331 Estelle H. Rosenblum Thesis/Dissertation Award

AMOUNT: None Specified DEADLINE: March 1
FIELDS/MAJORS: Nursing

Awards are available at the University of New Mexico for nursing students pursuing a master's degree. Must have a minimum GPA of 3.5. Write to the address below or contact the school of nursing for more details.

University of New Mexico, Albuquerque
Office of Financial Aid
Albuquerque, NM 87131

332 Ethel Tingley Scholarship

AMOUNT: $1410 DEADLINE: February 1
FIELDS/MAJORS: Law

Award for entering female law student. Must demonstrate financial need. Renewable for three academic years for full-time student and four academic years for part-time student. Contact the Assistant Dean, Chase College of Law, for further information.

Northern Kentucky University
Chase College of Law
Admissions Office
Highland Heights, KY 41099

333 Ethnic Minority and Women's Enhancement Programs

AMOUNT: $1400 DEADLINE: February 15
FIELDS/MAJORS: Intercollegiate Athletics Administration

Post-graduate scholarships, internships, and curricula vitae bank for women and minorities who intend to pursue careers in coaching, officiating, or athletic administration. Ten awards for women and ten for minorities. Contact the athletic director of the financial aid office at an NCAA member institution for details, or write to the Director of Personal Development at the address below for details.

National Collegiate Athletic Association
6201 College Boulevard
Overland Park, KS 66211

334 Ethnic Minority Fellowship Program

AMOUNT: $11946 DEADLINE: January 15
FIELDS/MAJORS: Nursing, Behavioral Sciences, Clinical Research, Biomedical Research, Mental Health

Fellowships for minorities with a commitment to a career in nursing related to minority mental health; and/or the research training program for careers in behavioral science or the clinical training program for careers in psychiatric nursing. For pre- or postdoctoral study. Must be a U.S. citizen or permanent resident and a R.N. Write to the address below for more information.

American Nurse's Association, Inc.
Minority Fellowships Office
600 Maryland Avenue, SW, Suite 100 West
Washington, DC 20024

335 Evans-Titus Scholarship

AMOUNT: None Specified DEADLINE: April 15
FIELDS/MAJORS: Medicine

Awards for students enrolled in the School of Medicine. Based on financial need, character, aptitude, and intellectual promise of success. Contact the address below for further information or the financial aid office at your school's location.

University of North Dakota—School of Medicine
Sandra Elshaug, Financial Aid Office
PO Box 9037—501 N. Columbia Road
Grand Forks, ND 58202

336 Executive Fellowship Program

AMOUNT: $19656   DEADLINE: February 19
FIELDS/MAJORS: California Govt., Public Policy, Service, Affairs, Administration

Fellows will be enrolled at CSUS as graduate students/employees for the academic year and placed in offices throughout the executive branch to work as professionals and gain experience. Also includes weekly meetings and seminars. Graduates from all disciplines may apply, and a knowledge of California government is highly recommended. Contact the address below for further information.

Center for California Studies at CA State University, Sacramento
6000 J Street
Sacramento, CA   95819

337 Faculty Disadvantaged Student Fund

AMOUNT: None Specified   DEADLINE: March 1
FIELDS/MAJORS: Medicine

Awards are available at the University of New Mexico for medical students with emergency financial need. Write to the address below for more information.

University of New Mexico, Albuquerque
Office of Financial Aid
Albuquerque, NM   87131

338 Faculty/Administrators Development

AMOUNT: None Specified   DEADLINE: June 1
FIELDS/MAJORS: Education

Minority American teachers or administrators at, or alumni of, sponsoring Arkansas public colleges or universities who have been admitted as full-time, in-residence doctoral program students. Write to the address below for more information.

Arkansas Department of Higher Education
Financial Aid Division
114 East Capitol
Little Rock, AR   72201

339 Family Practice Medical Scholarship

AMOUNT: $7500   DEADLINE: May 1
FIELDS/MAJORS: Medicine

Applicants must be Maryland residents attending the University of Maryland at Baltimore Medical School. Based primarily on financial need. Write to the address below for details.

Maryland State Higher Education Commission
16 Francis Street
Annapolis, MD   21401

340 Fannie and John Hertz Foundation Graduate Fellowship Program

AMOUNT: $20000   DEADLINE: February 25
FIELDS/MAJORS: Applied Physical Sciences

Applicants must have at least a bachelor's degree to be eligible for these fellowships for doctoral studies in the physical sciences. Tenable at thirty-four different graduate schools. Must have a GPA of at least 3.8 and be a U.S. citizen (or in process of naturalization). Renewable. Write to the address below for complete details.

Fannie and John Hertz Foundation
PO Box 5032
Livermore, CA   94551

341 Fanny Bullock Workman Fellowship

AMOUNT: Maximum: $3000   DEADLINE: December 16
FIELDS/MAJORS: All Areas of Study

Fellowships for Wellesley alumnae. For graduate study in any field. Contact the address below for further information.

Wellesley College, Fellowships for Wellesley Alumnae
Sec'y, Committee on Graduate Fellowships
106 Central Street, Career Center
Wellesley, MA   02181

342 Fanny Gerber Scholarship

AMOUNT: Maximum: $250
DEADLINE: March 1
FIELDS/MAJORS: Liberal Studies

Open to outstanding students at the completion of one year of study in the Master of Liberal Studies Program. Contact the address listed for further information. At least 3.2 GPA required.

Brooklyn College
Office of the V.P. for Student Life
2113 Boylan Hall
Brooklyn, NY   11210

343 Fargo First District Medical Society Scholarship

AMOUNT: None Specified   DEADLINE: April 15
FIELDS/MAJORS: Medicine

Awards for students enrolled in the School of Medicine who have been residents of North Dakota for a minimum of two years. Must demonstrate satisfactory academics. Contact the address below for further information or the financial aid office at your school's location.

University of North Dakota—School of Medicine
Sandra Elshaug, Financial Aid Office
PO Box 9037—501 N. Columbia Road
Grand Forks, ND   58202

344 Farm Foundation Extension Fellowships

AMOUNT: None Specified
DEADLINE: March 1
FIELDS/MAJORS: Social and Political Sciences, Education, Business Admin., Agriculture

Scholarships for agricultural extension workers. Emphasis is placed on improving managerial and supervisory abilities. Candidates must be recommended by extension director, accepted by the university, and selected and approved by the committee of the Farm Foundation. For graduate study. Write for complete details.

Farm Foundation
1211 W. 22nd Street
Oak Brook, IL   60521

345 Fellowship Awards in Pharmacology-Morphology

AMOUNT: $28585   **DEADLINE:** January 15
FIELDS/MAJORS: Pharmacology-Morphology

Post-doctoral fellowships to support research in drug actions, specifically cellular and tissue changes. Fellowships are for two years. Five awards annually. Must be U.S. citizen or permanent resident. Write to the address below for details.

Pharmaceutical Manufacturers Association Foundation, Inc.
1100 15th Street, NW
Washington, DC   20005

346 Fellowship in Aerospace History

AMOUNT: $16000–$30000
DEADLINE: February 1
FIELDS/MAJORS: American Aerospace History

Fellowships are available to Ph.D.s and Ph.D. candidates at the dissertation stage. Must have superior academic ability to engage in significant and sustained advanced research in NASA Aerospace Science, Technology, Management, or Policy. Applicants must be U.S. citizens. Write to the address below for details.

American Historical Association—NASA
AHA Administrative Assistant
400 A Street, SE
Washington, DC   20003

347 Fellowship on Women and Public Policy

AMOUNT: None Specified   **DEADLINE:** May 30
FIELDS/MAJORS: All Areas of Study

Fellowships are available to encourage greater participation of women in the public policy process, develop public policy leaders, and encourage the formulation of state policy which recognizes and responds to the need of women and families. Applicants must be female graduate students with at least 12 credit hours completed in an accredited New York University and plans to continue her education in New York. Write to the address below for information.

University at Albany, Center for Women in Government
Joeanna Hurston Brown, Director
135 Western Avenue, Draper Hall, Room 302
Albany, NY   12222

348 Fellowship Program in Academic Medicine

AMOUNT: $6000   **DEADLINE:** August 31
FIELDS/MAJORS: Biomedical Research and Academic Medicine

Scholarships, fellowships, and awards for minority medical students. Minorities are defined here as African-American, Mexican-American, mainland Puerto Rican, and American Indian. Must be a U.S. citizen. Thirty-five awards are presented annually. Send a SASE to the address below for additional information.

National Medical Fellowships, Inc.
110 West 32nd Street, 8th Floor
New York, NY   10001

349 Fellowship Research Grants

AMOUNT: Maximum: $20200
DEADLINE: None Specified
FIELDS/MAJORS: Government, International Affairs, Philosophy, Economics

Research grants are available to individuals for postdoctoral research. The applicant must be associated with educational or research institutions and the effort supported should lead to the advancement of knowledge through teaching, lecturing, or publication. Write to the address below for information.

Earhart Foundation
2200 Green Road, Suite H
Ann Arbor, MI   48105

350 Fellowships and Junior Fellowships

AMOUNT: None Specified
DEADLINE: November 1
FIELDS/MAJORS: Byzantine Studies, Pre-Columbian Studies, Landscape Architecture

Applicants must hold a doctorate or have established themselves in their field and wish to pursue their own research at the Harvard University Dumbarton Oaks Research Facilities (residential fellowships). Scholars who have fulfilled all preliminary requirements for the Ph.D. (or other terminal degree) are eligible for the junior fellowships. All fellows are expected to be able to communicate satisfactorily in English. Write to the address below for details.

Dumbarton Oaks
Office of the Director
1703 32nd Street, NW
Washington, DC   20007

351
Fellowships at the Smithsonian Astrophysical Observatory

AMOUNT: None Specified   DEADLINE: None Specified
FIELDS/MAJORS: Astronomy, Astrophysics and Related Fields

Fellowships are available to graduate and post-graduate students at the Smithsonian Astrophysical Observatory. Write to address below for details. Request the publication "Smithsonian Opportunities for Research and Study."

Smithsonian Astrophysical Observatory
Office of the Director
60 Garden Street, Mailstop 47
Cambridge, MA   02138

352
Fellowships for Advanced Predoctoral Training in Pharmaceutics

AMOUNT: $12000   DEADLINE: October 1
FIELDS/MAJORS: Pharmacology, Pharmacy, Academic Pharmaceutics

Advanced predoctoral fellowships to support promising students during thesis research. Fellowships are for one to two years. Must be U.S. citizen or permanent resident. Write to the address below for details. Additional funding for research expenses is available.

Pharmaceutical Manufacturers Association Foundation, Inc.
1100 15th Street, NW
Washington, DC   20005

353
Fellowships for Careers in Clinical Pharmacology

AMOUNT: $25000   DEADLINE: October 1
FIELDS/MAJORS: Pharmacology, Toxicology, Morphology, Pharmaceutics

Research starter grants open to postdoctoral instructors, assistant professors, and investigators. This program is intended to assist them in establishing careers as independent investigators in pharmacology, toxicology, morphology, and pharmaceutics. Applicants must be U.S. citizens. Write to the address below for details.

Pharmaceutical Manufacturers Association Foundation, Inc.
1100 15th Street, NW
Washington, DC   20005

354
Fellowships for Scientists

AMOUNT: None Specified
DEADLINE: February 17
FIELDS/MAJORS: Natural Science, Engineering

Fellowships are available at Stanford for an opportunity to explore a research topic in an interdisciplinary environment. Scientist and engineers who have demonstrated excellence in their specialties are urged to apply. Write to the address below or call 415-497-9625 for information.

Stanford University—Center for Int'l. Security and Arms Control
Ms. Barbara Platt
320 Galvez Street
Stanford, CA   94305

355
Fellowships in Arts and the Humanities

AMOUNT: None Specified
DEADLINE: None Specified
FIELDS/MAJORS: Arts and Humanities

Postdoctoral fellowships offered as a year or six-month visiting fellowships at selected academic and non-academic institutions. Will support scholars and writers whose research aids understanding of contemporary social and cultural issues. For a list of host institutions offering fellowships please write to "Arts and Humanities Fellowships" at the address below.

Rockefeller Foundation
Arts and Humanities Division
420 Fifth Avenue
New York, NY   10018-2702

356
Film and Fiction Scholarship

AMOUNT: Maximum: $10000   DEADLINE: January 15
FIELDS/MAJORS: Film, Fiction Writing, and Playwriting

Scholarships for graduate MFA students in the areas of film, fiction, or playwriting with an interest in the classical liberal or libertarian principles. Write to the address below or visit the website http://osf1.GMU.edu/~IHS/ for more information. Application requests will only be taken in the fall preceding the January deadline.

Institute for Humane Studies at George Washington University
4084 University Drive
Suite 101
Fairfax, VA   22030

357
Financial Assistance for Disadvantaged Students

AMOUNT: None Specified   DEADLINE: March 1
FIELDS/MAJORS: Medicine

Awards are available at the University of New Mexico for full-time medical students with exceptional financial need. Includes programs of financial assistance for disadvantaged health profession students, exceptional financial need scholarships, and scholarships for disadvantaged students. Applicants must be U.S. citizens or permanent residents. Write to the address below for more information.

University of New Mexico, Albuquerque
Office of Financial Aid
Albuquerque, NM   87131

358
Financial Awards at Washington University in St. Louis

AMOUNT: None Specified   DEADLINE: January 1
FIELDS/MAJORS: All Areas of Study

Several fellowship and scholarship programs are available to graduate students at Washington University in St. Louis. Contact the Office of Financial Aid for details.

Washington University
Office of Financial Aid
Campus Box 1041
St. Louis, MO   63130

359
Fine Fellowship Program

AMOUNT: $7000–$10000
DEADLINE: None Specified
FIELDS/MAJORS: Education

Scholarships are available at the University of Oklahoma, Norman for full-time master's or doctoral level graduate students who are of Native American heritage. Write to the address below for information.

University of Oklahoma, Norman
College of Education
Room 105, ECH
Norman, OK   73019

360
Five College Fellowship Program for Minority Scholars

AMOUNT: $25000   DEADLINE: None Specified
FIELDS/MAJORS: All Areas of Study

Program for minority graduate students in the final phase of the doctoral degree. While the emphasis is on completing the dissertation, fellows may be expected to teach a single one-semester course within the hosting department. Applicants must attend Amherst, Hampshire, Mount Holyoke, or Smith Colleges or the University of Massachusetts. Write to the address below for more information. Award also includes office space, housing assistance, and library privileges at the five colleges.

Five Colleges, Inc.
Fellowship Program Committee
97 Spring Street
Amherst, MA   01002

361
Flatbush Federal Savings and Loan Association Scholarship

AMOUNT: Maximum: $250   DEADLINE: March 1
FIELDS/MAJORS: Economics, Accounting

Open to graduating seniors who have shown excellence in economics or accounting. For graduate study and planned teaching. Contact the address listed for further information. At least 3.1 GPA required.

Brooklyn College
Office of the V.P. for Student Life
2113 Boylan Hall
Brooklyn, NY   11210

362
Flavin Fellowships

AMOUNT: None Specified   DEADLINE: None Specified
FIELDS/MAJORS: Management

Awards for M.B.A./M.S. degree candidates. Based on academic merit, financial need, and volunteer services. Applications for School of Management scholarships will be available in the SOM Development Office, Room 206.

University of Massachusetts, Amherst
School of Management
SOM Development Office, Room 206
Amherst, MA   01003

363
Flemish Community Fellowship

AMOUNT: None Specified
DEADLINE: January 15
FIELDS/MAJORS: Art, Music, Humanities, Social/Political Science, Law, Economics

Fellowships are available to American post-graduate students who wish to study at a Flemish university in Flanders, Belgium. Awards are given to candidates doing research in one of the fields listed above or in the science/medical fields, and their affiliation with the Flemish community. Applicant must hold at least a bachelor's degree, be under age thirty-five, and be a U.S. citizen. Write to the address below for information.

Embassy of Belgium
Flemish Community Fellowship
3330 Garfield Street, NW
Washington, DC   20008

364
Florence A. Carter Fellowships in Leukemia Research

AMOUNT: $25000   DEADLINE: None Specified
FIELDS/MAJORS: Leukemia Research

Fellowships open to researchers to help with their investigative efforts in the area of leukemia. Must be under forty years of age. Contact the address below for further information.

AMA—Education and Research Foundation
Rita M. Palulonis
515 N. State Street
Chicago, IL   60610

365
Florida Dental Association Student Loans

AMOUNT: None Specified   DEADLINE: March 31
FIELDS/MAJORS: Dentistry

Must be resident of Florida and have successfully completed one academic year in any dental college to be eligible for this loan. Academic standing, financial need, and potential will be considered in granting a loan. Renewable. Loans for postdoctoral candidates also available. Write to the Task Group on Student Loans at the address below for details.

Florida Dental Association
Task Group on Student Loans
3021 Swann Avenue
Tampa, FL   33609

366
Florida Library Association Graduate Grants

AMOUNT: $2000   DEADLINE: March 1
FIELDS/MAJORS: Library Science

Grants for master's level library science students attending Florida State University or the University of South Florida. Must be a Florida resident. Write to the address below for additional information.

Florida Library Association
Chair, FLA Scholarship Committee
1133 W. Morse Boulevard, Suite 201
Winter Park, FL   32789

367
Ford Foundation Doctoral Fellowships for Minorities

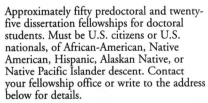

AMOUNT: $6000–$18000
DEADLINE: November 4
FIELDS/MAJORS: Social and Life Sciences, Humanities, Engineering, Math, Physics

Approximately fifty predoctoral and twenty-five dissertation fellowships for doctoral students. Must be U.S. citizens or U.S. nationals, of African-American, Native American, Hispanic, Alaskan Native, or Native Pacific Islander descent. Contact your fellowship office or write to the address below for details.

National Research Council
The Fellowship Office/FFPD
2101 Constitution Avenue, NW
Washington, DC   20418

368
Ford Foundation Postdoctoral Fellowships for Minorities

AMOUNT: $25000   DEADLINE: January 3
FIELDS/MAJORS: Social and Life Sciences, Humanities, Engineering, Math, Physics

Postdoctoral fellowships are available for scholars in the fields above. Renewable. Must be U.S. citizen or U.S. national and of African-American, Native American, Hispanic, Native Alaskan, or Native Pacific Islander descent. Twenty awards offered annually. Contact your fellowship office or write to the address below for details.

National Research Council
The Fellowship Office/FFPD
2101 Constitution Avenue, NW
Washington, DC   20418

369
Foreign Language and Area Studies Fellowships

AMOUNT: $4038–$10538   DEADLINE: None Specified
FIELDS/MAJORS: Arabic Studies

Awards are available for graduate students training in the Arabic language in combination with area studies, international studies, or international aspects of professional fields. Two fellowships for the academic year and two for summer term. Write to the address below for more information.

Portland State University
Middle East Studies Center
Sixth Avenue Building
Portland, OR   97207

370
Foster G. McGaw Student Scholarship

AMOUNT: $3000   DEADLINE: March 31
FIELDS/MAJORS: Hospital and Health Services Administration

Scholarships are available to graduate students in hospital administration. Student must show good character/potential for success and academic promise. Must be student associate of American College of Healthcare Executives and be a U.S. or Canadian citizen. To apply, obtain an application from your program director. For further details, inquire to address below.

Foundation of the American College of Healthcare Executives
1 North Franklin Street, Suite 1700
Chicago, IL   60606

371 Fraiser McConnell Memorial Scholarship

AMOUNT: None Specified
DEADLINE: March 31
FIELDS/MAJORS: Library and Information Sciences

Award open to graduate students who are majoring in library or information sciences. Must have minimum GPA of 3.0. Contact the address below for further information.

University of North Texas
Scholarship Office
Marquis Hall, #218
Denton, TX   76203

372 Frances Weitzenhoffer Memorial Fellowship in Art History

AMOUNT: $4000   **DEADLINE:** March 1
FIELDS/MAJORS: Art History

Fellowships are available at the University of Oklahoma, Norman for full-time graduate art history majors. One award offered annually. Write to the address below for information.

University of Oklahoma, Norman
Director, School of Art
540 Parrington, Room 122
Norman, OK   73019

373 Francile E. Clark Graduate Nursing Scholarship

AMOUNT: None Specified   **DEADLINE:** None Specified
FIELDS/MAJORS: Nursing

Scholarships are available for graduate nursing students at the University of Oklahoma with a GPA of at least 3.3 and financial need. One award offered annually. Write to the address below for information.

University of Oklahoma, Norman
Director, Office of Financial Aid
OUHSC, PO Box 73190
Oklahoma City, OK   73190

374 Frank and Otelia Kraft Scholarship

AMOUNT: $800   **DEADLINE:** November 1
FIELDS/MAJORS: English

Open to graduate students in English. Contact the address below for further information.

University of Northern Iowa
Michael Janopoulos, Dept. of English
15 Baker
Cedar Falls, IA   50614

375 Frank Gouin Scholarship Fund

AMOUNT: $1000   **DEADLINE:** March 1
FIELDS/MAJORS: Geology, Geophysics

Scholarships are available at the University of Oklahoma, Norman for full-time graduate student geology or geophysics majors, with GPAs of at least 3.0. Preference is given to students residing in Rotary District 577. Must be a U.S. citizen. Write to the address below for information.

University of Oklahoma, Norman
Director, School of Geology and Geophysics
100 East Boyd Street, Room 810
Norman, OK   73019

376 Frank J. Broilo, Harry and Margaret Basehart Memorial Scholarship

AMOUNT: None Specified   **DEADLINE:** March 1
FIELDS/MAJORS: Archaeology, Ethnology

Scholarships are available at the University of New Mexico for archaeology graduate students and ethnology graduate students. Write to the address below for information.

University of New Mexico, Albuquerque
Anthropology Department
Albuquerque, NM   87131

377 Frank M. Chapman Memorial Grants

AMOUNT: $200–$1000   **DEADLINE:** January 15
FIELDS/MAJORS: Ornithology

Open to young scientists and graduate students to encourage research in ornithology. Funds are to be used for modest support of museum/field/or laboratory research projects (i.e., not for tuition, etc.). Collection study grants are also available. Write to the address below for complete details.

American Museum of Natural History
Central Park West at 79th Street
New York, NY   10024

378 Frank Roberts Community Service Scholarship

AMOUNT: $1500   **DEADLINE:** April 15
FIELDS/MAJORS: All Areas of Study

Award is available at Portland State University for graduate students who are involved in community service related to the graduate student's academic program. One award offered annually. Contact the Office of Graduate Studies and Research for more information.

Portland State University
Office of Graduate Studies and Research
105 Neuberger Hall
Portland, OR   97207

379 Franklin Mosher Baldwin Memorial Fellowships

AMOUNT: $17000   **DEADLINE:** January 2
FIELDS/MAJORS: Anthropology

Fellowships for African students who seek an advanced degree at a major institution. Priority is given to students involved in disciplines related to human evolution. Write to the address below for more information.

L.S.B. Leaky Foundation
Grants Administration
77 Jack London Square, Suite M
Oakland, CA   94607

380 Fred Coffey Class of 1925 Memorial Scholarship

AMOUNT: None Specified   **DEADLINE:** March 31
FIELDS/MAJORS: All Areas of Study

Award open to graduate students who are physically or learning impaired. Must have a minimum GPA of 3.0. Contact the address below for further information.

University of North Texas
Scholarship Office
Marquis Hall, #218
Denton, TX   76203

381 Fred M. Chreist Sr. Scholarship

AMOUNT: None Specified
DEADLINE: March 1
FIELDS/MAJORS: Communicative Disorders

Awards are available at the University of New Mexico for full-time graduates majoring in the fields of communicative disorders. Based on academics. Write to the address below for information. At least 3.2 GPA required.

University of New Mexico, Albuquerque
Office of Financial Aid
Albuquerque, NM   87131

382 Freda Len '75 Memorial Scholarship

AMOUNT: None Specified   **DEADLINE:** March 1
FIELDS/MAJORS: Law, Paralegal

Open to graduating seniors who intend to become paralegals or who have been accepted by a law school. Contact the address listed for further information.

Brooklyn College
Office of the V.P. for Student Life
2113 Boylan Hall
Brooklyn, NY   11210

383 Frederic G. Melcher Scholarships

AMOUNT: $6000   **DEADLINE:** April 1
FIELDS/MAJORS: Library Science, Children's

Applicants must be graduate students entering an ALA-accredited master's program and specializing in children's libraries. Must be U.S. or Canadian citizen. Recipients are expected to work in the children's library field for a minimum of one year. Write to the address shown for details.

American Library Association
Assn. for Library Service to Children
50 E. Huron Street
Chicago, IL   60611

384 Freeman Fellowship

AMOUNT: $3000–$5000   **DEADLINE:** February 20
FIELDS/MAJORS: Civil Engineering

Applicant must be a national ASCE member in the first year of graduate study. Award to be used for experiments, observations and compilations to discover new and accurate data that will be useful in engineering, particularly hydraulics. Write to the address below for complete details.

American Society of Civil Engineers
Student Services Department
1801 Alexander Bell Drive
Reston, VA   20191

385 Fresno-Madera Medical Society Scholarships

AMOUNT: $1000   **DEADLINE:** May 15
FIELDS/MAJORS: Medicine

Applicants must be legal residents of Fresno or Madera Counties, California, for at least one year and be attending or accepted in a medical school. Based on need, academics, and prospects for completion of curriculum. Write to the address below for complete details.

Fresno-Madera Medical Society
Scholarship Foundation
PO Box 31
Fresno, CA   93707

386 Friedrich Ebert Doctoral Research Fellowships

AMOUNT: None Specified   **DEADLINE:** February 28
FIELDS/MAJORS: German Studies (Political Science, Sociology, History, Economics)

Fellowships for students in the above area of study who have an approved dissertation proposal. Applicants must be U.S. citizens and provide evidence that they have knowledge of German that is adequate for research purposes. Approximately five awards offered annually. These fellowships are for stays in Germany of between five and twelve months. Write to the address below for more information.

Friedrich Ebert Foundation
New York Office
950 Third Avenue, 28th Floor
New York, NY   10022

387 Friedrich Ebert Postdoctoral/Young Scholar Fellowships

AMOUNT: None Specified   DEADLINE: February 28
FIELDS/MAJORS: German Studies (Political Science, Sociology, History, Economics)

Fellowships for scholars in the above area of study who have a Ph.D., and at least two years of research or teaching experience at a university or institution. Applicants must be U.S. citizens and be able to prove that they have a knowledge of German that is adequate for their research purposes. Approximately five awards offered annually. Write to the address below for more information.

Friedrich Ebert Foundation
New York Office
950 Third Avenue, 28th Floor
New York, NY   10022

388 Friedrich Ebert Pre-Dissertation/ Advanced Graduate Fellowships

AMOUNT: None Specified   DEADLINE: February 28
FIELDS/MAJORS: German Studies (Political Science, Sociology, History, Economics)

Fellowships for students in the above area of studies who intend to pursue a doctoral degree. Applicants must be U.S. citizens, have completed two years of graduate study, and provide proof that they have knowledge of German. Approximately five awards offered annually. These fellowships will be granted for stays of between five and twelve months in Germany. Write to the address below for more information.

Friedrich Ebert Foundation
New York Office
950 Third Avenue, 28th Floor
New York, NY   10022

389 Friends of Rochester Hills Public Library Scholarship

AMOUNT: $2000   DEADLINE: August 1
FIELDS/MAJORS: Library Science

Awards for graduate students from the greater Rochester area who are studying in the area of library science. Must be currently enrolled or accepted in an accredited program. Must be a U.S. citizen. One award per year. Write to the address below for more information.

Friends of Rochester Hills Public Library
Scholarship Committee
500 Olde Town Road
Rochester, MI   48307

390 Friends of the Library of Hawaii Scholarships

AMOUNT: $500–$2000   DEADLINE: June 1
FIELDS/MAJORS: Library Science, Information Science

Open to graduate students enrolled in library science at the University of Hawaii. For master's level study. Twelve awards are given annually. Write to the address listed for further information.

University of Hawaii
School of Library and Information Studies
2550 The Mall
Manoa, HI   96822

391 Fritz Halbers Fellowship

AMOUNT: $3000
DEADLINE: November 1
FIELDS/MAJORS: Jewish Studies

Fellowships are available for research at the Leo Baeck Institute for current predoctoral scholars who are studying the social, communal, and intellectual history of German-speaking Jewry. Applicants must be U.S. citizens. Write to the address below for information.

Leo Baeck Institute
Fellowship Programs
129 East 73rd Street
New York, NY   10021

392 FSU University Fellowship Program

AMOUNT: $10000   DEADLINE: February 1
FIELDS/MAJORS: All Areas of Study

University wide fellowships, competitively awarded, are available to master's and doctoral students at FSU. Includes out-of-state fee waivers for non-resident students. Must have a minimum GPA of 3.5 and a GRE score of 1150 or higher. The university urges students to make specific inquiry to each program, with reference to both deadline and eligibility. Departmental fellowships are also available. Information for those is available at each departmental office.

Florida State University
Dean of Graduate Studies
408 Westcott, R-3
Tallahassee, FL   32306

393 Fulbright Awards

AMOUNT: None Specified   DEADLINE: None Specified
FIELDS/MAJORS: International Studies

Available to master's degree candidates to foster mutual understanding among nations through educational and cultural exchanges. The program enables U.S. students to benefit from unique resources and gain international competence in an increasingly interdependent world. Must be a U.S. citizen at the time of application. Write to the address below for information.

Institute of International Education
Fulbright Awards
809 United Nations Plaza
New York, NY   10017

394 Fund for Podiatric Medical Education

AMOUNT: None Specified   DEADLINE: May 1
FIELDS/MAJORS: Podiatric Medicine

Open to third- and fourth-year students studying podiatric medicine at any of the following seven schools: Barry University School of Podiatric Medicine, California College of Podiatric Medicine, College of Podiatric Medicine and Surgery, Scholl College of Podiatric Medicine, New York College of Podiatric Medicine, Ohio College of Podiatric Medicine, and the Pennsylvania College of Podiatric Medicine. Information available at the financial aid offices of the listed participating schools.

Fund for Podiatric Medical Education
9312 Old Georgetown Road
Bethesda, MD   20814

395 G. Michael Sims Memorial Scholarship

AMOUNT: $250   DEADLINE: February 1
FIELDS/MAJORS: Health and Sports Sciences

Scholarships are available at the University of Oklahoma, Norman for graduate students in one of the areas listed above. Requires a GPA of at least 3.5. Two awards offered annually. Write to the address below for information.

University of Oklahoma, Norman
Dept. of Health and Sports Sciences
Houston Huffman Center, Room 104
Norman, OK   73019

396 Garden Club of America Awards in Tropical Botany

AMOUNT: $5500   DEADLINE: December 31
FIELDS/MAJORS: Tropical Botany

Financial aid for study in tropical botany. Awards for field study to Ph.D. candidates. Two awards offered annually. Write to the address below for more details.

Garden Club of America
Ms. Marlar Oo, World Wildlife Fund
1250 24th Street, NW
Washington, DC   20037

397 GEM Fellowships

AMOUNT: Maximum: $12000
DEADLINE: December 1
FIELDS/MAJORS: Engineering, Sciences, Mathematics

Applicants must be engineering or science majors in their senior year or beyond. Must be U.S. citizen and one of the following minorities: Native, African, Hispanic, or Puerto Rican Americans. For graduate use only. Must have a GPA of at least 2.8 if in a master's program and a minimum GPA of 3.0 if pursuing a doctorate. Write to the address below for details. Please note if you are seeking a master's or doctoral degree.

Consortium for Graduate Degrees for Minorities
GEM Central Office
PO Box 537
Notre Dame, IN   46556

398 Geo-Centers Fellowship

AMOUNT: None Specified   DEADLINE: March 1
FIELDS/MAJORS: Chemistry

Awards for graduate students in the department of chemistry. Contact the chemistry department for more information.

University of Massachusetts, Amherst
Chemistry Department
Amherst, MA   01003

399 George J. Berlin Urban Planning and Policy Scholarship

AMOUNT: $2500   DEADLINE: March 5
FIELDS/MAJORS: Urban Planning, Policy Issues

Scholarship is available to a graduate student who demonstrates financial need and academic excellence in urban planning and/or policy issues. Write to the address below for more information.

Florida International University
College of Urban and Public Affairs
Office of the Dean—AC1 200
North Miami, FL   33181

400 George Miskovsky Sr. and Nelly Miskovsky Scholarship

AMOUNT: $1000   DEADLINE: September 1
FIELDS/MAJORS: Law

Scholarships are available at the University of Oklahoma, Norman for full-time law students from Oklahoma. Two awards offered annually. Write to the address below for information.

University of Oklahoma, Norman
Admissions and Records, Law Center
Room 22, 300 Timberdell Road
Norman, OK   73019

401 George T. Gibson Scholarship

AMOUNT: $500   DEADLINE: April 1
FIELDS/MAJORS: Industrial Engineering

Scholarships are available at the University of Oklahoma, Norman for full-time senior industrial engineering majors, who will be pursuing a master's degree and have a minimum GPA of 3.0. Also available to undergraduates who work part-time and carry 9 to 15 hours with a minimum GPA of 2.75. Two awards offered annually. Contact the address below for further information.

University of Oklahoma, Norman
Director, Industrial Engineering
Room 124, CEC
Norman, OK   73019

402
George W. and Eva Glaspel/ Keith and Elaine Wold Scholarships

AMOUNT: None Specified   **DEADLINE:** April 15
FIELDS/MAJORS: Medicine

Awards for students enrolled in the School of Medicine. Based on need and satisfactory academics. Contact the address below for further information or the financial aid office at your school's location.

University of North Dakota—School of Medicine
Sandra Elshaug, Financial Aid Office
PO Box 9037—501 N Columbus Road
Grand Forks, ND   58202

403
Gerber Prize for Excellence in Pediatrics

AMOUNT: $2000   **DEADLINE:** August 31
FIELDS/MAJORS: Pediatric Medicine

Scholarships, fellowships, and awards for minority medical students in pediatrics. Minorities are defined here as African-American, Mexican-American, mainland Puerto Rican, and American Indian. For study at Michigan medical schools. Academics is primary consideration; need is considered. Must be a U.S. citizen. One award presented annually. Write to "special programs" at the address below for details.

National Medical Fellowships, Inc.
110 West 32nd Street, 8th Floor
New York, NY   10001

404
Geriatrics Clinician of the Year Award

AMOUNT: $2000   **DEADLINE:** December 8
FIELDS/MAJORS: Geriatrics

Awards are available for geriatrics clinicians whose primary focus is the delivery of patient care in the office, hospital, long-term care facility or community. Must be AGS members who are maintaining a high level of professional competence through continuing medical education. Applicants must be nominated via a letter of nomination, at least one letter of support from colleagues and the nominee's curriculum vitae. Write to the address listed for more information.

American Geriatrics Society
770 Lexington Avenue, Suite 300
New York, NY   10021

405
German-American Society of Tulsa Graduate Scholarship

AMOUNT: None Specified   **DEADLINE:** March 1
FIELDS/MAJORS: Foreign Language—German

Scholarships are available at the University of Oklahoma, Norman for full-time graduate students majoring in German. Based on academic ability. Write to the address below for information.

University of Oklahoma, Norman
Modern Languages Department
780 Van Vleet Oval
Norman, OK   73019

406
Gertrude and Harry G. Fins Scholarship

AMOUNT: None Specified
DEADLINE: March 1
FIELDS/MAJORS: Law

Scholarships for Jewish men and women who are legal residents of the Chicago area. Must be attending/planning to attend DePaul University, Loyola University, IIT-Chicago/Kent, John Marshall, Southern Illinois University, or the University of Illinois at Urbana/Champaign for their law studies. Write to the address below for details after December 1.

Jewish Vocational Service
Attn: Academic Scholarship Program
One South Franklin Street
Chicago, IL   60606

407
GHI Dissertation Scholarships

AMOUNT: Maximum: $1100
DEADLINE: May 15
FIELDS/MAJORS: German Studies, German History, German American History

Awards for doctoral students working on topics related to the institute's general scope of interest. Twelve awards are offered annually. Write to the address below for more information.

German Historical Institute
1607 New Hampshire Avenue, NW
Washington, DC   20009

408
Gilbert Chinard Scholarships

AMOUNT: $1000
DEADLINE: January 15
FIELDS/MAJORS: French History, Literature, Art, and Music

Awards for research in France for Ph.D. dissertation or the Ph.D. held no longer than six years before time of application. A two-page description of research project and trip as well as a recommendation from the dissertation director will be required. Three awards offered annually. Write to the address below for additional information. Contact: Catherine A. Maley, President, Institut Francais De Washington.

University of North Carolina—Institut Francais De Washington
Department of Romance Languages
CB 3170
Chapel Hill, NC   27599

409 Gilbert F. White Postdoctoral Fellowship Program

AMOUNT: None Specified DEADLINE: February 28
FIELDS/MAJORS: Natural Resources, Energy, Environmental Sciences

Fellowship is for researchers in Social Science or Public Policy programs in the areas of Natural Resources, Energy, or the Environment. Applicants must have completed doctoral requirements and preference will be given to those with teaching and/or research experience. This is a residential fellowship. Write to the address below for details.

Resources for the Future
Coordinator for Academic Programs
1616 P Street NW
Washington, DC   20036

410 Gilbreth Memorial Fellowship

AMOUNT: $2500 DEADLINE: November 15
FIELDS/MAJORS: Industrial Engineering

Scholarships are available for graduate industrial engineering majors who are enrolled on a full-time basis, members of the institute, and have a GPA of at least 3.4. Students must be nominated by their IIE department heads. Five awards offered annually. Contact your school's industrial engineering department head for information.

Institute of Industrial Engineers
Scholarship Program
25 Technology Park/Atlanta
Norcross, GA   30092

411 Gillette Hayden Memorial Foundation Loans

AMOUNT: None Specified DEADLINE: August 1
FIELDS/MAJORS: Dentistry

Loans are available to women junior, senior, or graduate level dental students. Applicants will be judged on financial need, academic ability, and current amount of indebtedness. Write to address below for details.

American Association of Women Dentists
Gillette Hayden Memorial Foundation
401 N. Michigan Avenue
Chicago, IL   60611

412 Gillian Buchanan Scholarship

AMOUNT: $500 DEADLINE: March 1
FIELDS/MAJORS: Music

Award for graduate students at Eastern New Mexico University who are majoring in music. Write to the address below for more information.

Eastern New Mexico University
College of Fine Arts
Station 16
Portales, NM   88130

413 Gladys Agell Award for Excellence in Research

AMOUNT: None Specified DEADLINE: June 15
FIELDS/MAJORS: Art Therapy

Designed to encourage student research, this award will go to the most outstanding project, completed within the past year, by an art therapist using statistical measure in the area of applied art therapy. Must be a graduate student in an AATA approved program and be a student member of AATA. Write to the address below for complete details.

American Art Therapy Association, Inc.
Chair, Research Committee
1202 Allanson Road
Mundelein, IL   60060

414 Glenn Snoeyenbos Award

AMOUNT: None Specified DEADLINE: None Specified
FIELDS/MAJORS: Animal Science

Scholarships are awarded to an outstanding graduate student based on GPA, research progress, presentations at meetings, and recommendations. Contact the Chair, Scholarship Committee, Veterinary and Animal Sciences, for more information.

University of Massachusetts, Amherst
Chair, Scholarship Committee
Veterinary and Animal Sciences
Amherst, MA   01003

415 Global and Complex Systems Centennial Fellowships

AMOUNT: Maximum: $1000000
DEADLINE: December 15
FIELDS/MAJORS: Global and Complex Systems

The intent of the Centennial Fellowships is to support and encourage exceptional scientists and scholars in the early stages of their careers. Candidates should be able to demonstrate great scholarly promise, but have not yet achieved full academic maturity and/or professional recognition. Applicants must be actively engaged in research and have a commitment to teaching and demonstrate a superior ability to communicate their work to broad audiences. Candidates should be less than forty years of age at time of application or not more than twelve years from the completion of their academic training (receipt of Ph.D.). Fellowships awarded in this category will support scholarship and research involving the development of theories and models that can be applied to the study of complex systems. It is likely that nominees for this award category will be pursuing research on subject matter areas such as biodiversity, energy, climate, demography, epidemiology, and economic or technological change. Contact the address below for further information and instructions.

James S. McDonnell Foundation
1034 S. Brentwood Boulevard, Suite 1850
St. Louis, MO   63117

416 Golden Key Scholar Awards

AMOUNT: $10000   **DEADLINE:** February 15
FIELDS/MAJORS: All Areas of Study

Awards are available for graduate students who were members of the Golden Key National Honor Society. Applicants may be undergraduates or recent alumni, but they must hold the bachelor's degree by the time the scholarship is received. Based on academics, activities, and recommendations. Six awards offered annually. Write to the address below for more information. Applications will become available in October.

Golden Key National Honor Society
1189 Ponce De Leon Avenue
Atlanta, GA   30306

417 Grace Frank Fellowship Fund

AMOUNT: None Specified   **DEADLINE:** January 2
FIELDS/MAJORS: Humanities

Award open to graduate students in humanities. Contact the address below for further information.

Bryn Mawr Graduate School of Arts and Sciences
101 N. Merion Avenue
Bryn Mawr, PA   19010

418 Grace Legendre Fellowship

AMOUNT: $1000   **DEADLINE:** February 28
FIELDS/MAJORS: All Areas of Study

Applicants must be women who are New York state residents and pursuing a full-time graduate program at an accredited New York state college or university. Must be U.S. citizens. Write to address below for details.

Business and Professional Women's Clubs of New York State
212 Mayro Building
239 Genessee Street
Utica, NY   13501

419 Graduate and Post-Graduate Research Grants

AMOUNT: Maximum: $2500   **DEADLINE:** February 1
FIELDS/MAJORS: Natural Resources Research

Graduate and post-graduate research grants for the support of research in which the natural resources of the Huyck Preserve are utilized. Must also work on the Preserve. Housing and lab space are provided at the Preserve. Please contact address below for complete information.

Edmund Niles Huyck Preserve
PO Box 189
Rensselaerville, NY   12147

420 Graduate and Research Support Funds

AMOUNT: $150–$1000   **DEADLINE:** None Specified
FIELDS/MAJORS: All Areas of Study

Programs for Wayne State University graduate students to help defray unusual expenses or pay for any travel necessary to the students research. Write to the address below for further details.

Wayne State University
Graduate School
4300 Faculty/Administration Building
Detroit, MI   48202

421 Graduate Assistantships

AMOUNT: $6500   **DEADLINE:** January 1
FIELDS/MAJORS: Pharmacology

Awards open to full-time graduate students in the pharmacology doctoral program. Two awards offered annually. Contact the address below for further information.

University of Oklahoma, Norman—College of Medicine
Department of Pharmacology
OUHSC, PO Box 26901, Library 121
Oklahoma City, OK   73190

422 Graduate Assistantships and Fellowships

AMOUNT: None Specified   **DEADLINE:** February 1
FIELDS/MAJORS: All Areas of Study

Programs for graduate students at Penn State. Programs are offered through the graduate school, the office of financial aid, and the departments at Penn State. Includes Graham Fellowship and Academic Computer Fellowship, for students who use practical and innovative computer applications in their research. Forty awards are given annually. Contact the address below for further information.

Pennsylvania State University
Fellowships and Awards Office
313 Kern Graduate Building
University Park, PA   16802

423 Graduate Assistantships

AMOUNT: None Specified   **DEADLINE:** None Specified
FIELDS/MAJORS: All Areas of Study

Assistantships are available at the University of Oklahoma, Norman for full-time graduate students as teaching assistants or research assistants. Contact your department or write to the address below for information.

University of Oklahoma, Norman
Graduate College
1000 Asp Avenue, Room 313
Norman, OK   73019

424 Graduate Awards

AMOUNT: None Specified   DEADLINE: April 1
FIELDS/MAJORS: All Areas of Study

Applicants must be graduate students of Japanese ancestry and members or the JACL. Several programs are available. Applications and information may be obtained from local JACL chapters, district offices, and national headquarters at the address below. Please indicate your level of study and be certain to include a legal-sized SASE (offices in San Francisco, Seattle, L.A., Chicago, and Fresno).

Japanese American Citizens League
National Scholarship and Award Program
1765 Sutter Street
San Francisco, CA   94115

425 Graduate Chemistry Awards

AMOUNT: None Specified   DEADLINE: None Specified
FIELDS/MAJORS: Chemistry

Scholarships are available at the University of Oklahoma, Norman for graduate students in chemistry. Includes the Apex Scholarships, Belle W. Goodman Graduate Fellowship, Conoco Graduate Fellowship, Dow Chemistry Fellowship, and J. Clarence Karcher Fellowship. Individual award requirements may vary. Minimum of thirty-four awards offered annually. Write to the address below for information.

University of Oklahoma, Norman
Chemistry Department
620 Parrington Oval, Room 208
Norman, OK   73019

426 Graduate Dean's Multicultural Award

AMOUNT: $6600   DEADLINE: None Specified
FIELDS/MAJORS: All Areas of Study

Awards for graduate students at UW, Oshkosh who are members of an underrepresented minority group. Contact the graduate school and research, UW, Oshkosh for more details.

University of Wisconsin, Oshkosh
Financial Aid Office, Dempsey 104
800 Algoma Boulevard
Oshkosh, WI   54901

427 Graduate Fellowship Program for Native Americans

AMOUNT: $6000   DEADLINE: November 1
FIELDS/MAJORS: Political Science

Fellowships open to Native Americans who have received their baccalaureates and are planning to enroll in a political science doctoral program. Must have a record of outstanding academic achievement. Contact the address below for further information.

American Political Science Association
Director of Minority Affairs
1527 New Hampshire Avenue, NW
Washington, DC   20036

428 Graduate Fellowships

AMOUNT: $1000–$7000   DEADLINE: February 1
FIELDS/MAJORS: All Fields of Study

Fellowships are open to active members of Phi Kappa Phi who will be enrolling as first-year graduate students. Nomination by current chapter or the chapter in which you were initiated is required. Fifty awards per year. Thirty honorable mention awards of $1000 are awarded yearly. Application forms are available through the chapter secretaries. Contact your chapter's secretary to indicate your interest in becoming the chapter's nominee.

Phi Kappa Phi Honor Society
Louisiana State University
PO Box 16000
Baton Rouge, LA   70893

429 Graduate Fellowships and Scholarships

AMOUNT: None Specified   DEADLINE: March 3
FIELDS/MAJORS: All Areas of Study

Scholarships and fellowships available to students at Wayne State who are pursuing advanced or professional degrees. Many departmental awards are also available. Contact the university at the address below for details. For departmental awards, contact your department.

Wayne State University
Graduate Scholarship/Fellowship Office
4302 Faculty Administration Building
Detroit, MI   48202

430 Graduate Fellowships at National Laboratories and Cooperating Facilities

AMOUNT: None Specified   DEADLINE: February 1
FIELDS/MAJORS: Science, Engineering

Program open to qualified college and university faculty members in science, mathematics, engineering, and technology. Awards open to qualified master's and doctoral degree candidates. Purpose is to provide the opportunity to conduct thesis or dissertation research or to explore research career options at a cooperating facility. Fellowships range from one to twelve months. Awards may include a monthly stipend of $1300, tuition assistance, and a travel allowance.

Associated Western Universities, Inc.
4190 South Highland Drive
Suite 211
Salt Lake City, UT   84124

431 Graduate Fellowships for African-American Students

AMOUNT: $6000 **DEADLINE:** November 1
FIELDS/MAJORS: Political Science

Graduate fellowships for African-American doctoral students. Preference will be given to students just starting their doctoral program. Must be a U.S. citizen. Based on potential for success in graduate studies and financial needs. Fellowships will be awarded on an annual basis. Write to the address below for complete details.

American Political Science Association
1527 New Hampshire Avenue, NW
Washington, DC   20036

432 Graduate Fellowships for Chicano and Latino Students

AMOUNT: $6000 **DEADLINE:** November 1
FIELDS/MAJORS: Political Science

Graduate fellowships for Hispanic students. APSA fellows must enroll in doctoral programs. Priority will be given to those about to enter graduate school. Must be a U.S. citizen. Based on potential for success in graduate studies and financial needs. Fellowships will be awarded on an annual basis. Write to the address below for details.

American Political Science Association
1527 New Hampshire Avenue, NW
Washington, DC   20036

433 Graduate Fellowships for Minorities and Women in the Physical Sciences

AMOUNT: Maximum: $15000
DEADLINE: November 15
FIELDS/MAJORS: Physical Science or Related Fields

Six-year fellowship program for current college seniors or recent graduates not enrolled in a post-graduate program, who want to obtain a Ph.D. and are an underrepresented minority and/or female. Must be a U.S. citizen, and have at least a GPA of 3.0. For study at a participating NPSC member university. Recipients must agree to work two summers at a consortium member employer. Write to L. Nan Snow, Executive Director, at the address below for more information.

National Physical Science Consortium
New Mexico State University
Box 30001, Dept 3 NPS
Las Cruces, NM   88003

434 Graduate Fellowships

AMOUNT: None Specified **DEADLINE:** January 10
FIELDS/MAJORS: Graphic Communications

Open to graduate student in graphic communications with more than one year of study to complete, and graduating college seniors who wish to pursue advanced training. Write to the address below for details. Please specify that you are interested in support for graduate studies.

National Scholarship Trust Fund of the Graphic Arts
4615 Forbes Avenue
Pittsburgh, PA   15213

435 Graduate Fellowships

AMOUNT: None Specified **DEADLINE:** None Specified
FIELDS/MAJORS: All Areas of Study

Applicants must be graduate students who have been accepted to the Catholic University of America. Knights of Columbus members as well as their dependents are eligible. Write to the address below for details.

Knights of Columbus
Catholic University of America
Attn: Director of Financial Aid
Washington, DC   20064

436 Graduate Fellowships, Teaching and Research Assistantships

AMOUNT: None Specified **DEADLINE:** February 15
FIELDS/MAJORS: Geography

Privately funded and University funded awards for M.A., M.S., and Ph.D. students in the department of geography at the University of Illinois. Most are awarded competitively. Contact the department at the address below for details. Request the brochure "Financial Support for Graduate Study in Geography."

University of Illinois, Urbana-Champaign
220 Davenport Hall, Dept. of Geography
607 S. Matthews Avenue
Urbana, IL   61801

437 Graduate Journalism and Mass Communications Awards

AMOUNT: None Specified **DEADLINE:** March 15
FIELDS/MAJORS: Journalism and Mass Communications

Scholarships are available at the University of Oklahoma, Norman for graduate students in journalism. Includes the Chester H. Westfall, Fayette Copeland Memorial, John Scott Graduate Fellowship, Julie Blakley, Mrs. Walter B. Ferguson Memorial, and O.H. Lachenmeyer scholarships. Individual award requirements may vary. Minimum of ten awards offered annually. Write to the address below for information.

University of Oklahoma, Norman
School of Journalism and Mass Communications
860 Van Vleet Oval
Norman, OK   73019

438 Graduate Psychology Award

AMOUNT: None Specified   DEADLINE: None Specified
FIELDS/MAJORS: Psychology

Award open to graduate students who are U.S. citizens. Contact the psychology department for further information.

University of North Carolina, Greensboro
Financial Aid Office
723 Kenilworth Street
Greensboro, NC   27412

439 Graduate Research Assistant Program

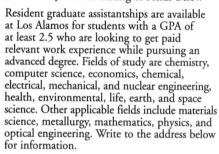

AMOUNT: None Specified
DEADLINE: None Specified
FIELDS/MAJORS: See Listing of Fields Below

Resident graduate assistantships are available at Los Alamos for students with a GPA of at least 2.5 who are looking to get paid relevant work experience while pursuing an advanced degree. Fields of study are chemistry, computer science, economics, chemical, electrical, mechanical, and nuclear engineering, health, environmental, life, earth, and space science. Other applicable fields include materials science, metallurgy, mathematics, physics, and optical engineering. Write to the address below for information.

Los Alamos National Laboratory
Personnel Services Division
Mail Stop P282
Los Alamos, NM   87545

440 Graduate Research Fellowships (Viets Fellowship)

AMOUNT: $3000   DEADLINE: March 15
FIELDS/MAJORS: Neuromuscular Medicine

Fellowships are available for medical or graduate students involved in basic or clinical research related to Myasthenia Gravis (MG). Write to the address below for information.

Myasthenia Gravis Foundation of America
Fellowship Program
222 S. Riverside Plaza, Suite 1540
Chicago, IL   60606

441 Graduate Scholarship

AMOUNT: Maximum: $250
DEADLINE: March 1
FIELDS/MAJORS: Arts, Social Sciences, Physical Sciences

Open to graduating seniors for graduate study. Contact the address listed for further information.

Brooklyn College
Office of the V.P. for Student Life
2113 Boylan Hall
Brooklyn, NY   11210

442 Graduate Scholarship Program

AMOUNT: Maximum: $7200
DEADLINE: None Specified
FIELDS/MAJORS: All Areas of Study

Renewable award given to New Mexico resident graduate students, with preference given to women and minorities in the fields of business, engineering, computer science, mathematics, and agriculture. Applicants must continue education in a New Mexico public university and serve ten hours per week in an unpaid internship or assistantship. Contact the dean of graduate studies at a New Mexico four-year public post-secondary institution.

New Mexico Commission on Higher Education
Financial Aid and Student Services
PO Box 15910
Santa Fe, NM   87506

443 Graduate Scholarship Program

AMOUNT: None Specified
DEADLINE: February 1
FIELDS/MAJORS: Counseling, Psychology, Mental Health, Mental Retardation, Speech Pathology

Scholarships for graduate students who intend to work directly with children in fields related to the areas above, as well as exceptional children, remedial skills development, hearing impaired, and gifted and talented. Based on commitment to children with special needs, scholarship, recommendations, and motivation and goals. Official application forms are available ONLY between September 1st and November 15th. They are available from Junior Auxiliary Chapters, colleges and universities, and from the address below. Requests made at any other time will not be accepted.

National Association of Junior Auxiliaries
NAJA Scholarship Committee
PO Box 1873
Greenville, MS   38702

444 Graduate Scholarship Program

AMOUNT: None Specified
DEADLINE: June 1
FIELDS/MAJORS: Dental Hygiene, Dental Research

Scholarships for students who have at least been accepted to a full-time master's or doctoral program. Minimum GPA of 3.0. Licensure as a dental hygienist is required. Write to the address below for more information.

American Dental Hygienists' Association Institute for Oral Health
444 N. Michigan Avenue, Suite 3400
Chicago, IL   60611

445
Graduate Scholarship Program

AMOUNT: None Specified   DEADLINE: June 15
FIELDS/MAJORS: Medicine, Dentistry

Applicants must be Georgia residents who are pursuing a degree in one of the above majors. Must be able to demonstrate financial need. Write to the address below for details.

Ty Cobb Educational Foundation
PO Box 725
Forest Park, GA   30051

446
Graduate Scholarships and Fellowships

AMOUNT: $1250–$5000   DEADLINE: February 1
FIELDS/MAJORS: Food Science and Technology

Graduate fellowships to encourage and support research in food science and technology at accredited institutions in the U.S. or Canada. In addition, the Arthur T. Schramm Fellowship will provide tuition assistance for needy Ph.D. candidates. Thirty-nine awards offered annually. Write to the address below for details. Please specify your year in school or what degree you are pursuing. You may request information and an application via phone at 312-782-8424 or "fax on demand" 800-234-0270. Graduates must request document #3440.

Institute of Food Technologists
Scholarship Department
221 North LaSalle Street
Chicago, IL   60601

447
Graduate Scholarships in Chemistry

AMOUNT: None Specified   DEADLINE: March 1
FIELDS/MAJORS: Chemistry

Awards are available at the University of New Mexico for graduate students studying chemistry who have an outstanding record in the chemistry department. Write to the address below for information.

University of New Mexico, Albuquerque
Office of Financial Aid
Albuquerque, NM   87131

448
Graduate Scholarships in the Marine Sciences

AMOUNT: $3000   DEADLINE: March 1
FIELDS/MAJORS: Marine Sciences

Scholarships are available to qualified graduate students of Marine Science. Personal qualifications considered include: character, academics, and relative need. Write to the address below for more information.

International Women's Fishing Association Scholarship Trust
PO Drawer 3125
Palm Beach, FL   33480

449
Graduate Scholarships

AMOUNT: None Specified   DEADLINE: April 15
FIELDS/MAJORS: All Areas of Study

Awards are available at Plymouth State for full-time graduate students who exhibit outstanding academic ability and financial need. Write to the address below for information. GPA of at least 3.0 required.

Plymouth State College
Office of Graduate Studies
Plymouth, NH   03264

450
Graduate Scholarships

AMOUNT: None Specified
DEADLINE: January 31
FIELDS/MAJORS: Aerospace Education, Science

Applicants must be CAP members and majoring in aerospace education or science. For graduate study. Write to the address below for details.

Civil Air Patrol
National Headquarters Cap(TT)
Maxwell AFB, AL   36112

451
Graduate Student English Awards

AMOUNT: $1000   DEADLINE: January 15
FIELDS/MAJORS: English

Award open to beginning and returning graduate students who are enrolled full-time (9 hours or more). Must have a minimum GPA of 3.0 overall and at least a 3.5 in English. Contact the address below for further information.

Fort Hays State University
Office of Student Financial Aid
600 Park Street
Hays, KS   67601

452
Graduate Student Researchers Program (Minority and Disabled Focus)

AMOUNT: Maximum: $22000
DEADLINE: February 1
FIELDS/MAJORS: Engineering, Physics, Math, Computer Science, Biology, Aeronautics

Applicants must be sponsored by their graduate department chair or faculty advisor; enrolled in a full-time graduate program at an accredited U.S.

college or university; studying in one of the fields listed above. Student must be highly motivated to pursue their plans of study in NASA related research. Applicant must be a U.S. citizen. Write to the Program Manager at the address below for information. The focus of this program is to bring underrepresented racial minorities and students with disabilities into these fields of study.

NASA Graduate Student Researchers Program
NASA Headquarters
Scholarships and Fellowships
Washington, DC   20546

453 Graduate Student Scholarships

AMOUNT: $2000–$4000
DEADLINE: June 21
FIELDS/MAJORS: Speech—Language Pathology, Communications Disorders

Awards for master's level studies in communication sciences and disorders programs. Four general awards per year. Also available are one award for a foreign or minority student, and one award giving preference to a disabled student pursuing graduate studies in the field. Up to six awards total. Write to the address below for complete details.

American Speech-Language-Hearing Foundation
10801 Rockville Pike
Rockville, MD   20852

454 Graduate Student Workshop

AMOUNT: Maximum: $200
DEADLINE: March 1
FIELDS/MAJORS: Law and Legal Education

Awards for students in law who are enrolled in a doctoral program and plan to enter academic careers. Award is to be used to offset the cost of attending the workshop in July. Forty awards are offered annually. Write to the address below for more information.

Law and Society Association
Hampshire House, Box 33615
University of Massachusetts
Amherst, MA   01003

455 Graduate Study Scholarships for Handicapped Learner Certificate

AMOUNT: $3183   DEADLINE: July 1
FIELDS/MAJORS: Special Education

Award for outstanding graduate students admitted to the special education program. Ten awards offered annually. Contact the Dean's office in the School of Education.

Portland State University
Student Services
204 School of Education Building
Portland, OR   97207

456 Graduate Study-Library Science Scholarship

AMOUNT: None Specified   DEADLINE: May 15
FIELDS/MAJORS: Library Science, Information Science

Tuition and fee assistance for Pennsylvania residents enrolled in an ALA approved program of graduate work in an institution located in Pennsylvania. Based on need, scholarship, motivation, and experience. Write to Ms. Margaret Bauer, Executive Director, at the address below for complete details.

Pennsylvania Library Association
1919 N. Front Street
Harrisburg, PA   17102

457 Grant and Programs for Theological Studies

AMOUNT: None Specified   DEADLINE: None Specified
FIELDS/MAJORS: Theology, Religion

Grants for theology students at the graduate level of study who are members of the Presbyterian Church, U.S.A. Applicants must be U.S. citizens, demonstrate financial need, and be recommended by an academic advisor or church pastor. Write to the address below for more information.

Presbyterian Church, U.S.A.
Office of Financial Aid
100 Witherspoon Street
Louisville, KY   40202

458 Grant Program for Medical Studies

AMOUNT: $500–$1500
DEADLINE: None Specified
FIELDS/MAJORS: Medicine

Grants for medical students at the graduate level of study who are members of the Presbyterian Church, U.S.A. Applicants must be U.S. citizens, demonstrate financial need, and be recommended by an academic advisor or church pastor. Write to the address below for more information.

Presbyterian Church, U.S.A.
Office of Financial Aid
100 Witherspoon Street
Louisville, KY   40202

459 Grant Program for New Investigators

AMOUNT: Maximum: $12500
DEADLINE: None Specified
FIELDS/MAJORS: Pharmacy, Pharmacology

Fellowships for graduate students in pharmacy who are nearing the end of their last year of graduate study (earning Ph.D.). Information may be available from your pharmacy school. Write to the below address if necessary.

American Foundation for Pharmaceutical Education
One Church Street
Suite 202
Rockville, MD   20850

460 Grant Program

AMOUNT: Maximum: $3000
DEADLINE: July 15
FIELDS/MAJORS: Parapsychology

Grants for research in parapsychology (ESP, psychic phenomena, psychokinesis). Not for travel, graduate, or undergraduate studies. For persons studying parapsychology directly (not those with merely a general interest in the subject). Write to the address below for details.

Parapsychology Foundation, Inc.
Eileen J. Garrett Library
228 E. 71st Street
New York, NY   10021

461 Grant-in-Aid for Graduate Students

AMOUNT: $7500   DEADLINE: December 15
FIELDS/MAJORS: Air Conditioning/Refrigeration, HVAC Engineering

Grant for full-time, graduate students in ASHRAE related fields. Program is designed "to encourage the student to continue his/her preparation for service in the HVAC&R Industry." Relevance of proposed research is considered. Not renewable. Applications are made by your advisor on your behalf. Consult with your advisor and write to the address below for further details and application forms. Please specify that your interest is in the graduate student Grant-in-Aid program.

American Society of Heating, Refrigerating, and AC Engineers
Manager of Research
1791 Tullie Circle, NE
Atlanta, GA   30329

462 Grant-in-Aid for Wildlife Research

AMOUNT: None Specified   DEADLINE: November 1
FIELDS/MAJORS: Wildlife, Large Game Animal Research

Awards for graduate students and more advanced investigators to support research on wildlife, and particularly North American big game animals and/or their habitat. Write to the address below for more information.

Boone and Crockett Club
Old Milwaukee Depot
250 Station Drive
Missoula, MT   59801

463 Grant-in-Aid of Research

AMOUNT: $500–$2000
DEADLINE: January 31
FIELDS/MAJORS: American History, Political History

Grants for researchers of subjects that are addressed by the holdings of the LBJ Library. Research is done at the library. Twenty awards are offered annually. Interested applicants must contact the library at the address below (or call 512-482-5137) to obtain information about materials available in the library on the proposed research topic.

Lyndon Baines Johnson Foundation
Archives, Lyndon B. Johnson Library
2313 Red River Street
Austin, TX   78705

464 Grants and Fellowships in Arthritis Research

AMOUNT: None Specified   DEADLINE: September 1
FIELDS/MAJORS: Arthritis Research

Various fellowship and grant programs open to doctors and scientists to further their training in patient care and research into arthritis. Doctoral dissertation awards are also available. Write to the address below for complete details.

Arthritis Foundation
Research Department
1314 Spring Street, NW
Atlanta, GA   30309

465 Grants for Field Research

AMOUNT: Maximum: $1200   DEADLINE: January 31
FIELDS/MAJORS: Science

Grants for graduate students in support of exploration and field research. Expeditions aided will be for specific scientific purposes, in accordance with the Club's stated objective, "to broaden our knowledge of the universe." Write to the address below for more information.

Explorers Club Exploration Fund
Exploration Fund Committee
46 East 70th Street
New York, NY   10021

466 Grants for Graduate Study and Advanced Research in French

AMOUNT: None Specified   DEADLINE: None Specified
FIELDS/MAJORS: French Studies

Grants for graduate students or postdoctorates in the field of French language or culture. Applicants must be U.S. citizens. Some programs are for travel to France. Write to the address below for more information.

Cultural Services of the French Embassy
972 Fifth Avenue
New York, NY   10021

467 Grants for Orchid Research

AMOUNT: $500–$12000 DEADLINE: January 1
FIELDS/MAJORS: Floriculture, Horticulture

Grants for experimental projects and fundamental and applied research on orchids. Qualified graduate students with appropriate interests may apply for grants in support of their research if it involves or applies to orchids. Purpose of award is to advance the scientific study of orchids in every aspect and to assist in the publication of scholarly and popular scientific literature on orchids. A second deadline date used is August 1 of each year. Post-graduates may only apply on behalf of the accredited institution or appropriate research institute they are associated with. Contact address below for complete details.

American Orchid Society
Research Grants
6000 South Olive Avenue
West Palm Beach, FL   33405

468 Grants-in-Aid

AMOUNT: $650–$2400
DEADLINE: None Specified
FIELDS/MAJORS: History of Business, Technology, and Society

Grants-in-aid are available to scholars at all levels who are working within the Hagley's research collection topics. Stipends are for a minimum of two weeks and a maximum of two months at $1200 per month. Hagley offers three deadlines per year: March 31, June 30, and October 31. Write to Dr. Philip B. Scranton at the address shown below for details.

Hagley Museum and Library
PO Box 3630
Wilmington, DE   19807

469 Grants-in-Aid

AMOUNT: Maximum: $2000   DEADLINE: January 15
FIELDS/MAJORS: Petroleum Geology, Geology, Geophysics, Paleontology

Grants are available to graduate students in studies relating to the earth science aspects of the petroleum industry. Several grant programs are offered by the AAPG. Write to the address listed for more details.

American Association of Petroleum Geologists
W.A. Morgan, Chairman/AAPG Grants CTME.
PO Box 979
Tulsa, OK   74101

470 Grants-in-Aid Program in Support of Anthropological Research

AMOUNT: Maximum: $15000   DEADLINE: May 1
FIELDS/MAJORS: Anthropology

Open to qualified scholars affiliated with accredited institutions and organizations. Awards are for individual postdoctoral research or for dissertation thesis research. Write to the address below for details.

Wenner-Gren Foundation for Anthropological Research
Grants Programs
220 Fifth Avenue
New York, NY   10001

471 Graphic Design Scholarships

AMOUNT: None Specified
DEADLINE: February 4
FIELDS/MAJORS: Graphic Design

Open to graduates in graphic design. Contact the address below for further information. At least 3.0 GPA required.

University of Northern Iowa
William W. Lew, Art Department Head
104 Kamerick Art Building
Cedar Falls, IA   50614

472 Grass Fellowships in Neurophysiology

AMOUNT: None Specified   DEADLINE: December 1
FIELDS/MAJORS: Neurophysiology

Summer fellowships for late predoctoral or early postdoctoral researchers who are academically prepared for independent research in neurophysiology. This is a resident fellowship at the Marine Biological Laboratory at Woods Hole, Massachusetts. Requires research proposal, budget and recommendation. Interested persons should write to the address below for further information. Request bulletin FA-296.

Grass Foundation
77 Reservoir Road
Quincy, MA   02170

473 Gratis Scholarship

AMOUNT: None Specified   DEADLINE: March 1
FIELDS/MAJORS: Medicine

Awards are available at the University of New Mexico for medical students from New Mexico who have financial need. Write to the address below for more information.

University of New Mexico, Albuquerque
Office of Financial Aid
Albuquerque, NM   87131

474 Greater Albuquerque Medical Association Scholarship

AMOUNT: None Specified   DEADLINE: March 1
FIELDS/MAJORS: Medicine

Awards are available at the University of New Mexico for medical students from Bernalillo County, New Mexico, who demonstrate academic achievement and financial need. Write to the address below for more information.

University of New Mexico, Albuquerque
Office of Financial Aid
Albuquerque, NM   87131

475
Greater New York Savings Bank Scholarship

AMOUNT: Maximum: $500 DEADLINE: March 1
FIELDS/MAJORS: Economics

Open to a graduating senior majoring in economics. Contact the address listed for further information.

Brooklyn College
Office of the V.P. for Student Life
2113 Boylan Hall
Brooklyn, NY 11210

476
Guggenheim Fellowship at the National Air and Space Museum

AMOUNT: $14000–$25000 DEADLINE: January 15
FIELDS/MAJORS: Aeronautics, Astronomy, Astrophysics, Space Research

Residential fellowship for researchers in the above areas. Persons holding Ph.D. must have received doctorate within seven years of award. Doctoral candidates must have completed preliminary coursework. Write to the Fellowship Coordinator, Museum Programs, at the address below for details.

National Air and Space Museum, Smithsonian Institution
Aeronautics Department
Fellowship Coordinator, Room 3312, MRC 312
Washington, DC 20560

477
Guggenheim Foundation Dissertation Awards and Research Grants

AMOUNT: $15000–$35000 DEADLINE: August 1
FIELDS/MAJORS: Subspecialties Directly Related to Violence, Aggression, and Dominance

Fellowships supporting the writing (i.e., not the preliminary work) of Ph.D. dissertations and grants supporting advanced research in areas of concern to the Foundation. Priority given to research that can increase understanding and amelioration of urgent problems in the modern world related to these topics. Research area must be directly related to these topics. August 1 is the deadline for decisions announced in December. Write for details. Dissertation applicants are asked to take particular care in deciding to apply and in organizing and completing application.

Harry Frank Guggenheim Foundation
Research Grants and Dissertation Awards
527 Madison Avenue
New York, NY 10022

478
Guy D. and Mary Edith Halladay Scholarships

AMOUNT: $500–$2500 DEADLINE: April 15
FIELDS/MAJORS: All Areas of Study

Scholarships for graduate students of Kent County who are studying at a school in western Michigan. Based upon academic ability and demonstrated financial need. Requires a minimum GPA of at least 3.0. Write to the address below for details.

Grand Rapids Foundation
209-C Waters Building
161 Ottawa Avenue, NW
Grand Rapids, MI 49503

479
H. Delight and Orlo H. Maughan Scholarship

AMOUNT: None Specified
DEADLINE: February 1
FIELDS/MAJORS: Agricultural Economics, Food Science

Award is open to graduate students who are able to demonstrate financial need. Available for agricultural economics in odd-numbered years and available for food science in even-numbered years. Contact the address below for further information.

Washington State University—Scholarship Committee
College of Agriculture and Home Economics
423 Hulbert Hall
Pullman, WA 99164

480
H. Thomas Austern Memorial Writing Competition

AMOUNT: $1000–$3000 DEADLINE: May 16
FIELDS/MAJORS: Law

Writing competition open to law students interested in the areas of law that affect foods, drugs, devices, and biologics. Submitted papers are judged by a committee of practicing attorneys with relevant expertise on a variety of factors. Write to the address below for more information.

Food and Drug Law Institute
Director of Academic Programs
1000 Vermont Avenue, NW, Suite 200
Washington, DC 20005

481
H.A. Miller Foundation Medical/Dental School Loans

AMOUNT: None Specified DEADLINE: None Specified
FIELDS/MAJORS: Medicine, Dentistry

Low interest loans to graduates of Curry County, NM, high schools who are attending medical or dental schools. Write to the address below for details.

H.A. Miller Foundation
c/o Rowley Law Firm, Attorneys at Law
PO Box 790, 305 Pile
Clovis, NM 88101

482
H.J. Holden Medical Scholarship Fund

AMOUNT: None Specified   DEADLINE: March 1
FIELDS/MAJORS: Medicine

Awards are available at the University of New Mexico for students accepted for attendance at UNM School of Medicine. Based on merit and financial need. Write to the address below for more information.

University of New Mexico, Albuquerque
Office of Financial Aid
Albuquerque, NM   87131

483
Hagley Winterthur Fellowships in Arts and Industries

AMOUNT: $1200–$7200
DEADLINE: December 1
FIELDS/MAJORS: History, Art, Industry, Economics

Open to all scholars who are researching in the fields above and interested in relationships between economic life and the arts. Stipends are for period of one to six months at $1200 per month. Write to Dr. Philip B. Scranton at the address shown below for details.

Hagley Museum and Library
PO Box 3630
Wilmington, DE   19807

484
Harley French/Dr. Henry Hobart Ruger Scholarships

AMOUNT: None Specified   DEADLINE: April 15
FIELDS/MAJORS: Medicine

Awards to students enrolled in the School of Medicine. Based on financial need and satisfactory academics. Contact the address below for further information or the financial aid office at your school's location.

University of North Dakota—School of Medicine
Sandra Elshaug, Financial Aid Office
PO Box 9037—501 N. Columbia Road
Grand Forks, ND   58202

485
Harold E. Hardy Scholarship

AMOUNT: None Specified   DEADLINE: None Specified
FIELDS/MAJORS: Marketing

Awards for graduate students in the field of marketing with financial need. Contact the SOM Development Office, Room 206, for more information and an application.

University of Massachusetts, Amherst
SOM Development Office
Room 206
Amherst, MA   01003

486
Harold Huneke Endowed Scholarship

AMOUNT: $500   DEADLINE: March 1
FIELDS/MAJORS: Mathematics

Scholarships are available at the University of Oklahoma, Norman for doctoral candidates in mathematics. Write to the address below for information.

University of Oklahoma, Norman
Mathematics Department
420 PHSC
Norman, OK   73019

487
Harold J. Siebenthaler Scholarship

AMOUNT: None Specified   DEADLINE: February 1
FIELDS/MAJORS: Law

Awards for law students who demonstrate academic promise and financial need. Also must be residents of: Hamilton, Butler, Clermont, or Warren Counties in Ohio. Contact the Assistant Dean, Chase College of Law, for further information.

Northern Kentucky University
Chase College of Law
Office of Administration
Highland Heights, KY   41099

488
Harold Lancour Scholarship for Foreign Study

AMOUNT: $1000   DEADLINE: March 15
FIELDS/MAJORS: Library and Information Science

Applicants must be library students who plan to study abroad. For graduate study. Write to the Executive Secretary at the address below for details.

Beta Phi Mu International Library Science Honor Society
Executive Secretary, Beta Phi Mu
SLIS—Florida State University
Tallahassee, FL   32306

489
Harold Moore Memorial Award

AMOUNT: $500–$1500   DEADLINE: April 1
FIELDS/MAJORS: Botany, Plant Taxonomy, and Related Fields

Fellowships are available at Cornell for graduate students to support research in plant science. Four awards are given annually. Write to the address listed for information.

Cornell University
Director, L.H. Bailey Hortorium
467 Mann Library
Ithaca, NY   14853

490
Harriet A. Shaw Fellowship

AMOUNT: $3000   DEADLINE: December 16
FIELDS/MAJORS: Music

Fellowships are available at Wellesley for study or research in music or art, in the United States or abroad. Preference given to music candidates. Undergraduate work in history of art required of other candidates. Write to the address below for information.

Wellesley College
Committee on Graduate Fellowships
106 Central Street, Career Center
Wellesley, MA   02181

491
Harriet and Leon Pomerance Fellowship

AMOUNT: $3000   DEADLINE: November 1
FIELDS/MAJORS: Aegean Bronze Age Archaeology

Applicants must be working on a project of a scholarly nature relating to Aegean Bronze Age archaeology. Preference will be given to candidates whose project requires travel to the Mediterranean for purposes stated above. Must be U.S. or Canadian citizen. Write to the address below for details.

Archaeological Institute of America
Boston University
656 Beacon Street, 4th Floor
Boston, MA   02215

492
Harry and Sarah Zelzer Fellowship and Prize

AMOUNT: Maximum: $3500
DEADLINE: None Specified
FIELDS/MAJORS: Instrumental Music

Awards open to musicians in the early stages of their careers. Awards are cash, a weekly stipend, housing (up to four weeks), and round-trip airfare to Chicago. Applicants must be instrumentalists. Contact the address below for further information.

Newberry Library
Committee on Awards
60 W. Walton Street
Chicago, IL   60610

493
Harry Byrd Lee Adams Scholarship

AMOUNT: None Specified
DEADLINE: January 1
FIELDS/MAJORS: Housing, Interior Design

Award open to master's candidates in the above fields. Preference to residents of North Carolina. Contact the address below for further information.

University of North Carolina, Greensboro
Financial Aid Office
723 Kenilworth Street
Greensboro, NC   27412

494
Harry Nadler Memorial Fellowship

AMOUNT: None Specified   DEADLINE: March 1
FIELDS/MAJORS: Art—Painting, Drawing

Scholarships are available at the University of New Mexico for full-time graduate students in painting or drawing. Based on artistic excellence. Write to the address below for information.

University of New Mexico, Albuquerque
College of Fine Arts
Office of Graduate Studies
Albuquerque, NM   87131

495
Harry Shwachman Clinical Investigator Award

AMOUNT: Maximum: $60000   DEADLINE: August 1
FIELDS/MAJORS: Medical Research—Cystic Fibrosis

This three-year award provides the opportunity for clinically trained physicians to develop into independent biomedical research investigators who are actively involved in CF-related areas. It is also intended to facilitate the transition from postdoctoral training to a career in academic medicine. Support is available for up to $60000 per year plus up to $15000 for supplies. Must be U.S. citizen or permanent resident. Write to the address below for details.

Cystic Fibrosis Foundation
Office of Grants Management
6931 Arlington Road
Bethesda, MD   20814

496
Hartley B. Dean Medical Scholarship

AMOUNT: None Specified
DEADLINE: March 1
FIELDS/MAJORS: Medicine

Awards are available at the University of New Mexico for Native American medical students who are in the top half of class. Write to the address below for more information. At least 2.0 GPA required.

University of New Mexico, Albuquerque
Office of Financial Aid
Albuquerque, NM   87131

497
Harvey Fellows Program

AMOUNT: $12000
DEADLINE: November 30
FIELDS/MAJORS: See Fields Below

Awards for graduate students in certain disciplines at top schools, whose career goals include leadership positions in fields where Christians have little influence. Fields of study include: high-tech research, science, news media, international economics or finance, business, journalism, visual and performing arts, telecommunications, government, public policy, teaching, and law. Approximately twelve awards are given annually. Write to the address below or email to harvey@cccu.org for more information. Applications available through November 15.

Harvey Fellows Program
329 Eighth Street, NE
Washington, DC   20002

498
Haskell Awards

AMOUNT: $1000   DEADLINE: February 14
FIELDS/MAJORS: Architectural Writing

Awards given for fine writing on architectural subjects at an advanced level of study. Applicants may only submit unpublished works for consideration. Write to the address below for details.

American Institute of Architects, New York Chapter
Arnold W. Brunner Grant
200 Lexington Avenue
New York, NY   10016

499
Havig Medical Scholarship in Surgery

AMOUNT: None Specified   DEADLINE: April 15
FIELDS/MAJORS: Surgery

Awards for third-year students who excel in the field of surgery. Based on financial need. Contact the address below for further information or the financial aid office at your school's location.

University of North Dakota—School of Medicine
Sandra Elshaug, Financial Aid Office
PO Box 9037—501 N. Columbia Road
Grand Forks, ND   58202

500
Hayek Fund for Scholars

AMOUNT: $1000   DEADLINE: None Specified
FIELDS/MAJORS: All Areas of Study

Fund to help offset expenses for participating in professional meetings. For graduate students and untenured faculty members. Write to Attn: Hayek Scholars Program at the address below for details.

Institute for Humane Studies at George Mason University
Hayek Fund for Scholars
4400 University Drive
Fairfax, VA   22030

501
Health Professionals Loan Repayment Program

AMOUNT: None Specified   DEADLINE: July 1
FIELDS/MAJORS: See Below

Loans for students who are studying the following areas of health: osteopathic and allopathic physician and physician assistants, advanced practice nursing, allied healthcare providers, podiatrists, optometrists, and dentists. Applicants must be New Mexico residents. For post-graduate level study in New Mexico. Write to the address below for more information. Past student loans will be repaid if he/she agrees to work in shortage areas in New Mexico.

New Mexico Commission on Higher Education
Financial Aid and Student Services
PO Box 15910
Santa Fe, NM   87506

502
Health Sciences Scholarship Program

AMOUNT: $10000   DEADLINE: November 3
FIELDS/MAJORS: Allopathic, Osteopathic, Family, Internal, Pediatric Medicine, Nursing, Physician Asst.

Available for fourth-year medical students in the areas above or students in the final year of a primary care education program for nurse practitioners, physician assistants, or nurse-midwives. Must have an interest in primary care in West Virginia. Recipients are obligated to sign a contract to practice in an underserved rural area for two years upon graduation. Write to the address below for more information. Applicants must attend Marshall University, West Virginia University, or Alderson-Broaddus College.

University System of West Virginia
1018 Kanawha Boulevard E.
Suite 901
Charleston, WV   25301

503
Hearst Minority Fellowship

AMOUNT: $15000   DEADLINE: February 1
FIELDS/MAJORS: Philanthropic Research

Fellowship for minority students admitted to a master's level program in philanthropic studies at Indiana University. Non-renewable. Write to the address below for more information.

Indiana University Center on Philanthropy
550 West North Street, Suite 301
Indianapolis, IN   46202

504
Helen James Scholarship

AMOUNT: None Specified
DEADLINE: March 1
FIELDS/MAJORS: Medicine

Awards are available at the University of New Mexico for female students enrolled in the UNM school of medicine. This scholarship is only awarded every three years and is based on financial need. Write to the address below for more information.

University of New Mexico, Albuquerque
Office of Financial Aid
Albuquerque, NM   87131

505
Helen M. Fields Scholarship

AMOUNT: None Specified
DEADLINE: None Specified
FIELDS/MAJORS: Education

Award open to graduate students with excellent academic records in the field of English and/or English education. Contact the address below for further information.

University of Toledo
Dean, College of Education
301 Snyder Memorial
Toldeo, OH   43606

506
Helen M. Fields Scholarship

AMOUNT: None Specified
DEADLINE: None Specified
FIELDS/MAJORS: English, English Education

Award open to full-time graduate students with excellent academics. Contact the address below for further information.

University of Toledo
Associate Dean for Graduate Studies
University Hall, Room 2230
Toldeo, OH   43606

507
Helen M. Woodruff Fellowship

AMOUNT: None Specified
DEADLINE: November 15
FIELDS/MAJORS: Archaeology and Classical Studies

A predoctoral or postdoctoral fellowship for study of the fields listed above has been established by the Institute at the Academy of Rome. This fellowship combined with other funds from the American Academy in Rome, will support a Rome prize fellowship which will be open to citizens or permanent residents of the U.S. Write to the address below for details.

Archaeological Institute of America
American Academy in Rome
7 East 60th Street
New York, NY   10022

508
Helena Rubinstein Fellowship in Art History and Museum Studies

AMOUNT: None Specified   DEADLINE: April 1
FIELDS/MAJORS: Art History/Museum Studies

Program is open to graduate students, post-graduate candidates, and undergraduates with the capacity for advanced scholarship. This is a residential program. Ten fellowships are available. Write to address below for details.

Whitney Museum of American Art Independent Study Program
384 Broadway, 4th Floor
New York, NY   10013

509
Henry A. Murray Dissertation Award Program

AMOUNT: $2500   DEADLINE: April 1
FIELDS/MAJORS: Social and Behavioral Sciences

Three grants supporting doctoral candidates performing research in the social or behavioral sciences studying individuals in context, in-depth, and across time. Write to the address below for details.

Radcliffe College
Henry A. Murray Research Center
10 Garden Street
Cambridge, MA   02138

510
Henry Belin Du Pont Fellowship

AMOUNT: $6000   DEADLINE: November 15
FIELDS/MAJORS: History, Art, Industry, Economics, Museum Studies

Open to doctoral candidates who have completed all but the dissertation. This is a residential fellowship for four months and provides housing, use of computer, email, Internet access, and an office along with the stipend. Write to address shown below for details.

Hagley Museum and Library
PO Box 3630
Wilmington, DE   19807

511
Henry G. Halladay Awards

AMOUNT: $760   DEADLINE: August 31
FIELDS/MAJORS: Medicine

Five supplemental scholarships are presented annually to African-American men enrolled in the first year of medical school who have overcome significant obstacles to obtain a medical education. Must be a U.S. citizen. Write to "special programs" at the address below for details.

National Medical Fellowships, Inc.
110 West 32nd Street, 8th Floor
New York, NY   10001

512

Henry J. Reilly Memorial Scholarship

AMOUNT: $500 DEADLINE: None Specified
FIELDS/MAJORS: All Areas of Study

Scholarships for active or associate members of the Reserve Officers Association. Must be accepted for graduate study at a regionally-accredited U.S. college or university. Must provide evidence of a GPA of at least 3.3. Also based on character and leadership. Write to the address below for details. When requesting information, please specify your year in school.

Reserve Officers Association
Henry J. Reilly Scholarship Program
One Constitution Avenue, NE
Washington, DC   20002

513

Henry Joel Cadbury Fellowship Fund

AMOUNT: None Specified DEADLINE: January 2
FIELDS/MAJORS: Humanities

Award open to advanced graduate students in humanities. Contact the address below for further information.

Bryn Mawr Graduate School of Arts and Sciences
101 N. Merion Avenue
Bryn Mawr, PA   19010

514

Henry Luce Foundation/ ACLS Fellowship for Scholarship in American Art

AMOUNT: $18500 DEADLINE: November 15
FIELDS/MAJORS: American Art

Fellowships for dissertation research in visual art in America. Must be a U.S. citizen or permanent resident. Fellowships are for a one-year non-renewable term beginning in the summer. Write to the address below for details.

American Council of Learned Societies
Office of Fellowships and Grants
228 E. 45th Street
New York, NY   10017

515

Herbert Hoover Presidential Fellowships and Grants

AMOUNT: $500–$1200 DEADLINE: March 1
FIELDS/MAJORS: American History, Political Science, Public Policy

Scholarships are awarded to current graduate students, postdoctoral scholars, qualified non-academic researchers. Priority given to proposals that have the highest probability of publication and use by educators and policymakers. Write to the address below for details.

Hoover Presidential Library Association
Ms. Patricia A. Hand
PO Box 696
West Branch, IA   52358

516

Herbert Scoville Jr. Peace Fellowships

AMOUNT: $7000 DEADLINE: October 15
FIELDS/MAJORS: Arms Control, International Peace, Military Science, and Related

Fellowships are available for graduate students to support four to six months of full-time work on arms control research and/or action activities in Washington, D.C. Write to the address below for information.

Scoville Peace Fellowship Program
110 Maryland Avenue, NE
Suite 211
Washington, DC   20002

517

Herman Kahn Resident Fellowships

AMOUNT: Maximum: $18000
DEADLINE: April 1
FIELDS/MAJORS: Political Science, Economics, International Relations, Education

Residential fellowships for candidates who have completed all requirements for Ph.D. except dissertation. Fellows are expected to spend 50% of their time on projects the Institute assigns in their general area. Areas of fellowship are in education, domestic political economy, international political economics, political theory, and national security studies. Postdoctoral fellowships also available. Application is made with vitae, three letters of recommendation (two academic, one non-academic), recent publications and theses proposal, and graduate school transcripts. Contact the Institute at the address below for details.

Hudson Institute
Herman Kahn Center
PO Box 26-919
Indianapolis, IN   46226

518

Hermon Dunlap Smith Center for the History of Cartography

AMOUNT: Maximum: $2400 DEADLINE: March 2
FIELDS/MAJORS: History of Cartography

Fellowships for scholars in the study of cartography history are available through the Hermon Dunlap Smith Center for the History of Cartography. Fellowships usually last three months and the award is $800 per month. One or two awards offered annually. Write to the address below for details.

Newberry Library
The Smith Center Scholarship Committee
60 W. Walton Street
Chicago, IL   60610

519
Herzog August Bibliothek Wolfenbuttel Fellowship

AMOUNT: None Specified **DEADLINE:** None Specified
FIELDS/MAJORS: Library Science

Awards open to doctorate students, at the Newberry Library, for a period in residence in Wolfenbuttel, Germany. Proposed project should link the collections of both libraries. Award is a monthly stipend and travel expenses. Contact the address below for further information.

Newberry Library
Committee on Awards
60 W. Walton Street
Chicago, IL   60610

520
Hettie M. Anthony Fellowship

AMOUNT: $2000 **DEADLINE:** January 15
FIELDS/MAJORS: Home Economics/Related Fields

Applicants must be Kappa Omicron Nu members and doctoral candidates at Northwest Missouri State University. Awards will be announced April 1. Write to the address below for details.

Kappa Omicron Nu Honor Society
4990 Northwind Drive, Suite 140
East Lansing, MI   48823

521
HHMI Research Training Fellowships for Medical Students Program

AMOUNT: $14500 **DEADLINE:** None Specified
FIELDS/MAJORS: Medicine

Fellowships are available for students currently enrolled in a U.S. medical school who wish to spend a year doing intensive research. Recipients are selected on the basis of a national competition. Research may be conducted at any academic or non-profit research institution in the U.S. except NIH in Bethesda, Maryland. Approximately sixty awards offered annually. Write to the address below for additional information.

Howard Hughes Medical Institute
Research Training Fellowships/GSE 94
4000 Jones Bridge Road
Chevy Chase, MD   20815

522
HHMI-NIH Research Scholars Program

AMOUNT: $16800 **DEADLINE:** January 10
FIELDS/MAJORS: Medicine

This program is available at NIH in Bethesda, Maryland for medical students to spend a year doing intensive research in the following fields: cell biology and regulation, epidemiology and biostatistics, genetics, immunology, neuroscience, and structural biology. Write to the address below for additional information.

Howard Hughes Medical Institute
HHMI-NIH Research Scholars Program
1 Cloister Court
Bethesda, MD   20814

523
Higgins-Quarles Award

AMOUNT: $1000 **DEADLINE:** January 8
FIELDS/MAJORS: American History

Awards are available for minority graduate students at the dissertation stage of their Ph.D. programs. To apply, students should submit a brief two-page abstract of the dissertation project, along with a one page budget explaining the travel and research plans for the funds requested. Write to the address below for more information.

Organization of American Historians
Award and Prize Committee Coordinator
112 N. Bryan Street
Bloomington, IN   47408

524
Higher Education Loan Program (HELP)

AMOUNT: None Specified **DEADLINE:** March 1
FIELDS/MAJORS: Obstetrics and Gynecology

Must be citizen of a country represented by the ACOG. Must be resident who has completed one year in approved training program in obstetrics or gynecology and has a membership in ACOG as a junior fellow. Write to the address below for more information.

American College of Obstetricians and Gynecologists
Attn: Higher Education Loan Program
409 12th Street, SW
Washington, DC   20024

525
Hirsh Student Writing Award

AMOUNT: $1000 **DEADLINE:** February 1
FIELDS/MAJORS: Dentistry, Podiatry, Nursing, Pharmacy, Health Science or Admin.

Writing competition for students in one of the areas listed above who are currently attending an accredited school in the United States or Canada. Papers must be at least 3000 words in length, must contain only uncollaborated original work, and may relate to research done by the author. Write to the address below for more information.

American College of Legal Medicine
Student Writing Competition
611 East Wells Street
Milwaukee, WI   53202

526 History and Philosophy of Science Centennial Fellowships

AMOUNT: Maximum: $1000000
DEADLINE: December 15
FIELDS/MAJORS: History and Philosophy of Science

The intent of the Centennial Fellowships is to support and encourage exceptional scientists and scholars in the early stages of their careers. Candidates should be able to demonstrate great scholarly promise, but have not yet achieved full academic maturity and/or professional recognition. Applicants must be actively engaged in research and have a commitment to teaching and demonstrate a superior ability to communicate their work to broad audiences. Candidates should be less than forty years of age at time of application or not more than twelve years from the completion of their academic training (receipt of Ph.D.). Fellowships in this category will support research on the practices, methods and consequences of science and technology, past and present. Of particular interest are: (i) studies exploring the reciprocal relations of science and technology with human self-conceptions, values, and society and (ii) studies informing our understanding of scientific processes and their significance. Contact the address below for further information and instructions.

James S. McDonnell Foundation
1034 S. Brentwood Boulevard, Suite 1850
St. Louis, MO   63117

527 History Graduate Award

AMOUNT: None Specified
DEADLINE: January 15
FIELDS/MAJORS: History

Scholarships are awarded to graduate students based on academic merit. Write to the address below for more information.

Fort Hays State University
Office of Student Financial Aid
600 Park Street
Hays, KS   67601

528 History Graduate Travel

AMOUNT: None Specified
DEADLINE: None Specified
FIELDS/MAJORS: History

Awards for graduate students at UMass to support academic travel. Contact the Chairperson, Department of History at the address below for more information.

University of Massachusetts, Amherst
Chairperson of the Department of History
Amherst, MA   01003

529 History of Science Research Award

AMOUNT: $175
DEADLINE: January 31
FIELDS/MAJORS: History of Science

Scholarships are available at the University of Oklahoma, Norman for graduate students in history of science, given for excellence in research accomplishments. Written research work up to 10,000 words may be considered. Write to the address below for information.

University of Oklahoma, Norman
Department of History of Science
PHSC, Room 622
Norman, OK   73019

530 Hollaender Distinguished Postdoctoral Fellowship Program

AMOUNT: $40500   DEADLINE: January 15
FIELDS/MAJORS: Biomedical, Life, and Environmental Sciences

These fellowships are for positions at the U.S. Department of Energy and the Office of Health and Environmental Research, to assist in understanding the health and environmental effects associated with energy technologies. Applicant must have received the Ph.D. within the past two years and be a citizen of the United States. Fellowship is for two years. Write to the address below for information.

Oak Ridge Associated Universities
Hollaender Postdoctoral Fellowships
PO Box 117, Science/Engineering Ed Div.
Oak Ridge, TN   37831

531 Hollingworth Award

AMOUNT: $2000   DEADLINE: January 15
FIELDS/MAJORS: Research: Education/
Psychology Relating to Gifted/Talented Children

Research grants for graduate students, teachers, professors, educational administrators, psychologists, etc. Supports educational or psychological research of potential benefit to the gifted and talented. Research must be of publishable quality. Based on abstract and research proposal. Write for details.

Intertel Foundation, Hollingworth Award Committee
Dr. Roxanne Herrick Cramer, Chairman
4300 Sideburn Road
Fairfax, VA   22030

532 Holly A. Cornell Scholarship

AMOUNT: $5000
DEADLINE: December 15
FIELDS/MAJORS: Science or Engineering Relating to Water Supply and Treatment

Scholarships are available to encourage and support outstanding female and/or minority students wishing to pursue advanced training in the field of water supply and treatment. For master's degree candidates. Write to the address below for information.

American Water Works Association
Scholarship Coordinator
6666 W. Quincy Avenue
Denver, CO   80235

Horton-Hollowell Fellowship

AMOUNT: Maximum: $4000   DEADLINE: December 16
FIELDS/MAJORS: All Areas of Study

Fellowships for Wellesley alumnae for graduate study in any field, preferably in the last two years of candidacy for the Ph.D., or its equivalent, or for private research of equivalent standard. Contact the address below for further information.

Wellesley College, Fellowships for Wellesley Alumnae
Sec'y, Committee on Graduate Fellowships
106 Central Street, Career Center
Wellesley, MA   02181

Howard A. Peters Scholarship

AMOUNT: None Specified
DEADLINE: None Specified
FIELDS/MAJORS: Environmental Health Science

Awards for graduate students at UMass in the environmental health sciences. Contact the Chair, Environmental Health Science Program, for more information.

University of Massachusetts, Amherst
Chairperson
Environmental Health Science Program
Amherst, MA   01003

Howard and Hermina Hallgarth, George Tamaki Memorial Scholarships

AMOUNT: None Specified   DEADLINE: February 1
FIELDS/MAJORS: Entomology

Awards open to graduate students with a minimum GPA of 3.5. Hallgarth Scholarship alternates with the department of civil engineering. Contact the address below for further information about both awards.

Washington State University—Scholarship Committee
College of Agriculture and Home Economics
423 Hulbert Hall
Pullman, WA   99164

Howard Hughes Predoctoral Fellowships in Biological Sciences

AMOUNT: $15000   DEADLINE: November 15
FIELDS/MAJORS: See Listing of Fields Below

Fellowships for doctoral students in their first year of graduate study in one of these fields: biochemistry, biophysics, biostatistics, cell biology, developmental biology, epidemiology, mathematical biology, microbiology, neuroscience, molecular biology, pharmacology, physiology, structural biology, genetics, and virology. Eighty awards offered annually. Write to the address below for further information.

Howard Hughes Medical Institute
Office of Grants and Special Programs
2101 Constitution Avenue
Washington, DC   20418

Howard Lehman Goodhart Fellowship Fund

AMOUNT: None Specified   DEADLINE: January 2
FIELDS/MAJORS: Medieval Studies

Award open to graduate students in medieval studies. Contact the address below for further information.

Bryn Mawr Graduate School of Arts and Sciences
101 N. Merion Avenue
Bryn Mawr, PA   19010

Howard M. Soule Graduate Fellowships in Educational Leadership

AMOUNT: $500–$1500   DEADLINE: May 1
FIELDS/MAJORS: Educational Administration

Open to Phi Delta Kappa members who are full-time students enrolled in a doctoral, master's, or specialist program. Write to the address below for complete details.

Phi Delta Kappa
International Headquarters
PO Box 789
Bloomington, IN   47402

Howard S. Brembeck Scholarship

AMOUNT: $5000   DEADLINE: April 1
FIELDS/MAJORS: Agricultural Engineering

Award open to graduate students with an interest in development of poultry-related equipment. Must hold a degree in agricultural engineering and be able to provide proof of being accepted into a graduate program offering studies "specializing in any and all equipment that would be considered necessary to sustain animal life during the production process." Contact the address below for further information.

Midwest Poultry Consortium, Inc.
Box 191, 13033 Ridgedale Drive
Minneapolis, MN   55343

Hubbard Scholarship

AMOUNT: $3000   DEADLINE: May 1
FIELDS/MAJORS: Library Science

The scholarship's purpose is to recruit excellent librarians for Georgia and will be used to provide financial assistance to qualified candidates for a year's study in completing a master's degree in library science. Must be completing senior year in an accredited college or university or be a graduate of such an institution. Preference to Georgia residents. Write to the address below for complete details.

Georgia Library Association
Hubbard Scholarship Committee c/o SOLNET
1438 W. Peachtree Street NW #200
Atlanta, GA   30309-2955

541 Hughes Aircraft Company Fellowship/Scholarship Program

AMOUNT: None Specified   DEADLINE: March 1
FIELDS/MAJORS: Engineering

Awards are available at the University of New Mexico for doctoral fellows in an engineering program. Contact Hughes Aircraft Company Corporate Fellowship and Rotation Programs, Technical Education Center, 200 N. Sepulveda Boulevard, El Segunda, CA 90245 for more information.

University of New Mexico, Albuquerque
Office of Financial Aid
Albuquerque, NM   87131

542 Human Cognition Centennial Fellowships

AMOUNT: Maximum: $1000000
DEADLINE: December 15
FIELDS/MAJORS: Human Cognition

The intent of the Centennial Fellowships is to support and encourage exceptional scientists and scholars in the early stages of their careers. Candidates should be able to demonstrate great scholarly promise, but have not yet achieved full academic maturity and/or professional recognition. Applicants must be actively engaged in research and have a commitment to teaching and demonstrate a superior ability to communicate their work to broad audiences. Candidates should be less than forty years of age at time of application or not more than twelve years from the completion of their academic training (receipt of Ph.D.). Fellowships awarded in this category will support research in the fields of cognitive neuroscience, cognitive science, or philosophy that promises to significantly enhance our understanding of the human mind/brain, or that applies the findings of cognitive science to pressing societal problems in such areas as child development, education, or rehabilitation. Applications must be submitted Contact the address below for further information and instructions.

James S. McDonnell Foundation
1034 S. Brentwood Boulevard, Suite 1850
St. Louis, MO   63117

543 Human Genetics Centennial Fellowships

AMOUNT: Maximum: $1000000
DEADLINE: December 15
FIELDS/MAJORS: Human Genetics

The intent of the Centennial Fellowships is to support and encourage exceptional scientists and scholars in the early stages of their careers. Candidates should be able to demonstrate great scholarly promise, but have not yet achieved full academic maturity and/or professional recognition. Applicants must be actively engaged in research and have a commitment to teaching and demonstrate a superior ability to communicate their work to broad audiences. Candidates should be less than forty years of age at time of application or not more than twelve years from the completion of their academic training (receipt of Ph.D.). Fellowships awarded in this category will support fundamental research in genetics to understand human development, gene function, evolution, diversity, molecular medicine, and the promotion of wellness throughout life. Interdisciplinary approaches based primarily on genetics are encouraged. Applications must be submitted by the sponsoring institution. Contact the address below for further information and instructions.

James S. McDonnell Foundation
1034 S. Brentwood Boulevard, Suite 1850
St. Louis, MO   63117

544 Hyland R. Johns Grant Program

AMOUNT: $5000–$20000   DEADLINE: May 1
FIELDS/MAJORS: Arboriculture

Awards are available for research in the field of arboriculture. Recipients must be qualified researchers for projects of interest and benefit to the arboriculture industry. Write to the address below for more information.

International Society of Arboriculture
ISA Research Trust
PO Box GG
Savoy, IL   61874

545 I.V. Payne Endowed Scholarship

AMOUNT: $600–$1000   DEADLINE: March 1
FIELDS/MAJORS: Education Administration

Award for a graduate student in the master's program in education with an emphasis on education administration. Must have at least one year of successful teaching experience in a public school. Financial need is a consideration. Write to the address below for more information.

Eastern New Mexico University
College of Education and Technology
Station 25
Portales, NM   88130

546 IAPA—Inter-American Press Association Scholarships

AMOUNT: Maximum: $10000   DEADLINE: August 1
FIELDS/MAJORS: Journalism

Scholarships for Latin American journalists under the age of thirty-five who are or will be studying in the U.S. or Canada. Must be citizen of Latin American country. Reciprocal scholarships for citizens of the U.S. and Canada (to study in a Latin American country) are also available. Fluency in the language of the country of study is required. Contact the address below for details.

Inter-American Press Association
2911 NW 39th Street
Miami, FL   33142

547 IBD Foundation Graduate Fellowship

AMOUNT: Maximum: $5000
DEADLINE: April 8
FIELDS/MAJORS: Interior Design

Awards are available for individuals who have completed their undergraduate study and are practicing commercial interior design full- or part-time or are enrolled in or intending to continue graduate studies in interior design. Three or four awards are offered annually. Write to the address below for more information.

International Interior Design Association
Headquarters
341 Merchandise Mart
Chicago, IL   60654

548
Ida and Benjamin Alpert Scholarships

AMOUNT: None Specified   DEADLINE: May 14
FIELDS/MAJORS: Law

Scholarships for Michigan residents who are or will be attending law school. Attendance at a Michigan law school is not necessary. Based on essay (1000 to 1500 words). In addition to the amounts listed, honorable mention awards will be given as funds allow. Write to the address below for details.

Ida and Benjamin Alpert Foundation
c/o David J. Szymanksi
1303 City-County Building
Detroit, MI   48226

549
Illinois NWSA Manuscript Prize

AMOUNT: $1000   DEADLINE: January 31
FIELDS/MAJORS: Women's Studies

Annual award for best book-length manuscript in women's studies. Along with the $1000 prize, the University of Illinois Press will publish the manuscript. Manuscripts can be on any subject in women's studies that expands our understanding of women's lives and gender systems. Interdisciplinary studies and discipline-specific studies are equally welcome. Write to the NWSA for details.

National Women's Studies Association
7100 Baltimore Avenue, Suite 301
College Park, MD   20740

550
Illinois State Library Training Grants

AMOUNT: $7500   DEADLINE: May 1
FIELDS/MAJORS: Library Science, Information Science

Up to fifteen scholarships for Illinois residents who are or will be attending an Illinois graduate school and pursuing a master's degree in library or information science. Must be a U.S. citizen and agree to work in an Illinois library after graduation. For full-time or part-time study. Write to the address below for details.

Illinois State Library
Training Grant Program
300 South Second Street
Springfield, IL   62701

551
IMF Education Fund Loans

AMOUNT: Maximum: $8000   DEADLINE: May 30
FIELDS/MAJORS: Medicine

Loans for residents of Iowa studying toward becoming a doctor. Must be a junior or senior in medical school. Financial need is seriously considered. Write to the address below for details.

Iowa Medical Foundation
IMF Education Fund
1001 Grand Avenue
West Des Moines, IA   50265

552
Imogen and Naomi Adams Memorial Medical Scholarship Endowment

AMOUNT: None Specified   DEADLINE: April 15
FIELDS/MAJORS: Medicine

Awards for students enrolled in the School of Medicine. Based on financial need and satisfactory academics. Contact the address below for further information or the financial aid office at your school's location.

University of North Dakota—School of Medicine
Sandra Elshaug, Financial Aid Office
PO Box 9037—501 N. Columbia Road
Grand Forks, ND   58202

553
Indian Fellowship and American Indian Graduate Center Fellowship Program

AMOUNT: None Specified   DEADLINE: December 3
FIELDS/MAJORS: All Areas of Study

Open to Native Americans in a post-baccalaureate program. Must be enrolled full-time, demonstrate financial need, and be certified as Indian by tribe. The federal government funds both programs, selects the eligible students, and determines amount of each student's fellowship. Contact the address below for further information about both fellowships.

Marquette University
Office of Admissions
1217 W. Wisconsin Avenue
Milwaukee, WI   53233

554
Indian Health Service Scholarships

AMOUNT: None Specified
DEADLINE: None Specified
FIELDS/MAJORS: Dentistry

Open to full-time students certified as Indian by tribe. These fellowships include tuition, books, instruments, and stipend. For information and application materials, contact the Indian Health Scholarship Programs Office.

Marquette University
Office of Admissions
1217 W. Wisconsin Avenue
Milwaukee, WI   53233

555
Industry Research Scholar Awards

AMOUNT: $50000 DEADLINE: September 10
FIELDS/MAJORS: Gastroenterology, Hepatology, Related Fields

Awards for investigators who hold full-time faculty positions at universities or professional institutes. Those who have been at the assistant professor level or equivalent for more than five years are not eligible. Applicants goals must be research careers in gastroenterology and hepatology. Contact the address below for further information or web sites: http://www.gastro.org; http://www.asge.org; or http://hepar-sfgh.ucsf.edu.

American Digestive Health Foundation
Ms. Irene Kuo
7910 Woodmont Avenue, 7th Floor
Bethesda, MD   20814

556
Inez McDavid Memorial Scholarship

AMOUNT: None Specified
DEADLINE: March 1
FIELDS/MAJORS: Communicative Disorders

Awards are available at the University of New Mexico for graduate students majoring in the fields of communicative disorders. Write to the address below for information.

University of New Mexico, Albuquerque
Office of Financial Aid
Albuquerque, NM   87131

557
Inmon Memorial Scholarship

AMOUNT: None Specified
DEADLINE: March 31
FIELDS/MAJORS: Guidance, Counseling

Student must be a full-time graduate guidance and counseling major with financial need. Must have a GPA of 3.0 or better and be a U.S. citizen. Preference is given to native Missourians. Contact the guidance and counseling department for more information.

Southwest Missouri State University
Office of Financial Aid
901 South National Avenue
Springfield, MO   65804

558
Institute of Nutrition Fellowship

AMOUNT: None Specified
DEADLINE: January 1
FIELDS/MAJORS: Food, Nutrition, Food Service

Award open to graduate students who are conducting research. Must have a minimum GPA of 3.75. Contact the address below for further information.

University of North Carolina, Greensboro
Financial Aid Office
723 Kenilworth Street
Greensboro, NC   27412

559
Institute of Paper Science and Technology Scholarships and Fellowships

AMOUNT: Maximum: $20000
DEADLINE: None Specified
FIELDS/MAJORS: Chemistry, Chemical Engineering, Physics, Math, Pulp/Paper Technology

Open to graduate students who are U.S., Canadian, or Mexican citizens or legal residents and hold a B.S. degree in the above fields. For pursuit of a master's or doctoral degree at the Institute. Applicants must have a GPA of at least 3.0. Write to address below for complete details.

Institute of Paper Science and Technology
Director of Admissions
500 10th Street, NW
Atlanta, GA   30318

560
Integrated Manufacturing Predoctoral Fellowships

AMOUNT: $1500–$20000 DEADLINE: December 5
FIELDS/MAJORS: Integrated Manufacturing, Product Design

Twelve awards are available for students who possess a master's degree and are pursuing a Ph.D. in one of the areas of study listed above. Must be a U.S. citizen or permanent resident. Write to the address listed for more information.

U.S. Department of Energy, Fellowship Office
National Research Council
2101 Constitution Avenue
Washington, DC   20418

561
Integrated Manufacturing Predoctoral Fellowships

AMOUNT: $20000–$35000 DEADLINE: December 6
FIELDS/MAJORS: Manufacturing Engineering or Related Field

Fellowships are available for doctoral candidates who wish to further their education in a field directly relating to integrated manufacturing. A cost-of-education allowance of up to $15000 is also available. Applicants must be U.S. citizens or nationals. Fellows must be enrolled full-time. Write to the address below for additional information or see the fellowship home page: http://fellowships.nas.edu.

National Research Council, U.S. Department of Energy
Fellowship Office
2101 Constitution Avenue
Washington, DC   20418

562
Interchange Fellowship and Martin McLaren Scholarship

AMOUNT: None Specified DEADLINE: November 15
FIELDS/MAJORS: Horticulture, Landscape Architecture, and Related Fields

Program for U.S. graduate students to spend a year in Great Britain studying horticulture or landscape architecture as well as working at American universities and botanical gardens in the U.K. Funds two graduate students annually. Send a SASE to the address below for more information.

Garden Club of America
Ms. Shelley Burch
598 Madison Avenue
New York, NY 10022

563 Interdisciplinary Artists Fellowships

AMOUNT: $14000   DEADLINE: January 10
FIELDS/MAJORS: Art

Four fellowships offered to artists. Submit application form, six copies of your resume, work samples, work sample information (six copies of screening list or notes), and return shipping. Must be a resident of Minnesota for a minimum of twelve months. For information and application form, contact the address below. Information on "diverse visions," another program administered by intermedia arts.

Intermedia Arts/McKnight
2822 Lyndale Avenue South
Minneapolis, MN 55408

564 International Fellows Program

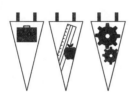

AMOUNT: None Specified
DEADLINE: April 5
FIELDS/MAJORS: Social and Physical Sciences, Health, English Education, Computer, Marketing

Tuskegee University offers a nine-month fellowship program to support the participation of graduate students in technical and educational transfer of expertise to areas of need in Africa and other third world countries. Write to the address below for details.

Tuskegee University
International Fellows Program
Office of International Programs
Tuskegee, AL 36088

565 International Fellowships

AMOUNT: $15160   DEADLINE: December 2
FIELDS/MAJORS: All Areas of Study

Fellowships for one year of graduate study or advanced research in the U.S. to women of outstanding ability who are citizens of countries other than the U.S. Applicants must hold the equivalent of a U.S. bachelor's degree. Forty-three awards offered annually. Write to the address below for details. Previous and current recipients of AAUW Fellowships are ineligible. Also six fellowships for members of International Federation of University Women to study in any country except their home country.

American Association of University Women Educational Foundation
2201 N. Dodge Street
Iowa City, IA 52243

566 International Fellowships in Jewish Studies

AMOUNT: $5000   DEADLINE: October 31
FIELDS/MAJORS: Jewish Studies

Applicants must be qualified scholars, researchers, or artists who process the knowledge and experience to formulate and implement a project in a field of Jewish specialization. Write to the address below for details.

Memorial Foundation for Jewish Culture
15 East 26th Street, Room 1901
New York, NY 10010

567 International Predissertation Fellowship Program

AMOUNT: None Specified   DEADLINE: None Specified
FIELDS/MAJORS: Economics, Political Science, Sociology, Social Sciences

Program is open to Ph.D. candidates in the above majors and enrolled at selected universities. Primary purpose is to provide funding for overseas study. Applicants must be in the early phases of their training. Check with your school to determine if it is one of the participants. Applications must be submitted by the participating university. Write to the International Predissertation Fellowship Program at the address below for details.

Social Science Research Council
605 Third Avenue
New York, NY 10158

568 International Reading Association Research Grants and Awards

AMOUNT: $500–$5000   DEADLINE: None Specified
FIELDS/MAJORS: Reading Research and Disabilities

Grant and award programs designed to support research in and recognize contributions to the field of reading research and reading disabilities. Open to recent and current Ph.D. candidates (for dissertations) and to teachers, reporters, writers, and researchers. Some awards limited to IRA members. Write for complete details on membership and award programs. Information can also be found in the spring issues of "Journal of Reading," "Lectura Y Vida," "Reading Research Quarterly," "The Reading Teacher," and "Reading Today."

International Reading Association
800 Barksdale Road
PO Box 8139
Newark, DE 19714

569
International Research Scholars Program

AMOUNT: None Specified   DEADLINE: None Specified
FIELDS/MAJORS: Biomedical Research

Fellowships are available for international scholars who have made significant contributions to fundamental biomedical research—to the understanding of basic biological processes and disease mechanisms. Awards are intended for researchers whose careers are still developing. Applicant must hold a full-time academic or research appointment at a non-profit facility. Write to the address below for additional information.

Howard Hughes Medical Institute
Office of Grants and Special Programs
4000 Jones Bridge Road
Chevy Chase, MD   20815

570
Iowa Federation of Labor, AFL-CIO, Graduate Assistantship

AMOUNT: Maximum: $6500   DEADLINE: March 1
FIELDS/MAJORS: All Areas of Study

Open to University of Iowa graduate students who are members or children of members of any local Iowa unions affiliated with the Iowa Federation of Labor AFL-CIO. One award is offered annually. Write to the address below for complete details.

Iowa Federation of Labor, AFL-CIO
Mark L. Smith, Secretary-Treasurer
2000 Walker Street, #A
Des Moines, IA   50317

571
Irene and Daisy MacGregor Memorial and Alice W. Rooke Scholarship

AMOUNT: $5000   DEADLINE: April 15
FIELDS/MAJORS: Medicine, Psychiatric Nursing

Scholarship available to students who have been accepted into an accredited school of medicine to pursue an M.D. or are studying in the field of psychiatric nursing (graduate level). All applicants must be sponsored by a local DAR chapter and be U.S. citizens. Contact your local DAR chapter or send a SASE to the address for more information.

National Society Daughters of the American Revolution
NSDAR Scholarship Committee
1776 D Street, NW
Washington., DC   20006

572
Irene F. and W.J. Billinger Scholarship

AMOUNT: None Specified   DEADLINE: January 15
FIELDS/MAJORS: Special Education

Award open to graduate special education major. This award is renewable. Contact the address below for further information.

Fort Hays State University
Office of Student Financial Aid
600 Park Street
Hays, KS   67601

573
Irene Thompson Scholarships

AMOUNT: $500   DEADLINE: None Specified
FIELDS/MAJORS: Business Administration

Open to full-time graduate students in good standing. Must have a minimum GPA of 3.0. Contact the address below for further information.

University of Northern Iowa
Elizabeth Peterson
204 Business
Cedar Falls, IA   50614

574
Irwin A. Dyer, Margaret Nicholson Schafer Fellowships

AMOUNT: None Specified   DEADLINE: February 1
FIELDS/MAJORS: Nutrition

Awards open to graduate students with a minimum GPA of 3.5. Contact the address below for further information about both awards.

Washington State University—Scholarship Committee
College of Agriculture and Home Economics
423 Hulbert Hall
Pullman, WA   99164

575
ISI Scholarship Program

AMOUNT: $1000   DEADLINE: October 31
FIELDS/MAJORS: Library and Information Science

The ISI scholarship will be granted only for beginning graduate study leading to a Ph.D. from a recognized program in library science, information science, or related fields of study. Applicants must be members of the Special Libraries Association and have worked in a special library. Applicants must submit evidence of financial need. One award is offered annually. Because ISI awards medical librarianship scholarships through the Medical Library Association, persons planning careers in medical librarianship cannot be considered. Write to the address below for details.

Special Libraries Association
SLA Scholarship Committee
1700 Eighteenth Street, NW
Washington, DC   20009

576 Ittleson and Andrew W. Mellon Fellowships

AMOUNT: Maximum: $16000
DEADLINE: November 15
FIELDS/MAJORS: Visual Art, Art History and Theory, Architecture, and Related Areas

Two-year fellowship for doctoral student doing dissertation research in the fields of study above. Scholars are expected to spend half a year at the National Gallery of Art, half a year doing research anywhere in the U.S. or abroad, and the second year at the Center to complete the dissertation. Applicants must know two languages related to the topic of their dissertation. Fellowship is only available to U.S. citizens or legal residents. Contact the chairperson of the graduate department of art history at your school (or other appropriate department) or write to the address below for more information.

National Gallery of Art
Center for Study in the Visual Arts
Predoctoral Fellowship Program
Washington, DC   20565

577 J. Franklin Jameson Fellowship in American History

AMOUNT: $10000   **DEADLINE:** January 15
FIELDS/MAJORS: American History

One semester fellowship is to support research at the Library of Congress by young historians. Applicants must hold the Ph.D. or equivalent, must have received this degree within the last five years, and must not have published or had accepted for publication a book-length historical work. Write to the address below for details.

American Historical Association
Awards Administrator
400 A Street, SE
Washington, DC   20003

578 J. Waldo Smith Hydraulic Fellowship

AMOUNT: $4000   **DEADLINE:** February 20
FIELDS/MAJORS: Civil Engineering/Hydraulics

Applicant must be a national ASCE member in good standing in a graduate program. Award is used for research in the field of experimental hydraulics. Write for complete details.

American Society of Civil Engineers
Student Services Department
1801 Alexander Bell Drive
Reston, VA   20191

579 J.E. Caldwell Centennial Scholarships

AMOUNT: $2000   **DEADLINE:** February 15
FIELDS/MAJORS: Historical Preservation

Scholarships for graduate students in the area of historic preservation. Must be sponsored by a DAR chapter and be a U.S. citizen. Contact your local or state DAR chapter or send a SASE to the address listed for details. GPA of at least 3.2 required.

National Society Daughters of the American Revolution
NSDAR Scholarship Committee
1776 D Street, NW
Washington, DC   20006

580 J.J. Barr Scholarship

AMOUNT: $5000   **DEADLINE:** April 1
FIELDS/MAJORS: Water Utility Industry

Scholarship for graduate students pursuing a degree in the water utility industry. Must be a U.S. citizen. Write to the address below for more information.

National Association of Water Companies
Scholarship Committee
1725 K Street, NW, Suite 1212
Washington, DC   20006

581 Jake Gimbel Loan Program

AMOUNT: None Specified   **DEADLINE:** March 31
FIELDS/MAJORS: Education, or Any Graduate Program

Special loans are available for residents of Santa Barbara County, who have attended grades 7–12 in Santa Barbara County, and are either pursuing a teaching career, or are in any graduate program in the state of California. Write to the address below for further information

Santa Barbara Foundation
Student Aid Director
15 East Carrillo Street
Santa Barbara, CA   93101

582 James Abbott Scholarship

AMOUNT: None Specified   **DEADLINE:** March 1
FIELDS/MAJORS: Foreign Language—Spanish

Scholarships are available at the University of Oklahoma, Norman for full-time graduate students majoring in Spanish. Based on academic ability. Write to the address below for information.

University of Oklahoma, Norman
Modern Languages Department
780 Van Vleet Oval
Norman, OK   73019

583 James Clark Memorial Scholarship

AMOUNT: $100 DEADLINE: March 2
FIELDS/MAJORS: Physical Education

Open to graduate students who have been accepted for an M.A. degree in physical education. Contact Rip Marsten at the address below for further information.

University of Northern Iowa
Health, Physical Ed. and Leisure Services
203 W. Gym
Cedar Falls, IA   50614

584 James E. Ryabik Graduate Scholarship

AMOUNT: None Specified
DEADLINE: January 15
FIELDS/MAJORS: Psychology

Award open to graduates with a minimum GPA of 3.5. Recipients must be active participants in activities related to psychology at Fort Hays State University. Contact the address below for further information.

Fort Hays State University
Office of Student Financial Aid
600 Park Street
Hays, KS   67601

585 James G. Oxnard Memorial Scholarship

AMOUNT: None Specified DEADLINE: March 1
FIELDS/MAJORS: Medicine

Awards are available at the University of New Mexico for first-year students in the medical school with academic ability and financial need. Write to the address below for more information.

University of New Mexico, Albuquerque
Office of Financial Aid
Albuquerque, NM   87131

586 James R. Nicholl Memorial Foundation Scholarships

AMOUNT: None Specified DEADLINE: None Specified
FIELDS/MAJORS: Medical Fields

Scholarships for graduate students in the field of medicine who are from Lorain County, Ohio. Write to the address below for further information.

Bank One Ohio Trust Co., N.A.—Lorain
Internal Zip 873
1949 Broadway
Lorain, OH   44052

587 James W. Cochran Memorial Scholarship

AMOUNT: $1000 DEADLINE: September 1
FIELDS/MAJORS: Law

Scholarship available at the University of Oklahoma, Norman for full-time law students who reside in Oklahoma, or are honorably discharged veterans, or both. Based on financial need. One award offered annually. Write to the address below for information.

University of Oklahoma, Norman
Admissions and Records, Law Center
Room 22, 300 Timberdell Road
Norman, OK   73019

588 Jane Coffin Childs Fund Postdoctoral Fellowships

AMOUNT: $26000 DEADLINE: February 1
FIELDS/MAJORS: Cancer Research, Oncology

Fellowship is for a three-year period with increases in stipend each year. Applicants must hold the M.D. or Ph.D. and submit a research proposal. For study into the causes, origins, and treatment of cancer. No restrictions on citizenship or institution. Recipients in general should not have more than one year of post-doctoral experience. Write to the address below for details.

Jane Coffin Childs Memorial Fund for Medical Research
Office of the Director
333 Cedar Street, PO Box 3333
New Haven, CT   06510

589 Janet M. Glasgow Essay Award

AMOUNT: $1500 DEADLINE: May 31
FIELDS/MAJORS: Medicine

This award is presented to an AMWA student member for the best essay of approximately 1000 words identifying a woman physician who has been a significant role model. Write to the address below for details.

American Medical Women's Association
Glasgow Essay Award
801 N. Fairfax Street, Suite 400
Alexandria, VA   22314

590 Japan Fellowships

AMOUNT: None Specified
DEADLINE: November 15
FIELDS/MAJORS: Japan-Related Studies

Fellowships are available for Japanese studies students enrolled in a U.S. doctoral program. Applicants must have completed all the requirements of the doctoral program and be at any stage in the dissertation process except the final write-up. Write to the address below for information.

Social Science Research Council
Fellowships and Grants
605 Third Avenue
New York, NY   10158

591 Japanese Government Scholarship

AMOUNT: None Specified   **DEADLINE:** March 1
FIELDS/MAJORS: All Areas of Study

Awards are available at the University of New Mexico for graduate students of Japanese descent who are under thirty-five years old and are U.S. citizens. Contact: Consulate General of Japan, 250 East First Street, Suite 1110, Los Angeles, CA 90012 for more details.

University of New Mexico, Albuquerque
Office of Financial Aid
Albuquerque, NM   87131

592 Jean-Luc Miossec Memorial Scholarship

AMOUNT: None Specified   **DEADLINE:** March 1
FIELDS/MAJORS: Earth and Planetary Sciences

Awards are available at the University of New Mexico for graduates in the fields of earth and planetary sciences. Contact the Earth and Planetary Sciences Department or the address below for more information.

University of New Mexico, Albuquerque
Office of Financial Aid
Albuquerque, NM   87131

593 Jeanette Trum Granoff '35 Graduate Scholarship

AMOUNT: Maximum: $1250   **DEADLINE:** March 1
FIELDS/MAJORS: Science

Open to an outstanding graduating senior entering a master's program in science. Contact the address listed for further information. At least 3.5 GPA required.

Brooklyn College
Office of the V.P. for Student Life
2113 Boylan Hall
Brooklyn, NY   11210

594 Jeanne Humphrey Block Dissertation Award

AMOUNT: $2500   **DEADLINE:** April 1
FIELDS/MAJORS: Psychology, Sociology, Behavioral Science

Dissertation grant for women doctoral students researching psychological development of women/girls. Must have completed coursework and be current doctoral candidate. Write to the address below for details.

Radcliffe College
Henry A. Murray Research Center
10 Garden Street
Cambridge, MA   02138

595 Jeannette Mowery Scholarship

AMOUNT: None Specified
DEADLINE: March 1
FIELDS/MAJORS: Law, Medicine, Dentistry

Open to graduate law, medicine, or dentistry students attending any school in Oregon. Must be U.S. citizens and residents of Oregon. Applicants may apply and compete annually. Contact the address below for further information.

Oregon State Scholarship Commission
Private Awards
1500 Valley River Drive, #100
Eugene, OR   97401-2130

596 Jefferson-Pilot Corporation Fellowship

AMOUNT: None Specified
DEADLINE: January 1
FIELDS/MAJORS: Food, Nutrition, Food Service

Award open to graduate students who are conducting research in nutrition. Contact the address below for further information.

University of North Carolina, Greensboro
Financial Aid Office
723 Kenilworth Street
Greensboro, NC   27412

597 Jerome Playwright-in-Residence Fellowship

AMOUNT: $750   **DEADLINE:** January 15
FIELDS/MAJORS: Playwriting/Drama/Theatre

Applicants must not have had more than two works produced by professional theaters and must spend the fellowship period as a member of the Playwrights' Center. Four to six scholarships are offered annually. Write to the address below for details.

Playwrights' Center
2301 Franklin Avenue, East
Minneapolis, MN   55406

598 Jerry L. Pettis Memorial Scholarship

AMOUNT: $2500   **DEADLINE:** January 31
FIELDS/MAJORS: Medicine

Awards for junior or senior medical students with demonstrated interest in communication of science. Write to the address below for more information.

American Medical Association—Education and Research
    Foundation
Rita M. Palulonis
515 N. State Street
Chicago, IL   60610

599 Jessup/McHenry Awards

AMOUNT: $500–$1000   DEADLINE: March 1
FIELDS/MAJORS: Botany

Grants for pre- and post-doctoral students who require the resources of the Academy of Natural Sciences of Philadelphia. Studies are performed under the supervision of a member of the curatorial staff of the Academy. The McHenry Fund is limited to the study of botany. A second deadline date for this award is October 1. Students from the Philadelphia area are not eligible. Write to Dr. Schuyler, Chairman of the Jessup-McHenry Fund Committee, at the address below for details.

Academy of Natural Sciences of Philadelphia
Dr. A.E. Schuyler, Jessup-McHenry Fund
1900 Benjamin Franklin Parkway
Philadelphia, PA   19103

600 Jewell Gardiner Memorial Fund Scholarship

AMOUNT: None Specified   DEADLINE: August 1
FIELDS/MAJORS: Library Science

Candidates must be a northern California resident enrolled in or accepted into an accredited graduate school of library science in California. Write for complete details.

California Media and Library Educators Association
Jewel Gardiner Memorial Fund Chairperson
1499 Old Bayshore Highway, Suite 142
Burlingame, CA   94010

601 Jimmy Rice Memorial Mathematics Fund Scholarships

AMOUNT: None Specified   DEADLINE: January 15
FIELDS/MAJORS: Mathematics

Award open to math majors who have been accepted into graduate school. Contact the address below for further information.

Fort Hays State University
Office of Student Financial Aid
600 Park Street
Hays, KS   67601

602 Joann Turner Cox Fellowship

AMOUNT: None Specified   DEADLINE: None Specified
FIELDS/MAJORS: Education

Awards are available to a graduate student in the teacher training program. Contact the address listed for further information.

Chapman University
333 N. Glassell
Orange, CA   92866

603 John A. Hartford/AFAR Medical Student Geriatric Scholars Program

AMOUNT: Maximum: $3000   DEADLINE: February 5
FIELDS/MAJORS: Geriatrics

Open to medical students, particularly budding researchers, who are considering geriatrics as a career. The program provides an opportunity for to train at an acclaimed center of excellence in geriatrics. Write to the address below for more information.

American Federation for Aging Research
1414 Avenue of the Americas
New York, NY   10019

604 John C. Geilfuss Fellowship

AMOUNT: Maximum: $2000
DEADLINE: February 1
FIELDS/MAJORS: Business, Economic History of Wisconsin and/or the American Midwest

This fellowship is awarded for graduate-level research in business and economics history of Wisconsin and the American Midwest. Recipients generally will be ineligible for more than one award. Contact the address below for further information.

State Historical Society of Wisconsin
Dr. Michael E. Stevens, State Historian
816 State Street
Madison, WI   53706-1488

605 John Carew Memorial Scholarship

AMOUNT: $1500   DEADLINE: April 1
FIELDS/MAJORS: Horticulture

Scholarships for graduate students who are pursuing a major in horticulture, with a specific interest in bedding plants or flowering potted plants. Write to the address below for details. The BPFI also sponsors two awards through Future Farmers of America (check with your FFA advisor).

Bedding Plants Foundation, Inc.
Scholarship Program
PO Box 27241
Lansing, MI   48909

606 John D. and Catherine T. MacArthur Fellowships

AMOUNT: $17500–$37500   DEADLINE: November 15
FIELDS/MAJORS: Foreign Policy, International Relations, International Security, Etc.

Approximately six dissertation and six postdoctoral fellowships supporting research into the implications of recent changes in several countries on worldwide security issues. These fellowships require fellows to gain competence in skills not previously acquired; i.e., a significant departure from earlier works. Write to "Program on Peace and Security in a Changing World" at the below address for further information.

Social Science Research Council
605 Third Avenue
New York, NY   10158

University of North Dakota—School of Medicine
Sandra Elshaug, Financial Aid Office
PO Box 9037—501 N. Columbia Road
Grand Forks, ND   58202

607 John D. Clark and Marian Clark Person Memorial Award in Chemistry

AMOUNT: None Specified   DEADLINE: March 1
FIELDS/MAJORS: Chemistry

Awards are available at the University of New Mexico for graduate students studying chemistry and working in the department as teaching assistants. Write to the address below for information.

University of New Mexico, Albuquerque
Office of Financial Aid
Albuquerque, NM   87131

608 John F.Y. Stambaugh Scholarship

AMOUNT: $1000   DEADLINE: February 8
FIELDS/MAJORS: Accounting

Scholarships are available at the University of Oklahoma, Norman for full-time master's candidates in accounting who come from the Tulsa area. Write to the address below for information.

University of Oklahoma, Norman
College of Business Administration
200 Adams Hall
Norman, OK   73019

609 John Halvor Leek Memorial Scholarship

AMOUNT: None Specified
DEADLINE: March 1
FIELDS/MAJORS: Political Science, Public Administration, Congressional Studies

Scholarships are available at the University of Oklahoma, Norman for full-time graduate students majoring in one of the above areas. Requires a minimum GPA of 3.5. Two to six awards offered annually. Write to the address below for information.

University of Oklahoma, Norman
Political Science Department
455 West Lindsey
Norman, OK   73019

610 John J. Ayash Memorial Scholarship Fund

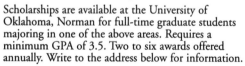

AMOUNT: None Specified   DEADLINE: April 15
FIELDS/MAJORS: Medicine

Awards for North Dakota students completing their second or third year at the School of Medicine. Based on need. Contact the address below for further information or the financial aid office at your school's location.

611 John M. Olin Pre/Postdoctoral Fellowship in National Security

AMOUNT: $16500–$28000   DEADLINE: January 15
FIELDS/MAJORS: National Security, Economics

Residential fellowships at the Center for International Affairs of Harvard for Ph.D. candidates (course work completed before beginning of fellowship) and postdoctoral scholars. Supports investigation of causes and conduct of war, military strategy and history, defense policy and institutions, economic security, defense economics, and the defense industrial base. Contact Inga Peterson at the address below for program details and application guidelines.

Harvard University, Center for International Affairs
CFIA Student Programs and Fellowships
1737 Cambridge Street
Cambridge, MA   02138

612 John Miller Musser Memorial Forest and Society Fellowship

AMOUNT: None Specified   DEADLINE: September 1
FIELDS/MAJORS: Forestry, Environmental Science

Fellowships are available to postdoctoral scholars to support research, outside of the U.S., in an area of interest to the foundation, including those areas mentioned above. Tenure is two years. Applicants must be age thirty-six or less and have a good command of written/spoken English . Second deadline date is April 1 for a June decision. Write to the address below for information.

Institute of Current World Affairs
Gary L. Hansen, Program Administrator
4 West Wheelock Street
Hanover, NH   03755

613 John N. Stern Fellowships for Oberlin College Faculty

AMOUNT: $1000–$3000   DEADLINE: None Specified
FIELDS/MAJORS: History (American and European), Humanities, Literature

Fellowships are available for Oberlin College faculty studying one of the fields above, who wish to spend up to three months in residence at the Newberry. Contact the Dean of the college for more details.

Newberry Library
Committee on Awards
60 W. Walton Street
Chicago, IL   60610

614
John O. Butler Graduate Scholarships

AMOUNT: None Specified   DEADLINE: April 1
FIELDS/MAJORS: Dental Hygiene

Awarded to a candidate enrolled in a master's degree program in dental hygiene or dental hygiene education. Seven awards per year. Write to the address below for more information.

American Dental Hygienists' Association Institute for Oral Health
444 North Michigan Avenue, Suite 3400
Chicago, IL   60611

615
John O. Crane Memorial Fellowship

AMOUNT: None Specified   DEADLINE: September 1
FIELDS/MAJORS: International Studies—Middle East, Eastern Europe

Fellowships are available to postdoctoral scholars to support research, outside the U.S., in an area of interest to the foundation, including those areas mentioned above. Tenure is two years. Applicants must be age thirty-six or less and have a good command of written/spoken English. Second deadline date is April 1 for a June decision. Write to the address below for information.

Institute of Current World Affairs
Gary L. Hansen, Program Administrator
4 West Wheelock Street
Hanover, NH   03755

616
John Robinson Memorial Fellowship

AMOUNT: None Specified   DEADLINE: None Specified
FIELDS/MAJORS: Communication

Award open to full-time graduate students. Contact the address below for further information.

University of North Carolina, Greensboro
Financial Aid Office
723 Kenilworth Street
Greensboro, NC   27412

617
John Stephen Larson Memorial Scholarship

AMOUNT: None Specified
DEADLINE: March 2
FIELDS/MAJORS: Environmental, Civil Engineering

Award open to students majoring in either of the above fields. Must have a minimum GPA of 3.0. Preference to graduates in M.S. civil and environmental engineering programs. Contact the address below for further information.

California Polytechnic State University
Financial Aid Office
212 Administration Building
San Luis Obispo, CA   93407

618
John Thomson Memorial Scholarship

AMOUNT: None Specified   DEADLINE: February 1
FIELDS/MAJORS: Law

Awards for entering law students who exhibit high academic promise. Preference will be given to J.D./M.B.A. candidates. Contact the Assistant Dean, Chase College of Law, for further information.

Northern Kentucky University
Chase College of Law
Office of Admissions
Highland Heights, KY   41099

619
John W. Lindsey Scholarship

AMOUNT: None Specified   DEADLINE: None Specified
FIELDS/MAJORS: Psychology

Award open to graduate students who are U.S. citizens majoring in psychology. Contact the address below for further information.

University of North Carolina, Greensboro
Financial Aid Office
723 Kenilworth Street
Greensboro, NC   27412

620
Jonas Salk Scholarship

AMOUNT: Maximum: $3500   DEADLINE: March 1
FIELDS/MAJORS: Medicine

Open to students enrolled/accepted into medical school. Contact the address listed for further information.

Brooklyn College
Office of the V.P. for Student Life
2113 Boylan Hall
Brooklyn, NY   11210

621
Joseph E. Motherway Fellowship

AMOUNT: None Specified
DEADLINE: March 1
FIELDS/MAJORS: Mechanical Engineering

Awards for graduates of UMass who are enrolled in a graduate program in the department of mechanical engineering. Based on academic excellence. The applicants thesis or dissertation should be in the area of design. Contact the Department Head, Mechanical Engineering for more information. At least 2.8 GPA required.

University of Massachusetts, Amherst
255 Whitmore Administration Building
Box 38230
Amherst, MA   01003

622
Joseph F. Rarick American Indian Law Scholarship

AMOUNT: $300 DEADLINE: September 1
FIELDS/MAJORS: Law

Scholarships are available at the University of Oklahoma, Norman for full-time Native American law students in their third year of study. One award offered annually. Write to the address below for information.

University of Oklahoma, Norman
Admissions and Records
Law Center, Room 221, 300 Timberdell Road
Norman, OK 73019

623
Joseph L. Boscov Scholarship

AMOUNT: None Specified DEADLINE: March 1
FIELDS/MAJORS: All Areas of Study

Awards for students accepted for admission to the graduate school at UMass. Preference given to women over the age of thirty-five whose studies will equip them for increased service to the needs of people and/or the environment. Students must file a FAFSA as soon as possible after January 1 and before the March 1 financial aid priority consideration date. You will automatically be considered for this scholarship if you are enrolled at the University and apply for financial aid. Separate applications, requests, or inquiries are not required and cannot be honored.

University of Massachusetts, Amherst
Office of Financial Aid Services
255 Whitmore Admin. Building, Box 38230
Amherst, MA 01003

624
Joseph L. Fisher Dissertation Award

AMOUNT: $12000 DEADLINE: February 28
FIELDS/MAJORS: Natural Resources, Energy, Environmental Sciences

Fellowship is for doctoral candidate dissertation research in economics on issues relating to natural resources, energy, or the environment. Write to the address below for details.

Resources for the Future
Coordinator for Academic Programs
1616 P Street, NW
Washington, DC 20036

625
Joseph P. Fitzpatrick S.J. Doctoral Fellowship

AMOUNT: $14000 DEADLINE: February 1
FIELDS/MAJORS: All Areas of Study

Fellowships open to exceptionally qualified minority students seeking the doctoral degree. Contact the address below for further information. At least 3.1 GPA required.

Fordham University
Graduate Admissions Office—Keating 216
Fordham University
Bronx, NY 10458

626
Joseph Troll Turfgrass Research Fund

AMOUNT: None Specified DEADLINE: May 1
FIELDS/MAJORS: Turfgrass Management and Research

Awards for graduate students doing research in the areas of turfgrass management and/or related areas. Contact the Dean, College of Food and Natural Resources, for more information.

University of Massachusetts, Amherst
Dean
College of Food and Natural Resources
Amherst, MA 01003

627
Josie Nance White Fellowship

AMOUNT: None Specified
DEADLINE: January 1
FIELDS/MAJORS: Human Development, Family Studies, Elementary Education

Award open to doctoral students in any of the above fields. Contact the address below for further information.

University of North Carolina, Greensboro
Financial Aid Office
723 Kenilworth Street
Greensboro, NC 27412

628
Josie Nance White Fellowship

AMOUNT: None Specified
DEADLINE: None Specified
FIELDS/MAJORS: Home Economics, Teaching

Award open to doctoral students in either of the above fields. Contact the address below for further information.

University of North Carolina, Greensboro
Financial Aid Office
723 Kenilworth Street
Greensboro, NC 27412

629
Judge Averill Graduate Fellowship

AMOUNT: None Specified DEADLINE: None Specified
FIELDS/MAJORS: Business Administration

Available to outstanding full-time students pursuing a master's degree in business administration. Contact the address listed for further information.

Columbus State University
Financial Aid Office
4225 University Avenue
Columbus, GA 31907

630 Judge Judy West Scholarship

AMOUNT: None Specified DEADLINE: February 1
FIELDS/MAJORS: Law

Awards for Kentucky residents who are entering law students. Must demonstrate academic promise, commitment to community affairs, and devotion for the study of law. Contact the Assistant Dean, Chase College of Law, for further information.

Northern Kentucky University
Chase College of Law
Office of Admissions
Highland Heights, KY 41099

631 Judith Graham Poole Postdoctoral Research Fellowship

AMOUNT: $35000 DEADLINE: December 1
FIELDS/MAJORS: Hemophilia Research

Post-doctorate (M.D. or Ph.D.) fellowships for hemophilia-related research. Number of awards per year dependent on available funding. Topics that the NHF has expressed an interest in are clinical or basic research on biochemical, genetic, hematologic, orthopedic, psychiatric, or dental aspects of the hemophilias or Von Willebrand Disease. Contact the address below for complete details. The NHF has listed related topics of interest as rehabilitation, therapeutic modalities, psychosocial issues, or AIDS/HIV.

National Hemophilia Foundation
Karen O'Hagen
110 Greene Street, Suite 303
New York, NY 10012

632 Julia Buchanan Tappan Fund

AMOUNT: None Specified DEADLINE: March 1
FIELDS/MAJORS: Medicine

Awards are available at the University of New Mexico for medical students with financial need. Write to the address below for more information.

University of New Mexico, Albuquerque
Office of Financial Aid
Albuquerque, NM 87131

633 Julius F. Neumueller Awards in Optics

AMOUNT: $500 DEADLINE: June 1
FIELDS/MAJORS: Optometry

Award for students pursuing a doctor of optometry degree. Based on paper (not to exceed 3000 words) on one of the following topics: geometrical optics, physical optics, ophthalmic optics, or optics of the eye. Cash award. Write to the address below for more information.

American Academy of Optometry
College of Optometry
University of Houston
Houston, TX 77204

634 Justinian Society of Lawyers/DuPage County Chapter

AMOUNT: $1000 DEADLINE: April 1
FIELDS/MAJORS: Law

Applicant must have completed one semester of law school and be of Italian heritage. Will also need to include a statement indicating his/her professional objectives and any special factors that should be considered. Must be U.S. citizen. Write to below address for information and application.

Marsha H. Cellucci, Chairwoman—Scholarship
Cellucci, Yacobellis & Holman
1155 S. Washington Street, #100
Naperville, IL 60540

635 Juvenile Diabetes Foundation Awards

AMOUNT: None Specified DEADLINE: September 15
FIELDS/MAJORS: Medical Research (Juvenile Diabetes)

Post-doctoral grants and fellowships supporting basic and applied research on diabetes and related disorders. Includes research grants, career development awards, postdoctoral fellowships, and new training for established scientist awards. Write to the address below for more information.

Juvenile Diabetes Foundation International
Ruth Marsch, Grant Administrator
120 Wall Street
New York, NY 10005

636 Kappa Beta Pi Scholarship

AMOUNT: $100–$200 DEADLINE: September 1
FIELDS/MAJORS: Law

Scholarship available at the University of Oklahoma, Norman for full-time, second- or third-year female law students. Based on merit and financial need. One award offered annually. Write to the address below for information.

University of Oklahoma, Norman
Admissions and Records, Law Center
Room 22, 300 Timberdell Road
Norman, OK 73019

637 Kappa Epsilon—AFPE Nellie Wakeman Scholarship

AMOUNT: $4000 DEADLINE: January 15
FIELDS/MAJORS: Pharmacy

Awards for Kappa Epsilon members in financial good standing with the fraternity who have completed one quarter/semester of advanced studies in the pharmaceutical sciences. Contact your local Kappa Epsilon executive office or write to the address below for more information.

American Foundation for Pharmaceutical Education
One Church Street
Suite 202
Rockville, MD 20850

638 Karcher Award

AMOUNT: None Specified   DEADLINE: None Specified
FIELDS/MAJORS: Mathematics

Scholarships are available at the University of Oklahoma, Norman for graduate students in mathematics who demonstrate academic excellence. Write to the address below for information.

University of Oklahoma, Norman
Mathematics Department
420 PHSC
Norman, OK   73019

639 Karen and Elvira Lynner Medical Scholarship

AMOUNT: None Specified   DEADLINE: April 15
FIELDS/MAJORS: Medicine

Awards for medical students who are residents of North Dakota, preferably from Maddock or Benson Counties. Based on financial need and satisfactory academics. Contact the address below for further information or the financial aid office at your school's location.

University of North Dakota—School of Medicine
Sandra Elshaug, Financial Aid Office
PO Box 9037—501 N. Columbia Road
Grand Forks, ND   58202

640 Karen D. Carsel Memorial Scholarship

AMOUNT: $500   DEADLINE: April 1
FIELDS/MAJORS: All Areas of Study

Scholarship open to full-time graduate student who presents evidence of economic need. Student must submit evidence of legal blindness, three letters of recommendation, and transcripts of grades from the college he/she is attending. Write to the address below for complete details.

American Foundation for the Blind
Scholarship Committee
11 Penn Plaza, Suite 300
New York, NY   10001

641 Kate B. and Hall J. Peterson, Stephen Botein Fellowships

AMOUNT: $5700–$11400   DEADLINE: January 15
FIELDS/MAJORS: American History, History of Publishing, 18th Century Studies, Etc.

Six- to twelve-month fellowships in support of research utilizing the collections of the American Antiquarian Society. Must hold Ph.D. or be involved in dissertation research. Write to the address below for information.

American Antiquarian Society
Director of Research and Publication
185 Salisbury Street, Room 100
Worcester, MA   01609

642 Kate Neal Kinley Memorial Fellowship

AMOUNT: $7000   DEADLINE: February 1
FIELDS/MAJORS: Art, Music, Architecture

Fellowships for graduate students in the College of Fine and Applied Arts at the University of Illinois, Urbana-Champaign. Three awards per year. Contact the office of the Dean of the College of Fine and Applied Arts at the address below for details.

University of Illinois, Urbana-Champaign, College of Fine and Applied Arts
College of Fine and Applied Arts
608 E Lorado Taft, 110 Architecture Building
Champaign, IL   61820

643 Katherine J. Schutze Memorial Scholarship

AMOUNT: None Specified   DEADLINE: March 15
FIELDS/MAJORS: Theology

Applicants must be women members of the Christian Church (Disciples of Christ) who are preparing for the ordained ministry. For full-time study. Financial need is considered. Write to the address below for details. GPA of at least 2.3 required.

Christian Church (Disciples of Christ)
Attn: Scholarships
PO Box 1986
Indianapolis, IN   46206

644 Kathryn McAllister England Theatre Scholarship

AMOUNT: None Specified   DEADLINE: None Specified
FIELDS/MAJORS: Theatre

Award open to graduate students who are U.S. citizens. Contact the address below for further information.

University of North Carolina, Greensboro
Financial Aid Office
723 Kenilworth Street
Greensboro, NC   27412

645 Kay McKay Scholarship in Orthopedics

AMOUNT: None Specified   DEADLINE: March 1
FIELDS/MAJORS: Medicine

Awards are available at the University of New Mexico for students in their second-year orthopedics residency. Applicants must be New Mexico residents with an intent to practice in a rural area of New Mexico. Write to the address below for more information.

University of New Mexico, Albuquerque
Office of Financial Aid
Albuquerque, NM   87131

646
Keepers Preservation Education Fund Fellowship

AMOUNT: $500 DEADLINE: None Specified
FIELDS/MAJORS: Historical Preservation

Awards are available for graduate students in the field of historical preservation to attend the annual meeting of the Society of Architectural Historians. Write to the address below for more information.

Society of Architectural Historians
1365 North Astor Street
Chicago, IL   60610

647
Ken Dawson Award

AMOUNT: $5000 DEADLINE: March 15
FIELDS/MAJORS: Gay and Lesbian History

Award for study in gay and lesbian history. Applicants must submit a vitae and a ten-page narrative proposal that includes a summary of work already done in gay and lesbian history. No university affiliation is required. Write to the address below for more information.

Center for Lesbian and Gay Studies
City University of New York
33 West 42nd Street, Room 404N
New York, NY   10036

648
Kenan T. Erim Award

AMOUNT: $4000 DEADLINE: November 1
FIELDS/MAJORS: Archaeology/Classical Studies

This award will be given to an American or international research and/or excavating scholar working on Aphrodisias material. If the project involves work at Aphrodisias, candidates must submit written approval from the field director with their applications. Write to the address below for details.

Archaeological Institute of America—American Friends of
    Aphrodisias
Boston University
656 Beacon Street, 4th Floor
Boston, MA   02215

649
Kentucky Bar Association/Worker's Compensation Section Scholarship

AMOUNT: None Specified DEADLINE: February 1
FIELDS/MAJORS: Law

Awards for law students who are Kentucky residents. Must demonstrate financial need and academic promise. Contact the Assistant Dean, Chase College of Law, for further information.

Northern Kentucky University
Chase College of Law
Office of Admissions
Highland Heights, KY   41099

650
Kepler Scholarship

AMOUNT: $10000–$2000 DEADLINE: April 1
FIELDS/MAJORS: Healthcare Related

Scholarships for students accepted into a medical school accredited in conjunction with the American Medical Association or the American Osteopathic Association. This award must be repaid within twenty-four months of graduation or recipient must establish a medical practice in the La Porte hospital service area and become a member of the medical staff. Preference to local residents. Write or visit the Office of Development for details.

La Porte Hospital/La Porte Hospital Foundation
Office of Development
PO Box 250
La Porte, IN   46352

651
Kimberly A. Soucy Scholarship

AMOUNT: None Specified DEADLINE: None Specified
FIELDS/MAJORS: Communication Disorders

Awards for seniors in the department of communication disorders who intend to continue as graduate students in audiology at UMass. Recipients should excel academically and demonstrate qualities of inner strength, high spirit, perseverance, and dignity. Contact the Chair, Department of Communication Disorders, for more information.

University of Massachusetts, Amherst
Chair
Department of Communication Disorders
Amherst, MA   01003

652
King-Chavez-Parks Fellowship Program

AMOUNT: $6250 DEADLINE: June 2
FIELDS/MAJORS: All Areas of Study

Scholarships for African-American, Native American, or Hispanic students studying at the doctoral level at Wayne State University. Must be U.S. citizen or permanent resident. Recipients should have the intention of teaching in a Michigan post-secondary institution within one year of receiving their degree. Information and application may be obtained through the Scholarship and Fellowship Office at the address below.

Wayne State University
Graduate Scholarship/Fellowship Office
4302 Faculty Administration Building
Detroit, MI   48202

653
Kingsley Alcid Brown Educational Fund

AMOUNT: None Specified DEADLINE: April 1
FIELDS/MAJORS: All Areas of Study

Awards for graduates of Washington County high schools to provide financial support for higher education at the graduate school level. Applicants must be accepted into an accredited graduate degree program to receive an award. Write to the address below for more information.

Maine Community Fund
PO Box 148
Ellsworth, ME   04605

654
Kit C. King Graduate Scholarship Fund

AMOUNT: $500   DEADLINE: March 1
FIELDS/MAJORS: Photojournalism

Scholarship for a person pursuing an advanced degree in photojournalism. Must be accepted into a graduate program. Portfolio and a statement of goals and philosophy relating to documentary photojournalism will be required. Write to Scott C. Sines, Director of Photography and Graphics, at the below address for more information.

National Press Photographers Foundation
The Spokesman Review
West 999 Riverside Avenue
Spokane, WA   99210

655
Knight Science Journalism Fellowships

AMOUNT: None Specified
DEADLINE: None Specified
FIELDS/MAJORS: Journalism: Science Writing

Mid-career nine-month residential fellowship program reserved for science journalists (either print or broadcast). Contact David Ansley, Acting Director, at the address below for details.

Massachusetts Institute of Technology
Knight Scholarships, Building 9, Room 315
77 Massachusetts Avenue
Cambridge, MA   02139

656
Kress Dissertation Fellowships

AMOUNT: $10000
DEADLINE: February 28
FIELDS/MAJORS: Art History

Applicants must be doctoral candidates who have completed the research for the dissertation. Must be nominated by the art history department of your university and be a U.S. citizen or foreign student matriculated at U.S. institutions. Ten awards offered annually. Consult your art history department advisor for further information. If necessary, write to the foundation at the address below.

Samuel H. Kress Foundation
174 East 80th Street
New York, NY   10021

657
Kress Travel Fellowships

AMOUNT: $1000–$12000
DEADLINE: November 30
FIELDS/MAJORS: Art History

Awards for travel to view material essential for the completion of dissertation research. For U.S. citizens to travel abroad or international students at American universities. Must be nominated by the art history department. Fifteen to twenty awards offered annually. Consult your art history department advisor for further information.

Samuel H. Kress Foundation
174 E. 80th Street
New York, NY   10021

658
L. Dudley Phillips Memorial Fellowship

AMOUNT: None Specified
DEADLINE: March 1
FIELDS/MAJORS: History

Awards are available at the University of New Mexico for graduate students in history to support the completion of the dissertation project. Applicant must have completed all parts of the Ph.D. program except the dissertation. Write to the address below for more information.

University of New Mexico, Albuquerque
Office of Financial Aid
Albuquerque, NM   87131

659
L.S.B. Leaky Foundation General Research Grants

AMOUNT: $3000–$12000   DEADLINE: August 15
FIELDS/MAJORS: Human Evolution

Grants are available for advanced predoctoral students as well as established scientists in the fields of human evolution. Write to the address below for more information.

L.S.B. Leaky Foundation
Grants Administration
77 Jack London Square, Suite M
Oakland, CA   94607

660
L.S.B. Leaky Foundation Special Research Grants

AMOUNT: $20000   DEADLINE: October 15
FIELDS/MAJORS: Human Evolution, Paleontology

Grants are available for postdoctoral scholars in the field of human evolution and paleontology. Most periods of research are expected to last for two years. Write to the address below for more information.

L.S.B. Leaky Foundation
Grants Administration
77 Jack London Square, Suite M
Oakland, CA   94607

661 Lachenmeyer Media Management Fellowship

AMOUNT: None Specified
DEADLINE: March 15
FIELDS/MAJORS: Journalism and Mass Communications

Scholarships are available at the University of Oklahoma, Norman for graduate students in journalism and mass communications, with GPAs of at least 3.5. Student must be planning a career in media management and have prior work experience in journalism. Five awards offered annually. Write to the address below for information.

University of Oklahoma, Norman
School of Journalism and Mass Communications
860 Van Vleet Oval
Norman, OK   73019

662 Ladd S. Gordon Memorial Scholarship

AMOUNT: None Specified   **DEADLINE:** March 1
FIELDS/MAJORS: Wildlife Science

Awarded to one or more graduate students enrolled in wildlife science. Recipient must have demonstrated financial need. Write to the address below for more information.

New Mexico State University
College of Agriculture and Home Economics
Box 30001, Box 3AG
Las Cruces, NM   88003-8003

663 Lakewood Medical Center Foundation Scholarship

AMOUNT: None Specified   **DEADLINE:** March 1
FIELDS/MAJORS: Medicine, Nursing, Pharmacy

Awards for students currently enrolled in an accredited school of medicine, nursing, or pharmacy who are from one of the following California cities: Artesia, Bellflower, Cerritos, Compton, Cypress, Downey, Hawaiian Gardens, Lakewood, Long Beach, Norwalk, Paramount, or Signal Hill. Write to the address below for more information.

Lakewood Medical Center Foundation
PO Box 6070
Lakewood, CA   90712

664 Landscape Architecture Foundation Student Research Grants

AMOUNT: $350–$2000   **DEADLINE:** May 4
FIELDS/MAJORS: Landscape Architecture

Scholarships are available at the University of Oklahoma, Norman for graduate students in landscape architecture. Twelve awards are offered annually. Write to the address below for information.

University of Oklahoma, Norman
Faculty, Landscape Architecture
Carnegie Building, Room 307
Norman, OK   73019

665 Lange, Quill, and Powers, P.S.C. Scholarship

AMOUNT: $1000   **DEADLINE:** February 1
FIELDS/MAJORS: Law

Applicant must be a second year law student who is a Kentucky resident. Contact the Assistant Dean, Chase College of Law, for further information.

Northern Kentucky University
Chase College of Law
Office of Admissions
Highland Heights, KY   41099

666 Larry Ratner Scholarship

AMOUNT: $500   **DEADLINE:** March 2
FIELDS/MAJORS: Business Administration

Award open to disadvantaged minority M.B.A. candidates. Must be active university or community activities and be able to demonstrate financial need. Must have a minimum GPA of 2.5. Contact the address below for further information.

California Polytechnic State University
Financial Aid Office
212 Administration Building
San Luis Obispo, CA   93407

667 Larson Aquatic Research Support Scholarship

AMOUNT: $3000–$5000   **DEADLINE:** November 15
FIELDS/MAJORS: Water Industry, Aquatic, Analytical, and Environmental Chemistry

Scholarships are available to encourage outstanding graduate students in science or engineering dedicated to research to improve water quality. Also for master's and Ph.D. level scholars conducting research in corrosion control, treatment, and distribution of domestic and industrial water supplies. Two awards per year. Write to the address below for information. The deadline for doctoral scholars is January 5; for master's students, the deadline is November 15.

American Water Works Association
Fellowship Coordinator
6666 W. Quincy Avenue
Denver, CO   80235

668 Latin American and Caribbean Fellowship Program

AMOUNT: Maximum: $30000
DEADLINE: March 28
FIELDS/MAJORS: Social Sciences/Humanities

Fellowships for Latin American and Caribbean practitioners and researchers whose work in grassroots development would benefit from advanced academic experience in the U.S. Fellowships are awarded to master's candidates and higher. Must demonstrate interest in the problems of poverty and development and be nominated by home institution. Up to forty fellowships are offered per year. Write to the address below for details.

Inter-American Foundation
IAF Fellowship Programs, Dept. 555
901 N. Stuart Street, 10th Floor
Arlington, VA   22203

669 Laura Hamilton Billingsley Memorial Scholarship

AMOUNT: None Specified   **DEADLINE:** March 15
FIELDS/MAJORS: Journalism, Mass Communications

Scholarships are available at the University of Oklahoma, Norman for students at master's level in journalism and mass communications, with minimum GPAs of 3.0. Preference is given to students of Native American descent. Four awards offered annually. Write to the address below for information.

University of Oklahoma, Norman
School of Journalism and Mass Communications
860 Van Vleet Oval
Norman, OK   73019

670 Laurance Reid Scholarship for Natural Gas Processing

AMOUNT: $800   **DEADLINE:** March 1
FIELDS/MAJORS: Chemical Engineering, Petroleum Engineering

Scholarships are available at the University of Oklahoma, Norman for full-time graduate students in chemical or petroleum engineering who demonstrate an interest in natural gas. Write to the address below for information.

University of Oklahoma, Norman
Chemical Engineering and Materials Science
100 East Boyd Street, Energy Center
Norman, OK   73019

671 Law Scholarships

AMOUNT: None Specified   **DEADLINE:** April 1
FIELDS/MAJORS: Law

Applicants must be of Japanese ancestry and entering or enrolled at an accredited law school. Must also be members of the JACL. Applications and information may be obtained from local JACL chapters, district offices, and the national headquarters at the address below. Please indicate your level of study and be certain to include a legal-sized SASE.

Japanese American Citizens League
National Scholarship and Award Program
1765 Sutter Street
San Francisco, CA   94115

672 Lawrence E. Hart Music Scholarship

AMOUNT: None Specified   **DEADLINE:** None Specified
FIELDS/MAJORS: Music

Award open to graduate music students. Contact the address below for further information.

University of North Carolina, Greensboro
Financial Aid Office
723 Kenilworth Street
Greensboro, NC   27412

673 Legislative Fellows Program

AMOUNT: None Specified   **DEADLINE:** None Specified
FIELDS/MAJORS: Political Science, Government, Public Affairs

Fellows must be full-time graduate students, a New York state citizen or a student enrolled on an accredited campus in New York state, and intending to pursue a career in public service. Fellowship term is usually about one year. Up to fourteen fellows per year. Write to Dr. Russell J. Williams, Director, at the address below for details.

New York State Senate
Senate Student Programs
90 South Swan Street, Room 401
Albany, NY   12247

674 Leopold E. Wrasse Scholarship

AMOUNT: $1000   **DEADLINE:** March 2
FIELDS/MAJORS: Agribusiness

Award open to M.B.A. students following the agribusiness specialization. Contact the address below for further information.

California Polytechnic State University
Financial Aid Office
212 Administration Building
San Luis Obispo, CA   93407

675
Lerner-Scott Prize

AMOUNT: $1000 DEADLINE: November 1
FIELDS/MAJORS: American and Women's History

Awards are available for the best doctoral dissertation submitted in U.S. women's history. Finalists will be asked to submit a complete copy of the dissertation. Write to the address below for more information.

Organization of American Historians
Award and Prize Committee Coordinator
112 N. Bryan Street
Bloomington, IN   47408

676
Lerner-Gray Fund for Marine Research

AMOUNT: $200–$1000 DEADLINE: March 15
FIELDS/MAJORS: Marine Research, Marine Zoology

For postdoctoral scholars and marine scientists. Submit details of educational and scientific backgrounds and a description of project to be undertaken. For study of systematics, evolution, ecology, and field-related research of marine animal behavior. Not for botany or biochemistry. Information on collection study grants is also available from the sponsor. Write to the address below for details.

American Museum of Natural History
Central Park West at 79th Street
New York, NY   10024

677
Leroy Matthews Physician/Scientist Award

AMOUNT: Maximum: $46000 DEADLINE: September 1
FIELDS/MAJORS: Medical Research—Cystic Fibrosis

Grants are available to newly trained pediatricians and internists (M.D.s and M.D./Ph.D.s) to complete subspecialty training, develop into independent investigators, and initiate a research program. Awards range from $36000 (stipend) plus $10000 (R&D) for one year to $60000 (stipend) plus $15000 (R&D) for year six. Write to the address below for details.

Cystic Fibrosis Foundation
Office of Grants Management
6931 Arlington Road
Bethesda, MD   20814

678
Leslie T. Posey and Frances U. Posey Scholarships

AMOUNT: $1000–$4000 DEADLINE: March 1
FIELDS/MAJORS: Art, Painting, Sculpture

Applicants must be full-time graduate art majors in traditional painting or sculpture. If student is just starting their master's program, evidence of acceptance must be provided. Write to Robert E. Perkins, Administrator, at the address below for details.

Leslie T. Posey and Frances U. Posey Foundation
1800 Second Street, Suite 905
Sarasota, FL   34236

679
Lester Auer Jaffe Memorial Fund

AMOUNT: $1200 DEADLINE: February 1
FIELDS/MAJORS: Law

Awards for law students who demonstrate academic promise and financial need. Renewable for three academic years for full-time students and four academic years for part-time students. Contact the Assistant Dean, Chase College of Law, for further information.

Northern Kentucky University
Chase College of Law
Office of Admission
Highland Heights, KY   41099

680
Letourneau Student Writing Award

AMOUNT: $1000 DEADLINE: February 1
FIELDS/MAJORS: Law

Writing competition for students in the field of law who are currently attending an accredited school in the United States or Canada. Papers must be at least 3000 words in length, must contain only uncollaborated original work, and may relate to research done by the author. Write to the address below for more information.

American College of Legal Medicine
Student Writing Competition
611 East Wells Street
Milwaukee, WI   53202

681
Lettie Pate Whitehead Foundation Fellowship

AMOUNT: None Specified DEADLINE: March 1
FIELDS/MAJORS: Nursing

Award open to students in the Graduate School of Nursing. Contact the address below for further information.

University of North Carolina, Greensboro
Financial Aid Office
723 Kenilworth Street
Greensboro, NC   27412

682
Library Education Scholarship, Continuing Education Scholarship

AMOUNT: None Specified DEADLINE: September 15
FIELDS/MAJORS: Library/Information Sciences

Scholarship for Wisconsin residents who will be attending a master's level program in Wisconsin for the study of library or information science. Based on academic and professional accomplishments, as well as on financial need. Write to the address below for complete details.

Wisconsin Library Association
Chair, Library Careers Committee
4785 Hayes Road
Madison, WI   53704

683
Linda E. Jennett Endowed Fellowship

AMOUNT: None Specified
DEADLINE: March 1
FIELDS/MAJORS: Civil Engineering

Awards are available at the University of New Mexico for female civil engineering graduate students enrolled full-time. Write to the address below for more information.

University of New Mexico, Albuquerque
Office of Financial Aid
Albuquerque, NM 87131

684
Linda Isaacs Memorial Scholarship, Outstanding Student Award

AMOUNT: $250 DEADLINE: None Specified
FIELDS/MAJORS: Human Relations

Scholarships are available at the University of Oklahoma, Norman for graduate students in human relations, based on academic achievement, financial need, and professional promise. Write to the address below for information.

University of Oklahoma, Norman
Department of Human Relations
501 Elm, Room 730
Norman, OK 73019

685
Linda M. Lampe Memorial Scholarship

AMOUNT: None Specified
DEADLINE: February 1
FIELDS/MAJORS: Law

Awards for female law students who are employed full-time and entering their fourth year of study. Academic promise and financial need are considered. Contact the Assistant Dean, Chase College of Law, for further information.

Northern Kentucky University
Chase College of Law
Office of Admissions
Highland Heights, KY 41099

686
Link Foundation Energy Fellowship Program

AMOUNT: Maximum: $18000 DEADLINE: December 1
FIELDS/MAJORS: Energy Research

Fellowships are available at the University of Rochester for dissertation research in the development of energy resources and their conservation. To enhance both the theoretical and practical knowledge and application of energy research. Preference given to proposals dealing directly with energy and exploring ideas not yet fully tested, rather than developed programs in progress and can be implemented in the relatively near term. Write to the address listed for further information.

Center for Governmental Research, Inc.
Link Foundation Energy Fellowship
37 S. Washington Street
Rochester, NY 14608

687
LITA/GEAC-CLSI Scholarship

AMOUNT: $2500 DEADLINE: April 1
FIELDS/MAJORS: Information Science

Applicants must be entering an ALA-accredited master's program with an emphasis on library automation. Previous experience will be considered. One award per year. Write to the address shown for details.

American Library Association
Library and Information Technology Assn.
50 E. Huron Street
Chicago, IL 60611

688
LITA/OCLC and LITA/LSSI Minority Scholarships

AMOUNT: $2500 DEADLINE: April 1
FIELDS/MAJORS: Information Science

Applicants must be Native American, Asian-American, African-American, or Hispanic graduate students who are entering or enrolled in an ALA-accredited master's program with an emphasis on library automation. Previous experience is considered and U.S. or Canadian citizenship is required. Two awards per year. Write to the address shown for details.

American Library Association
Library and Information Technology Assn.
50 E. Huron Street
Chicago, IL 60611

689
Littleton-Griswold Research Grant

AMOUNT: $1000 DEADLINE: February 1
FIELDS/MAJORS: American Legal History

Grant available to American Historical Association members to support research in American legal history and the field of law and society. Write to the address below for details.

American Historical Association
Award Administrator
400 A Street, SE
Washington, DC 20003

690
Liver Scholar Award Program

AMOUNT: $30000 DEADLINE: December 31
FIELDS/MAJORS: Liver Research

Award open to trained investigators who hold an M.D. or Ph.D. wishing a career in liver disease research. Applicants must have three to four years of relevant postdoctoral experience prior to award and apply within the first three years of faculty appointment. Recipient is responsible to the sponsoring institution. Contact the address below for further information.

American Liver Foundation
1425 Popton Avenue
Cedar Grove, NJ   07009

691
Lloyd Lewis Fellowships in American History

AMOUNT: Maximum: $40000
DEADLINE: January 20
FIELDS/MAJORS: American History

Fellowships for established scholars in any field of American history that is appropriate to the collections of the library. Must hold Ph.D. Must be U.S. citizen or permanent resident. Write to the address below for details.

Newberry Library
Committee on Awards
60 W. Walton Street
Chicago, IL   60610

692
Lofty L. Basta, M.D., Scholarship

AMOUNT: None Specified DEADLINE: None Specified
FIELDS/MAJORS: Medicine

Scholarship available for freshmen medical students who are legal residents of Oklahoma, with one or more years of work history within the health field. One award offered annually. Write to the address below for information.

University of Oklahoma, Norman
Director, Office of Financial Aid
OUHSC, PO Box 73190
Oklahoma City, OK   73190

693
Logan-Hetherington Memorial Medical Awards

AMOUNT: None Specified DEADLINE: April 15
FIELDS/MAJORS: Medicine

Awards for upperclassmen in the School of Medicine who are interested in primary care. Awards rotate between Grand Forks and Bismarck natives. Contact the address below for further information or the financial aid office at your school's location.

University of North Dakota—School of Medicine
Sandra Elshaug, Financial Aid Office
PO Box 9037—501 N. Columbia Road
Grand Forks, ND   58202

694
Loh-Van Scherrenburg Graduate Scholarship

AMOUNT: $1000 DEADLINE: February 7
FIELDS/MAJORS: Accounting

Students must be admitted to the M.B.A. or Master of Accountancy program, with a combined GMAT and GPA admission score of 1100 or higher. Recipient must enroll in 9 hours each semester. Two awards are offered annually. Contact the COBA office for more information.

Southwest Missouri State University
Office of Financial Aid
901 South National Avenue
Springfield, MO   65804

695
Long-Term Research Fellowships

AMOUNT: $13375 DEADLINE: January 15
FIELDS/MAJORS: Humanities/Social Science

Five-month research fellowships are available for postdoctoral study. Must be United States citizens or residents for at least three years preceding the fellowship term. Residency at the John Carter Brown Library is required. Write to address below for details.

John Carter Brown Library
Attn: Director
Box 1894, Brown University
Providence, RI   02912

696
Lorain County Medical Scholarship Foundation Scholarships

AMOUNT: None Specified DEADLINE: May 15
FIELDS/MAJORS: Medicine, Nursing, and Related Health Fields

Scholarships for Lorain County (OH) students who are currently enrolled or formally admitted to medical school (not pre-med) nursing students who have completed one year of study or are enrolled/admitted to courses in the health related field. Must be able to demonstrate academic competence and financial need. Write to the address below for details.

Lorain County Medical Scholarship Foundation
5320 Hoag Drive, Suite D
Elyria, OH   44035

697
Los Alamos County Medical Society Memorial Scholarship

AMOUNT: None Specified DEADLINE: None Specified
FIELDS/MAJORS: Medicine

Awards for residents of Los Alamos or Northern New Mexico who are enrolled in medical school. Must demonstrate financial need and merit. Write to the address below for more information.

University of New Mexico, Albuquerque
Office of Financial Aid
Albuquerque, NM   87131

698
Louis P. Goldberg Memorial Scholarship

AMOUNT: Maximum: $500
DEADLINE: March 1
FIELDS/MAJORS: Political Science, Economics, Sociology

Open to a graduating senior enrolling in a master's degree program. Contact the address listed for further information.

Brooklyn College
Office of the V.P. for Student Life
2113 Boylan Hall
Brooklyn, NY   11210

699
Louis Pelzer Memorial Award

AMOUNT: $500   DEADLINE: November 30
FIELDS/MAJORS: All Areas of Study

Award for the graduate student who submits the best essay in American history. Author must be enrolled in graduate program in any field. Write to the address below for more information.

Organization of American Historians
Journal of American History
1125 E. Atwater, Indiana University
Bloomington, IN   47401

700
Louise Carter Hoffler Scholarship

AMOUNT: None Specified   DEADLINE: January 1
FIELDS/MAJORS: Clothing, Textiles

Award open to graduate students engaged in textile research. Contact the address below for further information.

University of North Carolina, Greensboro
Financial Aid Office
723 Kenilworth Street
Greensboro, NC   27412

701
Louise Giles Minority Scholarships

AMOUNT: $3000   DEADLINE: April 1
FIELDS/MAJORS: Library Science

Applicants must be Native American, Asian-American, African-American, or Hispanic graduate students entering or enrolled in an ALA-accredited master's program. United States or Canadian citizenship is required. Must not have completed more than 12 semester hours toward master's degree. Write to the address shown for details.

American Library Association
Staff Liaison, ALA Scholarship Juries
50 E. Huron Street
Chicago, IL   60611

702
Luce Fellowship

AMOUNT: None Specified
DEADLINE: February 1
FIELDS/MAJORS: Biological Sciences

Fellowships open to female graduates. Fellowship includes a stipend and tuition remission. Contact the address below for further information.

Fordham University
Graduate Admissions Office—Keating 216
Fordham University
Bronx, NY   10458

703
Luise Meyer-Schutzmeister Award

AMOUNT: $500   DEADLINE: January 15
FIELDS/MAJORS: Physics

Scholarship for female doctoral student in physics. For U.S. citizens to study in U.S. or abroad, or for foreign students to study in U.S. (the AWIS also publishes a directory of financial aid). Write to the address below for details.

Association for Women in Science Educational Foundation
National Headquarters
1200 New York Avenue NW, #650
Washington, DC   20005

704
Lyle Mamer, Julia Kiene Fellowship in Electrical Energy

AMOUNT: $1000–$2000   DEADLINE: March 1
FIELDS/MAJORS: Electrical Related Fields

Open to women who are graduating seniors or those who have a degree from an accredited institution. The applications are judged on scholarship, character, financial need, and professional interest in electrical energy. The college or university selected by the recipient for advanced study must be accredited and approved by the EWRT Fellowship Committee. One award given for each fellowship. Write to the address below for further information.

Electrical Women's Round Table, Inc.
Executive Director
PO Box 292793
Nashville, TN   37229

705
Lynn Meier Medical Scholarship

AMOUNT: None Specified   DEADLINE: April 15
FIELDS/MAJORS: Medicine

Awards for third-year students in the School of Medicine. Scholastic achievement, high moral character, financial need, and potential for achievement in the medical profession will be considered. Contact the address below for further information or the financial aid office at your school's location.

University of North Dakota—School of Medicine
Sandra Elshaug, Financial Aid Office
PO Box 9037—501 N. Columbia Road
Grand Forks, ND   58202

706
Lynnford L. Peterson Scholarship

AMOUNT: None Specified   DEADLINE: March 1
FIELDS/MAJORS: Medicine

Awards are available at the University of New Mexico for medical students with financial need and demonstrated merit. Write to the address below for more information.

University of New Mexico, Albuquerque
Office of Financial Aid
Albuquerque, NM   87131

707
M.A. Cartland Shackford Medical Fellowship

AMOUNT: Maximum: $3500
DEADLINE: December 16
FIELDS/MAJORS: Medicine

Scholarship for women studying medicine (on the graduate level). Fellowships are intended to support women with a career objective in general practice, not psychiatry. Write to the address below for information.

Wellesley College
Committee on Graduate Fellowships
106 Central Street, Career Center
Wellesley, MA   02181

708
M.B.A. Scholarships

AMOUNT: $2500–$10000
DEADLINE: March 31
FIELDS/MAJORS: All Areas of Business

Awards for minority students who are enrolled in full-time graduate or doctoral business programs. Based on financial need, activities, and GPA. Write to the address below for more information.

National Black M.B.A. Association, Inc.
180 N. Michigan Avenue
Suite 1515
Chicago, IL   60601

709
M.C. Roberts Memorial Law Scholarship

AMOUNT: None Specified   DEADLINE: June 1
FIELDS/MAJORS: Law

Applicants must be five-year residents of the county of Peoria, IL. Must have completed all studies that would allow for student to enroll in an accredited J.D. program. Scholarship is open to unmarried male applicants only. Based on need. Write to address below for details.

First of America Trust Company
Trustee of the M.C. Roberts Fund
301 Southwest Adams Street, PO Box 749
Peoria, IL   61652

710
Mabelle Wilhelmina Boldt Memorial Scholarship

AMOUNT: $2000   DEADLINE: March 4
FIELDS/MAJORS: Interior Design

Scholarship for graduate level students who have worked in the field for at least five years and are returning to school for further studies. Based on academic/creative accomplishment. Preference given to students with a focus on design research. One award per year. Send a SASE to the address below for details.

American Society of Interior Designers Educational Foundation
Scholarship and Awards Program
608 Massachusetts Avenue, NE
Washington, DC   20002

711
MacArthur Fellowships

AMOUNT: $16000–$28000   DEADLINE: February 3
FIELDS/MAJORS: International Relations and Security, Arms Control

Fellowships are available at Stanford for doctoral dissertation research in an area related to the field listed above. Write to the address below or call 415-497-9625 for information.

Stanford University
Center for Int'l Security and Arms Control
320 Galvez Street
Stanford, CA   94305

712
Magoichi and Shizuko Kato Memorial Scholarship

AMOUNT: None Specified   DEADLINE: April 1
FIELDS/MAJORS: Medicine, Theology/Religion

Open to graduate students of Japanese ancestry majoring in medicine or the ministry. Must be a member of the JACL to apply. Applications and information may be obtained from local JACL chapters, district offices, and the national headquarters at the address below. Please indicate your level of study and be certain to include a legal-sized SASE.

Japanese American Citizens League
National Scholarship and Award Program
1765 Sutter Street
San Francisco, CA   94115

713 Maine Osteopathic Association Memorial Scholarship

AMOUNT: $1000 **DEADLINE:** May 1
FIELDS/MAJORS: Osteopathic Medicine

Award for a first-year student who is a Maine resident and presents proof of enrollment at an approved college of osteopathic medicine. Write to the address below for more information.

Maine Osteopathic Association
Executive Director
RR 2 Box 1920
Manchester, ME   04351

714 Maine Osteopathic Association Scholarship

AMOUNT: $1000 **DEADLINE:** May 1
FIELDS/MAJORS: Osteopathic Medicine

Award for a first-year student who is a Maine resident and presents proof of enrollment at an approved college of osteopathic medicine. Write to the address below for more information.

Maine Osteopathic Association
Executive Director
RR 2 Box 1920
Manchester, ME   04351

715 MALDEF Law School Scholarship Program

AMOUNT: None Specified **DEADLINE:** June 30
FIELDS/MAJORS: Law

Open to full-time law students of Hispanic descent accepted to/enrolled in an accredited law school. Varying number of awards per year. Recipients must demonstrate a commitment to serve the Hispanic community after graduation. Write to the address below for details.

Mexican American Legal Defense and Educational Fund
MALDEF Law School Scholarship Program
634 S. Spring Street, 11th Floor
Los Angeles, CA   90014

716 Manpower Access-to-Community Health (MATCH Program)

AMOUNT: Maximum: $38000 **DEADLINE:** January 15
FIELDS/MAJORS: Public Health

Must be a public health graduate student. To qualify as a candidate for the program, an individual must complete a written application, essay, resume, minimum of three references, and undergo a formal interview. Approximately twenty fellows will be selected each year. Write to the address below for more information.

Florida International University
M.S., Ches, MATCH Program Coordinator
1330 New Hampshire, NW, #122
Washington, DC   20036

717 Marcus Foster Fellowship, Fontaine Fellowship

AMOUNT: None Specified **DEADLINE:** February 5
FIELDS/MAJORS: Education

Fellowships for minority Ph.D./Ed.D. students in the GSE at the University of Pennsylvania. Foster Fellowship is renewable. Contact the Financial Aid Office at the address below for details.

University of Pennsylvania, Graduate School of Education
Financial Aid Office
3700 Walnut Street
Philadelphia, PA   19104

718 Margaret and Charles E. Stewart Scholarship Fund

AMOUNT: $500 **DEADLINE:** April 30
FIELDS/MAJORS: Religion, Theology

Awards for African-American full-time seminary students enrolled as candidates for the Master of Divinity degree, in preparation for the pastorate in the Black Church of any Protestant denomination. Write to the address below for more information.

Philadelphia Foundation
1234 Market Street
Suite 1900
Philadelphia, PA   19107

719 Margaret Freeman Bowers Fellowship

AMOUNT: $1500 **DEADLINE:** December 16
FIELDS/MAJORS: Social Work, Law, Public Policy, Public Administration

Fellowships for graduates of Wellesley College studying any in any of the above fields or studying for a M.B.A. with career goals in the field of social services. Preference given to candidates with financial need. Contact the address below for further information.

Wellesley College, Fellowships for Wellesley Alumnae
Sec'y, Committee on Graduate Fellowships
106 Central Street, Career Center
Wellesley, MA   02181

720 Margaret Gilman and Anne Cutting Jones & Edith Melcher Fund Awards

AMOUNT: None Specified **DEADLINE:** January 2
FIELDS/MAJORS: French

Award open to graduate students studying French. Contact the address below for further information about both awards.

Bryn Mawr Graduate School of Arts and Sciences
101 N. Merion Avenue
Bryn Mawr, PA   19010

721 Margaret Hard Home Economics Research Award

AMOUNT: None Specified   DEADLINE: February 1
FIELDS/MAJORS: Home Economics

Award open to master's student who has completed one semester of graduate-level home economics. Must have a minimum GPA of 3.5. Contact the address below for further information.

Washington State University—Scholarship Committee
College of Agriculture and Home Economics
423 Hulbert Hall
Pullman, WA   99164

722 Margaret McNamara Memorial Fund Fellowships

AMOUNT: Maximum: $6000   DEADLINE: February 2
FIELDS/MAJORS: All Areas of Study

Fellowships are available to women from developing countries, with a record of service to women/children. Applicants must be twenty-five years of age or older and planning to return to their country of origin within two years of the grant date. Must be able to demonstrate financial need. Write to the address below for information.

Margaret McNamara Memorial Fund
1818 H Street, NW, Room G-1000
Washington, DC   20433

723 Marguerite Bartlett Hamer and Bertha Haven Putman Fellowships

AMOUNT: None Specified   DEADLINE: January 2
FIELDS/MAJORS: History

Awards open to graduate students in history. Contact the address below for further information about both awards.

Bryn Mawr Graduate School of Arts and Sciences
101 N. Merion Avenue
Bryn Mawr, PA   19010

724 Marian Franklin Counseling Fellowship

AMOUNT: None Specified
DEADLINE: None Specified
FIELDS/MAJORS: Counseling, Specialized Education

Award open to graduates students who are U.S. citizens. Contact the address below for further information.

University of North Carolina, Greensboro
Financial Aid Office
723 Kenilworth Street
Greensboro, NC   27412

725 Mariani Award

AMOUNT: None Specified   DEADLINE: March 1
FIELDS/MAJORS: Psychology

Awards are available at the University of New Mexico for graduate students in psychology with outstanding graduate work. Write to the address below for more information.

University of New Mexico, Albuquerque
Office of Financial Aid
Albuquerque, NM   87131

726 Marie Hutton Memorial Scholarship

AMOUNT: None Specified   DEADLINE: March 1
FIELDS/MAJORS: Medicine

Awards are available at the University of New Mexico for medical students with financial need. Write to the address below for more information.

University of New Mexico, Albuquerque
Office of Financial Aid
Albuquerque, NM   87131

727 Marjorie Roy Rothermel Scholarship

AMOUNT: $1500   DEADLINE: February 15
FIELDS/MAJORS: Mechanical Engineering

Applicants must be master's students in mechanical engineering and ASME members. Write to the address below for details. Please be certain to enclose a SASE with your request.

American Society of Mechanical Engineers Auxiliary, Inc.
Mrs. Otto Prochaska
332 Valencia Street
Gulf Breeze, FL   32561

728 Mark Lindsey Memorial Scholarship

AMOUNT: None Specified   DEADLINE: March 1
FIELDS/MAJORS: Medicine

Awards are available at the University of New Mexico for students in need of assistance due to medical conditions or other restrictions. If this criteria cannot be met, then the scholarship shall be awarded to any deserving student. Write to the address below for more information.

University of New Mexico, Albuquerque
Office of Financial Aid
Albuquerque, NM   87131

729

Mark O. Hatfield Scholarship

AMOUNT: Maximum: $2000
DEADLINE: None Specified
FIELDS/MAJORS: Public Policy

Award for a scholar to do research in the fields above and produce a paper of publishable quality which will reflect the spirit and interests of Senator Mark Hatfield. Write to the address listed for more information.

Ripon Educational Fund
Executive Director
227 Massachusetts Avenue, NE, Suite 201
Washington, DC   20002

730

Mary Adeline Connor Professional Development Scholarship Program

AMOUNT: Maximum: $6000   DEADLINE: October 31
FIELDS/MAJORS: Library and Information Science

Scholarships for members of the Special Libraries Association who have worked in special libraries for at least five years. For post-MLS study. Preference is given to persons who display an aptitude for special library work. One or more awards per year. Write to the address below for details.

Special Libraries Association
SLA Scholarship Committee
1700 Eighteenth Street, NW
Washington, DC   20009

731

Mary C. Crossman Memorial Scholarship

AMOUNT: None Specified   DEADLINE: March 1
FIELDS/MAJORS: Communicative Disorders

Awards are available at the University of New Mexico for full-time graduate students majoring in the fields of communicative disorders. Must demonstrate financial need. Write to the address below for information.

University of New Mexico, Albuquerque
Office of Financial Aid
Albuquerque, NM   87131

732

Mary Davis Fellowship

AMOUNT: $13000   DEADLINE: November 15
FIELDS/MAJORS: Western Art, Visual Art, and Related Areas

Two-year fellowship is available for doctoral scholars researching for the dissertation. One year will be spent on research, and one year will be spent at the National Gallery of Art. Applicants must know two foreign languages related to the topic of their dissertation and be U.S. citizens or legal residents. Write to the address below for information.

National Gallery of Art
Center for Advanced Study in Visual Arts
Predoctoral Fellowship Program
Washington, DC   20565

733

Mary Elizabeth Barwick and Carl Jackson Sink Fellowship

AMOUNT: None Specified   DEADLINE: None Specified
FIELDS/MAJORS: Humanities

Award open to first year graduate students. Contact the Dean, College of Arts and Sciences, for further information.

University of North Carolina, Greensboro
Financial Aid Office
723 Kenilworth Street
Greensboro, NC   27412

734

Mary Elizabeth Barwick and Carl Jackson Sink Fellowship

AMOUNT: None Specified   DEADLINE: None Specified
FIELDS/MAJORS: Humanities

Award open to first-year graduate students in humanities. Contact the address below for further information.

University of North Carolina, Greensboro
Financial Aid Office
723 Kenilworth Street
Greensboro, NC   27412

735

Mary Elvira Stevens Traveling Fellowship

AMOUNT: $20000   DEADLINE: December 16
FIELDS/MAJORS: All Areas of Study

Fellowship is for a full year of travel or study abroad. Candidates must have graduated from Wellesley and be at least twenty-five years of age in the year of application. Any scholarly, artistic, or cultural purpose may be considered. Merit and financial need will also be considered. Contact the address below for further information.

Wellesley College
Alumnae Office
106 Central Street
Wellesley, MA   02181

736

Mary Frances Johnson, Sangster Parrott, H.W. Wilson Library Scholarship

AMOUNT: None Specified   DEADLINE: None Specified
FIELDS/MAJORS: Library, Information Studies

Awards open to graduate students who are able to demonstrate financial need. Contact the address below for further information about all three awards.

University of North Carolina, Greensboro
Financial Aid Office
723 Kenilworth Street
Greensboro, NC   27412

737
Mary Macklanburg Scholarship

AMOUNT: None Specified   DEADLINE: May 1
FIELDS/MAJORS: Dentistry

Scholarships are available at the University of Oklahoma, Norman for full-time graduate dentistry students, who are residents of Oklahoma. Three awards offered annually. Write to the address below for information.

University of Oklahoma, Norman
College of Dentistry
1001 Stanton L. Young Boulevard
Oklahoma City,. OK   73190

738
Mary McEwen Schimke Scholarship

AMOUNT: Maximum: $1000
DEADLINE: December 16
FIELDS/MAJORS: Literature, History

Scholarship for women studying on the graduate level. Purpose of the award is to provide relief from household and child care while studying. Based on scholarly expectation and identified need. Must be over thirty years of age. Preference is given to American studies. Candidates may have graduated from any American institution. Contact the address below for further information.

Wellesley College
Sec'y, Committee on Graduate Fellowships
106 Central Street, Career Center
Wellesley, MA   02181

739
Mary O'Day Memorial Fellowship

AMOUNT: $600   DEADLINE: January 6
FIELDS/MAJORS: Public Health Services

Open to full-time master's degree students planning a career in gerontology. Must be U.S. citizens or permanent residents. Contact the address below for further information.

University of California, Berkeley
Office of Financial Aid Graduate Unit
201 Sproul Hall, #1960
Berkeley, CA   94720

740
Mary Roberts Rinehart Awards

AMOUNT: $5000   DEADLINE: November 30
FIELDS/MAJORS: Creative Writing, Poetry

Awards are available for unpublished writers who need financial assistance to complete works of fiction, poetry, drama, biography, autobiography, or history with strong narrative quality. Applicants must be nominated by a program faculty member, a sponsoring writer, agent, or editor. Submit writing samples of up to thirty pages. Write to the address below for information.

George Mason University—Department of English
Mary Roberts Rinehart Fund
4400 University Drive
Fairfax, VA   22030

741
Mass Media Science and Engineering Fellows Program

AMOUNT: None Specified   DEADLINE: January 15
FIELDS/MAJORS: Engineering/Science

This program offers an opportunity for advanced students in the natural and social sciences and engineering to spend ten weeks during the summer working as reporters, researchers, or production assistants with media organizations nationwide. A modest stipend is included to help cover living expenses. Must be U.S. citizen and have a Ph.D. Write to the address below for further information.

American Association for the Advancement of Science
Amie E. King, Coordinator
1200 New York Avenue NW
Washington, DC   20005

742
Master's Thesis Fellowships

AMOUNT: Maximum: $2500   DEADLINE: May 1
FIELDS/MAJORS: U.S. Military and Naval History

Awards are available for master's degree thesis research in any area of history relevant to the Marine Corps (military and naval history, etc.). Applicants must be U.S. citizens or nationals. It is expected that part of the research will be undertaken at the Marine Corps Historical Archives in Washington, D.C. Write to the address below for information

Marine Corps Historical Center
Building 58
Washington Navy Yard
Washington, DC   20374

743
Match Administrative Fellowship Program

AMOUNT: None Specified   DEADLINE: June 1
FIELDS/MAJORS: Primary Healthcare

Open to professionals who at minimum, hold a baccalaureate degree, a five-year employment history, commitment to community health, possess strong written and verbal communication skills, and are U.S. citizens or permanent residents. Contact the address below for further information.

National Association of Community Health Centers
Match Program Office
1330 New Hampshire Avenue, NW, #122
Washington, DC   20036

744 Mattie Pattison Paddock Memorial Scholarship

AMOUNT: None Specified
DEADLINE: February 1
FIELDS/MAJORS: Home Economics

Award for graduate students working toward an advanced degree in home economics. Must have a minimum GPA of 3.5. Contact the address below for further information.

Washington State University—Scholarship Committee
College of Agriculture and Home Economics
423 Hulbert Hall
Pullman, WA 99164

745 Maurice Yonover Scholarship

AMOUNT: None Specified DEADLINE: March 1
FIELDS/MAJORS: Helping Professions

Open to master's and doctoral candidates with career goals in the "helping professions." Must be legally domiciled in Cook County, the Chicago metro area, or Northwest Indiana. Contact the address below for further information after December 1. At least 2.8 GPA required.

Jewish Vocational Service
Academic Scholarship Program
1 S. Franklin Street
Chicago, IL 60606

746 Maurie Clark Fellowship

AMOUNT: $5600 DEADLINE: March 15
FIELDS/MAJORS: Urban and Public Affairs

Awards are available to outstanding Ph.D. candidates in the school of urban and public affairs. Recipients must have an approved dissertation outline and intend to use the fellowship to support research activities. One award offered annually. Write to the address below for more information.

Portland State University
Dean's Office
101 School of Urban and Public Affairs
Portland, OR 97207

747 Max Richter Fellowship Fund

AMOUNT: None Specified DEADLINE: January 2
FIELDS/MAJORS: International Affairs

Awards open to advanced graduate students. May be used to fund dissertation overseas. Applicants must be U.S. citizens. Contact the address below for further information.

Bryn Mawr Graduate School of Arts and Sciences
101 N. Merion Avenue
Bryn Mawr, PA 19010

748 McAlester Scottish Rite Graduate Fellowship

AMOUNT: None Specified DEADLINE: April 1
FIELDS/MAJORS: Engineering

Scholarships are available at the University of Oklahoma, Norman for full-time graduate students in engineering who plan to pursue an academic faculty career. One award offered annually. Write to the address below for information.

University of Oklahoma, Norman
College of Engineering
Room 107, CEC
Norman, OK 73019

749 McKnight Awards in Neuroscience

AMOUNT: None Specified DEADLINE: None Specified
FIELDS/MAJORS: Neuroscience

Awards for students at the doctoral or postdoctoral level who are doing research in the area of neuroscience. Write to the address below for more information.

McKnight Endowment Fund for Neuroscience
600 TCF Tower
121 South Eighth Street
Minneapolis, MN 55402

750 McKnight Black Doctoral Fellowship Program

AMOUNT: Maximum: $5000 DEADLINE: January 15
FIELDS/MAJORS: See Below

Fellowships for African-American doctoral students at participating Florida universities. For areas of study except: M.D., D.B.A., D.D.S., J.D., or D.V.M. The applicant must be a U.S. citizen. Write to the address below for details or contact the academic department heads of your school.

Florida Endowment Fund for Higher Education
201 E. Kennedy Boulevard, Suite 1525
Tampa, FL 33602

751 Medical and Physician Assistant Student Loan for Service Program

AMOUNT: Maximum: $12000 DEADLINE: None Specified
FIELDS/MAJORS: Medicine

$12000 annual loan available to New Mexico resident graduate students in medicine. Loan may be repaid or forgiven by working in a medically underserved area of New Mexico. Must be U.S. citizen or legal resident who demonstrates financial need and attends a New Mexico school. Write to the address below for further information.

New Mexico Commission on Higher Education
Financial Aid and Student Services
PO Box 15910
Santa Fe, NM 87506

752
Medical Scholarship Program

AMOUNT: Maximum: $2500   DEADLINE: May 15
FIELDS/MAJORS: Medicine (All Areas), Osteopathic Medicine

Scholarships for Georgia residents who have been accepted or matriculated into an M.D. or D.O. program. Recipient must agree to practice in a selected town in Georgia (all of the selected towns have populations of less than 15,000) one year for each year of the award. Write to the address below for details.

Georgia State Medical Education Board
244 Washington Street, SW, Room 574 J
Atlanta, GA   30334

753
Medical Student Fellowships

AMOUNT: $2000   DEADLINE: March 1
FIELDS/MAJORS: Medicine-Epilepsy Research

Research grants for medical students to perform research project related to epilepsy. A faculty advisor/preceptor must accept responsibility and supervision of the study. Write to the address below for details.

Epilepsy Foundation of America
Fellowship Programs
4351 Garden City Drive
Landover, MD   20785

754
Medical Student Loan Program

AMOUNT: $500–$3000   DEADLINE: October 15
FIELDS/MAJORS: Medicine

Open to any student who has completed at least one semester at a Minnesota medical school and is a member of the Minnesota Medical Association and a local medical society. Interview required. Interest rates: 0% during schooling, 8% after graduation. Thirty-five awards are given annually. Write to the address below for details.

Minnesota Physicians Foundation
Minnesota Medical Association
2221 University Avenue, SE, Suite 400
Minneapolis, MN   55414

755
Medical Student Loan Program

AMOUNT: $6000   DEADLINE: None Specified
FIELDS/MAJORS: Medicine

Open to medical students who have resided in Kent County, Michigan, or surrounding counties. Applicants must have completed the first year of medical school and demonstrate financial need. Write to the address below for details.

Kent Medical Foundation
220 Cherry Street, SE
Grand Rapids, MI   49503

756
Medical/Science Research Grants

AMOUNT: Maximum: $35000   DEADLINE: March 1
FIELDS/MAJORS: Cancer Research

Grants for younger faculty or scientists beginning new projects. Must be investigators at Massachusetts institutions. A second deadline date is September 1. Contact the address below for further information.

American Cancer Society
30 Speen Street
Framingham, MA   01701

757
Melinda Bealmear Endowed Memorial Scholarship

AMOUNT: None Specified   DEADLINE: March 1
FIELDS/MAJORS: Biology

Scholarships are available at the University of New Mexico for full-time graduate biology majors. Write to the address below for information.

University of New Mexico, Albuquerque
Department of Student Financial Aid
Mesa Vista Hall North
Albuquerque, NM   87131

758
Mellon Fellowships in Humanistic Studies

AMOUNT: $13750   DEADLINE: December 31
FIELDS/MAJORS: Humanities

Beginning graduate students only. Program is designed to attract and support fresh talent of outstanding ability enrolled in a program leading to a Ph.D. in one of the humanistic disciplines. Must be a U.S. citizen or permanent resident. Fellowships do not support the more quantifiable social sciences (law, library science, social work, education). Eighty awards offered annually. Write to the address below for details. The deadline to request an application is December 9. At least 3.0 GPA required.

Woodrow Wilson National Fellowship Foundation
Cn 5329
Princeton, NJ 08543

759
Mellon Post-Doctoral Fellowship Program

AMOUNT: Maximum: $30000
DEADLINE: January 3
FIELDS/MAJORS: Asian Studies, Classics, German Studies, Romance Studies, Russian Lit.

Fellowships for scholars and non-tenured teachers in the above fields who completed their Ph.D. requirements in the last five years. U.S. citizenship, Canadian citizenship, or permanent residency required. These are residential fellowships at Cornell. Three or four fellows per year. Write to address below for details. Must have Ph.D. completed at time of application.

Cornell University
Agnes Sirrine, Program Administrator
27 East Avenue, A.D. White Center
Ithaca, NY   14853

American Geriatrics Society
770 Lexington Avenue, Suite 300
New York, NY   10021

 760

Melodee Siegel Kornacker Fellowship

AMOUNT: None Specified   DEADLINE: January 2
FIELDS/MAJORS: Biology, Chemistry, Geology, Physics, Psychology

Awards open to graduate students in any of the above fields. Contact the address below for further information.

Bryn Mawr Graduate School of Arts and Sciences
101 N. Merion Avenue
Bryn Mawr, PA   19010

 761

Memorial Education Fellowship

AMOUNT: $2000   DEADLINE: March 1
FIELDS/MAJORS: Varies

Applicants must be women maintaining legal residence in Massachusetts for at least five years and present a letter of endorsement from the sponsoring Women's Club in your community. These awards are for graduate study. Write to the address below for details, be sure to include a SASE.

General Federation of Women's Clubs of Massachusetts
Chairman of Trustees, 245 Dutton Road
PO Box 679
Sudbury, MA   01776

 762

Mental Health Minority Research Fellowship Program

AMOUNT: None Specified   DEADLINE: February 28
FIELDS/MAJORS: Mental Health Research

Awards for minorities who have a master's degree in social work and will begin full-time study leading to a doctoral degree or are already in a doctoral social work program. Applicants must be U.S. citizens or permanent residents and be pursuing a career in mental health research. Write to the address below for more information.

National Institute of Mental Health
1600 Duke Street, #300
Alexandria, VA   22314

763

Merck/AGS New Investigator Awards

AMOUNT: $2000   DEADLINE: December 8
FIELDS/MAJORS: Geriatrics

Awards are restricted to fellows-in-training and new junior investigators holding an academic appointment not longer than five years post-fellowship. Awards will be chosen based on originality, scientific merit, relevance of the research, and overall academic accomplishments. Write to the address listed for more information.

 764

Metropolitan Life Foundation Program for Excellence in Medicine

AMOUNT: $2500   DEADLINE: None Specified
FIELDS/MAJORS: Medicine

Awards for minority students from Los Angeles, San Francisco, CA; Denver, CO; Tampa, FL; Atlanta, GA; Chicago/Aurora, IL; Wichita, KS; New York, NY; Tulsa, OK; Pittsburgh, Scranton, PA; Warwick/Providence, RI; Greenville, SC; or Houston, TX in their second or third year of medicine. Based on academics, leadership, and potential for contributions in medicine. Send a SASE to the address below for more information.

National Medical Fellowships, Inc.
110 West 32nd
8th Floor
New York, NY   10001

 765

Michael Kraus Research Grants

AMOUNT: Maximum: $800   DEADLINE: February 1
FIELDS/MAJORS: History—American Colonial

Grants are available to American Historical Association members for research in American colonial history, with preference given to the intercultural aspects of American and European relations. Write to the address below for details.

American Historical Association
Award Administrator
400 A Street, SE
Washington, DC   20003

 **766**

Michael Reese Women's Board Scholarship

AMOUNT: None Specified
DEADLINE: March 1
FIELDS/MAJORS: Medicine

Open to women medical students who have completed at least one year of medical school, accredited by the American Medical Association, with a minimum GPA of 3.0. Must be legally domiciled in Cook County or the Chicago metro area. Information and applications available after December 1 from the address below.

Jewish Vocational Service
Academic Scholarship Program
1 S. Franklin Street
Chicago, IL   60606

767

Mike Watts Memorial Engineering Graduate Fellowship

AMOUNT: $800   DEADLINE: March 1
FIELDS/MAJORS: Civil Engineering

Three awards at least $800 annually for U.S. citizens who have completed a B.S. degree and who are graduate students in good standing in civil engineering. Write to the address below for more information.

New Mexico State University
College of Engineering
Complex I, Box 30001, Dept. 3449
Las Cruces, NM   88003

768

Mike Watts Memorial Excellence Award

AMOUNT: $800   DEADLINE: March 1
FIELDS/MAJORS: Civil Engineering

$800 awarded to a civil engineering graduate student who is a U.S. citizen. Write to the address below for more information.

New Mexico State University
College of Engineering
Complex I, Box 30001, Dept. 3449
Las Cruces, NM   88003

769

Mildred Clarke Pressinger/ Mildred and Carl Otto Von Kienbusch Fellowship

AMOUNT: None Specified   DEADLINE: January 2
FIELDS/MAJORS: All Areas of Study

Awards open to students working toward the doctorate. Contact the address below for further information about both awards.

Bryn Mawr Graduate School of Arts and Sciences
101 N. Merion Avenue
Bryn Mawr, PA   19010

770

Miles and Shirley Fiterman Foundation Basic Research Awards

AMOUNT: $25000   DEADLINE: January 9
FIELDS/MAJORS: Gastrointestinal, Liver Function, or Related Diseases

Applicants must be MD's. or Ph.D.s holding full-time faculty positions at universities or institutions. Must be an individual member of any of the ADHF member organizations and below the level of assistant professor. Awards to those whose goal is a research career. Two awards are given annually. Contact the address below for further information or websites: http://www.gastro.org; http://www.asge.org; or http://hepar-sfgh.ucsf.edu.

American Digestive Health Foundation
Ms. Irene Kuo
7910 Woodmont Avenue, 7th Floor
Bethesda, MD   20814

771

Miles and Shirley Fiterman Foundation Clinical Research Awards

AMOUNT: $25000   DEADLINE: January 9
FIELDS/MAJORS: Clinical Research in Hepatology, Nutrition, or Gastroenterology

Applicants should be active investigators, with considerable achievements to date, but with ongoing research. Must be an individual member of any of the ADHF member organizations. Young and mid-level investigators are encouraged to apply. Contact the address below for further information or websites: http://www.gastro.org; http://www.asge.org; or http://hepar-sfgh.ucsf.edu.

American Digestive Health Foundation
Ms. Irene Kuo
7910 Woodmont Avenue, 7th Floor
Bethesda, MD   20814

772

Millender Fellowship Program

AMOUNT: $20000   DEADLINE: March 31
FIELDS/MAJORS: Public Serv., Law, Political Science, Business, Public Administration

Applicants must demonstrate a record of successful accomplishment in some graduate educational program and/or through equivalent experience, broadly related to public service careers (as listed above) which would demonstrate a capacity for high-level accomplishment. Applicants must have completed a master's degree or equivalent professional degree. Write to the address below for more information. At least 3.8 GPA required.

Wayne State University
Academic Programs
4116 Faculty/Administration Building
Detroit, MI   48202

773

Milton Topping Research Assistantship

AMOUNT: None Specified   DEADLINE: None Specified
FIELDS/MAJORS: Biology

Student must be enrolled in the biology graduate studies program and submit a summer research proposal. Preference is given to an entering graduate student. Contact the biology department for more information.

Southwest Missouri State University
Office of Financial Aid
901 South National Avenue
Springfield, MO   65804

774
Ministerial Education Scholarship

AMOUNT: None Specified
DEADLINE: None Specified
FIELDS/MAJORS: Theology, Ministerial

Awards for members of a Unitarian Universalist congregation enrolled full-time in a Master of Divinity degree leading to ordination as a UU minister. Write to the address below for more information.

Unitarian Universalist Association of Congregations
Office of Ministerial Education
25 Beacon Street
Boston, MA   02108

775
Minna B. Crook, Myrtle C. Lytle and Martha Chickering Fellowships

AMOUNT: $1800–$2700   **DEADLINE:** January 6
FIELDS/MAJORS: Social Services

Open to full-time master's degree students planning a career in public social services. Must be U.S. citizens or permanent residents. Contact the address below for further information.

University of California, Berkeley
Office of Financial Aid Graduate Unit
201 Sproul Hall, #1960
Berkeley, CA   94720

776
Minority Affairs Graduate Program

AMOUNT: None Specified   **DEADLINE:** March 15
FIELDS/MAJORS: All Areas of Study

Awards open to minority students accepted into the graduate school of the University of Wyoming. Must be a U.S. citizen attending school full-time. Contact the address below for further information.

University of Wyoming
Director MAGP
PO Box 3808
Laramie, WY   82071

777
Minority Dental Laboratory Technician Scholarship

AMOUNT: $1000   **DEADLINE:** August 15
FIELDS/MAJORS: Dental Laboratory Technology

Applicants must be U.S. citizens and must be enrolled or planning to enroll in a dental lab technology program accredited by the Commission on Accreditation of the American Dental Association. Students must have a minimum GPA of 2.8 and demonstrate financial need. These awards are for minority students. Write to the address below for details.

ADA Endowment and Assistance Fund, Inc.
211 East Chicago Avenue
Chicago, IL   60611

778
Minority Dental Student Scholarship Program

AMOUNT: $2000   **DEADLINE:** July 1
FIELDS/MAJORS: Dentistry

Awards for African-American, Hispanic, or Native American students entering their second year of a dental school accredited by the Commission on Dental Accreditation. Must demonstrate financial need and have a GPA of at least 2.5. Must be a U.S. citizen. Contact your school's financial aid office for more information.

ADA Endowment and Assistance Fund, Inc.
211 East Chicago Avenue
Chicago, IL   60611

779
Minority Doctoral Assistance Loan-for-Service Program

AMOUNT: Maximum: $25000   **DEADLINE:** January 1
FIELDS/MAJORS: Most Areas of Study

Awards for minority doctoral students who attend a New Mexico institution and who are also New Mexico residents. Must be U.S. citizens or permanent residents and enrolled in full-time study. Women are considered a minority for this award. Contact the graduate dean of your four-year public institution in New Mexico.

New Mexico Commission on Higher Education
Financial Aid and Student Services
PO Box 15910
Santa Fe, NM   87506

780
Minority Doctoral Study Grant Program

AMOUNT: $6000   **DEADLINE:** None Specified
FIELDS/MAJORS: All Areas of Study

Grants are available for minority doctoral candidates studying at Oklahoma institutions. This program was created as an incentive to increase the number of minority faculty and staff in the Oklahoma state system of higher education. Recipients must agree to teach in a state system institution two years for each year of aid. Must be an Oklahoma resident. Write to the address below for information.

Oklahoma State Regents for Higher Education
State Capitol Complex
500 Education Building
Oklahoma City, OK   73105

781
Minority Fellowship Program

AMOUNT: $8340–$10008
DEADLINE: January 15
FIELDS/MAJORS: Psychology

Fellowships for ethnic minority students pursuing doctoral degrees in APA accredited doctoral programs in psychology. Must be a U.S. citizen or a permanent resident. Applicants must be in at least their second year of training. Fellowships are from ten to twelve months with a stipend of $834 per month. Write to the address below for more information.

American Psychological Association
Minority Fellowship Program
750 First Street, NE
Washington, DC   20002

782
Minority Fellowship Program

AMOUNT: None Specified
DEADLINE: None Specified
FIELDS/MAJORS: Psychiatry

Fellowships for Psychiatric minority residents in their PGY-II year or residency. Must be U.S. citizens. Write to the address below for more information.

American Psychiatric Association
Office of Minority/National Affairs
1400 K. Street, NW
Washington, DC   20005

783
Minority Fellowships

AMOUNT: $7800   DEADLINE: None Specified
FIELDS/MAJORS: Human Resource Management, Industrial Relations

Open to full-time minority students who are pursuing graduate degrees in human resource management/industrial relations at one of thirteen consortium graduate schools. Must be a U.S. citizen. Write to the address below for more information.

Industrial Relations Council on Goals
PO Box 4363
East Lansing, MI   48826

784
Minority Graduate Emergency Aid Fund

AMOUNT: Maximum: $1000
DEADLINE: None Specified
FIELDS/MAJORS: All Areas of Study

Awards are available at Portland State University for minority graduate students who find themselves in short-term straitened circumstances. Contact the Office of Graduate Studies and Research for more information.

Portland State University
Office of Graduate Studies and Research
105 Neuberger Hall
Portland, OR   97207

785
Minority Master's Fellows Loan Program

AMOUNT: $2500–$7500   DEADLINE: June 1
FIELDS/MAJORS: Mathematics, Science, Foreign Languages, Education

African-American students who are admitted to a master's program in mathematics, the sciences, or foreign languages, or to African-American students in the fifth year of a teacher education program who were recipients of the minority teacher scholarship. Students must be full-time during fall/spring; can go part-time for three summers. Recipients are required to teach full-time in an Arkansas public school or institution for two years to receive total forgiveness of the loan. Write to the address below for more information.

Arkansas Department of Higher Education
Financial Aid Division
114 East Capitol
Little Rock, AR   72201

786
Minority Medical Faculty Development Program

AMOUNT: $75000   DEADLINE: March 28
FIELDS/MAJORS: Medicine/Education

Applicants must be minority physicians who are U.S. citizens, have excelled in their education, are now completing or will have completed formal clinical training, and are committed to academic careers. Minorities here are African- and Mexican-Americans, Native Americans, and mainland Puerto Ricans who have completed college on the mainland. Fellowships aid research and last four years. Write to the address below for additional information.

Robert Wood Johnson Foundation
James R. Gavin III, M.D, Ph.D., Program
4733 Bethesda Avenue, Suite 350
Bethesda, MD   20814

787
Minority Presence Fellowship

AMOUNT: $4000   DEADLINE: March 1
FIELDS/MAJORS: All Areas of Study

Award open to doctoral candidates who are African-American, U.S. citizens, North Carolina residents, and attending school full-time. Must be able to demonstrate financial need. Contact the address below for further information.

University of North Carolina, Greensboro
Financial Aid Office
723 Kenilworth Street
Greensboro, NC   27412

788

Minority Presence Fellowship

AMOUNT: $4000   DEADLINE: March 1
FIELDS/MAJORS: All Areas of Study

Award open to full-time graduate students who are African-American, U.S. citizens, and residents of North Carolina. Must be able to demonstrate financial need. Contact the address below for further information.

University of North Carolina, Greensboro
Financial Aid Office
723 Kenilworth Street
Greensboro, NC   27412

789

Minority Professional Study Grant Program

AMOUNT: $4000   DEADLINE: None Specified
FIELDS/MAJORS: Medicine, Dentistry, Law, Veterinary Medicine, Optometry

Grants are available for minority students studying at Oklahoma institutions. This program was created as an incentive to increase the number of minority groups in the programs listed above. Must be a U.S. citizen. Write to the address below for information.

Oklahoma State Regents for Higher Education
State Capitol Complex
500 Education Building
Oklahoma City, OK   73105

790

Minority Scholars Program Fellowship

AMOUNT: Maximum: $13000
DEADLINE: None Specified
FIELDS/MAJORS: All Areas of Study

Programs for African-American, Hispanic, and Native American graduate students at Pennsylvania State. Based upon academic excellence. Twenty fellowships and sixty assistantships are available. Contact the address below for further information.

Pennsylvania State University
Fellowships and Awards Office
313 Kern Graduate Building
University Park, PA   16802

791

Minority Scholarship Program

AMOUNT: $2500   DEADLINE: October 15
FIELDS/MAJORS: Psychology

Award for ethnic minority students accepted into a doctoral level psychology program in the state of California. Based on community involvement, leadership, knowledge of ethnic minority/cultural issues, career plans, and financial need. Scholarships are given to students in their first year of study. Write to the address below for more information.

California Psychological Association Foundation
1010 Eleventh Street
Suite 202
Sacramento, CA   95814

792

Minority Scholarship Program

AMOUNT: Maximum: $2500
DEADLINE: October 15
FIELDS/MAJORS: Psychology

Scholarships open to minority students who have been accepted in a first-year, full-time doctoral level psychology program in a California school. Candidates must be considered a member of one or more of these established ethnic minority groups: African/Hispanic/Latino/Asian-American, Native American, Alaskan Native, or Pacific Islander. Scholarships are not made based solely on financial need, but it is taken into account. Winners will be announced in mid-December. Information and applications are sent to the financial aid offices of California graduate schools in early summer. Get the information from that source instead of writing to the address indicated.

California State Psychological Association Foundation
CSPA Scholarship Department
1022 G Street
Sacramento, CA   95814-0817

793

MLA Doctoral Fellowship

AMOUNT: $2000   DEADLINE: December 1
FIELDS/MAJORS: Medical Librarianship

Fellowship for doctoral candidates in medical librarianship. Supports research or travel. Write to the address below for details.

Medical Library Association/Institute for Scientific Information
Professional Development Department
6 N. Michigan Avenue, Suite 300
Chicago, IL   60602

794

MLA Scholarship

AMOUNT: Maximum: $2000
DEADLINE: December 1
FIELDS/MAJORS: Medical Library Science

Graduate scholarship for students entering graduate school in medical librarianship or have at least half of the requirements to complete during the year following the granting of the scholarship. Must be studying in an ALA accredited school. Grants support research, etc., into projects which will enhance the field of health science librarianship. Write to the address below for details.

Medical Library Association
Professional Development
6 N. Michigan Avenue, Suite 300
Chicago, IL   60602

795

MLS Alumni Scholarship

AMOUNT: $500   DEADLINE: None Specified
FIELDS/MAJORS: Liberal Studies

Scholarships are available at the University of Oklahoma, Norman for full-time Master of Liberal Studies majors. Write to the address below for information.

University of Oklahoma, Norman
Dean, College of Liberal Studies
Room 226, OCCE
Norman, OK   73019

796

MLS Scholarship for Minority Students

AMOUNT: $2000   DEADLINE: December 1
FIELDS/MAJORS: Medical Librarianship

Scholarship for minority students entering or continuing graduate school in Health Science Librarianship. Must be studying in an ALA-accredited school. Write to the address below for details.

Medical Library Association
Program Services
6 N. Michigan Avenue, Suite 300
Chicago, IL   60602

797

Monticello College Foundation Fellowship for Women

AMOUNT: $12000   DEADLINE: January 20
FIELDS/MAJORS: History (Western and American), Women's Studies, Literature

Open to women with Ph.D. degrees. Preference will be given to applicants who are particularly concerned with the study of women, but study may be proposed in any field appropriate to Newberry's Collections. Must be a U.S. citizen. Fellowship is for six months work in residence at the Newberry Library. Write to the address below for complete details.

Newberry Library
Committee on Awards
60 W. Walton Street
Chicago, IL   60610

798

Morrison Center MSW Minority Scholarship

AMOUNT: $6000   DEADLINE: March 1
FIELDS/MAJORS: Social Work

Award for a graduate student in social work. Requires demonstrated interest and commitment to providing mental health services for children, youth, and families. Applicant must be in the MSW program and be a minority student entering their second year of field placement. One award offered annually. Contact the Graduate School of Social Work for more information.

Portland State University
Graduate School of Social Work
300 University Center Building
Portland, OR   97207

799

Munich Fellowships

AMOUNT: None Specified   DEADLINE: April 1
FIELDS/MAJORS: All Areas of Study

Fellowships are available for Wayne State graduate students who have written and oral competence in the German language to study for ten months at the University of Munich. Applicants must be U.S. citizens. Write to the address below for further details.

Wayne State University
Graduate School
Office of the Dean
Detroit, MI   48202

800

Muscular Dystrophy Association Research Fellowship Program

AMOUNT: None Specified   DEADLINE: January 10
FIELDS/MAJORS: Medical Research, Neurology

Postdoctoral research fellowships for investigators (in U.S.A. or abroad) who hold a Ph.D., M.D., or equivalent. Most grants are for two years. Special consideration given to young investigators. Write to the address below for complete details.

Muscular Dystrophy Association, Inc.
Karen Mashburn, Grants Program Manager
3300 E. Sunrise Drive
Tucson, AZ   85718

801

Music Scholarships

AMOUNT: None Specified
DEADLINE: None Specified
FIELDS/MAJORS: Music

Scholarships are available at the Catholic University of America for students studying music. Includes the John Paul Music Scholarship, the David Burchuk Memorial Scholarship, the Clifford E. Brown Scholarship, the William Masselos Scholarship, and the Benjamin T. Rome Endowment Scholarship. Individual award requirements may vary. For graduate study. Contact the financial aid office at the address below for details.

Catholic University of America
Office of Admissions and Financial Aid
Washington, DC   20064

802

Myasthenia Gravis Foundation Fellowships

AMOUNT: None Specified   DEADLINE: November 1
FIELDS/MAJORS: Neuromuscular Medicine

Fellowships are available for postdoctoral scholars involved in clinical research related to Myasthenia Gravis (MG). Write to the address below for information.

Myasthenia Gravis Foundation of America
Fellowship Program
222 S. Riverside Plaza, Suite 1540
Chicago, IL   60606

803
Myasthenia Gravis Foundation Nurses Research Fellowship

AMOUNT: None Specified   DEADLINE: February 1
FIELDS/MAJORS: Research Nursing

Award for currently licensed or registered professional nurses who are interested in research pertaining to problems faced by Myasthenia Gravis patients. Must be U.S. or Canadian citizens or permanent residents. Write to the address below for more information.

Myasthenia Gravis Foundation of America
222 S. Riverside Plaza
Suite 1540
Chicago, IL   60606

804
Myra Levick Scholarship Fund

AMOUNT: None Specified
DEADLINE: June 15
FIELDS/MAJORS: Art Therapy

Scholarships for graduate students who have demonstrated academic excellence and are in an AATA approved art therapy program. Applicants must demonstrate financial need and have a minimum undergraduate GPA of 3.0. Write to the address below for complete details.

American Art Therapy Association, Inc.
Scholarship Committee
1202 Allanson Road
Mundelein, IL   60060

805
NAACP Willems Scholarship—Graduate

AMOUNT: $3000   DEADLINE: April 30
FIELDS/MAJORS: Engineering, Chemistry, Physics, Computer Science, Mathematics

Applicants must be an graduate students who are members of the NAACP with at least a GPA of 3.0. Renewable. Write to the address below for details and include the scholarship name on the envelope.

NAACP Special Contribution Fund
Education Department
4805 Mount Hope Drive
Baltimore, MD   21215

806
NABWA Scholarships

AMOUNT: $5000–$10000
DEADLINE: February 15
FIELDS/MAJORS: Law

Scholarships for female minority law students in their first or second year of law school or those in their third year of a four-year program. Four to six awards offered annually. Write to the address below for information and an application.

National Association of Black Women Attorneys
Office of the President, Mabel D. Haden
3711 Macomb Street, NW
Washington, DC   20016

807
NASA Earth Science Graduate Student Research Program

AMOUNT: None Specified   DEADLINE: March 12
FIELDS/MAJORS: Earth Related Sciences (Geology, Meteorology, Hydrology, etc.)

Fellowships for students enrolled full-time in a graduate program at a U.S. university and in a field supporting the study of earth as a system. Fifty awards per year. Additional information is available electronically via the internet at: http://www.hp.nasa.gov/office/MTPE/or via anonymous FTP at: ftp.hp.nasa.gov/pub/MTPE. Paper copies of information received online will only be available to those who do not have access to the Internet.

NASA Earth System Science Fellowship Program
Code YSP-44
Attn: Dr. Ghassem Asrar
Washington, DC   20546

808
National Alumni Fellowship

AMOUNT: $1000   DEADLINE: April 1
FIELDS/MAJORS: Home Economics/Related Fields

Applicants must be members of Kappa Omicron Nu and a master's candidate. Awards will be announced May 15. Write to the address below for details.

Kappa Omicron Nu Honor Society
4990 Northwind Drive, Suite 140
East Lansing, MI   48823

809
National Association of Social Workers Scholarship (Oregon Chapter)

AMOUNT: $1000   DEADLINE: March 1
FIELDS/MAJORS: Social Work

Award for a graduate student who will agree to attend metro district board meetings regularly and will be actively involved in a minimum of one targeted district project. One award offered annually. Contact the Graduate School of Social Work for more information.

Portland State University
Graduate School of Social Work
300 University Center Building
Portland, OR   97207

810

National Doctoral Fellowships in Business and Management

AMOUNT: $10000   DEADLINE: February 8
FIELDS/MAJORS: Business Administration

Scholarships are available at the University of Oklahoma, Norman for full-time Ph.D. candidates in business administration or management, who are citizens of the U.S. or Canada with a high GMAT and GPA. Write to the address below for information.

University of Oklahoma, Norman
College of Business Administration
307 W. Brooks
Norman, OK   73019

811

National Endowment for the Humanities Fellowships

AMOUNT: $30000   DEADLINE: December 15
FIELDS/MAJORS: Renaissance, 19th and 20th Century Literature, Colonial America

Awards for established postdoctoral level scholars pursuing scholarship in a field appropriate to the Huntington's collection. Contact the address below for further information.

Huntington Library, Art Collections and Botanical Gardens
Robert C. Ritchie, Director of Research
1151 Oxford Road
San Marion, CA   91108

812

National Endowment for the Humanities Fellowships

AMOUNT: Maximum: $30000   DEADLINE: January 20
FIELDS/MAJORS: History, Humanities, Linguistics

Six- to eleven-month fellowships are available for postdoctoral research in any subject relevant to the library materials. Applicants must be citizens of the U.S. or foreign nationals who have been residents in the U.S. for at least three years. Preference is given to applicants who have not held major fellowships or grants in the previous three years. Write to the address below for details.

Newberry Library
Committee on Awards
60 W. Walton Street
Chicago, IL   60610

813

National Health Service Corps Loan Repayment Program

AMOUNT: None Specified   DEADLINE: None Specified
FIELDS/MAJORS: Medicine, Social Work, Nursing, Dentistry, Psychology, Family Therapy

Loan repayment program for fully-trained medical personnel in primary care to work in a priority shortage area for at least two years. Applicants must be U.S. citizens with a valid, unrestricted state license. Program includes a competitive salary, a percentage of loans repaid and a stipend. Must have completed one year of medical school or training. Write to the address below for more information or call 800-221-9393.

National Health Service Corps
2070 Chain Bridge Road, #450
Vienna, VA   22182

814

National Health Service Corps Scholarship Program

AMOUNT: None Specified   DEADLINE: None Specified
FIELDS/MAJORS: Medicine, Osteopathy, Nursing, Medical Assisting

Scholarship program for students in one of the areas listed above. For each year of support, recipients are obligated to serve one year in full-time clinical practice of their profession, or work for the National Health Service Corps, a component of the U.S. Public Health Service. Assignments will be in eligible health shortage manpower areas in the U.S. Applicants must be U.S. citizens who have completed one year of medical school. Write to the address below for more information.

National Health Service Corps
Scholarship Program
2070 Chain Bridge Road, #450
Vienna, VA   22182

815

National Museum of American Art Intern Programs

AMOUNT: None Specified   DEADLINE: March 1
FIELDS/MAJORS: Art History, American Studies, Studio Art

Internships for graduate students seeking degrees in the above areas of study. Opportunity exists to earn course credits during internship. Write to the address below for details.

Smithsonian Institution—National Museum of American Art
Intern Program Officer
Research and Scholars Center
Washington, DC   20560

816

National Osteopathic Foundation Scholarships and Loan Fund

AMOUNT: $400–$2000   DEADLINE: None Specified
FIELDS/MAJORS: Osteopathic Medicine

Open to third- or fourth-year medical students at an osteopathic college. Includes the McCaughan Scholarship, the William B. Strong Scholarship, and the Avallone Scholarship. Information should be available at the financial aid office of your school. If not, write to the address below for details.

National Osteopathic Foundation
5775-G Peachtree-Dunwoody Road
Suite 500
Atlanta, GA   30342

817
National Potato Council Auxiliary Scholarship

AMOUNT: $1500   DEADLINE: April 1
FIELDS/MAJORS: Any Field Related to the Potato Industry

Fellowships are available for graduate students enrolled in any field pursuing advanced studies that will enhance the potato industry, such as agriculture, agronomy, crop and soil sciences, entomology, food sciences, horticulture, and plant pathology. Write to the address below for information.

National Potato Council
Ms. Kathy Polatis
174 S. 1075 W.
Blackfoot, ID   83221

818
National Restaurant Association Teacher Work-Study Grants

AMOUNT: $3000   DEADLINE: February 15
FIELDS/MAJORS: Foodservice, Hospitality

Awards available to foodservice/hospitality educators and administrators who wish to add hands-on work experience to gain a better understanding of day-to-day operations. Must currently be a full-time high school or college educator or administrator of a foodservice/hospitality program. Consulting work is not eligible for this program. Eight awards offered annually. Contact the address below for further information.

National Restaurant Association Educational Foundation
250 S. Wacker Drive #1400
Chicago, IL   60606

819
National Science Foundation Minority Graduate Research Fellowships

AMOUNT: Maximum: $24500
DEADLINE: November 6
FIELDS/MAJORS: Science, Mathematics, Engineering

Open to minorities who are U.S. citizens or permanent residents for graduate study leading to research based master's or doctoral degrees in the fields listed above. Based on all available documentation of ability, including academic records, recommendations regarding the applicant's qualifications, and GRE scores. Fellowships include a stipend of $15000 for twelve-month tenure and a cost of education allowance or $9500 per tenure year. Contact the address below for further information.

National Science Foundation
Oak Ridge Associated Universities
PO Box 3010
Oak Ridge, TN   37831

820
National Society to Prevent Blindness Grants-in-Aid

AMOUNT: $1000–$12000   DEADLINE: March 1
FIELDS/MAJORS: Ophthalmology

Grants are for the funding of studies that have limited or no research funding. They are used to help defray the costs of personnel, equipment, and supplies. Write to the address below for details.

Fight for Sight Research Division
National Society to Prevent Blindness
500 E. Remington Road
Schaumburg, IL   60173

821
National Society to Prevent Blindness Postdoctoral Research Fellowship

AMOUNT: $28000   DEADLINE: March 1
FIELDS/MAJORS: Ophthalmology

Research fellowship for basic or clinical work at the early postdoctoral stage in ophthalmology, vision, or related sciences. Write to the address below for details.

Fight for Sight Research Division
National Society to Prevent Blindness
500 E. Remington Road
Schaumburg, IL   60173

822
National Wool Growers Memorial Fellowship

AMOUNT: $2500   DEADLINE: June 1
FIELDS/MAJORS: Sheep Industry

Fellowships are available for graduate students enrolled in sheep-related programs who wish to pursue a career in the sheep industry. Write to the address below for information.

American Sheep Industry Association
Attn: Memorial Fellowship
6911 South Yosemite
Englewood, CO   80112

823
NAWE Women's Research Awards

AMOUNT: $750   DEADLINE: October 1
FIELDS/MAJORS: Women's Studies

Supports research on any topic about the education, personal, and professional development of women and girls. Awards for graduate students and for persons at any career/professional level. Membership not required. Write to the address below for details. Please be certain to enclose a SASE with your request for information.

National Association for Women in Education
Anna Roman-Koller, Ph.D.
Dept. of Pathology, 701 Scaife Hall
Pittsburgh, PA   15261

824 NCAR Graduate Research Assistantships

AMOUNT: $15695   DEADLINE: July 1
FIELDS/MAJORS: Atmospheric Sciences, Related Area

This program is designed to foster cooperative research between NCAR and academic institutions by providing support for doctoral candidates who are willing to work on their thesis in cooperation with an NCAR program. U.S. or foreign applicants. Three to four awards are offered annually. Tenure usually not more than two years. Write to Barbara McDonald, Coordinator, at the address below for details.

National Center for Atmospheric Research
Advanced Study Program
PO Box 3000
Boulder, CO   80307

825 NCTE Grants-in-Aid

AMOUNT: Maximum: $12500
DEADLINE: February 15
FIELDS/MAJORS: English/Education

The grant program is for research in the field of English/reading education and is open to graduate students and educators. Must be member of NCTE. Write to the address below for details.

National Council of Teachers of English Research Foundation
Project Assistant
1111 W. Kenyon Road
Urbana, IL   61801

826 NDSEG Fellowships

AMOUNT: $17000–$19000
DEADLINE: January 15
FIELDS/MAJORS: Mathematics, Engineering, Physics, Marine and Biological Sciences

Research fellowships are available for students at the beginning of their graduate studies in one of the areas listed above. Applicants must be U.S. citizens. Minority, handicapped, and female candidates are encouraged to apply. Write to the address below for information.

National Defense Science and Engineering Fellowship Program
Dr. George Outterson
200 Park Drive, Suite 211, PO Box 13444
Research Triangle, NC   27709

827 Near and Middle Eastern Fellowships

AMOUNT: None Specified
DEADLINE: November 1
FIELDS/MAJORS: Middle Eastern Studies

Fellowships are available for scholars enrolled in a doctoral program. Must have completed all the requirements except for the dissertation. Research to be done through training and study in the Middle East (defined as North Africa, Middle East, Afghanistan, and Turkey). Must be a U.S. citizen or permanent resident. Write to the address below for information.

Social Science Research Council
Fellowships and Grants
605 Third Avenue
New York, NY   10158

828 NEH Fellowship in Classical and Byzantine Studies

AMOUNT: Maximum: $30000   DEADLINE: November 15
FIELDS/MAJORS: Classical and Byzantine Studies

Awards are available for postdoctoral scholars in the fields of classical and Byzantine studies. Must be a U.S. citizen or permanent resident. Write to the address below for more information.

American School of Classical Studies at Athens
Committee on Admissions and Fellowships
6-8 Charlton Street
Princeton, NJ   08540

829 New Initiatives Grant

AMOUNT: $3000   DEADLINE: February 15
FIELDS/MAJORS: Home Economics/Related Fields

Applicants must be Kappa Omicron Nu members. Awarded annually from the Kappa Omicron Nu New Initiatives Fund. Awards announced April 15. Write to the address below for details.

Kappa Omicron Nu Honor Society
4990 Northwind Drive, Suite 140
East Lansing, MI   48823

830 New Jersey Medical Society Medical Student Loans

AMOUNT: None Specified   DEADLINE: None Specified
FIELDS/MAJORS: Medicine

Loans at 7% interest for medical students. Must be U.S. citizens and residents of New Jersey for at least five years. Must be (or become) member of MSNJ-student association and in the third or fourth year of medical school. Repayment begins two years after graduation from medical school. Write to the chairman of the committee on medical student loan fund at the address below for details.

Medical Society of New Jersey
Committee on Medical Student Loan Fund
Two Princess Road
Lawrenceville, NJ   08648

831 New Jersey Osteopathic Education Foundation Scholarships

AMOUNT: None Specified   DEADLINE: April 30
FIELDS/MAJORS: Osteopathic Medicine

Scholarships for New Jersey residents entering their first year of study at an osteopathic college. Must have an undergraduate GPA of at least 3.0. Based on grades, need, motivation, and professional promise. Recipients must agree to practice in New Jersey for two years after education and training is complete. Approximately five scholarships are awarded each year. Application forms may be obtained from your medical advisor or by writing to the administrator at the address below.

New Jersey Osteopathic Education Foundation
One Distribution Way
Monmouth Junction, NJ   08852

832
New Mexico Orthopedic Shoe Shop Scholarship

AMOUNT: None Specified   DEADLINE: March 1
FIELDS/MAJORS: Orthopedic Medicine

Awards are available at the University of New Mexico for seniors in medical school who plan to specialize in orthopedic surgery. Write to the address below for more information.

University of New Mexico, Albuquerque
Office of Financial Aid
Albuquerque, NM   87131

833
New Mexico Space Grant Graduate Fellowship

AMOUNT: $4000   DEADLINE: March 1
FIELDS/MAJORS: Astronomy, Biology, Chemistry, Physics, Computer and Earth Science, Math

Up to $4000 awarded to graduate students in the college of engineering or in the college of arts and sciences majoring in astronomy, biology, chemistry, physics, computer science, earth science, or math. Students must have a cumulative GPA of 3.0 and be U.S. citizens. Preference will be given to women and minorities. Applications available from Financial Aid or the Space Grant Office.

New Mexico State University
Student Financial Aid Office
Box 30001, Dept. 5100
Las Cruces, NM   88003

834
Nicholas and Elizabeth Melnick Instructional Leadership Scholarship

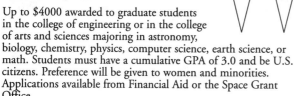

AMOUNT: None Specified   DEADLINE: February 1
FIELDS/MAJORS: Education Administration

Awards for students who have been admitted to the education administration graduate program in the school of education. Preference will be given to minority students. Must be a resident of Kentucky. Contact the school of education for further information.

Northern Kentucky University
Financial Aid Office—Nunn Drive
Administrative Center, #416
Highland Heights, KY   41099

835
Nicholas Bauer Scholarship

AMOUNT: None Specified   DEADLINE: February 1
FIELDS/MAJORS: Law

Awards for law students who demonstrate academic promise. Contact the Assistant Dean, Chase College of Law, for further information.

Northern Kentucky University
Chase College of Law
Office of Admissions
Highland Heights, KY   41099

836
NIDR Individual Fellows

AMOUNT: $19608–$32300   DEADLINE: April 5
FIELDS/MAJORS: Dental Research

Postdoctoral fellowship provides health scientists an opportunity to receive full-time research training in areas that reflect the national need for biomedical and behavioral research. Must have received a D.D.S./M.D. or Ph.D. Must be U.S. citizens or legal residents. Must arrange to work with a sponsor who is affiliated with (and has the staff and facilities needed for) the proposed training. Write for complete details.

National Institute of Dental Research
Special Asst. for Manpower Development
Westwood Building, Room 510
Bethesda, MD   20205

837
NIDR Short-Term Training for Dental Research

AMOUNT: None Specified   DEADLINE: February 1
FIELDS/MAJORS: Dental Research

Award is designed to interest dental students at an early stage in their development in pursuing a career in biomedical research. Apply through institution. Must be U.S. citizens. Institutions and individuals seeking additional information on short-term training programs and a list of participating dental schools should contact address below.

National Institute of Dental Research
Special Asst. for Manpower Development
Westwood Building, Room 510
Bethesda, MD   20205

838
NIGMS Predoctoral Fellowships

AMOUNT: Maximum: $1500
DEADLINE: November 15
FIELDS/MAJORS: Medical Science

Awards are available for minority graduate students working toward their Ph.D. in medical science. Must be U.S. citizens. Write to the address below for additional information.

National Institute of General Medical Sciences
National Institute of Health
45 Center Drive MSC 6200, Room 2AS.43
Bethesda, MD   20892

839
NJLA Member, George M. Lamonte and Sarah B. Askew Scholarships

AMOUNT: $500–$4000   DEADLINE: February 15
FIELDS/MAJORS: Library Science

Scholarships for New Jersey residents admitted to an ALA-accredited, graduate level library science program. Financial need is required. Three separate awards offered. Write to the address below for further information.

New Jersey Library Association
Scholarship Committee, Linda Defelice
1400 Tanyard Road
Sewell, NJ   08080

840
Noble Foundation Scholarships

AMOUNT: $1000–$5000   DEADLINE: February 8
FIELDS/MAJORS: Business Administration, Economics

Scholarships are available at the University of Oklahoma, Norman for full-time M.B.A. and Ph.D. candidates in business administration, who are U.S. citizens or permanent residents. Must have at least 85% on the GMAT. Write to the address below for information.

University of Oklahoma, Norman
College of Business Administration
307 W. Brooks
Norman, OK   73019

841
Non-Profit Sector Research Fund Grants

AMOUNT: $20000–$50000   DEADLINE: January 2
FIELDS/MAJORS: Public Policy, Political Science

Grants are available to encourage graduate students and scholars in the early stages of their careers to conduct research to expand understanding of non-profit activities, including philanthropy and its underlying values. For dissertation and advanced research. Write to the address below for information.

Aspen Institute
Nonprofit Sector Research Fund
1333 New Hampshire Avenue, Suite 1070
Washington, DC   20036

842
Non-Resident Tuition Waiver Scholarships for Graduate Assistants

AMOUNT: $1000   DEADLINE: March 1
FIELDS/MAJORS: All Areas of Study

Scholarships are available at the University of Oklahoma, Norman for full-time students, who are residents of a state other than Oklahoma, and are graduate assistants or research assistants. Write to the address below for information.

University of Oklahoma, Norman
Office of Financial Aid
Norman, OK   73019

843
Non-Resident Tuition Waiver Scholarships for Minority Students

AMOUNT: $1000   DEADLINE: March 1
FIELDS/MAJORS: All Areas of Study

Scholarships are available at the University of Oklahoma, Norman for full-time graduate minority students, who are residents of a state other than Oklahoma. Write to the address below for information.

University of Oklahoma, Norman
Graduate College
1000 Asp Avenue, Room 313
Norman, OK   73019

844
Nora M. and Patrick J. Healy Scholarship Fund

AMOUNT: None Specified   DEADLINE: January 2
FIELDS/MAJORS: Arts and Sciences, Social Work, Social Research

Awards open to graduate students in any of the above fields. Contact the address below for further information.

Bryn Mawr Graduate School of Arts and Sciences
101 N. Merion Avenue
Bryn Mawr, PA   19010

845
North American Loon Fund Grants

AMOUNT: None Specified   DEADLINE: December 15
FIELDS/MAJORS: Ornithology—Loon Research

Grants to support specific research, management, and educational projects which may yield results useful to the NALF in furtherance of its goals and which will promote and enhance the conservation and management of loons in North America. Write to the address below for more information.

North American Loon Fund
Grant Committee
6 Lily Pond Road
Gilford, NH   03246

846
North American Student Fund

AMOUNT: None Specified
DEADLINE: March 1
FIELDS/MAJORS: Medicine

Awards are available at the University of New Mexico for Native American students who are unable to finance his or her own education. Write to the address below for more information.

University of New Mexico, Albuquerque
Office of Financial Aid
Albuquerque, NM   87131

847
North Dakota Physician Loan Repayment Program

AMOUNT: Maximum: $10000
DEADLINE: None Specified
FIELDS/MAJORS: Medicine

This program offers repayment of student loans for physicians and psychiatrists who agree to practice in specialized areas in North Dakota with limited access to medical care. Up to $10000 per year for four years of student loan indebtedness may be canceled. Write to the address listed for information.

North Dakota Primary Care Cooperative—Center for Rural Health
Mary Amundson, Director
PO Box 9037
Grand Forks, ND   58202

848
Novartis Pharmaceuticals/ Oncology Foundation Post-Master's Awards

AMOUNT: $3000   DEADLINE: February 1
FIELDS/MAJORS: Oncology Nursing

Awards available to students enrolled in, or applying to, a post-master's nurse practitioner certificate bearing program in an NLN-accredited school of nursing. Applicants must be currently licensed registered nurses, have a master's degree and a commitment to oncology nursing. Contact the address listed for further information about both awards.

Oncology Nursing Foundation
501 Holiday Drive
Pittsburgh, PA   15220

849
NSF Graduate Research Fellowships

AMOUNT: Maximum: $24500
DEADLINE: November 6
FIELDS/MAJORS: Mathematics, Science, Engineering

Fellowships for graduate study leading to research based master's or doctoral degrees in the fields listed above. Applicants must be U.S. citizens or permanent residents. Based on all available documentation of ability, including academic records, recommendations regarding the applicant's qualifications, and GRE scores. Fellowships include a stipend of $15000 for twelve-month tenure and a cost of education allowance of $9500 per tenure year. Write to the address listed for details. Information is also available from departmental offices at many colleges and universities.

National Science Foundation
Oak Ridge Associated Universities
PO Box 3010
Oak Ridge, TN   37831

850
Nursing Economics Foundation Scholarships

AMOUNT: $5000   DEADLINE: May 1
FIELDS/MAJORS: Nursing

Scholarships are available to master's and doctoral candidates in nursing science, with an emphasis on nursing administration or management. Write to the address below for complete details.

Nursing Economics Foundation
East Holly Avenue, Box 56
Pitman, NJ   08701

851
Nursing Student Assistant Program

AMOUNT: $2000–$4000   DEADLINE: July 10
FIELDS/MAJORS: Nursing

Assistantships are available at the University of Oklahoma, Norman for full-time graduate nursing students, who are U.S. citizens and Oklahoma residents. Contact the physician commission manpower training at 405-271-5848 for more details.

University of Oklahoma, Norman
College of Nursing
PO Box 26901
Oklahoma City, OK   73190

852
NWSA Graduate Scholarship in Lesbian Studies

AMOUNT: $500   DEADLINE: February 15
FIELDS/MAJORS: Women's Studies—Lesbian Studies

Scholarship for graduate student researching for master's thesis or Ph.D. dissertation. Write to the address below for information and an application.

National Women's Studies Association
University of Maryland
7100 Baltimore Avenue, Suite 301
College Park, MD   20740

853
NWSA Scholarship in Jewish Women's Studies

AMOUNT: $500   DEADLINE: February 15
FIELDS/MAJORS: Jewish Women's Studies

Scholarship for graduate student whose area is Jewish women's studies. Write to the address below for details.

National Women's Studies Association
University of Maryland
7100 Baltimore Avenue, Suite 301
College Park, MD   20740

854
O.H. Ammann Fellowship

AMOUNT: $5000   DEADLINE: February 20
FIELDS/MAJORS: Structural Engineering

Applicant must be a national ASCE member in good standing in any grade. Award is used for purposes of encouraging the creation of new knowledge in the field of structural design and construction. Write to the address below for complete details.

American Society of Civil Engineers
Student Services Department
1801 Alexander Bell Drive
Reston, VA   20191

855 Oklahoma Garden Club Scholarship

AMOUNT: $300–$500 **DEADLINE:** April 15
FIELDS/MAJORS: Landscape Architecture

Scholarships are available at the University of Oklahoma, Norman for graduate students in landscape architecture who demonstrate financial need. Write to the address below for information.

University of Oklahoma, Norman
Landscape Architecture
Gould Hall #150
Norman, OK 73019

856 Oklahoma Rural Scholarship

AMOUNT: None Specified **DEADLINE:** March 1
FIELDS/MAJORS: Medicine

Scholarships are available at the University of Oklahoma for medical students who declare an intent to practice in a rural area of Oklahoma. Write to the address below for information.

University of Oklahoma, Norman
Director, Office of Financial Aid
OUHSC, PO Box 73190
Oklahoma City, OK 73190

857 Olfactory Research Fund

AMOUNT: None Specified **DEADLINE:** January 15
FIELDS/MAJORS: Otolaryngology

Fund is to support research that seeks to integrate the study of olfaction with current issues in developmental, perceptual, social, and cognitive psychology and related disciplines. For those who are currently specializing in olfaction or those who wish to redirect their research. Applicant must possess a doctoral degree in a related field. Contact the address below for additional information.

Olfactory Research Fund, Ltd.
145 E. 32nd Street
New York, NY 10016

858 Olin Fellowships

AMOUNT: $1000–$3000 **DEADLINE:** March 15
FIELDS/MAJORS: Fisheries, Marine Biology, and Related Areas

ASF Fellowships are offered annually to individuals seeking to improve their knowledge or skills in advanced fields related to Atlantic salmon (biology, management, or conservation). For use at any accredited university, research laboratory, or active management program. Must be U.S. or Canadian citizen. Application forms may be obtained from the Atlantic Salmon Federation at the address below or from Box 429, St. Andrews, N.B., E0G 2X0, Canada.

Atlantic Salmon Federation
PO Box 807
Calais, ME 04619

859 Olivia James Traveling Fellowship

AMOUNT: $15000 **DEADLINE:** November 1
FIELDS/MAJORS: Classics, Sculpture, Architecture, Archaeology, and History

Competition is open to students who are citizens or permanent residents of the United States. The award is to be used for travel and study in: Greece, the Aegean Islands, Sicily, Southern Italy, Asia Minor, or Mesopotamia. Preference will be given to individuals engaged in dissertation research or to recent recipients of the Ph.D. Write to the address below for details.

Archaeological Institute of America
Boston University
656 Beacon Street, 4th Floor
Boston, MA 02215

860 Olympus Advanced Endoscopic Training Scholarship

AMOUNT: $40000 **DEADLINE:** September 3
FIELDS/MAJORS: Gastroenterology, Endoscopic Procedures

Candidates must have completed (or currently completing) a minimum of eighteen months of formal accredited gastroenterology training or equivalent endoscopic training within an accredited surgical training program. The physician should be committed to assuming a faculty position at an academic center. Two awards are given annually. Contact the address below for further information or websites: http://www.gastro.org; http://www.asge.org; or http://hepar-sfgh.ucsf.edu.

American Digestive Health Foundation
Ms. Irene Kuo
7910 Woodmont Avenue, 7th Floor
Bethesda, MD 20814

861 Omicron Nu Research Fellowship

AMOUNT: $2000 **DEADLINE:** January 15
FIELDS/MAJORS: Home Economics/Related Fields

Applicants must be members of Kappa Omicron Nu and enrolled in a Ph.D. program in Home Economics. Awards will be announced April 1. Write to the address below for details.

Kappa Omicron Nu Honor Society
4990 Northwind Drive, Suite 140
East Lansing, MI 48823

862 Oncological Research Awards

AMOUNT: None Specified **DEADLINE:** March 1
FIELDS/MAJORS: Oncology

The American Cancer Society provides support for junior investigators as well as established researchers into areas related to cancer. Both basic and applied research is supported. Must hold Ph.D. at the time application for funding is made. Write to the address below or call 404-329-7558 for details and policies.

American Cancer Society, Inc.
Extramural Grants and Awards
1599 Clifton Road, NE
Atlanta, GA   30329

863
Oncology Nursing Certification Corporation Master's Scholarships

AMOUNT: $3000   DEADLINE: February 1
FIELDS/MAJORS: Oncology Nursing

Scholarships available to master's students in the field of oncology nursing. All applicants must be currently licensed registered nurses. For full-time or part-time studies at an NLN-accredited school of nursing. Write to the address listed for more information.

Oncology Nursing Foundation
501 Holiday Drive
Pittsburgh, PA   15220

864
Oncology Nursing Ethnic Minority Master's Scholarships

AMOUNT: $3000   DEADLINE: February 1
FIELDS/MAJORS: Oncology Nursing

Scholarships available to ethnic minority master's students enrolled in the field of oncology nursing. All applicants must be currently licensed registered nurses. For full-time or part-time students. Write to the address listed for more information.

Oncology Nursing Foundation
501 Holiday Drive
Pittsburgh, PA   15220

865
Oncology Nursing Foundation and Glaxo Wellcome Master's Scholarships

AMOUNT: $3000   DEADLINE: February 1
FIELDS/MAJORS: Oncology Nursing

Scholarships available to master's students in the field of oncology nursing. All applicants must be currently licensed registered nurses and currently enrolled, full- or part-time in a degree program in an NLN-accredited school of nursing. Write to the address listed for more information about both these awards.

Oncology Nursing Foundation
501 Holiday Drive
Pittsburgh, PA   15220

866
Opal Dancey Memorial Foundation

AMOUNT: $2500   DEADLINE: June 15
FIELDS/MAJORS: Theology

Grants awarded primarily in the Midwest. Preference given to McCormick, United, Garrett, Trinity, Asbury, and Methodist Theological School in Ohio. Given to students seeking a Master of Divinity degree only from accredited theological schools and seminaries. Renewable if recipients maintain satisfactory scholastic work. Applications sent January through May 31. Write to the address below for more information.

Opal Dancey Memorial Foundation
Rev. Gary R. Imms, Chairman
45 South Street
Croswell, MI   48422

867
Oregon Laurels Graduate Tuition Remission Program

AMOUNT: None Specified   DEADLINE: April 15
FIELDS/MAJORS: All Areas of Study

Merit-based awards are available at Portland State University for graduate students. Preference is given to Oregon residents. Contact the Office of Graduate Studies and Research for more information.

Portland State University
Office of Graduate Studies and Research
105 Neuberger Hall
Portland, OR   97207

868
Oregon Society for Hospital Social Work: Outstanding MSW Graduate

AMOUNT: $200   DEADLINE: April 15
FIELDS/MAJORS: Social Work

Cash award and plate with recipient's name honors outstanding academic and internship performance in the field of medical social work. One award offered annually. Contact the graduate school of social work for more information.

Portland State University
Graduate School of Social Work
300 University Center Building
Portland, OR   97207

869
Oregon Sports Lottery Graduate Scholarships Program

AMOUNT: None Specified   DEADLINE: April 15
FIELDS/MAJORS: All Areas of Study

Awards are available at Portland State University for full-time graduate students. Preference is given to doctoral students. Application is made by department nomination only. Contact the Office of Graduate Studies and Research for more information.

Portland State University
Office of Graduate Studies and Research
105 Neuberger Hall
Portland, OR   97207

870
Orentreich Foundation for the Advancement of Science, Inc.

AMOUNT: None Specified DEADLINE: None Specified
FIELDS/MAJORS: Science, Medicine

For recipients at or above post-graduate level in science or medicine at accredited universities or research institutions in the U.S. Write to the address below for more information.

Orentreich Foundation for the Advancement of Science, Inc.
Biomedical Research Station
Rd 2 Box 375, 855 Route 301
Cold Spring-on-Hudson, NY 10516

871
Orthopedic Research and Education Career Development Awards

AMOUNT: $75000 DEADLINE: August 1
FIELDS/MAJORS: Medicine: Orthopedics

Grants to encourage commitment to scientific research in orthopedic surgery. Must have completed residency within five years of application. Must have demonstrated sustained interest in research and clinical training. Write to the address below for details.

Orthopedic Research and Education Foundation
6300 N. River Road, Suite 700
Rosemont, IL 60018

872
Orthopedic Research and Education Foundation Grants

AMOUNT: $50000 DEADLINE: August 1
FIELDS/MAJORS: Medicine: Orthopedics

Grants to support and encourage young investigators by providing seed money and start up funding. Awards may be made for one or two years. Principal or co-principal must be an orthopedic surgeon working at an institution in the U.S. or Canada. Write to the address below for further information.

Orthopedic Research and Education Foundation
6300 N. River Road, Suite 700
Rosemont, IL 60018

873
Orthopedic Research and Education Foundation Resident Research Awards

AMOUNT: $15000 DEADLINE: May 31
FIELDS/MAJORS: Medicine: Orthopedics

Grants for one year are offered to residents in approved orthopedic programs to encourage the development of research interests. These grants provide funds for supplies and expenses but not for a resident's salary. Write to Katherine Walker, Director of Grants, at the address below for details.

Orthopedic Research and Education Foundation
6300 N. River Road, Suite 700
Rosemont, IL 60018

874
Oscar W. Rittenhouse Memorial Scholarship

AMOUNT: Maximum: $2500 DEADLINE: June 15
FIELDS/MAJORS: Law

Scholarship for New Jersey residents who are enrolled in or accepted into law school and who have an interest in pursuing a career in law enforcement. One-year scholarship grant. Persons may reapply in succeeding years. Write to the address below for details.

County Prosecutors Association of New Jersey Foundation
Prosecutors Supervisory Section
25 Market Street, CN-085
Trenton, NJ 08625

875
Otological Research Fellowships

AMOUNT: Maximum: $13500 DEADLINE: March 15
FIELDS/MAJORS: Otological Research

Fellowships supporting otological research by third-year medical students (or students in other doctoral programs related to otology (physiology, anatomy, pharmacology, etc.). Requires a leave of absence from studies. Write to the address below for additional information.

Deafness Research Foundation
The Deafness Research Foundation
9 East 38th Street
New York, NY 10016

876
Otto M. Stanfield Legal Scholarship

AMOUNT: None Specified
DEADLINE: February 15
FIELDS/MAJORS: Law

Open to active Unitarian Universalists who are entering law school and have financial need. Write to the address below for details.

Unitarian Universalist Association
Publication Department
25 Beacon Street
Boston, MA 02108

877
OU College of Law General Scholarships

AMOUNT: $250–$1200 DEADLINE: September 1
FIELDS/MAJORS: Law

Nineteen to twenty-two scholarships offered annually to full-time law students. Includes the A.L. Jeffrey Municipal Law, Albert G. Kulp Memorial, Baker & Hoster, College of Law Association, Dean's, George J. Fagin and the Judge W.A. and Mabel Woodruff scholarships. Individual award requirements may vary. Write to the address below for information.

University of Oklahoma, Norman
Admissions and Records, Law Center
Room 22, 300 Timberdell Road
Norman, OK 73019

878
OU Graduate Music Scholarships

AMOUNT: $100–$3000   DEADLINE: None Specified
FIELDS/MAJORS: Music

Scholarships are available at the University of Oklahoma, Norman for full-time graduate music majors. Includes the Benton-Schmidt, Barbara Tuttle, Derdeyn Memorial, Marjorie Martin Caylor, Martha Boucher Memorial, graduate fee waivers, Opera Guild Awards, Rejto Memorial, and Ruth Moore Memminger Scholarships. Individual requirements will vary. Twenty-one awards annually. Write to the address below for information.

University of Oklahoma, Norman
Director, School of Music
560 Parrington Oval
Norman, OK   73019

879
Outcomes Research Training Award

AMOUNT: Maximum: $100000
DEADLINE: September 10
FIELDS/MAJORS: Gastroenterology Medicine

Applicants must be M.D.s who are committed to academic careers and who have completed the clinical training necessary for board eligibility in gastroenterology (twelve months) at an accredited North American institution. Write to the address below for more information or websites: http://www.gastro.org; http://www.asge.org; or http://hepar-sfgh.uscf.edu.

American Digestive Health Foundation
Ms. Irene Kuo
7910 Woodmont Avenue, 7th Floor
Bethesda, MD   20814

880
Outstanding Educator Award

AMOUNT: $5000   DEADLINE: November 1
FIELDS/MAJORS: Civil Engineering or Construction

Award for a full-time teaching faculty member of an ABET- or ACCE-approved construction or civil engineering program. Applicants must have at least five years teaching experience at the undergraduate level. Write to the address below for more information.

Associated General Contractors
1957 E Street, NW
Washington, DC   20006

881
Outstanding Graduate Student Awards

AMOUNT: $100   DEADLINE: None Specified
FIELDS/MAJORS: Sociology

Scholarships are available at the University of Oklahoma, Norman for full-time graduate students majoring in sociology. Write to the address below for information.

University of Oklahoma, Norman
Sociology Department
601 Elm, Room 903
Norman, OK   73019

882
Pan American Round Table II Endowed Scholarships

AMOUNT: None Specified   DEADLINE: March 1
FIELDS/MAJORS: Latin American Studies

Awards are available at the University of New Mexico for female students in a Latin American studies program. Applicant must exhibit financial need and be enrolled in one of the dual degree graduate programs. Must be a legal resident of New Mexico. Write to the address below for more information.

University of New Mexico
Latin American Studies Graduate Program
525 Buena Vista SE
Albuquerque, NM   87131

883
Parker B. Francis Fellowship Grants

AMOUNT: None Specified   DEADLINE: September 1
FIELDS/MAJORS: Medical Research—Pulmonary and Anesthesiology

Non-residential fellowships providing stipends and modest incidental expenses in support of qualified postdoctoral candidates performing fundamental research in Pulmonary Medicine or Anesthesiology at a U.S. or Canadian institution. Sponsorship by an established investigator required. Application is made on the candidates behalf by the director of the program within an institution. Write to the address below for details.

Francis Families Foundation
Ms. Linda K. French
800 W. 47th Street, #717
Kansas City, MO   64112

884
Patrick L. Altringer and Wayne and Frieda Steinke Scholarships

AMOUNT: None Specified   DEADLINE: April 15
FIELDS/MAJORS: Medicine

Awards for students enrolled in the School of Medicine who can demonstrate satisfactory academics and financial need. Contact the address below for further information or the financial aid office at your school's location.

University of North Dakota—School of Medicine
Sandra Elshaug, Financial Aid Office
PO Box 9037—501 N. Columbia Road
Grand Forks, ND   58202

885 Paul Cuffe Memorial Fellowship

AMOUNT: $2400   DEADLINE: None Specified
FIELDS/MAJORS: Naval History

Fellowships are available for scholars researching the participation of Native Americans and African-Americans in maritime activities, using the scholarly resources of New England. Write to the address below for information.

Munson Institute of American Maritime Studies
Director
Box 6000, Mystic Seaport Museum
Mystic, CT   06355

886 Paul Dannelley Public Relations Scholarship

AMOUNT: $250   DEADLINE: February 15
FIELDS/MAJORS: Public Relations

Scholarships are available at the University of Oklahoma, Norman for master level students in public relations. Write to the address below for information.

University of Oklahoma, Norman
School of Journalism and Mass Communications
860 Van Vleet Oval
Norman, OK   73019

887 Paul J. Vollmar Jr. Memorial Scholarship

AMOUNT: None Specified   DEADLINE: March 1
FIELDS/MAJORS: Piano Music

Awards at the University of New Mexico for graduate students majoring in piano music. Must have artistic ability and financial need. Contact the College of Music for more information.

University of New Mexico, Albuquerque
Office of Financial Aid
Albuquerque, NM   87131

888 Paul Vouras, Robert D. Hodgson, and Otis Paul Starkey Funds

AMOUNT: $500   DEADLINE: December 31
FIELDS/MAJORS: Geography

Provides financial assistance for dissertation research or dissertation preparation to candidates in the field of geography. Must have been a member of AAG for at least one year. All course requirements must be completed in the academic term following the approval of the grant. Request application form from Elizabeth Beetschen at the address below.

Association of American Geographers
AAG Dissertation Research Grants
1710 16th Street, NW
Washington, DC   20009

889 Paula Milner Scholarship

AMOUNT: None Specified   DEADLINE: December 15
FIELDS/MAJORS: Environmental Conservation

Scholarships are awarded to full-time graduate students pursuing a master's degree in the environmental conservation program. Contact the Department Head, Forestry and Wildlife Management, for more information.

University of Massachusetts, Amherst
Department of Forestry and Wildlife Mgmt
Amherst, MA   01003

890 Peace Scholar Dissertation Fellowships

AMOUNT: $14000   DEADLINE: November 17
FIELDS/MAJORS: Areas Related to International Peace and Conflict Management

Fellowships are available for doctoral candidates who have demonstrated a clear interest in issues of international peace and conflict management, who have completed all required work except the dissertation. Dissertation study must reflect a topic that advances the state of knowledge about international peace and conflict management. Write to the address listed for information.

U.S. Institute of Peace
Jennings Randolph Fellowship Program
1550 M Street, NW, Suite 700
Washington, DC   20005

891 Pedro Morell Memorial Scholarship

AMOUNT: None Specified   DEADLINE: March 1
FIELDS/MAJORS: Classical Guitar Music

Awards are made at the University of New Mexico for graduate students studying classical guitar music. If no graduate students are eligible, award may be given to a junior. Write to the address below for more information.

University of New Mexico, Albuquerque
Office of Financial Aid
Albuquerque, NM   87131

892 Pergamon-NWSA Graduate Scholarship in Women's Studies

AMOUNT: $500–$1000   DEADLINE: February 15
FIELDS/MAJORS: Women's Studies

Award available for a woman researching for a master's thesis or Ph.D. dissertation in women's studies. Preference will be given to NWSA members and to those whose research projects focus on "color" or "class." Two awards per year. Write to the address below for details.

National Women's Studies Association
7100 Baltimore Avenue, Suite 301
University of Maryland
College Park, MD   20740

893 Petroleum and Geological Engineering Fellowships

AMOUNT: $3000–$7000 DEADLINE: March 1
FIELDS/MAJORS: Petroleum and Geological Engineering

Scholarships are available at the University of Oklahoma, Norman for full-time graduate students in petroleum or geological engineering. Includes the Exxon Education, International Petroleum Exposition, O.H. and Ruth Verne Davis Reaugh, Phillips, Shell Companies, Texaco Foundation, and Union Pacific Fellowships. Individual requirements may vary. Seven to seventeen awards offered annually. Write to the address below for information.

University of Oklahoma, Norman
Petroleum and Geological Engineering
Room F301 Energy Center
Norman, OK   73019

894 Pharmacia and Upjohn Master's Scholarship

AMOUNT: $3000 DEADLINE: February 1
FIELDS/MAJORS: Oncology Nursing

Awards to students who are registered nurses with an interest in and commitment to oncology nursing. Must be enrolled in a graduate nursing degree program with an application to oncology nursing, in an NLN-accredited school of nursing. May be attending school full- or part-time. Contact the address listed for further information.

Oncology Nursing Foundation
501 Holiday Drive
Pittsburgh, PA   15220

895 Phillips Petroleum Scholarship

AMOUNT: $2500 DEADLINE: September 1
FIELDS/MAJORS: Law

Scholarship available at the University of Oklahoma, Norman for full-time, second-year female law students. Based on merit. One award offered annually. Individual award requirements will vary. Write to the address below for information.

University of Oklahoma, Norman
Admissions and Records, Law Center
Room 22, 300 Timberdell Road
Norman, OK   73019

896 Physician Loan Repayment Program

AMOUNT: Maximum: $20000
DEADLINE: None Specified
FIELDS/MAJORS: Medicine

This program offers repayment of student loans for physicians who agree to practice in specialized areas in Ohio with limited access to medical care. Up to $20000 per year for four years of student loan indebtedness may be canceled. Write to the address below for information.

Ohio Student Aid Commission
Customer Service
PO Box 16610
Columbus, OH   43216

897 Physio-Control Advanced Practice Scholarship

AMOUNT: Maximum: $2000 DEADLINE: June 1
FIELDS/MAJORS: Nursing

Open to nurses pursuing an advanced clinical practice degree to become a nurse practitioner or clinical nurse specialist. Preference given to nurses focusing on cardiac nursing, including cardiac resuscitation. Write to the address below for more information.

Emergency Nurses Association (ENA) Foundation Funding
   Program
216 Higgins Road
Park Ridge, IL   60068

898 Pi Gamma Mu Scholarship

AMOUNT: $1000–$2000
DEADLINE: January 30
FIELDS/MAJORS: Social Science, Sociology, Anthropology, Political Science, History

Open to Pi Gamma Mu members who are full-time graduate students with financial need. Letters of recommendation are required. Intended primarily for first year graduate study. Ten awards offered annually. Write to the address below for details.

Pi Gamma Mu International Honor Society in Social Science
Executive Director
1001 Millington, Suite B
Winfield, KS   67156

899 Pilot Club of Tulsa Scholarship

AMOUNT: None Specified
DEADLINE: March 1
FIELDS/MAJORS: Dentistry

Scholarships are available at the University of Oklahoma, Norman for full-time female graduate dentistry or dental hygiene students, who are in their fourth year of study. One award offered annually. Write to the address below for information.

University of Oklahoma, Norman
College of Dentistry
1001 Stanton L. Young Boulevard
Oklahoma City, OK   73190

900
Plenum Scholarship Program

AMOUNT: $1000   DEADLINE: October 31
FIELDS/MAJORS: Library and Information Science

Scholarships for members of the special libraries association who have worked in special libraries. For doctoral study. Preference is given to persons who display an aptitude for special library work. One award per year. Based on academic achievement, evidence of financial need, and dissertation topic approval. Write to the address below for details.

Special Libraries Association
SLA Scholarship Committee
1700 Eighteenth Street, NW
Washington, DC   20009

901
Polingaysi Qoyawayma Teaching Program

AMOUNT: None Specified
DEADLINE: None Specified
FIELDS/MAJORS: Math/Science Education

Scholarships for student members of the American Indian Science and Engineering Society. Must be able to prove tribal enrollment. For graduate studies toward teaching certificate. Program is designed to support teachers who will work in teaching math and sciences to Native American students. Write to the address below for details.

American Indian Science and Engineering Society
Scholarship Coordinator
5661 Airport Boulevard
Boulder, CO   80301-2339

902
Population Council Fellowships in the Social Sciences

AMOUNT: None Specified   DEADLINE: January 2
FIELDS/MAJORS: Population Studies and Related Fields

Doctoral, postdoctoral, and midcareer research fellowships in population studies. Doctoral applicants should have made considerable progress toward their Ph.D. or an equivalent degree. Selection criteria will stress academic excellence and prospective contribution to the population field. Nineteen to twenty-one awards per year. Write for complete details. Include a brief description of your academic qualifications and a description of your research plans.

Population Council
Manager, Fellowship Prog., Research Div.
One Dag Hammarskjold Plaza
New York, NY   10017

903
Post-Doctoral Fellowship

AMOUNT: $30000   DEADLINE: November 1
FIELDS/MAJORS: Early American History and Culture

Post-doctoral residential fellowship. Must meet requirements for Ph.D. before beginning fellowship (ABD). Must have potential for eventual publication. Residence is maintained at the College of William and Mary. Applicants may not have previously published a book. Ph.D. holders who have begun careers in the field are welcome to apply. Tenure is for two years. Includes appointment as Assistant Professor. Write to the address below for more information.

Institute of Early American History and Culture
Office of the Director
PO Box 8781
Williamsburg, VA   23187

904
Post-Doctoral Fellowships

AMOUNT: None Specified   DEADLINE: October 15
FIELDS/MAJORS: Humanities

Post-doctoral fellowships offered to junior and senior scholars. Tenable at the university. For research on some aspect of the humanities. Must have doctorate at the time of application. Some priority given to studies in fields of interest of senior researchers at the institute. Write to the address below for further information.

Institute for Research in the Humanities
1401 Observatory Drive/Old Observatory
University of Wisconsin, Madison
Madison, WI   53706

905
Post-Doctoral Research Fellowships and Grants

AMOUNT: Maximum: $20000
DEADLINE: September 30
FIELDS/MAJORS: Social Sciences and Humanities

Applicants must be Ph.D. scholars who provide evidence of degree, field of specialization, research proposal, and project duration. U.S. citizenship or legal residency required. ACLS supports research in the humanities and the humanistic aspects of the social sciences. Write to the address below for complete details.

American Council of Learned Societies
Office of Fellowships and Grants
228 E. 45th Street
New York, NY   10017

906
Post-Graduate Scholarship Program

AMOUNT: None Specified
DEADLINE: February 15
FIELDS/MAJORS: All Areas of Study

Must be nominated by the faculty athletic representative or director of athletics of an NCAA member institution. Eligibility is restricted to student athletes attending NCAA member institutions. One hundred twenty five awards per year. Must be U.S. citizens and ethnic minorities. Selections are made in the academic year in which the student completes his or her final season of eligibility for intercollegiate athletics under NCAA legislation. Write to the address below for details.

National Collegiate Athletic Association
6201 College Boulevard
Overland Park, KS   66211

907 Postdoctoral Fellowship Program

AMOUNT: $24000–$30000   DEADLINE: September 1
FIELDS/MAJORS: Biology, Medicine, Relevant to Cancer Research

Fellowships are available for postdoctoral research at California institutions in the biological or medical sciences relevant to cancer research. There are no citizenship requirements but the applicant must already hold the Ph.D. Write to the address below for information.

American Cancer Society, California Division
Research Fellowship Program
PO Box 2061
Oakland, CA   94604

908 Postdoctoral Fellowship Program

AMOUNT: None Specified   DEADLINE: January 1
FIELDS/MAJORS: Sleep Disorders and Mechanisms

Research grants for postdoctoral scientists in the areas of study listed above. Must be a U.S. citizen or resident alien. Can be used for basic, applied, or clinical research. Write to the address below for more information.

National Sleep Foundation
1367 Connecticut Avenue, NW
Suite 200
Washington, DC   20036

909 Postdoctoral Fellowship, AHA California Affiliate

AMOUNT: $20300–$32300   DEADLINE: October 1
FIELDS/MAJORS: Cardiovascular Research

Postdoctoral fellowships for California residents or students at California institutions to support beginning investigators in areas relating to cardiovascular research. Must be a U.S. citizen or hold a current visa. Write to the address below for more information. Deadline to request applications is July 1.

American Heart Association, California Affiliate
Research Department
1710 Gilbreth Road
Burlingame, CA   94010

910 Postdoctoral Fellowship, Physician Research Training, Scholar Awards

AMOUNT: None Specified   DEADLINE: March 1
FIELDS/MAJORS: Cancer Research and Related Fields

The American Cancer Society provides support to new investigators to qualify for an independent career in cancer research. Both basic and applied research is supported. Must hold Ph.D. at the time application is made. Write to the address below or call 404-329-7558 for details and policies.

American Cancer Society, Inc.
Extramural Grants and Awards
1599 Clifton Road, NE
Atlanta, GA   30329

911 Postdoctoral Fellowships in Law and Social Science

AMOUNT: $30000   DEADLINE: February 3
FIELDS/MAJORS: Law, Social Science

Available to scholars who have completed all requirements for their Ph.D. within the past two years or are currently in the final stages of completing their dissertation. Research must be in the areas of: social scientific approaches to law, sociological studies, the legal profession, or legal institutions. Held in residence at the ABF. Minorities encouraged to apply. Write to the address below for information.

American Bar Foundation
Ann Tatalovich, Assistant Director
750 N. Lake Shore Drive
Chicago, IL   60611

912 Postdoctoral Fellowships

AMOUNT: Maximum: $29000
DEADLINE: None Specified
FIELDS/MAJORS: Toxicology and Related Disciplines

Postdoctoral research fellowships for recent recipients of D.V.M., M.D., or Ph.D. (biochemical, pharmacology, cell/molecular biology, genetics, immunology, chemistry, biophysics, mathematics, etc.). Supports original research related to chemical toxicity at CIIT's laboratory. Up to twenty-five awards per year. Write to the address below for details.

Chemical Industry Institute of Toxicology
6 Davis Drive
PO Box 12137
Research Triangle Park, NC   27709

913 Postdoctoral Research Fellow Program Award

AMOUNT: $7500   DEADLINE: December 31
FIELDS/MAJORS: Liver Research, Liver Physiology

Award open to M.D./Ph.D.s in the first or second year of appointment as a postdoctoral research fellow or trainee. Applicants must have a career goal to enter an academic career in liver disease research. Persons with more than two years of postdoctoral research training or already well established are ineligible for this award. Contact the address below for further information.

American Liver Foundation
1425 Pompton Avenue
Cedar Grove, NJ   07009

914

Postdoctoral Research Fellowships

AMOUNT: $30000   DEADLINE: November 30
FIELDS/MAJORS: Mathematics

Awards for scholars who have earned their Ph.D. in the field of mathematics in 1993 or later. Most fellowships last for a year, but a shorter period is possible, and in exceptional cases, two-year awards may be made. Awards will be announced by spring. Preference is given to U.S. citizens. Write to the address below for more information.

Mathematical Sciences Research Institute
1000 Centennial Drive, #5070
Berkeley, CA   94720

915

Postdoctoral Research Fellowships

AMOUNT: $30000–$33000   DEADLINE: September 1
FIELDS/MAJORS: Medical Research—Cystic Fibrosis

Fellowships for M.D.s and Ph.D.s interested in conducting basic or clinical research related to cystic fibrosis. Stipends are $30000 (first year), $31000 (second year), and $33000 (optional third year). Must be a U.S. citizen or permanent resident. Write to the address below for details.

Cystic Fibrosis Foundation
Office of Grants Management
6931 Arlington Road
Bethesda, MD   20814

916

Postdoctoral Research Fellowships for Basic and Physician Scientists

AMOUNT: $100000   DEADLINE: None Specified
FIELDS/MAJORS: Cancer Research (Oncology)

Open to the following degree holders: M.D., Ph.D., D.D.S., or D.V.M. who are involved in cancer research. Sponsorship by a senior member of the research community is required. The proposed investigation must be conducted at a university, hospital, or research institution. Write to the address below for details. The deadlines are August 15, December 15, and March 15.

Damon Runyon-Walter Winchell Cancer Fund
131 E. 36th Street
New York, NY   10016

917

Postdoctoral Research Fellowships for Physicians

AMOUNT: $40000–$57500   DEADLINE: None Specified
FIELDS/MAJORS: Medicine

Fellowships are available for scholars with the M.D., Ph.D., D.O., M.B.B.S., or equivalent degree who wish to further their education through research into basic biological processes and disease mechanisms. Applicant should have no more than two years of postdoctoral research training, and should have received first medical degree no more than ten years previously. Write to the address below for additional information.

Howard Hughes Medical Institute
Office of Grants and Special Programs
4000 Jones Bridge Road
Chevy Chase, MD   20815

918

Potash and Phosphate Institute Fellowship

AMOUNT: None Specified   DEADLINE: None Specified
FIELDS/MAJORS: Soil, Plant Sciences

Award open to graduates studying soil or plant sciences. Contact the address below for further information.

Washington State University
Department of Crop and Soil Sciences
Pullman, WA   99164

919

Pre-Dissertation Fellowship Program

AMOUNT: Maximum: $3000
DEADLINE: February 3
FIELDS/MAJORS: History, Sociology, Poly Sci, Anthropology, Economics, Geography

Research grants are available to those studying in the above fields and specializing in European studies. Must have completed a minimum of two years of graduate study. These are non-residential fellowships and are not for students in advanced stages of dissertation research. Must be a U.S. citizen or legal resident of the U.S. or Canada. Write to address below for details.

Council for European Studies
Columbia University
Box 44, Schermerhorn Hall
New York, NY   10027

920

Predoctoral Fellowship Program

AMOUNT: Maximum: $10000
DEADLINE: March 15
FIELDS/MAJORS: Social, Behavioral Sciences Relevant to Cancer Research

Fellowships are available for predoctoral research at California institutions in the areas above. Intended to provide support related to the dissertation. By award activation date, applicants must have been accepted to candidacy and the doctoral degree anticipated within two years. Write to the address below for information.

American Cancer Society, California Division
Research Fellowship Program
PO Box 2061
Oakland, CA   94604

921

Predoctoral Fellowship, AHA California Affiliate

AMOUNT: $16500   DEADLINE: October 1
FIELDS/MAJORS: Cardiovascular Research

Predoctoral fellowships for California residents or students at California institutions to support doctoral dissertation projects in areas relating to cardiovascular research. Must be a U.S. citizen or hold a current visa. Write to the address below for more information. Deadline to request applications is July 1.

American Heart Association, California Affiliate
Research Department
1710 Gilbreth Road
Burlingame, CA 94010

922 Presbyterian Ethnic Leadership Supplemental Grant

AMOUNT: $500–$1000   DEADLINE: None Specified
FIELDS/MAJORS: Ministry

Open to full-time students who are African, Asian, Hispanic, Native American, or Alaska Native. Must be enrolled in a Presbyterian Church seminary or theological institution approved by the Students' Committee on Preparation for Ministry. Must be studying for the first professional degree for a church occupation or a position within one of the ecumenical agencies in which the Presbyterian Church participates. Contact the address below for further information.

Presbyterian Church, U.S.A.
Office of Financial Aid for Studies
100 Witherspoon Street
Louisville, KY 40202-1396

923 Presbyterian Study Grant

AMOUNT: $500–$2000
DEADLINE: None Specified
FIELDS/MAJORS: Preparation for Ministry

Open to full-time students in a Presbyterian Church seminary or theological institution approved by the Students' Committee on Preparation for Ministry. Must be studying for the first professional degree for a church occupation or a position within one of the ecumenical agencies in which the Presbyterian Church participates. Contact the address below for further information.

Presbyterian Church, U.S.A.
Office of Financial Aid for Studies
100 Witherspoon Street
Louisville, KY 40202-1396

924 President's Grant in Aid

AMOUNT: $20000   DEADLINE: December 6
FIELDS/MAJORS: Medical Research (Allergy/Immunology)

Grants for members of the American Academy of Allergy and Immunology. To support a wide range of scholarly activities. Applicant must be an M.D. or Ph.D. and be sponsored by an AAAI fellow. Write to the address below for details.

American Academy of Allergy and Immunology
Jerome Schultz, Continuing Med. Educ. Mgr.
611 E. Wells Street
Milwaukee, WI 53202

925 President's Postdoctoral Fellowship Program

AMOUNT: Maximum: $27000
DEADLINE: December 1
FIELDS/MAJORS: Mathematics, Computer Science, Engineering, Physics

Twenty fellowships are available at Oakland for minority and female post-doctoral scholars committed to careers in university teaching or research. Applicants must be U.S. citizens or permanent residents, and hold, or will be holding the Ph.D. by the year of the award. Write to the address listed for information on these and other programs which are available.

University of California, Oakland
Office of the President
300 Lakeside Drive, 18th Floor
Oakland, CA 94612

926 President's Scholar Program Minority Scholarships

AMOUNT: None Specified   DEADLINE: None Specified
FIELDS/MAJORS: All Areas of Study

Scholarships available to African, Hispanic, Asian, and Native American graduate students. Must be able to demonstrate high achievement or unusual potential as artists, designers, or educators. Must be U.S. citizens or permanent residents. Financial need is a critical priority. Two awards offered annually. Contact the address below for further information. At least 3.0 GPA required.

Rhode Island School of Design
Financial Aid Office
2 College Street
Providence, RI 02903

927 Presidential Scholarship

AMOUNT: None Specified
DEADLINE: February 1
FIELDS/MAJORS: Psychology

Scholarships open to minority students enrolled in a psychology degree program. These awards may be given in concert with other awards or separately. Contact the address below for further information.

Fordham University
Graduate Admissions Office—Keating 216
Fordham University
Bronx, NY 10458

928 Professional Education Scholarship for Graduate Study

AMOUNT: Maximum: $1000   DEADLINE: May 1
FIELDS/MAJORS: Journalism

Must be women members of NFPW with a bachelor's or B.S. and two years membership. Based on academic and professional performance, career potential, and financial need. Write to the address below for details.

National Federation of Press Women
4510 W 89th Street, #110
Prairie Village, KS 66207

929 Professional Growth Scholarship

AMOUNT: None Specified   DEADLINE: April 15
FIELDS/MAJORS: Food Service/Management

For graduate students who have a minimum GPA of 2.7. Must be a member of the American School Food Service Association or a child of a member, and plan to have a career in food service. Renewable. Write to the address below for additional information.

American School Food Service Association
Scholarship Committee
1600 Duke Street, 7th Floor
Alexandria, VA   22314

930 Professional Opportunities for African-American Students and Graduates

AMOUNT: $1300   DEADLINE: April 15
FIELDS/MAJORS: All Areas of Study

Students must be admitted to graduate school for the first time, in the spring or summer semester. Must be U.S. citizens or permanent residents. This is a one time award for students of African-American descent. Write to the address below for more information.

Florida International University
Division of Graduate Studies, PC 520
University Park
Miami, FL   33199

931 Professor Elizabeth F. Fisher Fellowship

AMOUNT: $1000   DEADLINE: December 16
FIELDS/MAJORS: Geology, Geography, Urban/Environmental/Ecological Studies

Fellowship for Wellesley graduates to perform research or undertake further studies in one of the above fields. Preference is given to geology and geography. Contact the address below for further information.

Wellesley College, Fellowships for Wellesley Alumnae
Sec'y, Committee on Graduate Fellowships
106 Central Street, Career Center
Wellesley, MA   02181

932 Professor Emeritus Harry J. Hardenbrook, D.V.M., Scholarships

AMOUNT: $500–$1000   DEADLINE: February 9
FIELDS/MAJORS: Medicine: Veterinary

Scholarships for third year D.V.M. students at the University of Illinois. Funds are from the Illinois Standardbred and the Illinois Thoroughbred Breeders Fund Programs. Competitively awarded. Recipients determined by the dean of the College of Veterinary Medicine. Contact the dean's office for details.

Illinois Department of Agriculture
Bureau of Horse Racing—State Fairgrounds
PO Box 19281
Springfield, IL   62794

933 Professor Stanley Zimmering Prize in Biology

AMOUNT: Maximum: $300   DEADLINE: March 1
FIELDS/MAJORS: Biology

Open to graduating seniors who plan an academic career in research and teaching biology and have been accepted by graduate school. Contact the address listed for further information.

Brooklyn College
Office of the V.P. for Student Life
2113 Boylan Hall
Brooklyn, NY   11210

934 Program on Nonviolent Sanctions, Pre- and Postdoctoral Fellowships

AMOUNT: None Specified   DEADLINE: January 15
FIELDS/MAJORS: Arms Control and Disarmament

Residential fellowships at the Center for International Affairs of Harvard for Ph.D. candidates (coursework completed before beginning of fellowship) and postdoctoral scholars. Supports research on the degree to which, and how, nonviolent direct action provides an alternative to violence in resolving the problems of totalitarian rule, war, genocide, and oppression. Contact Pamela Slavsky at the address below for program details and application guidelines. Persons interested in applying should contact the program director to discuss research project before compiling application.

Harvard University, Center for International Affairs
CFIA Student Programs and Fellowships
1737 Cambridge Street
Cambridge, MA   02138

935 Program on U.S.-Japan Relations, Advanced Research Fellowships

AMOUNT: Maximum: $27000   DEADLINE: March 3
FIELDS/MAJORS: Japanese Culture—International Relations

Postdoctoral residential fellowship program at the Center for International Affairs of Harvard University. Supports investigation of issues or problems in contemporary U.S.-Japan relations, Japan's international relations, or other studies of Japan that contribute to the understanding of Japan's international behavior. Contact Dr. Frank Schwartz at the address below for program details and application guidelines. Preference is given to U.S. citizens; but others, especially from Pacific Rim countries, may apply.

Harvard University, Center for International Affairs
CFIA Student Programs and Fellowships
1737 Cambridge Street
Cambridge, MA   02138

936 Project Grants

AMOUNT: $3000–$10000
DEADLINE: November 1
FIELDS/MAJORS: Byzantine Studies, Pre-Columbian Studies, Archaeological Research

Grants available to assist with scholarly projects in the above fields. Projects supported are generally related to the study and or excavation of a site (Byzantine, pre-Columbian, or Garden), but other relevant projects will be considered. Write to the address below for details.

Dumbarton Oaks
Office of the Director
1703 32nd Street, NW
Washington, DC   20007

937 PTC Research Prizes

AMOUNT: $2000   DEADLINE: June 30
FIELDS/MAJORS: Telecommunications Research

Awards are available for the authors of the best research papers concerning telecommunications concerns of the Pacific region. Must hold at least a bachelor's degree. One to three awards offered annually. Write to the address below for more information.

Pacific Telecommunications Council
2454 Beretania Street
Suite 302
Honolulu, HI   96826

938 Public Health Student Recognition Award

AMOUNT: None Specified   DEADLINE: None Specified
FIELDS/MAJORS: Public Health

Awards for graduate students based on GPA and service to the school. Contact the Dean, School of Public Health, for more information.

University of Massachusetts, Amherst
Dean
School of Public Health
Amherst, MA   01003

939 Public Interest Law Graduate Fellow/Staff Attorney Fellowships

AMOUNT: $29000   DEADLINE: November 15
FIELDS/MAJORS: Law (Public Policy, Communications)

Two-year post-graduate (i.e., post-J.D./LL.B.) residential fellowships for law students. Provides extensive training and experience in public interest advocacy in the federal courts, administrative agencies, and legislative bodies. Fellows receive an LL.M. in advocacy at the end of the fellowship term. Four fellowships per year. Write to the address below for details.

Georgetown University Law Center
Institute for Public Representation
600 New Jersey Avenue, NW, Suite 312
Washington, DC   20001

940 Public Investor Scholarship

AMOUNT: $3000   DEADLINE: February 14
FIELDS/MAJORS: Public or Business Administration, Finance, Social Sciences

Scholarship for graduate students in the above areas of study who are planning to pursue a career in state or local government finance. For full- or part-time study. Must have superior academic record. One award per year. For U.S. or Canadian citizens or permanent residents. Information may be available from the head of your accounting department. If not, write to the address below. Applications are available in November for awards in the following spring. GPA of at least 2.8 required.

Government Finance Officers Association
Scholarship Committee
180 N. Michigan Avenue, Suite 800
Chicago, IL   60601

941 Puerto Rican Legal Defense and Education Fund Scholarship Fund

AMOUNT: $1000–$5000   DEADLINE: January 31
FIELDS/MAJORS: Law

Open to Puerto Rican or other Hispanic law students. Based on need, academic promise, and Latino community involvement. Generally, must be already enrolled into a J.D. program. Also have a summer law internship program. Please contact the address below for complete information.

Puerto Rican Legal Defense and Education Fund, Inc.
99 Hudson Street
New York, NY   10013

942 Purina Mills Research Fellowship

AMOUNT: $12500   DEADLINE: February 3
FIELDS/MAJORS: Animal Science and Nutrition

Fellowships for graduate students conducting research relating to the field of nutrition and companion animal sciences. For full-time study. Based on application, transcripts, grade reports, recommendations, and research proposal. Write to the address below to request an application packet.

Purina Mills, Inc.
Purina Research Awards Committee
PO Box 66812, c/o Joan Roslauski—2E
St. Louis, MO   63166

943
R. Robert and Sally D. Funderburg Research Scholar Award

AMOUNT: $25000   DEADLINE: September 10
FIELDS/MAJORS: Gastric Biology, Pathobiology

Awards for established investigators in the field of gastric biology who hold faculty positions at accredited institutions. Women and minorities are encouraged to apply. Individual members of the ADHF member societies will be given preference. One award is given annually. Contact the address below for further information or websites: http://www.gastro.org; http:www.asge.org; or http://hepar-sfgh.ucsf.edu.

American Digestive Health Foundation
Ms. Irene Kuo
7910 Woodmont Avenue, 7th Floor
Bethesda, MD   20814

944
Radcliffe Research Support Program

AMOUNT: Maximum: $5000   DEADLINE: October 15
FIELDS/MAJORS: History of Women, Human Development

This program offers grants to postdoctoral investigators for research drawing on the center's data resources. The center is a national repository for social science data on human development and social change, particularly the changing life experience of American women. Write to the address below for details.

Radcliffe College
Henry A. Murray Research Center
10 Garden Street
Cambridge, MA   02138

945
Ralph and Hazel Rhode Medical Scholarship

AMOUNT: None Specified   DEADLINE: April 15
FIELDS/MAJORS: Medicine, Medical Technology

Awards for deserving students studying medicine or medical technology. Contact the address below for further information or the financial aid office at your school's location.

University of North Dakota—School of Medicine
Sandra Elshaug, Financial Aid Office
PO Box 9037—501 N. Columbia Road
Grand Forks, ND   58202

946
Ralph and Margaret Lyon Graduate Scholarship

AMOUNT: $1200   DEADLINE: April 15
FIELDS/MAJORS: Education

Scholarship for graduate students who are majoring in education. Renewable for LU or UWA graduate students/teachers. Must be U.S. citizens or permanent residents. Write to the address below for more information.

University of West Alabama
Office of Admissions
Station 4
Livingston, AL   35470

947
Ralph E. Cooley Memorial Award

AMOUNT: None Specified
DEADLINE: None Specified
FIELDS/MAJORS: Cross Cultural Studies,
Native American Languages

Scholarships are available at the University of Oklahoma, Norman for graduate students in one of the areas listed above. Requires a GPA of at least 3.0. Write to the address below for information.

University of Oklahoma, Norman
Communications Department
780 Van Vleet Oval
Norman, OK   73019

948
Randall Jarrell Writing Scholarship

AMOUNT: None Specified   DEADLINE: None Specified
FIELDS/MAJORS: English

Awards open to graduate students majoring in English. Preference given to writers or poets. Contact the address below for further information.

University of North Carolina, Greensboro
Financial Aid Office
723 Kenilworth Street
Greensboro, NC   27412

949
Rawley Silver Scholarship Fund

AMOUNT: None Specified   DEADLINE: June 15
FIELDS/MAJORS: Art Therapy

Scholarships for graduate students who have demonstrated academic excellence and are in an AATA approved art therapy program. Applicants must demonstrate financial need in order to complete their program of study. Write to the address below for complete details.

American Art Therapy Association, Inc.
Scholarship Committee
1202 Allanson Road
Mundelein, IL   60060

950
Ray Kageler

AMOUNT: None Specified   DEADLINE: March 1
FIELDS/MAJORS: All Areas of Study

Open to graduate students who are U.S. citizens, residents of Oregon, and members of a credit union affiliated with the Oregon Credit Union League. Applicants may apply and compete annually. Contact the address below for further information.

Oregon State Scholarship Commission
Private Awards
1500 Valley River Drive, #100
Eugene, OR   97401-2130

951 Raymond A. and Ina C. Best Scholarship

AMOUNT: $10000   DEADLINE: January 15
FIELDS/MAJORS: Business Administration

Award open to member studying for his/her master's degree at Rensselaer Polytechnic Institute. Contact the address listed for further information.

Tau Beta Pi-Alabama Power Company
D. Stephen Pierre Jr., P.E., Director
150 St. Joseph Street, PO Box 2247
Mobile, AL   36652

952 Raymond Jonson Fellowship

AMOUNT: None Specified   DEADLINE: March 1
FIELDS/MAJORS: Art—Painting, Drawing

Scholarships are available at the University of New Mexico for full-time graduate students in painting or drawing who have completed at least one semester of coursework at UNM. Write to the address below for information.

University of New Mexico, Albuquerque
College of Fine Arts
Office of Graduate Studies
Albuquerque, NM   87131

953 Raymond P. Hutchens Scholarship

AMOUNT: None Specified   DEADLINE: February 1
FIELDS/MAJORS: Law

Awards for law students who are Ohio residents. Must demonstrate academic promise. Contact the Assistant Dean, Chase College of Law, for further information.

Northern Kentucky University
Chase College of Law
Office of Admissions
Highland Heights, KY   41099

954 Rebecca McCulloch Smith Fellowship

AMOUNT: None Specified   DEADLINE: January 1
FIELDS/MAJORS: Human Development, Family Studies

Award open to graduate students in the above fields. Contact the address below for further information.

University of North Carolina, Greensboro
Financial Aid Office
723 Kenilworth Street
Greensboro, NC   27412

955 Regents Graduate/ Professional Fellowships

AMOUNT: Maximum: $3500   DEADLINE: March 1
FIELDS/MAJORS: All Areas of Study

Scholarships are available to Ohio resident graduate students who continue their education in a Ohio school. Based upon academic ability. Write to the address below for information, or your school financial aid office.

Ohio Student Aid Commission
Customer Service
PO Box 16610
Columbus, OH   43216

956 Regents Health Care Scholarships for Medicine or Dentistry

AMOUNT: $1000–$10000   DEADLINE: None Specified
FIELDS/MAJORS: Medicine/Dentistry

Program for minority residents of New York for at least one year preceding date of award. Students must be enrolled in/accepted to approved medical/dental school in New York. Must agree to practice in a designated shortage area for at least twenty-four months. Renewable. Must be a U.S. citizen or legal resident. One hundred awards per year. Eighty awards for medicine and twenty awards for dentistry. Write to the address below for complete details.

New York State Education Department
Bureau of Post-secondary Grants Admin.
Cultural Education Center
Albany, NY   12230

957 Regents Physician Loan Forgiveness Program

AMOUNT: Maximum: $10000
DEADLINE: None Specified
FIELDS/MAJORS: Medicine

Must agree to practice medicine in an area of New York state for a period of twenty-four months for each award received. Must have completed residency training in medicine within the five years immediately preceding the period for which the award is granted, and must be licensed to practice medicine in New York prior to beginning the service commitment. Must be a legal resident of New York. May not have ever received a regents physician shortage scholarship. Preference will be given to applicants who have completed a residency in family practice or primary care. Eighty awards per year.

New York State Education Department
Bureau of Post-Secondary Grants Admin.
Cultural Education Center
Albany, NY   12230

958 Regents' Opportunity Scholarship

AMOUNT: None Specified   DEADLINE: None Specified
FIELDS/MAJORS: Public Administration or Business Administration

Awarded to Georgia residents who are economically-disadvantaged and enrolled in the master's degree programs for public administration or business administration. Contact the address listed for further information.

Columbus State University
Financial Aid Office
4225 University Avenue
Columbus, GA   31907

959 Regular Membership Fellowships

AMOUNT: $7840   DEADLINE: January 6
FIELDS/MAJORS: Classical Studies

Awards are available for graduate students in classical studies in the U.S. or Canada. Based on transcripts, recommendations, and examinations in Greek language, history, archaeology, or literature. Applicants may have taken one year of graduate work but not completed the Ph.D. Six awards offered annually. Write to the address below for more information.

American School of Classical Studies at Athens
Committee on Admissions and Fellowships
6-8 Charlton Street
Princeton, NJ   08540

960 Research and Education Grant

AMOUNT: Maximum: $5000   DEADLINE: January 31
FIELDS/MAJORS: Science, Horticulture

Graduate and postdoctoral grants are available for scholars with a proposed program of scientific, academic, or artistic investigation of herbal plants. Write to the address below for information.

Herb Society of America, Inc.
Research and Education Grants
9019 Kirtland Chardon Road
Kirtland, OH   44094

961 Research Assistance

AMOUNT: Maximum: $500
DEADLINE: October 1
FIELDS/MAJORS: Japanese Studies

Small grants are available for a variety of scholarly needs that are not covered by other funding sources, such as research assistance and manuscript typing. Applicants must clearly explain what the funds would be used for. Write to the address below for more information.

Northeast Asia Council Association for Asian Studies
1 Lane Hall
University of Michigan
Ann Arbor, MI   48109

962 Research Assistantship

AMOUNT: $14400   DEADLINE: January 15
FIELDS/MAJORS: Any Area of Study

Offered to graduate students in order to carry out thesis or dissertation work. For more information write to the address below.

Vanderbilt University
411 Kirkland Hall
Nashville, TN   37240

963 Research Awards and Grants Program

AMOUNT: Maximum: $35000   DEADLINE: January 1
FIELDS/MAJORS: Respiratory Disease, Medical Research, Epidemiology

Awards for scholars with two years of research experience or for doctoral candidates. Programs for funding include research training, pediatric pulmonary research, nursing research, Dalsemer Scholar, career investigator research grant, and behavioral science dissertation grants. Must be a Canadian citizen or a U.S. citizen or permanent resident. Write to the address below for information.

American Lung Association
Medical Affairs Division
1740 Broadway
New York, NY   10019

964 Research Awards at the Huntington Library

AMOUNT: None Specified
DEADLINE: December 15
FIELDS/MAJORS: American and British Literature, Art, Science, and Culture

For doctoral and postdoctoral students. Awards are for work which will sufficiently utilize the Huntington Collections. Applications should include a project outline, the period of proposed residence at the library, personal data, previous scholarly work, and references. For scholars of high merit. Write to the address below for complete details.

Huntington Library, Art Collections, and Botanical Gardens
Committee on Awards
1151 Oxford Road
San Marino, CA   91108

965 Research Fellowship

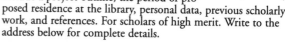

AMOUNT: None Specified
DEADLINE: November 1
FIELDS/MAJORS: Japanese Studies

Fellowships available to scholars who hold an academic position in a research institution and have substantial experience in research, teaching, or writing in their respective fields of study. Write to the address listed for additional information.

Japan Foundation
New York Office
152 West 57th Street
New York, NY   10019

966 Research Fellowships and Young Investigator Grant Program

AMOUNT: Maximum: $25000   DEADLINE: September 5
FIELDS/MAJORS: Nephrology, Urology

Research fellowships for clinical and basic research into understanding and cure of kidney and urologic diseases. Must be sponsored by member of NKF. At award activation, research candidates may not have completed more than four and a half years of research training beyond a doctoral degree. No more than ten years can have elapsed between last doctoral degree and this award. Young investigators candidate must be holding a position on a faculty or staff of a research institution. Awarded no later than three and a half years after initial appointment to position. Contact the address below for further information.

National Kidney Foundation
Research Fellowship Committee
30 East 33rd Street
New York, NY   10016

967 Research Fellowships in American History and Culture

AMOUNT: None Specified
DEADLINE: February 1
FIELDS/MAJORS: American History and Culture, Architectural History, Art History, Etc.

Fellowships are available for pre- and post-doctoral scholars to support research at the library company of Philadelphia in one of the areas listed above. Applicants are urged to inquire about the appropriateness of the research topic prior to applying. Call 215-546-3181 for information and to discuss your proposed research topic or write to the address below.

Library Company of Philadelphia
James Green, Assistant Librarian
1314 Locust Street
Philadelphia, PA   19107

968 Research Fellowships in New England History and Culture

AMOUNT: $1500   DEADLINE: January 31
FIELDS/MAJORS: History—New England

Research fellowships are available for graduate and post-graduate scholars conducting research into the history of New England, at the Peabody Essex Museum. Stipends will be awarded for up to two months. Write to the address below for information.

Peabody Essex Museum
Fellowship Program, Phillips Library
East India Square
Salem, MA   01970

969 Research Grants

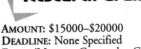

AMOUNT: $15000–$20000
DEADLINE: None Specified
FIELDS/MAJORS: Geography, Geology, Anthropology, Archaeology, Astronomy, Biology

Investigators who hold doctor's degrees and are associated with institutions of higher learning or other scientific and educational nonprofit organizations such as museums, are eligible to apply. For field research. Scholars in the fields of botany, oceanography, paleontology, and zoology are also encouraged to apply. Two hundred fifty grants are awarded per year. Address inquiries to Secretary, Committee for Research and Exploration, at the address below.

National Geographic Society
Committee for Research and Exploration
PO Box 98249
Washington, DC   20090

970 Research Grants

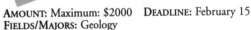

AMOUNT: Maximum: $2000   DEADLINE: February 15
FIELDS/MAJORS: Geology

Open to any master's or doctoral student at universities in the U.S., Canada, Mexico, or Central America. Award is intended to help support thesis research. GSA membership is not required. Approximately two hundred fifty awards per year. Write for complete details. Application forms should be available from your department or from the campus GSA representative. If necessary, write to the research grants administrator at the address below.

Geological Society of America
3300 Penrose Place
PO Box 9140
Boulder, CO   80301

971 Research in the Biology of Aging

AMOUNT: $5500   DEADLINE: February 26
FIELDS/MAJORS: Geriatrics

Open to predoctoral Ph.D. and M.D. students to undertake a three-month research project in an area of biomedical research in aging under the auspices of a mentor. The scholarships consist of $4000 for the student and $1500 for the mentor. Write to the address below for more information.

American Federation for Aging Research/Glenn Foundation
1414 Avenue of the Americas
New York, NY   10019

972 Research Professorships

AMOUNT: Maximum: $40000
DEADLINE: September 30
FIELDS/MAJORS: Mathematics

Awards for mid-career mathematicians who have earned their Ph.D. in the field of mathematics no later than 1992. The award is limited to a ceiling of $40000 and normally will not exceed half of the applicants salary. Awards will be announced mid-December. Write to the address below for more information.

Mathematical Sciences Research Institute
1000 Centennial Drive, #5070
Berkeley, CA   94720

973 Research Resident Scholar Fellowships

AMOUNT: None Specified
DEADLINE: December 1
FIELDS/MAJORS: Human Behavior, Culture, Humanities, Anthropology

Fellowships for pre- and postdoctoral scholars whose field work or basic research is complete. Applications will be evaluated on the basis of overall excellence and significance of the proposed project. Predoctoral applicants must be nominated by their degree granting department. Contact the address below for further information.

School of American Research
660 Garcia Street
PO Box 2188
Sante Fe, NM   87504

974 Research Resident Scholar-Katrin H. Lamon Native American Fellowship

AMOUNT: None Specified   DEADLINE: December 1
FIELDS/MAJORS: Human Behavior, Culture, Humanities, Anthropology

Fellowships for pre- and postdoctoral Native Americans whose field work or basic research is complete. Applications will be evaluated on the basis of overall excellence and significance of the proposed project. Predoctoral applicants must be nominated by their degree granting department. Contact the address below for further information.

School of American Research
660 Garcia Street
PO Box 2188
Sante Fe, NM   87504

975 Research Support Grants

AMOUNT: $18000–$22000   DEADLINE: December 15
FIELDS/MAJORS: Humanities, Arts, Social Sciences

Fellowships are available from the Getty Center Scholar Program. These are two-year pre- and postdoctoral residential fellowships. Evaluated in terms of how the dissertation or book bears upon the theme. Research projects that lead from the passions to issues about the nature and history of the humanities will be of special interest. Write to the address below for information.

Getty Research Institute for the History of Art and the Humanities
Scholars and Seminars Program
1200 Getty Center Drive, #1100
Los Angeles, CA   90049-1688

976 Research Training Fellowships for Medical Students

AMOUNT: $14500   DEADLINE: None Specified
FIELDS/MAJORS: Medicine

Fellowships for doctoral candidates enrolled in medical school, to encourage more M.D.s to pursue a career in biological research. Forty-four awards offered annually. Write to address below for further information.

Howard Hughes Medical Institute
Office of Grants and Special Programs
4000 Jones Bridge Road
Chevy Chase, MD   20815

977 Research Travel Grant— North America

AMOUNT: $1000   DEADLINE: October 1
FIELDS/MAJORS: Korean Research

Available to scholars engaged in research on Korea and wish to use museum, library, or other archival materials in the United States or Canada. Primarily intended to support postdoctoral research. Contact the address below for further information.

Association for Asian Studies, Inc.
University of Michigan
1 Lane Hall
Ann Arbor, MI   48109

978 Research Travel within the U.S.A.

AMOUNT: Maximum: $1500
DEADLINE: October 1
FIELDS/MAJORS: Japanese Studies

Awards for graduate students who are engaged in scholarly research on Japan and wish to use museum, library, or other archival materials located in the U.S. Applicants must be U.S. citizens or permanent residents. Though primarily to support postdoctoral research on Japan, Ph.D. candidates may also apply. Second deadline date is February 1 for the spring awards. Write to the address below for more information.

Northeast Asia Council Association for Asian Studies
1 Lane Hall
University of Michigan
Ann Arbor, MI   48109

979 Resident Junior Fellowships

AMOUNT: Maximum: $22000
DEADLINE: October 15
FIELDS/MAJORS: Greek Classical Studies

Fellowships are available for classical Greek studies to those who hold the Ph.D. and can demonstrate professional competence in ancient Greek. Preference will be shown to applicants in the early stages of their careers. Eleven resident fellowships are available. Write to the address below for details.

Center for Hellenic Studies
The Director
3100 Whitehaven Street, NW
Washington, DC   20008

980
Respiratory Diseases Research Award

AMOUNT: $25000   DEADLINE: December 6
FIELDS/MAJORS: Allergy/Immunology Medical Research

Grants for members of the American Academy of Allergy and Immunology (or persons who are awaiting acceptance into the academy) who are M.D.s or Ph.D.s, associated with an approved allergy and immunology or clinical and laboratory immunology training program. Write to the address below for details.

American Academy of Allergy and Immunology/Allen & Hanburys
Committee Chair to Grant Research Awards
611 E. Wells Street
Milwaukee, WI   53202

981
Retha Duggan Scholarship

AMOUNT: None Specified   DEADLINE: February 8
FIELDS/MAJORS: Accounting

Scholarships are available at the University of Oklahoma, Norman for full-time master's candidates in accounting who reside in Oklahoma. Three awards offered annually. Write to the address below for information.

University of Oklahoma, Norman
College of Business Administration
200 Adams Hall
Norman, OK   73019

982
Rev. and Mrs. G.D. Albanese Fellowship

AMOUNT: None Specified
DEADLINE: January 1
FIELDS/MAJORS: Food, Nutrition, Food Service

Award open to master's candidates in their second year studying in any of the above fields. Contact the address below for further information.

University of North Carolina, Greensboro
Financial Aid Office
723 Kenilworth Street
Greensboro, NC   27412

983
Rice-Cullimore Scholarship

AMOUNT: $2000   DEADLINE: February 15
FIELDS/MAJORS: Mechanical Engineering

Grants for foreign students studying mechanical engineering at a U.S. school on the graduate level. Applications are made through the Institute of International Education. Write to the address below for details.

American Society of Mechanical Engineers Auxiliary, Inc.
345 E. 47th Street
New York, NY   10017

984
Richard B. Irvine, M.D., Memorial Scholarship Award

AMOUNT: None Specified   DEADLINE: October 15
FIELDS/MAJORS: Medicine

Scholarships for medical students who were graduated from high schools, or who live in one of the following cities: Clayton, Concord, Pleasant Hill, Pacheco, or Martinez (Contra Costa County, California). Based on financial need. Contact the address below for further information.

Mt. Diablo Medical Center, Richard B. Irvine, M.D., Scholarship
2540 East Street
PO Box 4110
Concord, CA   94524-4110

985
Richard C. Maguire Scholarship

AMOUNT: $1000   DEADLINE: March 31
FIELDS/MAJORS: History and Related Fields (i.e., Museum Studies, Archaeology)

Scholarships for U.S. citizens doing post-graduate study in history or any related field. Must be pursuing a master's degree or higher. Based on grades, career goals, recommendations, transcripts, and extracurriculars. Send a SASE to the address below for details.

Rock Island Arsenal Historical Society
R. Maguire Scholarship Comm., R.I.A. Museum
Attn: Siori-Cfm, Rock Island Arsenal
Rock Island, IL   61299

986
Richard Cronin Fisheries Fund

AMOUNT: None Specified   DEADLINE: None Specified
FIELDS/MAJORS: Fisheries Research

Scholarships are awarded to graduate students to support fisheries research at UMass. Contact the Department Head, Forestry and Wildlife Management, for more information.

University of Massachusetts, Amherst
Department of Forestry and Wildlife Mgmt
Amherst, MA   01003

987
Richard H. Allen Memorial Scholarship

AMOUNT: None Specified   DEADLINE: March 1
FIELDS/MAJORS: Civil or Construction Engineering

Awards are available at the University of New Mexico for graduate students in the civil or construction engineering program. Must be a U.S. citizen. Write to the address below for more information.

University of New Mexico, Albuquerque
Office of Financial Aid
Albuquerque, NM   87131

988 Richard Klutznick Scholarship Fund

AMOUNT: Maximum: $2500
DEADLINE: April 1
FIELDS/MAJORS: Social Work

Applicants must be Jewish graduate students attending accredited schools studying social work and have records of good scholarship. Award recipients must agree to accept a two-year position with BBYO upon graduation. Write to the address below for details.

B'nai Brith Youth Organization
1640 Rhode Island Avenue, NW
Washington, DC   20036

989 Richard M. Weaver Fellowship and Salvatori Fellowship Awards Programs

AMOUNT: None Specified   DEADLINE: January 15
FIELDS/MAJORS: Teaching—College Level

One-year fellowship to encourage graduate work in preparation for college teaching. Must be U.S. citizen and ISI member. For study at any school in the U.S. or abroad. Write to the address below for complete details.

Intercollegiate Studies Institute
Fellowship Awards Programs
3901 Centerville Road, PO Box 4431
Wilmington, DE   19807

990 Richard P. Vann Memorial Scholarship

AMOUNT: None Specified   DEADLINE: March 1
FIELDS/MAJORS: Paleontology

Awards are available at the University of New Mexico for graduate students working on the paleontology of New Mexico or a related subdiscipline. Contact the Earth and Sciences Department for more information.

University of New Mexico, Albuquerque
Office of Financial Aid
Albuquerque, NM   87131

991 Richard W. and Florence B. Irwin Law Scholarship

AMOUNT: None Specified   DEADLINE: August 31
FIELDS/MAJORS: Law

Scholarships are available for Northampton residents who are attending or have been accepted into law school. Must have been a resident of Northampton for at least five years. Write to the address below for information.

Community Foundation of Western Massachusetts
PO Box 15769
1500 Main Street
Springfield, MA   01115

992 Richard W. Benfer Graduate Scholarship in Speech and Hearing Research

AMOUNT: None Specified   DEADLINE: March 1
FIELDS/MAJORS: Speech Pathology and Audiology

Scholarship awarded annually to a student actively engaged in ongoing research within the fields of speech pathology and audiology, while pursuing a graduate degree within the communication disorders faculty. Student must have a minimum GPA of 3.0. Write to the address below for details.

New Mexico State University
College of Education
Box 30001, Dept. 3AC
Las Cruces, NM   88003

993 Rita G. Rudel Award

AMOUNT: $20000   DEADLINE: May 31
FIELDS/MAJORS: Behavioral Neurology, Developmental Neuropsychology

Applicants must hold a Ph.D. or M.D. degree and should be in the early to middle stage of their postdoctoral careers. Must be doing research in the field of developmental neuropsychology or developmental behavioral neurology. Write to the address below for more information.

Rita G. Rudel Foundation
PO Box 674
Chappaqua, NY   10514

994 Riva Specht, Wurzel Family, and Fred Smith/ Don Catalano Fellowships

AMOUNT: $1800–$2700   DEADLINE: January 6
FIELDS/MAJORS: Public Social Services, Public Health Services

Open to full-time master degree students planning a career in public social and/or health services. Must be U.S. citizens or permanent residents. Contact the address below for further information.

University of California, Berkeley
Office of Financial Aid Graduate Unit
201 Sproul Hall, #1960
Berkeley, CA   94720

995 Riverside County Physicians Memorial Foundation Scholarship

AMOUNT: None Specified   DEADLINE: None Specified
FIELDS/MAJORS: Medicine

Award open to residents of Riverside County, California, who have been accepted by or currently enrolled (in good standing) in an accredited medical or osteopathic school. Must be able to demonstrate financial need. Contact the address below for further information.

Riverside County Physicians Memorial Foundation
3993 Jurupa Avenue
Riverside, CA   92506

996
Robert A. Welch Graduate Fellowships in Chemistry and Biochemistry

AMOUNT: None Specified   DEADLINE: March 1
FIELDS/MAJORS: Chemistry, Biochemistry

Fellowships for graduate students in the Department of Chemistry and Biochemistry at UT-Austin. Limited teaching duties and enhanced research potentials are afforded to these fellows. Graduate teaching and research assistantships are also available through the department. Contact the department for details.

University of Texas, Austin
Department of Chemistry and Biochemistry
Austin, TX   78712

997
Robert and Charlotte Bitter Graduate Scholarship

AMOUNT: $900   DEADLINE: February 7
FIELDS/MAJORS: Accounting

Student must be admitted to the M.B.A. or Master of Accountancy program, with a combined GMAT and GPA admission score of 1100 or higher. Must be enrolled in 12 hours each semester and have a GPA of 3.33 or better. Contact the COBA office for more information.

Southwest Missouri State University
Office of Financial Aid
901 South National Avenue
Springfield, MO   65804

998
Robert and Rosemary Low Memorial Scholarships

AMOUNT: None Specified   DEADLINE: April 15
FIELDS/MAJORS: All Areas of Study

Award is available at Portland State University for full-time graduate students with disabilities. Award is merit-based, but financial need may be considered. One award is offered. Contact the Office of Graduate Studies and Research for more information.

Portland State University
Office of Graduate Studies and Research
105 Neuberger Hall
Portland, OR   97207

999
Robert Bosch Foundation Fellowship

AMOUNT: $3500   DEADLINE: October 15
FIELDS/MAJORS: All Areas of Study

Fellowships are available for postdoctoral scholars to study in Germany. Applicant must be fluent in German, and be available to work in a government assignment for nine months, and in the private sector for four months. Twenty awards are given annually. Write to the address below for information.

CDS International, Inc.
330 7th Avenue, 19th Floor
New York, NY   10001

1000
Robert D. Watkins Minority Graduate Fellowship

AMOUNT: $12000   DEADLINE: May 1
FIELDS/MAJORS: Microbiological Sciences

One-year fellowship for students who are African-American, Hispanic-American, Native American, or Native Pacific Islander. Must have completed first year of doctoral studies in microbiological science, be ASM student members, and U.S. citizens or permanent residents. Project's mentor must also be an ASM member. Write to the address below for additional information.

American Society for Microbiology
Office of Education and Training
1325 Massachusetts Avenue, NW
Washington, DC   20005

1001
Robert G. Carr and Nona K. Carr Scholarships (Graduate)

AMOUNT: Maximum: $4500   DEADLINE: February 1
FIELDS/MAJORS: All Areas of Study

Scholarships for graduate students at Angelo State University who are academically accomplished and have high GRE/GMAT scores (GPA of at least 3.5). Write to the address below for details.

Angelo State University
Carr Academic Scholarship Program
Box 11007-C, ASU Station
San Angelo, TX   76909

1002
Robert H. and Clarice Smith Fellowship

AMOUNT: $16000   DEADLINE: None Specified
FIELDS/MAJORS: Art History–Dutch or Flemish

One-year fellowships are available for doctoral scholars researching for the dissertation. The Smith Fellow may use the grant to study either in the U.S. or abroad. Applicants must know two foreign languages related to the topic of their dissertation and be U.S. citizens or legal residents. Write to the address below for information.

National Gallery of Art
Center for Advanced Study in Visual Arts
Predoctoral Fellowship Program
Washington, DC   20565

1003

Robert L. Baker Graduate Student Scholarship

AMOUNT: None Specified   DEADLINE: None Specified
FIELDS/MAJORS: Horticulture/Garden Design

Applicants must be graduate students studying ornamental horticulture or garden design. Must be a Maryland resident. Write to the address below for details.

Federated Garden Clubs of Maryland, Robert Baker Scholarship
Mrs. Pauline Vollmer, Chairperson
6405 Murray Hill Road
Baltimore, MD   21212

1004

Robert M. Burger Fellowship

AMOUNT: None Specified   DEADLINE: February 1
FIELDS/MAJORS: Microelectronics

Fellowships are available at Duke University, North Carolina State University, and the University of North Carolina for graduate students pursuing a doctoral degree in areas related to microelectronics. Awards pay tuition and fees as well as a monthly stipend of $1400, and a $2000 gift to the university department with which the student is associated. Must be a U.S. citizen. Write to the address below for complete details and an application.

Semiconductor Research Corporation Education Alliance
Graduate Fellowship Program
PO Box 12053
Research Triangle Park, NC   27709

1005

Robert M. Dennis Scholarship

AMOUNT: $1200   DEADLINE: February 1
FIELDS/MAJORS: Law

Awards for law students who demonstrate financial need. Renewable for three academic years for full-time students; four academic years for part-time students. Contact the Assistant Dean, Chase College of Law, for further information.

Northern Kentucky University
Chase College of Law
Office of Admissions
Highland Heights, KY   41099

1006

Robert S. Morison Fellowship

AMOUNT: $40000   DEADLINE: November 1
FIELDS/MAJORS: Neurology, Neurosurgery

Fellowships for medical doctors who have been accepted into or completed residence in neurology or neurosurgery and in need of two years intensive research or training preparation for a career in academic neurology or neurosurgery. Write to the address below for complete details.

Grass Foundation
PO Box 850250
Braintree, MA   02185-0250

1007

Robert W. Tuttle/ Dean Theodore Harwood Memorial Scholarships

AMOUNT: None Specified   DEADLINE: April 15
FIELDS/MAJORS: Medicine

Awards for students enrolled in the School of Medicine. Based on need and satisfactory academics. Contact the address below for further information or the financial aid office at your school's location.

University of North Dakota—School of Medicine
Sandra Elshaug, Financial Aid Office
PO Box 9037—501 N. Columbia Road
Grand Forks, ND   58202

1008

Robert W. Woodruff Fellowship

AMOUNT: Maximum: $15000
DEADLINE: May 31
FIELDS/MAJORS: Public or Business Administration, Social Work, Recreation, and Leisure

This graduate fellowship program has two options for master's degree candidates and for those holding a master's. All applicants must be currently involved with the Boys and Girls Clubs and must make a commitment to a minimum of two years full-time employment at a Boys and Girls Club after completion of the program. Write to the address below for details.

Boys and Girls Clubs of America
Human Resource Group
1230 W. Peachtree Street, NW
Atlanta, GA   30309

1009

Rock Sleyster Memorial Scholarship

AMOUNT: $2500   DEADLINE: May 1
FIELDS/MAJORS: Psychiatry

Candidates must be high achieving rising seniors with demonstrated interest and financial need. Nomination by medical school is required. For U.S. citizens studying in the U.S. or Canada. Approximately twenty awards offered annually. Write to the address below for further information.

American Medical Association
Division of Undergraduate Medical Educ.
515 North State Street
Chicago, IL   60610

1010

Rockefeller Foundation Fellowships in Legal Humanities

AMOUNT: $40000   DEADLINE: November 15
FIELDS/MAJORS: Law, Humanities, Social Science

Postdoctoral fellowships are available at Stanford to support research on theories of interpretation, intention, narrative, and human agency in law and the humanities, especially as these affect subordinated populations. Twelve awards per year. Write to the address below for information.

Stanford University
Stanford Humanities Center
Mariposa House
Stanford, CA   94305

1011

Rodney C. Rhodes Memorial Scholarship

AMOUNT: None Specified   DEADLINE: March 1
FIELDS/MAJORS: Earth and Planetary Sciences, Geology

Awards are available at the University of New Mexico for graduates studying geology or students pursuing a graduate degree in the fields of earth and planetary science. Write to the address below for information.

University of New Mexico, Albuquerque
Office of Financial Aid
Albuquerque, NM   87131

1012

Roger Dodge Memorial Scholarships

AMOUNT: None Specified   DEADLINE: February 15
FIELDS/MAJORS: Reading

Awards for graduate students at UW, Platteville in the area of reading. One award is offered annually. Write to the address below for more information.

University of Wisconsin, Platteville
Office of Enrollment and Admissions
Platteville, WI   53818

1013

Rosann S. Berry Annual Meeting Fellowship

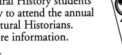

AMOUNT: $500   DEADLINE: None Specified
FIELDS/MAJORS: Architectural History

Awards are available for Architectural History students engaged in advanced graduate study to attend the annual meeting of the Society of Architectural Historians. Write to the address below for more information.

Society of Architectural Historians
1365 North Astor Street
Chicago, IL   60610

1014

Rosario Curletti Scholarship

AMOUNT: None Specified
DEADLINE: March 2
FIELDS/MAJORS: Agricultural Sciences

Awards open to graduate students showing professional promise. Must have a minimum GPA of 3.2. Contact the address below for further information.

California Polytechnic State University
Financial Aid Office
212 Administration Building
San Luis Obispo, CA   93407

1015

Rose Marie and Martin H. Boone Jr. Graduate Scholarship

AMOUNT: $1000   DEADLINE: None Specified
FIELDS/MAJORS: Religious Studies

Student must be admitted to the Master of Arts program in religious studies with a 3.25 undergraduate GPA and a 3.5 graduate GPA. Must have at least 3 hours each semester. Contact the religious studies department for more information.

Southwest Missouri State University
Office of Financial Aid
901 South National Avenue
Springfield, MO   65804

1016

Rosenblum Award

AMOUNT: None Specified   DEADLINE: March 1
FIELDS/MAJORS: Psychology

Awards are available at the University of New Mexico for outstanding clinical psychology graduate students involved in research and treatment of children and their families. Write to the address below for more complete details.

University of New Mexico, Albuquerque
Office of Financial Aid
Albuquerque, NM   87131

1017

Roth Journalism Fellowship

AMOUNT: None Specified   DEADLINE: None Specified
FIELDS/MAJORS: Journalism

Applicants must be graduate students who are New York state citizens attending a New York state college or university or a citizen from a different state attending a New York school. Must be pursuing a career in journalism or public relations. This is a fellowship program in the New York state legislature not an on-campus aid program. For U.S. citizens only. Write to Dr. Russell J. Williams, Director, at the address below for details.

New York State Senate
Senate Student Programs
90 South Swan Street, Room 401
Albany, NY   12247

1018 Rowley/Ministerial Education Scholarship

AMOUNT: None Specified
DEADLINE: March 15
FIELDS/MAJORS: Theology

Applicants must be members of the Christian Church (Disciples of Christ) who are preparing for the ordained ministry. Must be a full-time student. Financial need is considered. Write to the address below for details. GPA of at least 2.3 required.

Christian Church (Disciples of Christ)
Attn: Scholarships
PO Box 1986
Indianapolis, IN   46206

1019 Roy Hickman Family Fund Assistantship

AMOUNT: None Specified
DEADLINE: March 1
FIELDS/MAJORS: Sports Administration Program

Assistantship available at the University of New Mexico for graduate students in a sports administration program. Contact the Health Education Department for more information.

University of New Mexico, Albuquerque
Office of Financial Aid
Albuquerque, NM   87131

1020 Rozenwaig Single Mothers Scholarship Fund

AMOUNT: $2000   DEADLINE: March 5
FIELDS/MAJORS: Social Work

Scholarship is available to a graduate student in good academic standing in the school of social work. The student must be a single mother, over the age of thirty-five, and demonstrate financial need. Essay on family life required. Write to the address below for more information.

Florida International University
College of Urban and Public Affairs
Office of the Dean—AC1 200
North Miami, FL   33181

1021 Rural Kentucky Medical Scholarship Fund Loans

AMOUNT: Maximum: $12000   DEADLINE: April 1
FIELDS/MAJORS: Medicine

Loans for Kentucky residents who have been admitted to one of the two accredited medical schools in Kentucky. Recipients must agree to practice twelve months in an approved rural Kentucky county for each loan received. Write to the address below for more information.

Kentucky Medical Association
301 N. Hurstbourne Parkway
Suite 200
Louisville, KY   40222

1022 Ruth H. Skaggs Graduate Scholarships

AMOUNT: $1000   DEADLINE: February 28
FIELDS/MAJORS: All Areas of Study

Scholarships for full-time graduate students who reside in the Aurora area. Renewable for up to three years. Write to the address below for details.

Aurora Foundation
111 W. Downer Place, Suite 312
Aurora, IL   60506

1023 Ruth Ingersoll Goldmark Fellowship

AMOUNT: $1000   DEADLINE: December 16
FIELDS/MAJORS: English Literature, English Composition, Classics

Fellowships for Wellesley alumnae for graduate study in English literature, English composition, or the classics. Contact the address below for further information.

Wellesley College, Fellowships for Wellesley Alumnae
Sec'y, Committee on Graduate Fellowships
106 Central Street, Career Center
Wellesley, MA   02181

1024 Ruth Renfroe Scholarship

AMOUNT: $500   DEADLINE: March 1
FIELDS/MAJORS: Social Work

Award for a graduate student who agrees to fulfill a three-term, two-day a week field instruction assignment in a practicum serving the elderly. One award offered annually. Contact the Graduate School of Social Work for more information.

Portland State University
Graduate School of Social Work
300 University Center Building
Portland, OR   97207

1025 Ruth Satter Memorial Award

AMOUNT: $500–$1000   DEADLINE: January 15
FIELDS/MAJORS: All Areas of Study

Scholarship for women pursuing their doctorate who have taken at least three years off to raise children. Applications available after October 1. Write to the address below for more details.

Association for Women in Science Educational Foundation
National Headquarters
1200 New York Avenue, NW, #650
Washington, DC   20005

1026
Ruth Taylor Scholarship

AMOUNT: None Specified DEADLINE: June 15
FIELDS/MAJORS: Medicine, Social Work

Scholarships for Westchester County, New York, residents who are graduate students in social work or medicine. Based on need, ability, and interest in public service. Write to the commissioner's office at the address below for details.

Westchester County Department of Social Services
Ruth Taylor Award Fund Committee
112 E. Post Road
White Plains, NY   10601

1027
S.O. Graham Research Fellowship Fund

AMOUNT: None Specified DEADLINE: February 1
FIELDS/MAJORS: Plant Pathology

Award open to graduate students who can demonstrate financial need. Contact the address below for further information.

Washington State University—Scholarship Committee
College of Agriculture and Home Economics
423 Hulbert Hall
Pullman, WA   99164

1028
Samuel A. Laycock Memorial Scholarship

AMOUNT: $150 DEADLINE: September 1
FIELDS/MAJORS: Law

Scholarships are available at the University of Oklahoma, Norman for full-time, second-year male law students who are married, with a GPA of at least 1.7. Write to the address below for information.

University of Oklahoma, Norman
Admissions and Records, Law Center
Room 22, 300 Timberdell Road
Norman, OK   73019

1029
Samuel H. Kress Joint Athens-Jerusalem Fellowship

AMOUNT: $5500 DEADLINE: November 15
FIELDS/MAJORS: Classical Studies, Art History, Architecture, Archaeology

Awards are available for Ph.D. candidates in the areas of study above. Must be a U.S. citizen. Write to the address below for more information.

American School of Classical Studies at Athens
Committee on Admissions and Fellowships
6-8 Charlton Street
Princeton, NJ   08540

1030
Samuel R. Wallis Scholarship

AMOUNT: None Specified DEADLINE: April 20
FIELDS/MAJORS: Medicine

Scholarships available to residents of Hawaii who have been accepted by a medical school. Preference given to those who plan on practicing in Hawaii. Contact the address below for further information.

Wilcox Hospital Foundation
S.R. Wallis Scholarship Committee
3420 Kuhio Highway
Lihue, HI   96766

1031
Sarah Perry Wood Medical Fellowship

AMOUNT: Maximum: $24000 DEADLINE: December 16
FIELDS/MAJORS: Medicine

Fellowships for Wellesley alumnae for the study of medicine. Not renewable. Contact the address below for further information.

Wellesley College, Fellowships for Wellesley Alumnae
Sec'y, Committee on Graduate Fellowships
106 Central Street, Career Center
Wellesley, MA   02181

1032
Sarah Rebecca Reed Scholarship

AMOUNT: $1500 DEADLINE: March 15
FIELDS/MAJORS: Library and Information Science

Applicants must have been admitted to a graduate program in Library Science accredited by the ALA. For master's level study. Write to the executive secretary at the address below for details.

Beta Phi Mu International Library Science Honor Society
Executive Secretary, Beta Phi Mu
SLIS—Florida State University
Tallahassee, FL   32306

1033
Schechter Foundation Grants

AMOUNT: $1250 DEADLINE: July 1
FIELDS/MAJORS: Physical, Occupational Therapy

Grants for graduate students enrolled in one of the above programs at New York, Columbia, or Hahnemann universities. Twenty-five to thirty awards offered annually. Must be a U.S. citizens to apply. Contact the address below for further information.

Schechter Foundation
535 Madison Avenue, 28th Floor
New York, NY   10022

1034
Schering-Plough Dissertation Fellowship

AMOUNT: None Specified **DEADLINE:** February 1
FIELDS/MAJORS: Biological Sciences

Fellowships open to doctoral candidates in the form of stipends to allow students to complete their dissertations during the tenure of the fellowship. Contact the address below for further information.

Fordham University
Graduate Admissions Office—Keating 216
Fordham University
Bronx, NY 10458

1035
Scholars in Residence Program Fellowships

AMOUNT: Maximum: $30000
DEADLINE: January 13
FIELDS/MAJORS: Black Culture, History, Museum Administration

To assist scholars and professionals whose research in the black experience will benefit from extended access to the center's collections. Allows fellows to spend six months to a year in residence and includes seminars, forums, and conferences. Candidates for advanced degrees must have received the degree or completed all the requirements for it by the Center's deadline. Contact the address below for further information and application.

Schomburg Center for Research in Black Culture
515 Malcolm X Boulevard
New York, NY 10037

1036
Scholarship in Librarianship

AMOUNT: $3000 **DEADLINE:** May 1
FIELDS/MAJORS: Library Science

Must be Louisiana residents in a master's program at Louisiana State University School of Library and Information Science. Undergraduate GPA of at least 3.2 is required. Residency requirement is met by any of the following: 1) born in Louisiana, 2) lived in Louisiana for the past two years, or 3) either parent lived in Louisiana for at least five years. GRE score of 1050 required. Write to the address below for complete details.

Louisiana Library Association
PO Box 3058
Baton Rouge, LA 70821

1037
Scholarships for Foreign Students

AMOUNT: None Specified **DEADLINE:** June 1
FIELDS/MAJORS: Church-Related Studies, Theology

Scholarships for students from developing countries who are in some type of theological training within the Anglican Communion. Preference is given to students pursuing a master's degree, but it is open for all levels of study. Write to the address below for more details. Applications must be authorized or approved by the Diocesan Bishop, the Archbishop, or another provincial authority.

Episcopal Church Center
815 Second Avenue
New York, NY 10017

1038
Scholarships for Minority Ministries

AMOUNT: None Specified **DEADLINE:** June 1
FIELDS/MAJORS: Church Related Studies, Theology

Scholarships for Asian-American, African-American, Hispanic, and Native American students for assistance in pursuing theological education or a graduate-level degree at a church approved seminary or in an Episcopal studies program. Write to the address below for more details.

Episcopal Church Center
815 Second Avenue
New York, NY 10017

1039
School Librarians Workshop Scholarship

AMOUNT: $2500 **DEADLINE:** February 3
FIELDS/MAJORS: Library Science, Children's or Young Adult

Applicants must be entering an ALA-accredited master's program or a school library media program that meets ALA curriculum guidelines for an NCATE-accredited unit. Based on interest in working with children or young adults in a school library setting. Write to the address shown for details.

American Library Association
American Assn. of School Librarians
50 E. Huron Street
Chicago, IL 60611

1040
School of Social Work Graduate Awards

AMOUNT: None Specified **DEADLINE:** None Specified
FIELDS/MAJORS: Social Work

Scholarships are available at the University of Oklahoma, Norman for full-time graduate students majoring in social work. Includes the Deborah Grace Toops Memorial Scholarship, the George Rogers Scholarship, and the Interdisciplinary Graduate Training Awards. Individual award requirements may vary. Write to the address below for information.

University of Oklahoma, Norman
School of Social Work
217 Rhyn
Norman, OK 73019

1041
Schwartz Writing Competition Award

AMOUNT: $1000 **DEADLINE:** February 1
FIELDS/MAJORS: Medicine

Writing competition for medical students who are currently enrolled in an accredited school in the United States or Canada. Papers must be no less than 3000 words in length, contain only uncollaborated original work, may deal with any aspect of legal medicine, or relate to research done by the author. Write to the address below for more information.

American College of Legal Medicine
Student Writing Competition
611 East Wells Street
Milwaukee, WI   53202

1042
Science and Technology Fellowships

AMOUNT: $5000–$9500
DEADLINE: December 15
FIELDS/MAJORS: Architecture, Computer Science, Engineering, Mathematics, Statistics

Open to women who are citizens or permanent residents of the United States preparing to enter designated fields with low female participation. Available to candidates for the final year of a master's degree program. Write for complete details.

American Association of University Women Educational Foundation
2201 N. Dodge Street
Iowa City, IA   52243

1043
Science, Engineering and Diplomacy Fellows Program

AMOUNT: None Specified   DEADLINE: January 15
FIELDS/MAJORS: Engineering, Science

Applicants must be AAAS fellows or applying for membership. Two agencies are participating, the U.S. Agency for International Development (USAID) and the U.S. Department of State Foreign Policy Agency. Will work on scientific and technical subjects with regard to international affairs. Must be U.S. citizens. Write to the address below for details.

American Association for the Advancement of Science
1200 New York Avenue, NW
Washington, DC   20005

1044
Scientist Development Grant

AMOUNT: $65000   DEADLINE: None Specified
FIELDS/MAJORS: Medical Research (Cardiovascular and Other Related Areas)

Awards for beginning investigators in the areas of cardiovascular research. Applications may be submitted in the final year of a postdoctoral fellowship or within the first four years of a faculty appointment. Based on originality and scientific merit of proposed project, prior productivity of the applicant, and evidence that the award will promote independent status for the applicant. Write to the address below for more information.

American Heart Association
National Center
7272 Greenville Avenue
Dallas, TX   75231

1045
Scott Lakin Jones Memorial Fellowship

AMOUNT: None Specified   DEADLINE: March 1
FIELDS/MAJORS: Music

Awards are available at the University of New Mexico for full-time graduate students majoring in music. Contact the music department for more information.

University of New Mexico, Albuquerque
Office of Financial Aid
Albuquerque, NM   87131

1046
Second- and Third-Year Law Scholarships

AMOUNT: $100–$1000   DEADLINE: September 1
FIELDS/MAJORS: Law

Scholarships are available at the University of Oklahoma, Norman for full-time, second- or third-year law students. Includes the Bennie and Audrey Shultz, Gable and Gotwals Scholarship, Charles B. Memminger Memorial, J. Marshall Huser and Hartzog, Conger, Cason and Hargus scholarships. Award requirements may vary slightly. Contact the address below for further information.

University of Oklahoma, Norman
Admissions and Records, Law Center
Room 22, 300 Timberdell Road
Norman, OK   73019

1047
Second-Year Law Scholarships

AMOUNT: $200–$4000   DEADLINE: September 1
FIELDS/MAJORS: Law

Scholarships are available at the University of Oklahoma, Norman for full-time, second-year law students. Includes the Cecil L. Hunt Memorial, Charles B. Memminger Memorial, Frank C. Love Memorial, Maurice H. Merrill Memorial, Ray Teague, Robert J. Emery, Savage and Vivian Hood scholarships. Individual award requirements may vary. Write to the address below for information.

University of Oklahoma, Norman
Admissions and Records, Law Center
Room 22, 300 Timberdell Road
Norman, OK   73019

1048
Seix-Dow Fellowship

AMOUNT: None Specified
DEADLINE: February 1
FIELDS/MAJORS: Economics, International Development, International Economics

Fellowships open to Hispanic students enrolled in any of the above listed areas. Contact the address below for further information.

Fordham University
Graduate Admissions Office—Keating 216
Fordham University
Bronx, NY   10458

1049
Selected Professions Fellowship

AMOUNT: $5000–$9500
DEADLINE: December 17
FIELDS/MAJORS: Architecture, Business Admin., Engineering, Math, Computer Science

Fellowships are available for women who are in the final year of an advanced degree in the fields of architecture (master's), business administration (M.B.A.), engineering (M.E., M.S., Ph.D.), mathematics (Ph.D.), and computer science (Ph.D.) must be U.S. citizens or permanent residents. Write to the address below for information.

American Association of University Women
Fellowship Programs
2201 N. Dodge Street, Department 67
Iowa City, IA   52243

1050
Seminars on Teaching About Japan

AMOUNT: Maximum: $3000
DEADLINE: October 1
FIELDS/MAJORS: Japanese Studies

Grants are available for scholars to design seminars or courses to improve the teaching of the Japanese studies at the college or pre-college level. Applicants should be prepared to explain the character or rationale of their seminar and be able to prepare a budget estimate. Write to the address below for more information.

Northeast Asia Council Association for Asian Studies
1 Lane Hall
University of Michigan
Ann Arbor, MI   48109

1051
Senator Jeff Johnston Memorial Scholarship

AMOUNT: $1000   DEADLINE: September 1
FIELDS/MAJORS: Law

Scholarship available at the University of Oklahoma, Norman for full-time, second- or third-year law students who reside in eastern Oklahoma. Based on merit and financial need. One award offered annually. Write to the address below for information.

University of Oklahoma, Norman
Admissions and Records, Law Center
Room 22, 300 Timberdell Road
Norman, OK   73019

1052
Senior Merit Awards

AMOUNT: None Specified   DEADLINE: August 31
FIELDS/MAJORS: Medicine

Awards given to senior medical students in recognition of outstanding academic achievement, leadership, and community service. Includes the Irving Graef Memorial Scholarship, the William and Charlotte Cadbury Award, the Franklin C. McLean Award, and the James H. Robinson Memorial Prize. Send a SASE to the address below for additional information.

National Medical Fellowships, Inc.
110 West 32nd Street
New York, NY   10001

1053
Sequoyah Graduate Fellowships

AMOUNT: None Specified   DEADLINE: October 1
FIELDS/MAJORS: All Areas of Study

Fellowships are available for American Indian or Native Alaskan graduate students. Ten awards are offered for study in all areas. Write to the address below for details.

Association on American Indian Affairs, Inc.
Box 268
Sisseton, SD   57262

1054
Sertoma Communicative Disorders Scholarship Program

AMOUNT: $2500   DEADLINE: March 28
FIELDS/MAJORS: Audiology, Speech Pathology

Scholarships for master's level programs in Audiology or Speech Pathology. Applicants must be citizens of the U.S., Mexico, or Canada enrolled full-time in a U.S. institution accredited by ASHA's Council on Academic Accreditation. Must have a minimum GPA of 3.2 in college coursework. Thirty awards are offered annually. Information is available from the address below (must include a #10 SASE) or from NSSLHA chapters, universities, Sertoma Affiliates, Speech and Hearing Organizations, etc.

Sertoma International
Sertoma Scholarship
1912 East Meyer Boulevard
Kansas City, MO   64132

1055
Shirley N. and Frank B. Gilliam Scholarships

AMOUNT: None Specified   DEADLINE: March 1
FIELDS/MAJORS: Medicine

Awards are available at the University of New Mexico for full-time medical students who have completed at least one year of study at UNM medical center. Must demonstrate financial need and satisfactory academic standing. Write to the address below for more information.

University of New Mexico, Albuquerque
Office of Financial Aid
Albuquerque, NM   87131

1056
Short-Term Fellowships

AMOUNT: $1000–$2000
DEADLINE: December 1
FIELDS/MAJORS: Bibliography, History of Printing and Publishing

Graduate research fellowships for one or two months. Supports inquiry into research focusing on books or manuscripts (the physical objects themselves). Approximately eight awards per year. Three letters of recommendation are required. Award amount is per month. Write to the address below for details.

Bibliographical Society of America
BSA Executive Secretary
PO Box 397, Grand Central Station
New York, NY   10163

1057
Short-Term Research Fellowships

AMOUNT: $2000–$4000
DEADLINE: January 15
FIELDS/MAJORS: Humanities/Social Science

Two- to four-month research fellowships are available for pre- or postdoctoral study. Open to American citizens and foreign nationals. For study in any area in which the Library has holdings. Write to address below for details.

John Carter Brown Library
Attn: Director
Box 1894, Brown University
Providence, RI   02912

1058
Short-Term Resident Fellowships for Individual Research

AMOUNT: None Specified   DEADLINE: March 1
FIELDS/MAJORS: History (American and Western), Humanities, Literature

Scholars who hold a Ph.D. may apply. Applicants must be working on a specific research project in a field appropriate to the Newberry's Collection. Doctoral candidates who have completed all requirements except the dissertation are also invited to apply. For study and research involving the collections of the Newberry. Preference given to scholars from outside the Chicago area. Write to the address below for details.

Newberry Library
Committee on Awards
60 W. Walton Street
Chicago, IL   60610

1059
Short-Term Travel to Japan for Professional Purposes

AMOUNT: None Specified   DEADLINE: October 1
FIELDS/MAJORS: Japanese Studies

Awards for scholars who have a Ph.D. (or comparable professional qualification), and need time in Japan to complete their work. These grants are intended for short-term research trips by scholars who are already familiar with Japan and with their topic. Second deadline date is February 1 for the spring awards. Ph.D. candidates are not eligible to apply. Write to the address below for more information.

Northeast Asia Council Association for Asian Studies
1 Lane Hall
University of Michigan
Ann Arbor, MI   48109

1060
Sigma Phi Alpha Graduate Scholarship

AMOUNT: None Specified   DEADLINE: April 1
FIELDS/MAJORS: Dental Hygiene

Awarded to a candidate pursuing a graduate degree in dental hygiene or a related field. Candidates must include a statement of professional activities related to dental hygiene. Write to the address below for more information.

American Dental Hygienists' Association Institute for Oral Health
444 North Michigan Avenue, Suite 3400
Chicago, IL   60611

1061
Sigma Theta Tau American Nurses' Foundation Grant

AMOUNT: $6000   DEADLINE: May 1
FIELDS/MAJORS: Nursing

Grant for nurses who have completed master's degree study. Supports research of a clinical nature. One award per year. Request application forms for the ANF Grant Program from the address below.

Sigma Theta Tau International/American Nurses Foundation
American Nurses Foundation
600 Maryland Avenue, SW, Suite 100 West
Washington, DC   20024

1062
Sigma Theta Tau Int'l/ American Association of Diabetes Educators Grant

AMOUNT: Maximum: $6000   DEADLINE: October 1
FIELDS/MAJORS: Nursing

Grant for nurses who have completed master's degree study, to encourage them to contribute to the enhancement of quality and increase the availability of diabetes education and care research. One grant is offered annually. Request application forms for the AADE Grant Program from the address below.

Sigma Theta Tau International Honor Society of Nursing/AADE
AADE Education and Research Foundation
444 North Michigan Avenue, Suite 1240
Chicago, IL   60611

1063
Sigma Theta Tau Int'l/ Emergency Nursing Foundation Grant

AMOUNT: Maximum: $6000   DEADLINE: March 1
FIELDS/MAJORS: Nursing

Grant for nurses who have completed master's degree study, which will advance the specialized practice of emergency nursing. One grant is offered annually. Request application forms for the AADE Grant Program from the address below.

Sigma Theta Tau International/Emergency Nursing Foundation
Emergency Nursing Foundation
216 Higgins Road
Park Ridge, IL   60068

1064

Sigma Theta Tau Int'l/ Mead Johnson Nutritionals Perinatal Grants

AMOUNT: $10000   DEADLINE: June 1
FIELDS/MAJORS: Nursing

Grant for nurses who have completed master's degree study. Supports research relating to perinatal issues (up to one-year old). One award per year. Must be a U.S. citizen. Request application forms for the Mead Johnson Grant Program from the below address.

Sigma Theta Tau International Honor Society of Nursing
Program Department
550 West North Street
Indianapolis, IN   46202

1065

Sigma Theta Tau International/Glaxo Wellcome Research Grant

AMOUNT: Maximum: $5000   DEADLINE: October 1
FIELDS/MAJORS: Nursing

Grant for nurses who have completed master's degree study. Supports research relating to the prescribing practices of advanced practicing nurses. One award is offered annually. Request application forms for the Glaxo Grant Program from the address below.

Sigma Theta Tau International Honor Society of Nursing/
    Glaxo Wellcome
Program Department
550 West North Street
Indianapolis, IN   46202

1066

Sigma Theta Tau International Small Research Grants

AMOUNT: $3000   DEADLINE: March 1
FIELDS/MAJORS: Nursing

Grants for nurses who have completed master's degree study. No specific focus of this program; but pilot, multidisciplinary, and international research is encouraged. Ten to fifteen awards per year. Request application forms for the Small Grants Program from the address below.

Sigma Theta Tau International Honor Society of Nursing
Program Department
550 West North Street
Indianapolis, IN   46202

1067

Sigma Theta Tau International/Oncology Nursing Society Grant

AMOUNT: $10000   DEADLINE: December 1
FIELDS/MAJORS: Nursing

Grant for nurses who have completed master's degree study. Supports research of an oncology clinically-oriented topic. One award per year. Request application forms for the ONS Grant Program from the address below.

Sigma Theta Tau International Honor Society of Nursing
Oncology Nursing Foundation
501 Holiday Drive
Pittsburgh, PA   15220

1068

Sigma Theta Tau Nursing

AMOUNT: $3000–$10000   DEADLINE: March 1
FIELDS/MAJORS: Nursing

Grant for nurses who have completed master's degree study. Supports research relating to caregiving issues for HIV-positive persons. One award per year. Write to the address listed for more information.

Sigma Theta Tau International Honor Society of Nursing
Program Department
550 West North Street
Indianapolis, IN   46202

1069

Sigma Theta Tau/ American Assn. of Critical Care Nurses Grant

AMOUNT: $10000   DEADLINE: October 1
FIELDS/MAJORS: Nursing

Grant for nurses who have completed master's degree study. Supports research relating to Critical Care Nursing Practice. One award per year. Request application forms for the AACN Grant Program from the address below.

Sigma Theta Tau International/AACN
Department of Research
101 Columbia
Alison Viejo, CA   92656

1070

Silvio O. Conte Memorial Scholarship

AMOUNT: None Specified   DEADLINE: None Specified
FIELDS/MAJORS: Wildlife, Fisheries, Ecology, Natural Resources

Awards for graduate students in the fields listed above. Based on financial need, academic achievement, and potential for contribution to the profession. Contact the Associate Dean, College of Food and Natural Resources.

University of Massachusetts, Amherst
Associate Dean
College of Food and Natural Resources
Amherst, MA   01003

1071

Simmons Scholarships

AMOUNT: $2000   DEADLINE: July 28
FIELDS/MAJORS: Travel and Tourism

Awards are available for master's or doctoral students of travel and tourism at a recognized college, university, or proprietary travel school. Must be U.S. citizens or legal residents and have a GPA of at least 2.5. Two awards per year are given. Write to the address below for more information.

American Society of Travel Agents
Scholarship Committee
1101 King Street, Suite 200
Alexandria, VA   22314

1072
Simons-Minkler Graduate Scholarships

AMOUNT: Maximum: $1000   **DEADLINE:** February 28
FIELDS/MAJORS: All Areas of Study

Scholarships for students pursuing graduate or professional degrees in any field of study. Must be graduates of East Aurora, West Aurora, or Yorkville high schools. Write to the address below for details.

Aurora Foundation
111 W. Downer Place, Suite 312
Aurora, IL   60506

1073
Sinfonia Foundation Research Assistance Grants

AMOUNT: Maximum: $1000   **DEADLINE:** May 1
FIELDS/MAJORS: Music Research

Grants supporting research on American music or music in America. Must show history of scholarly writing in music or show unusual knowledge in area to be researched. Write to the address below for details.

Sinfonia Foundation
10600 Old State Road
Evansville, IN   47711

1074
Singer and Pollack Scholarship

AMOUNT: None Specified   **DEADLINE:** March 1
FIELDS/MAJORS: Medicine, Dentistry

Scholarships are available at the University of Oklahoma for medical or dental students. Four awards are offered annually. Write to the address below for information.

University of Oklahoma, Norman
Director, Office of Financial Aid
OUHSC, PO Box 73190
Oklahoma City, OK 73190

1075
SLA Scholarship Program

AMOUNT: $6000   **DEADLINE:** October 31
FIELDS/MAJORS: Library/Information Science

For study in librarianship leading to a master's degree at a recognized school of library or information science. Preference will be given to those who display an aptitude for and interest in special library work. Up to three awards given per year. Write to the address below for complete details.

Special Libraries Association
SLA Scholarship Committee
1700 Eighteenth Street, NW
Washington, DC   20009

1076
Sloan Research Fellowships

AMOUNT: Maximum: $30000
DEADLINE: None Specified
FIELDS/MAJORS: Chemistry, Computer Science, Economics, Math, Neuroscience, Physics

Postdoctoral fellowships for promising researchers early in their careers. Fellowships are for two years. The foundation also directly supports research in areas it feels are not sufficiently covered by agencies such as NSF and NIH. One hundred awards per year. Request the brochure "Sloan Research Fellowships" from the address below.

Alfred P. Sloan Foundation
Sloan Foundation Fellowship Programs
630 Fifth Avenue
New York, NY   10111

1077
Smith, Wolnitzek, Schachter & Rowekamp, P.S.C.

AMOUNT: None Specified   **DEADLINE:** February 1
FIELDS/MAJORS: Law

Awards for Kentucky residents who are second-year law students. Must demonstrate financial need and academic merit. Contact the Assistant Dean, Chase College of Law, for further information.

Northern Kentucky University
Chase College of Law
Office of Admissions
Highland Heights, KY   41099

1078
Smithsonian Fellowship Program

AMOUNT: $3000–$25000
DEADLINE: January 15
FIELDS/MAJORS: Humanities, Art Studies, Anthropology, Astrophysics, Biology, History

Fellowships are available to pre- and postdoctoral scholars for research in one of the above fields, or any field of interest to the Smithsonian. Write to the address below for details. Request the publication "Smithsonian Opportunities for Research and Study."

Smithsonian Institution
Office of Fellowships and Grants
955 L'Enfant Plaza, Suite 7000
Washington, DC   20560

1079

Smithsonian Marine Station at Link Port Fellowships

AMOUNT: None Specified   DEADLINE: February 15
FIELDS/MAJORS: Marine Sciences

Fellowships are available for pre- and postdoctoral scholars to support research in marine science at Link Port. Three levels of fellowships are offered: ten-week periods for graduate students, two- to twelve-month periods for recent Ph.D.s, and also for senior scholars who have held the Ph.D. for more than seven years. Write to the address below for information.

Smithsonian Institution
Smithsonian Marine Station at Link Port
Old Dixie Highway
Fort Pierce, FL   34946

1080

Society for the Humanities Postdoctoral Fellowships

AMOUNT: $32000   DEADLINE: October 21
FIELDS/MAJORS: Humanities

Six to ten fellowships for Ph.D. applicants with at least one year of college teaching experience. Ph.D. must have been awarded before applying for this fellowship program seeks to bring scholars from a wide variety of disciplines in the study of one topic. Write to the address below for details. Must have Ph.D. completed at time of application.

Cornell University
Agnes Sirrine, Program Administrator
27 East Avenue, A.D. White Center
Ithaca, NY   14853

1081

Solis Family Fellowship

AMOUNT: $600   DEADLINE: January 6
FIELDS/MAJORS: Public Services

Open to full-time Latino master degree students planning a career to serve Latino people and communities in the U.S. Must be U.S. citizens or permanent residents. Contact the address below for further information.

University of California, Berkeley
Office of Financial Aid Graduate Unit
201 Sproul Hall, #1960
Berkeley, CA   94720

1082

South Asian Fellowships, Southeast Asian Fellowships

AMOUNT: None Specified   DEADLINE: November 1
FIELDS/MAJORS: Asian Studies

Fellowships are available for scholars enrolled in a U.S. doctoral program. Applicants must have completed all the program requirements except for the dissertation. Research must be in Asian studies (including Sri Lanka, Nepal, Bangladesh, India, Pakistan, Brunei, Burma, Indonesia, Kampuchea, Laos, Malaysia, Singapore, Philippines, Thailand, and Vietnam.) Write to the address below for information.

Social Science Research Council
Fellowships and Grants
605 Third Avenue
New York, NY   10158

1083

South Carolina Graduate Incentive Fellowship Program

AMOUNT: Maximum: $10000   DEADLINE: None Specified
FIELDS/MAJORS: All Areas of Study

Fellowships for South Carolina residents who are members of a minority group attending a South Carolina public college or university. For graduate and doctoral study. Write to the address below for additional information.

South Carolina Commission on Higher Education
1333 Main Street, Suite 200
Columbia, SC   29201

1084

South Central Modern Languages Association Fellowships

AMOUNT: $800   DEADLINE: March 1
FIELDS/MAJORS: History (American and European), Humanities, Literature

Fellowships are available for work in residence by a member of the South Central Modern Language Association. Applicants must be postdoctoral scholars. Contact the address below for more details.

Newberry Library
Committee on Awards
60 W. Walton Street
Chicago, IL   60610

1085

Special Education Scholarship

AMOUNT: None Specified   DEADLINE: January 15
FIELDS/MAJORS: Special Education

Available to graduate students majoring in special education. Write to the address below for more information.

Fort Hays State University
Office of Student Financial Aid
600 Park Street
Hays, KS   67601

1086

Speech Language Pathologist Incentive Program

AMOUNT: None Specified   DEADLINE: April 15
FIELDS/MAJORS: Speech Pathology

Scholarship for students who meet academic requirements and enroll in a graduate speech pathology program. Commission makes final awards July 1. Write to the address below for more information.

Delaware Higher Education Commission
Carvel State Office Building
820 North French Street, #4F
Wilmington, DE   19801

1087 Spencer Dissertation Year Fellowships for Research in Education

AMOUNT: Maximum: $17000   **DEADLINE:** October 22
FIELDS/MAJORS: Education

Fellowships are available for doctoral students who have completed all program requirements except the dissertation. Dissertation topics must concern education and all pre-dissertation requirements must be completed by June 1, 1998. To encourage research relevant to the improvement of education. Approximately thirty awards offered annually. Write to the address listed for information.

Spencer Foundation, Inc.
Dissertation Fellowship Program
900 N. Michigan Avenue, Suite 2800
Chicago, IL   60611-1542

1088 Spencer Postdoctoral Fellowship Program

AMOUNT: $45000   **DEADLINE:** December 11
FIELDS/MAJORS: Education, Humanities, Social Science, Behavioral Sciences

Postdoctoral fellowships for persons in education, the humanities, or the social and behavioral sciences. They must describe research with relevance to education. Must have Ph.D. or Ed.D. within last five years. Up to thirty fellowships per year. Amount shown may be for one- or two-year awards. This is a non-residential fellowship. Write to the address below for complete details.

National Academy of Education
Stanford University, School of Education
CERAS-108
Stanford, CA   94305

1089 Spencer T. Olin Fellowships for Women in Graduate Study

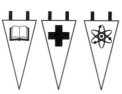

AMOUNT: $20000–$33000
DEADLINE: February 1
FIELDS/MAJORS: See Listing of Fields Below

Fellowships are available at Washington University for female scholars in one of the following fields: biology, biomedicine, humanities, physics, math, social science, behavioral science, architecture, business administration, engineering, fine arts, law, medicine, and social work. For master's and doctoral level study. Write to the address below for information.

Monticello College Foundation/
    Washington University
Margaret Watkins, Olin Fellowship Prog.
Campus Box 1187, One Brookings Drive
St. Louis, MO   63130

1090 SRC Education Alliance Graduate Fellowship

AMOUNT: None Specified   **DEADLINE:** February 3
FIELDS/MAJORS: Microelectronics

Must be U.S. or Canadian citizen or permanent resident and pursuing a Ph.D. program in areas relevant to microelectronics and is or will be performing research under the guidance of an SRC-designated faculty member. Should be interested in the possibility of an academic career in areas relevant to microelectronics at a U.S. university or employment with an SRC member. Write to the address below for complete details.

Semiconductor Research Corporation Education Alliance
Graduate Fellowship Program
PO Box 12053
Research Triangle Park, NC   27709

1091 SREB Doctoral Scholars Program

AMOUNT: $12000   **DEADLINE:** April 1
FIELDS/MAJORS: All Areas of Study

Awards are available for the purpose of encouraging ethnic minority students to pursue doctoral degrees and become college level teachers. Preference is given to science, engineering, and mathematics students. For residents of Alabama, Arkansas, Florida, Georgia, Kentucky, Louisiana, Maryland, Virginia, Mississippi, North Carolina, Oklahoma, South Carolina, Texas, Tennessee, and West Virginia. Write to the address below for information.

Southern Regional Education Board
592 Tenth Street, NW
Atlanta, GA   30318

1092 State Medical Board of Georgia Scholarships

AMOUNT: None Specified   **DEADLINE:** May 15
FIELDS/MAJORS: Medicine

Scholarships are available for Georgia resident medical students who plan to practice medicine in a rural area of Georgia upon graduation. Write to the address below for information.

State Medical Board of Georgia
270 Washington Street, SW, 7th Floor
Atlanta, GA   30334

1093 Stephen and Milah Lynn Endowment

AMOUNT: $600   **DEADLINE:** February 8
FIELDS/MAJORS: Marketing

Scholarships are available at the University of Oklahoma, Norman for full-time Ph.D. candidates in marketing who have not yet proposed their dissertation. One award offered annually. Write to the address below for information.

University of Oklahoma, Norman
College of Business Administration
307 W. Brooks
Norman, OK   73019

1094

Stoody-West Fellowship

AMOUNT: $6000   DEADLINE: February 15
FIELDS/MAJORS: Journalism (Religious)

Awards for Christian graduate students enrolled in journalism at accredited schools who plan a career in religious journalism. Write to the fellowship committee at the address below for details.

United Methodist Communications
Fellowship Committee, Public Media Div.
PO Box 320
Nashville, TN   37202

1095

Student Associate Membership Fellowships

AMOUNT: None Specified   DEADLINE: January 31
FIELDS/MAJORS: Anthropology, Art History, Classics

Awards are available for graduate students who have passed their qualifying examinations for the Ph.D. and do not intend to follow the regular program of the school. Write to the address below for more information.

American School of Classical Studies at Athens
Committee on Admissions and Fellowships
6-8 Charlton Street
Princeton, NJ   08540

1096

Student Award Program

AMOUNT: $3000   DEADLINE: April 30
FIELDS/MAJORS: Healthcare, Health Policy, Medicine (M.D., D.O., Ph.D.)

Stipends for doctoral (M.D. and Ph.D.) students interested in the improvement of health and medical care in the state of Michigan. Supports a wide range of activities including research, pilot projects, intervention/demonstration projects, feasibility studies, proposal development, and critical literature reviews. Must be a Michigan resident attending a Michigan school. Projects must address quality of care, cost containment, healthcare access, or a major public health/medical issue. Must focus (geographically) on the state of Michigan. Proposal required. Program announcement may be found in your department office or financial aid office. If unavailable, write to the address below.

Blue Cross Blue Shield of Michigan Foundation
Margie Nagel, Program Officer
600 Lafayette East, B243
Detroit, MI   48226

1097

Student Financial Aid—Loans

AMOUNT: $1000–$5000   DEADLINE: May 15
FIELDS/MAJORS: Medicine, Dentistry, Allied Health Fields

Delaware resident. Not for undergraduate study. In selecting applicants the academy considers academic record and need. The academy also administers the Delaware state "Delaware Institute of Medical Education and Research" program at the Jefferson Medical College. For full-time study. Write for complete details.

Delaware Academy of Medicine
1925 Lovering Avenue
Wilmington, DE   19806

1098

Student Loan Program

AMOUNT: Maximum: $5000   DEADLINE: February 1
FIELDS/MAJORS: Periodontology

Applicants must be postdoctoral candidates in periodontology. Must have completed at least four months of study in a periodontal speciality training program approved by the Council on Dental Education (ADA). Renewable. Twenty-two loans were made in 1992 (out of thirty-seven applications). Contact the address below for further information.

American Academy of Periodontology
Meeting and Membership Services Dept.
737 N. Michigan Avenue, #800
Chicago, IL   60611

1099

Student Loan Program

AMOUNT: None Specified   DEADLINE: None Specified
FIELDS/MAJORS: Osteopathic Medicine

Low interest loans to Washington residents who accept obligation to practice for three years in Washington state following training. Must be U.S. citizens. Must have completed at least one semester or quarter. Interest is at 6% per annum, commencing accrual at the completion of college. Write to the executive vice president at the address below for details.

Washington Osteopathic Foundation
PO Box 16486
Seattle, WA   98116

1100

Student Research Award

AMOUNT: $500   DEADLINE: December 8
FIELDS/MAJORS: Geriatrics

Awards will be given to the student presenting the most outstanding paper or poster at the AGS annual meeting. Awardee will be chosen based on originality, scientific merit, and relevance of the research. All abstracts must be submitted on the official AGS abstract form. Write to the address listed for more information. You may call AGS at 212-308-1414 to obtain copies of the abstract form.

American Geriatrics Society
770 Lexington Avenue, Suite 300
New York, NY   10021

1101

Student Research Fellowships

AMOUNT: $2100   DEADLINE: January 15
FIELDS/MAJORS: Dental Research

For students enrolled in an accredited D.D.S./D.M.D. or hygiene program at an accredited dental school within the U.S. Must be sponsored by a faculty member at that school. Should not be due to receive their degree in the year the award is given. Applicants may have an advanced degree in a basic science subject. Twenty-six awards offered annually. Contact the address below for complete information.

American Association for Dental Research
Patricia J. Reynolds
1619 Duke Street
Alexandria, VA   22314

1102

Student Research Fellowships in Liver/ Hepatic Research

AMOUNT: $2500   **DEADLINE:** December 31
FIELDS/MAJORS: Medicine, Medically Related Fields

Fellowships for M.D. and Ph.D. students to encourage them to gain exposure in the research laboratory, and possibly consider liver research as a career option. Fellowships are for three months. Must be full-time student at a graduate or medical school. Not for terminal Ph.D. funding. Write to the foundation at the address below for details.

American Liver Foundation
Student Research Fellowships
1425 Pompton Avenue
Cedar Grove, NJ   07009

1103

Student Research Grants in Sexuality

AMOUNT: None Specified   **DEADLINE:** February 1
FIELDS/MAJORS: Sexuality Studies

Grants for students doing scholarly research on sexuality. Applicants must be enrolled in a degree granting program. Write to the address below for more information.

Society for the Scientific Study of Sexuality
Ilsa L. Lottes, Ph.D.
PO Box 208
Mount Vernon, IA   52314

1104

Student Traineeship Research Grants

AMOUNT: $1500   **DEADLINE:** None Specified
FIELDS/MAJORS: Cystic Fibrosis Research

Doctoral (M.D. or Ph.D.) research grants for students who plan a career in research and have a lab project that can be completed in less than one year. Award intended to interest student in Cystic Fibrosis research and offset costs of the project. Contact the foundation for further information on application procedure.

Cystic Fibrosis Foundation
Medical/Research Programs
6931 Arlington Road
Bethesda, MD   20814

1105

Sub-Saharan Africa Dissertation Internship Awards

AMOUNT: $20000   **DEADLINE:** March 2
FIELDS/MAJORS: All Areas of Study

Fellowships are available to African scholars who have completed all the Ph.D. requirements except the dissertation. Award is to increase the quality of overseas advanced studies for outstanding African scholars and to enhance the relevance of their training to the process of economic development in Africa. Priority is given to agricultural and environmental majors. Write to the address listed for information.

Rockefeller Foundation
African Dissertation Internships
420 Fifth Avenue
New York, NY   10018

1106

Summer Fellowship Grants

AMOUNT: $2000   **DEADLINE:** May 15
FIELDS/MAJORS: Medical Research (Allergy/Immunology)

Grants for medical students pursuing a career in the fields of allergy and immunology. Grants support summer research. Must be a full-time medical students who have successfully completed at least eight months of medical school. Must be a U.S. or Canadian resident. Write to the address below for details.

American Academy of Allergy, Asthma, and Immunology
Summer Fellowship Grant
611 E. Wells Street
Milwaukee, WI   53202

1107

Summer Fellowships

AMOUNT: None Specified
DEADLINE: November 1
FIELDS/MAJORS: Byzantine Studies (and Related), Landscape Architecture

Fellowships are available for a period of four to nine weeks and are open to all scholars at any graduate level (resident fellowships). Write to the address below for details.

Dumbarton Oaks
Office of the Director
1703 32nd Street, NW
Washington, DC   20007

1108

Summer Fellowships of the Electrochemical Society, Inc.

AMOUNT: None Specified   **DEADLINE:** January 1
FIELDS/MAJORS: Electrochemistry and Related Fields

Awards are available for graduate students enrolled in a college or university in the U.S. or Canada. Applicants must be studying a field related to the objectives of the Electrochemical Society. Renewable. Write to the address below for more information.

Electrochemical Society, Inc.
10 South Main Street
Pennington, NJ   08534

1109
Summer Medical Student Fellowship

AMOUNT: $2200   DEADLINE: February 1
FIELDS/MAJORS: Urology

Fellowships allowing highly qualified medical students to work in urology research laboratories for two months in the summer. Write to the address below for additional information. At least 2.8 GPA is required.

American Foundation for Urologic Disease, Inc.
Research Scholar Division
300 West Pratt Street, Suite 401
Baltimore, MD   21201

1110
Summer Scholarships in Epidemiology

AMOUNT: $2000   DEADLINE: April 1
FIELDS/MAJORS: Medical Research—Cystic Fibrosis

Scholarships are available for M.D.s currently working in cystic fibrosis to increase skills in epidemiology. Awards cover tuition and expenses of up to $2000 for selected summer epidemiology programs. Coursework should include biostatics and epidemiology, particularly clinical epidemiology and/or clinical trials. Write to the address below for details.

Cystic Fibrosis Foundation
Office of Grants Management
6931 Arlington Road
Bethesda, MD   20814

1111
Summer Session Scholarships

AMOUNT: Maximum: $300   DEADLINE: March 15
FIELDS/MAJORS: Teaching, Counseling

Open to credentialed classroom teachers and counselors. Applications available after January 1. Send a legal-sized SASE to the address listed for an application.

California Congress of Parents, Teachers, and Students, Inc.
930 Georgia Street, PO Box 15015
Los Angeles, CA   90015

1112
Susan Shuttleworth Stout Fellowship

AMOUNT: None Specified   DEADLINE: March 1
FIELDS/MAJORS: Exercise and Sports Science

Award open to graduate students who are U.S. citizens. Contact the address below for further information.

University of North Carolina, Greensboro
Financial Aid Office
723 Kenilworth Street
Greensboro, NC   27412

1113
T.A. Liang Memorial Award

AMOUNT: $500   DEADLINE: None Specified
FIELDS/MAJORS: Photogrammetry, Remote Sensing

Applicants must be a student member of the Society who is currently pursuing graduate-level studies. Based on scholastic record, research plans, recommendations, and community service activities. Write to the address below for more information.

American Society for Photogrammetry and Remote Sensing
ASPRS Awards Program
5410 Grosvenor Lane, Suite 210
Bethesda, MD   20814

1114
Tau Beta Pi—Deuchler Fellowship

AMOUNT: $10000   DEADLINE: January 15
FIELDS/MAJORS: Water Supply, Waste-Water Treatment, Ecological Disciplines

Award open to graduate members in any of the above fields. Contact the address listed for further information.

Tau Beta Pi-Alabama Power Company
D. Stephen Pierre Jr., P.E., Director
150 St. Joseph Street, PO Box 2247
Mobile, AL   36652

1115
Tau Beta Pi—King Fellowship

AMOUNT: $10000   DEADLINE: January 15
FIELDS/MAJORS: Engineering

Award open to graduate members whose leadership and participation in his/her national technical society's branch are judged outstanding. Contact the address listed for further information.

Tau Beta Pi-Alabama Power Company
D. Stephen Pierre Jr., P.E., Director
150 St. Joseph Street, PO Box 2247
Mobile, AL   36652

1116
Tau Beta Pi— Spencer Fellowship

AMOUNT: $10000   DEADLINE: January 15
FIELDS/MAJORS: Engineering

Award open to graduate members of Tau Beta Pi. Based on contributions made to applicant's undergraduate chapter and college. Contact the address listed for further information.

Tau Beta Pi-Alabama Power Company
D. Stephen Pierre Jr., P.E., Director
150 St. Joseph Street, PO Box 2247
Mobile, AL   36652

1117
Tau Beta Pi—Stark Fellowship

AMOUNT: $10000 DEADLINE: January 15
FIELDS/MAJORS: Fluid Power

Award open to Tau Beta Pi members who plan graduate study in the field of fluid power. Contact the address listed for further information.

Tau Beta Pi-Alabama Power Company
D. Stephen Pierre Jr., P.E., Director
150 St. Joseph Street, PO Box 2247
Mobile, AL   36652

1118
Tau Beta Pi— Williams Fellowship

AMOUNT: $10000 DEADLINE: January 15
FIELDS/MAJORS: Education, Engineering

Award open to graduate member who possesses outstanding cultural and ethical attributes and plans to earn a doctoral degree and become an engineering teacher. Contact the address listed for further information.

Tau Beta Pi-Alabama Power Company
D. Stephen Pierre Jr., P.E., Director
150 St. Joseph Street, PO Box 2247
Mobile, AL   36652

1119
Teachers of Visually Impaired and Blind Students Scholarships

AMOUNT: $3183 DEADLINE: June 15
FIELDS/MAJORS: Blind/Visually Impaired Education

Award for graduate students enrolled in an education program for visually impaired students. Must have a GPA of 3.0 or better. Eight awards offered annually. Contact the special education office for more information.

Portland State University
Special Education Program Office
204 School of Education Building
Portland, OR   97207

1120
Teaching Assistantships

AMOUNT: $14400 DEADLINE: January 15
FIELDS/MAJORS: Any Area of Study

Awarded for one year and may be renewed. The teaching assistant is expected to pursue graduate studies and assist in supervised undergraduate teaching. A tuition scholarship is normally provided in addition to the stipend. For more information write to the address below.

Vanderbilt University
411 Kirkland Hall
Nashville, TN 37240

1121
Teaching Projects Grants

AMOUNT: Maximum: $1000
DEADLINE: October 1
FIELDS/MAJORS: Korean Education

Grant supports planning, workshops, and material related to teaching about Korea or integrating Korean Studies topics in broader categories of instruction. Contact the address below for further information.

Association for Asian Studies, Inc.
University of Michigan
1 Lane Hall
Ann Arbor, MI   48109

1122
Technology Scholarship Program for Alabama Teachers

AMOUNT: None Specified DEADLINE: None Specified
FIELDS/MAJORS: Teaching

A state scholarship loan not to exceed the graduate tuition and fees for attendance at a public college or university. Students who are full-time, regularly certified Alabama public school teachers enrolled in approved courses or programs that incorporate new technologies in the curriculum. Write to the address below for details.

Alabama Commission on Higher Education
PO Box 302000
Montgomery, AL   36130

1123
Texas Library Association Research Grant/DEMCO, Inc.

AMOUNT: Maximum: $2000 DEADLINE: January 31
FIELDS/MAJORS: Library Science

Grants for Texas students to support research involving library use, resource sharing, administrative study, etc. Pilot studies and experimental programs are encouraged. Write to the address below for more information.

Texas Library Association Briscoe Library
Daniel H. Jones, Chair
7703 Floyd Curl Drive
San Antonio, TX   78284

1124
Texas Library Association Scholarships

AMOUNT: $500–$2000 DEADLINE: January 31
FIELDS/MAJORS: Library Science

Awards are for Texas graduate students to study at an ALA-accredited school in Texas leading to a library science degree. Write to the address below for more information.

Texas Library Association Briscoe Library
Daniel H. Jones, Chair
7703 Floyd Curl Drive
San Antonio, TX   78284

1125 Theatre Assistantships, College Teaching Fellowship

AMOUNT: $4400–$5900 DEADLINE: None Specified
FIELDS/MAJORS: Drama/Theatre, Fine Arts, Costume Design

Assistantships and fellowships for students in the MFA program in the School of Theatre at Florida State University. Awarded competitively. Must have a minimum GPA of 3.2 and a GRE score of 1150 or better. Assistantships also include a tuition waiver for 9 credit hours. Contact Graduate Fellowship Coordinator, at the address below, for details.

Florida State University School of Theatre
Graduate Fellowships Coordinator
School of Theatre
Tallahassee, FL 32306

1126 Theodore N. Ely Fund Scholarship

AMOUNT: None Specified
DEADLINE: January 2
FIELDS/MAJORS: Archaeology, Art History

Award open to graduate students in either of the above fields. Contact the address below for further information.

Bryn Mawr Graduate School of Arts and Sciences
101 N. Merion Avenue
Bryn Mawr, PA 19010

1127 Theodore Roosevelt Memorial Fund

AMOUNT: $200–$1000 DEADLINE: February 15
FIELDS/MAJORS: Natural History

Grants for study of North American fauna including field research, study of the collections at the American Museum of Natural History, or for work at any of the museum's field stations. Write to the address below for complete information.

American Museum of Natural History
Central Park West at 79th Street
New York, NY 10024

1128 Third-Year Law Scholarships

AMOUNT: $500–$1000 DEADLINE: September 1
FIELDS/MAJORS: Law

Scholarships are available at the University of Oklahoma, Norman for full-time, third-year law students. Includes the Charles B. Memminger Memorial, Jones, Givens, Gotcher, & Bogan, and Robert B. Looper Memorial scholarships. Individual award requirements will vary. Write to the address below for information.

University of Oklahoma, Norman
Admissions and Records, Law Center
Room 22, 300 Timberdell Road
Norman, OK 73019

1129 Thomas C. Rumble University Graduate Fellowship

AMOUNT: $10250 DEADLINE: February 3
FIELDS/MAJORS: All Areas of Study

Recipients must be enrolled in a Ph.D., M.M., or M.F.A. program at WSU during the semesters for which the award is given. Recipients may not hold other fellowships, scholarships, assistantships, or internships or hold full-time employment during fellowship period. Only full-time students are eligible. The fellowships are awarded primarily on the basis of academic qualifications to eligible graduate students with clearly defined objectives in their field of specialization and demonstrated capacity for independent study; financial need is also a consideration. Write to the address below for details.

Wayne State University
4302 Faculty/Administration Building
Detroit, MI 48202

1130 Thomas Jordan Doctoral Scholarships

AMOUNT: $3000 DEADLINE: February 1
FIELDS/MAJORS: Oncology Nursing

Grants available to doctoral students in the field of oncology nursing. All applicants must be currently licensed registered nurses. Write to the address listed for more information.

Oncology Nursing Foundation
501 Holiday Drive
Pittsburgh, PA 15220

1131 Thomas R. Camp Scholarship

AMOUNT: $5000 DEADLINE: January 15
FIELDS/MAJORS: Drinking Water Research

One award is given to master's or doctoral students who are doing applied research in the drinking water field. Based on excellence of academic record and potential to provide leadership in research activities. Write to the address below for more information.

American Water Works Association
Scholarship Coordinator
6666 W. Quincy Avenue
Denver, CO 80235

1132 Thomas S. Morgan Scholarship and William E. Parrish Scholarship

AMOUNT: $500 DEADLINE: March 15
FIELDS/MAJORS: History

Grants are available to members of Phi Alpha Theta who are entering graduate school for the first time. Two awards, one from each of the above named scholarships, offered annually. Write to address below for details. Please indicate the name of your chapter. Information may be available from your chapter officers.

Phi Alpha Theta—International Honor Society in History
Headquarters Office
50 College Drive
Allentown, PA 18104

1133

Thurmond E. Williamson Scholarship Fund

AMOUNT: None Specified   DEADLINE: March 1
FIELDS/MAJORS: Latin-American Studies

Awards are available at the University of New Mexico for graduate students in a Latin-American studies program. Applicant must exhibit outstanding academic achievement. Write to the address below for more information.

University of New Mexico, Albuquerque
Office of Financial Aid
Albuquerque, NM 87131

1134

Timothy Bigelow Graduate Scholarship

AMOUNT: None Specified   DEADLINE: May 15
FIELDS/MAJORS: Horticulture

Award for graduate students from New England in the field of horticulture. Must have a GPA of 3.0 or better. Preference given to students who plan to work in the nursery industry following graduation or to applicants with financial need. Write to the address below for more information.

Horticulture Research Institute
1250 I Street, NW
Suite 500
Washington, DC 20005

1135

Tostlebe-Ray Graduate Art Scholarship

AMOUNT: $2566   DEADLINE: March 1
FIELDS/MAJORS: Art, Studio Art

Open to graduates who have an overall minimum GPA of 3.0 majoring in art with an emphasis in a studio area of the department of art. Contact the address below for further information.

University of Northern Iowa
William W. Lew, Art Department Head
104 Kamerick Art Building
Cedar Falls, IA 50614

1136

Tourette Syndrome Association Research and Training Grants

AMOUNT: $5000–$25000   DEADLINE: December 20
FIELDS/MAJORS: Tourette Syndrome Related (Biochem, Epidemiology, Psychology, etc.)

Postdoctoral training fellowships and basic or clinical research grants for researchers whose areas of study are specifically relevant to Gilles De La Tourette Syndrome. To receive an application packet and a review of TSA literature (including areas of interest to TSA), interested persons should call 718-224-2999 or fax 718-279-9596. Preliminary screening based on letter of intent: brief description scientific basis of proposed project and approximate level of funding sought.

Tourette Syndrome Association, Inc.
Research and Training Grants
42-40 Bell Boulevard
Bayside, NY 11361

1137

Training Fellowship for Minorities in Substance Abuse Research

AMOUNT: $5000   DEADLINE: None Specified
FIELDS/MAJORS: Substance Abuse and Treatment, Epidemiology, Health Policy

Awards for minority students in the second or third year of study an any of the fields listed above. Must be a U.S. citizen. Ten awards presented annually. Send a SASE to the address below for more information.

National Medical Fellowships, Inc.
110 West 32nd
8th Floor
New York, NY 10001

1138

Training in the Neurosciences for Minorities

AMOUNT: $10000–$18000   DEADLINE: January 15
FIELDS/MAJORS: Neurosciences

Fellowships for ethnic minority students pursuing doctoral degrees in APA accredited doctoral programs in Psychology or Neuroscience. Must be a U.S. citizen or permanent resident. Write to the address below or call 202-336-6027 for more information.

American Psychological Association
Minority Fellowship Program/Neuroscience
750 First Street, NE
Washington, DC 20002

1139

Travel Grants to Visit the Gerald R. Ford Library

AMOUNT: Maximum: $2000   DEADLINE: September 15
FIELDS/MAJORS: U.S. Government Domestic, Economic, Foreign and National Policies

Grants are available to assist graduate researchers in traveling to the Gerald R. Ford Library in Ann Arbor, Michigan. These grants are to give researchers in the fields listed above access to the archival collections of the library. Twenty awards are offered annually. Write to the address below or email to library@fordlib.nara.gov for more information.

Gerald R. Ford Library
Mr. William McNitt
1000 Beal Avenue
Ann Arbor, MI 48109

1140
Trent R. Dames and William W. Moore Fellowships

AMOUNT: $5000–$10000   DEADLINE: February 20
FIELDS/MAJORS: Civil Engineering

Awards for practicing engineers or earth scientists, professors, or graduate students. To be used for post-graduate research to aid in the creation of new knowledge for the benefit and advancement of the profession of civil engineering. Contact your local ASCE chapter or write to the address below for details.

American Society of Civil Engineers
ASCE Student Services
345 E. 47th Street
New York, NY   10017

1141
Tulsa County Medical Society Scholarships

AMOUNT: None Specified   DEADLINE: July 1
FIELDS/MAJORS: Medicine

Scholarships available for medical students residing in Tulsa County. Includes the Dr. O.C. Armstrong, Dr. Anna Lavern Hays, Glass-Nelson, William R.R. and Ruth G. Loney, Dr. Maxwell A. Johnson Memorial, Martha Jane and Richard Jackson, Dr. Frank L. and Jessie O. Flack, Dr. John G. Matt, Glenda Ann Cole, and Wilma Jean Bowden Memorial awards. Individual award requirements may vary. Write to the address below for information.

University of Oklahoma, Norman
2021 South Lewis
Suite 560
Oklahoma City, OK   74014

1142
Tyner Scholarship

AMOUNT: $1500   DEADLINE: None Specified
FIELDS/MAJORS: Special Education, Psychology

Award open to full-time master's students in special education or a graduate student majoring in psychology. Contact the address below for further information.

University of Toledo
Dean, College of Education
301 Snyder Memorial
Toldeo, OH   43606

1143
University African-American Graduate Fellowships

AMOUNT: None Specified   DEADLINE: March 1
FIELDS/MAJORS: All Areas of Study

Six fellowships for African-American graduate students enrolled full-time at Syracuse University. Must enroll in at least one course in African-American studies (3 credit hours). Contact the Graduate Admissions Office for details.

Syracuse University
Office of Financial Aid
200 Archbold
Syracuse, NY   13244

1144
University Fellowship

AMOUNT: $9800   DEADLINE: January 15
FIELDS/MAJORS: All Areas of Study.

Fellowships offered to graduate students. Service-free and student is expected to devote full time to study and have no other occupation. For more information write to the address below.

Vanderbilt University
411 Kirkland Hall
Nashville, TN   37240

1145
University Fellowships and Assistantships

AMOUNT: None Specified   DEADLINE: None Specified
FIELDS/MAJORS: Any Area of Study

University fellowships, university minority fellowship, teaching assistantship, and research assistantships offered to graduate students. Almost all of the graduate students receive university support for their studies. For more information write to the address below.

University of Texas, Austin
Director of Graduate Admissions
2608 Whittis
Austin, TX   78713

1146
University Fellowships, Teaching and Research Assistantships

AMOUNT: $9000–$11000   DEADLINE: January 5
FIELDS/MAJORS: Zoology, Biology, Ecology, and Evolutionary Biology, and Related Fields

Fellowships and assistantships for graduate students in the Department of Zoology at University of Texas at Austin. Write to the address below for details.

University of Texas, Austin
Graduate Coordinator
Department of Zoology
Austin, TX   78712

1147
Urban Fellows Program

AMOUNT: $18000   DEADLINE: January 20
FIELDS/MAJORS: Urban Government, Public Administration, Planning, Public Service

Full-time program lasting nine months that combines work in mayoral offices and city agencies with an intensive seminar component that explores key issues facing New York City government. For recent bachelor's degree holder (must have received degree within past two years). Must be New York residents. Write to the address below for complete details.

New York City Department of Personnel
Urban Fellows Program
2 Washington Street, 15th Floor
New York, NY   10004

1148 Urban Studies Awards

AMOUNT: None Specified   DEADLINE: None Specified
FIELDS/MAJORS: Urban Studies

Internships for graduate students in the School of Urban Studies at Wayne State University. Write to the address below for details.

Wayne State University
Center for Urban Studies
3049 Faculty Administration Building
Detroit, MI   48202

1149 Valerie D. and Phillip M. Anderson Scholarships

AMOUNT: None Specified
DEADLINE: February 15
FIELDS/MAJORS: Education

Awards for graduate students at UW, Platteville in the area of education. Must have a GPA of 3.5 or better. One award is offered annually. Write to the address below for more information.

University of Wisconsin, Platteville
Office of Enrollment and Admissions
Platteville, WI   53818

1150 Van Deren Coke Fellowship

AMOUNT: None Specified   DEADLINE: March 1
FIELDS/MAJORS: Photography

Scholarships are available at the University of New Mexico for full-time graduate art students with a concentration in photography. Must have completed one semester of graduate study at UNM. Write to the address below for information.

University of New Mexico, Albuquerque
College of Fine Arts
Office of the Dean
Albuquerque, NM   87131

1151 Verne Catt McDowell Corporation Scholarship

AMOUNT: None Specified   DEADLINE: None Specified
FIELDS/MAJORS: Theology/Religion

Applicants must be members of the Christian Church (Disciples of Christ) seeking to become ministers and accepted into a graduate program at an approved institution of theological education. Preference given to students from Oregon. Four students are supported at a time. Write to the address below for details.

Verne Catt McDowell Corporation
PO Box 1336
Albany, OR   97321-0440

1152 Vida Dutton Scudder Fellowship

AMOUNT: Maximum: $2000
DEADLINE: December 16
FIELDS/MAJORS: Social Sciences, Political Science, Literature

Fellowships for Wellesley alumnae. For study in the field of social science, political science, or literature. Contact the address below for further information.

Wellesley College, Fellowships for Wellesley Alumnae
Sec'y, Committee on Graduate Fellowships
106 Central Street, Career Center
Wellesley, MA   02181

1153 Villa I. Tatti Fellowships

AMOUNT: Maximum: $30000
DEADLINE: October 15
FIELDS/MAJORS: Italian Renaissance

Fellowship program for postdoctoral scholars in the field of Italian Renaissance studies. Based on applicant's scholarly excellence and promise and the importance of the proposed research topic. Program includes a period of study in Florence, Italy. Write to the address below for more information.

Harvard University Center for Italian Renaissance Studies
University Place
124 Mt. Auburn Street
Cambridge, MA   02138

1154 Vincent A. Kleinfeld Research Fellowship

AMOUNT: Maximum: $5000   DEADLINE: April 18
FIELDS/MAJORS: Law, as related to the fields of drugs and food.

Competition for law students to write a research paper of publishable quality on a subject relevant to the field of food and drug law. Contact the address below for further information.

Food and Drug Law institute
Julia K. Ogden
1000 Vermont Avenue, NW, #200
Washington, DC   20005

1155 W. Jeff Ward Scholarship

AMOUNT: $2000   DEADLINE: February 1
FIELDS/MAJORS: Law

Awards for full-time entering law students who demonstrate financial need and academic promise. Priority given to residents of one of the following Kentucky counties: Pike, Floyd, Johnson, Martin, Knott, or Perry. Contact the Assistant Dean, Chase College of Law, for further information.

Northern Kentucky University
Chase College of Law
Office of Admissions
Highland Heights, KY   41099

1156
W.M. Keck Foundation Fellowships

AMOUNT: $2300   DEADLINE: December 15
FIELDS/MAJORS: Renaissance, 19th and 20th Century Literature, Colonial America

Awards for research to complete a dissertation or to begin a new project. Contact the address below for further information.

Huntington Library, Art Collections and Botanical Gardens
Robert C. Ritchie, Director of Research
1151 Oxford Road
San Marion, CA   91108

1157
Walter Byers Post-Graduate Scholarship

AMOUNT: Maximum: $12500   DEADLINE: January 20
FIELDS/MAJORS: All Areas of Study

Two scholarships for students who have participated in varsity level sports at an NCAA institution. Must be nominated, have a GPA of at least 3.5, and be within 30 semester hours of receiving degree. Write to address below for details.

National Collegiate Athletic Association
6201 College Boulevard
Overland Park, KS   66211

1158
Walter S. Barr Graduate Fellowships

AMOUNT: None Specified   DEADLINE: February 1
FIELDS/MAJORS: All Areas of Study

Fellowships available to Hampden County residents who are furthering their education as full-time graduate students. Write to the Executive Secretary at the address below for details.

Horace Smith Fund
Executive Secretary
1441 Main Street
Springfield, MA   01102

1159
Wanda and Donald Atkinson Scholarship

AMOUNT: None Specified   DEADLINE: March 1
FIELDS/MAJORS: Medicine

Awards are available at the University of New Mexico for medical students who demonstrate academic ability and financial need. Write to the address below for more information.

University of New Mexico, Albuquerque
Office of Financial Aid
Albuquerque, NM   87131

1160
Washington Library Association Scholarships

AMOUNT: None Specified   DEADLINE: January 31
FIELDS/MAJORS: Library Science

Scholarships for master's level students who have completed at least two quarters of graduate school in library science at the University of Washington. Must be a member of the Washington Library Association. Write to the address below for details or email at wasla@wla.org or wasla@wla.com.

Washington Library Association
Gail Willis
4016—1st Avenue, NE
Seattle, WA   98105

1161
Washington University Graduate Architecture Scholarships

AMOUNT: $1000–$9000   DEADLINE: None Specified
FIELDS/MAJORS: Architecture

Graduate fellowships, assistantships, and scholarships for graduate students in the School of Architecture at Washington University in St. Louis. Criteria for programs varies. Contact Graduate Admissions of the school for complete details.

Washington University—St. Louis
Graduate Admissions, School of Architecture
1 Brookings Drive Campus Box 1079
St. Louis, MO   63130

1162
Wayne Kay Graduate Fellowship

AMOUNT: $5000   DEADLINE: March 1
FIELDS/MAJORS: Manufacturing or Industrial Engineering

Scholarships for graduate students who are enrolled in a graduate program in manufacturing or industrial engineering. Ten fellowships are given annually. Write to the address below for details. Information may also be available in your department office. If writing, please specify what scholarship(s) you are interested in.

Society of Manufacturing Engineering Education Foundation
One SME Drive
PO Box 930
Dearborn, MI   48121

1163
Weil Graduate Foreign Scholarship

AMOUNT: None Specified   DEADLINE: March 1
FIELDS/MAJORS: All Areas of Study

Award open to international graduate students. Contact the address below for further information.

University of North Carolina, Greensboro
Financial Aid Office
723 Kenilworth Street
Greensboro, NC   27412

1164

Weiss/Brown Publication Subvention Award

AMOUNT: $15000   DEADLINE: January 20
FIELDS/MAJORS: Renaissance French/Italian Literature, Culture, Music, Theatre

Applicants must be authors of scholarly books already accepted for publication. Awards are to subsidize the publication of other materials covering European Civilization before 1700. Contact the address below for further information.

Newberry Library—Center for Renaissance Studies
Office of Research and Education
60 W. Walton Street
Chicago, IL   60610

1165

Welfare Training Stipend

AMOUNT: $6000   DEADLINE: March 1
FIELDS/MAJORS: Social Work

Award for graduate minority students who are interested in a career in child welfare services and are entering the second year of field placement. One or more awards offered annually. Contact the Graduate School of Social Work for more information.

Portland State University
Graduate School of Social Work
300 University Center Building
Portland, OR   97207

1166

Wexner Graduate Fellowship Program

AMOUNT: None Specified
DEADLINE: February 1
FIELDS/MAJORS: Jewish Studies

Awards for North American students who are college graduates and plan to enter a graduate program in preparation for a career in Jewish Education, communal service, the Rabbinate, the Cantorate, or Jewish studies. Write to the address below for more information.

Wexner Foundation
158 W. Main Street
PO Box 668
New Albany, OH   43054

1167

Wharton Doctoral Fellowships in Risk and Insurance

AMOUNT: Maximum: $36000   DEADLINE: February 1
FIELDS/MAJORS: Insurance/Actuarial Science, Risk Management

Doctoral fellowships available at the Wharton School of Business. Must be a U.S. or Canadian citizen. Summer and postdoctoral fellowships are also available. Write to the address below for complete details.

S.S. Huebner Foundation for Insurance Education
Executive Director
3733 Spruce Street, 430 Vance Hall
Philadelphia, PA   19104

1168

Whiting Fellowships in the Humanities

AMOUNT: None Specified   DEADLINE: None Specified
FIELDS/MAJORS: Humanities

Dissertation fellowships for students in their final year of writing at one of the following schools: Bryn Mawr, University of Chicago, Columbia, Harvard, Princeton, Stanford, or Yale. Selection/nomination of candidates is made by their departments. The foundation does not send out or receive applications. Contact your department.

Mrs. Giles Whiting Foundation
1133 Avenue of the Americas
22nd Floor
New York, NY   10036

1169

WICHE Doctoral Scholars Program

AMOUNT: None Specified
DEADLINE: None Specified
FIELDS/MAJORS: All Areas of Study

Awards are available for the purpose of encouraging ethnic minority students to pursue doctoral degrees and become college level teachers. Preference is given to science, engineering and mathematics students. For residents of Alaska, Arizona, Colorado, Hawaii, Idaho, Montana, Nevada, Oregon, Utah, North Dakota, New Mexico, South Dakota, Washington, and Wyoming. Write to the address below for information.

Western Interstate Commission for Higher Education
PO Drawer P
Boulder, CO   80301

1170

WICHE Professional Student Exchange Program

AMOUNT: None Specified   DEADLINE: None Specified
FIELDS/MAJORS: See Listing Below

The student exchange program helps Alaska residents obtain access to eight fields of graduate education not available in Alaska, but made available at participating institutions in other western states at reduced tuition rate. Fields include dentistry, medicine, occupational therapy, optometry, podiatry, osteopathy, physical therapy, and veterinary medicine. Write to the address below for information.

Alaska Commission on Post-Secondary Education
WICHE Certifying Office
3030 Vintage Boulevard
Juneau, AK   99801

1171
Wiebe Public Service Fellowship

AMOUNT: None Specified   DEADLINE: None Specified
FIELDS/MAJORS: Public Service

Applicants must be full-time graduate students who are residents of New York or students attending New York schools. This is a fellowship in the New York state government, not on-campus financial aid. Applicants should be exceptionally well-suited for placement in a high level leadership office. Write to Dr. Russell J. Williams, Director, at the address below for details.

New York State Senate
Senate Student Programs
90 South Swan Street, Room 401
Albany, NY   12247

1172
Wilhelm-Frankowski Medical Education Scholarship

AMOUNT: $3500–$5000   DEADLINE: April 30
FIELDS/MAJORS: Medicine, Osteopathic Medicine

Open to student members in the first, second, or third year of medical or osteopathic medical school. Criteria included are community service, participation in women's health issues, and participation in student medical groups other than AMWA. Contact the address below for further information.

American Medical Women's Association Foundation
Maria Glanz
801 N. Fairfax Street, #400
Alexandria, VA   22314

1173
William A. Fischer Memorial Scholarship

AMOUNT: $2000   DEADLINE: None Specified
FIELDS/MAJORS: Remote Sensing

Award is to facilitate graduate-level studies and career goals adjudged to address new and innovative uses of remote sensing data/techniques that relate to natural, cultural, or agricultural resources. Awards are restricted to members of ASPRS. Write to the address below for more information.

American Society for Photogrammetry and Remote Sensing
ASPRS Awards Program
5410 Grosvenor Lane, Suite 210
Bethesda, MD   20814

1174
William and Mary Graduate Awards

AMOUNT: None Specified
DEADLINE: February 1
FIELDS/MAJORS: American History, American Culture, Historical Archaeology

For master's and doctoral students at William and Mary in the above areas. Master's awards are limited to one year of support. Apprenticeship and internship programs at the Institute of Early American History and Culture, the SWEM Library, and the Colonial Williamsburg Foundation are also available. Write to the address below for details. Request for consideration for financial aid programs for new students must be made at the same time as application to the graduate program.

College of William and Mary—Department of History
Director of the Graduate Program
PO Box 8795
Williamsburg, VA   23187

1175
William B. Keeling Dissertation Award

AMOUNT: $1500   DEADLINE: March 1
FIELDS/MAJORS: Hotel-Restaurant Administration, Travel and Tourism

Graduate students who have completed or are about to complete doctoral dissertation in a travel/tourism related area are eligible for this award. Applicants are asked to submit abstract. Finalists will be judged on final dissertation. Write to the address below for details.

Travel and Tourism Research Association
10200 W. 44th Avenue
Suite 304
Wheat Ridge, CO   80033

1176
William C. Ezell Fellowship

AMOUNT: Maximum: $6000   DEADLINE: May 15
FIELDS/MAJORS: Optometry

Fellowships are available for master's or doctoral candidates in optometry who are pursuing a degree on a full-time basis. Write to the address below or contact your department of optometry for information.

American Optometric Foundation
Ezell Fellowship
6110 Executive Boulevard, Suite 506
Rockville, MD   20852

1177
William C. Stokoe Scholarship

AMOUNT: $1000   DEADLINE: March 15
FIELDS/MAJORS: Deaf Education, Sign Language

Must be a deaf student who is pursuing part-time or full-time graduate studies in a field related to sign language or the deaf community, or is developing a special project on one of these topics. Write to the address below for details.

National Association of the Deaf
Stokoe Scholarship Secretary
814 Thayer Avenue
Silver Spring, MD   20910

1178
William F. Miller, M.D./ H. Frederic Helmholz Jr., M.D., Scholarships

AMOUNT: $1000–$3000   DEADLINE: June 30
FIELDS/MAJORS: Respiratory Therapy

Scholarship for a respiratory care practitioner who is pursuing a degree beyond the bachelor's level. GPA of at least 3.0 is required. Awards for research, master's thesis, or doctoral dissertation. Write to the address below for details.

American Respiratory Care Foundation
11030 Ables Lane
Dallas, TX 75229

1179
William G. and Kate Hodge Lane Fellowship

AMOUNT: None Specified   DEADLINE: None Specified
FIELDS/MAJORS: English

Award open to graduate students who are U.S. citizens. Preference to student with interest in 19th century British literature. Contact the address below for further information.

University of North Carolina, Greensboro
Financial Aid Office
723 Kenilworth Street
Greensboro, NC 27412

1180
William H. Greaves Scholarship

AMOUNT: $1410   DEADLINE: February 1
FIELDS/MAJORS: Law

Applicants must be accepted by the Chase College of Law. Incoming students will be considered by their undergraduate GPA and LSAT scores among other factors. Continuing students must have a GPA of 3.0 or higher. Contact the Assistant Dean, Chase College of Law, for further information.

Northern Kentucky University
Chase College of Law
Office of Admissions
Highland Heights, KY 41099

1181
Willis H. Carrier Graduate Research Fellowship

AMOUNT: Maximum: $20000   DEADLINE: December 1
FIELDS/MAJORS: Research

Open to graduate research students at Purdue University. Contact the address below for further information. At least 3.0 GPA required.

American Society of Heating, Refrigerating and Air-Conditioning Engineers
Scholarship Program
1791 Tullie Circle NE
Atlanta, GA 30329

1182
Wilson-Cook Endoscopic Research Scholar Award

AMOUNT: $36000   DEADLINE: January 9
FIELDS/MAJORS: Endoscopic Research

Applicants must hold full-time faculty positions at universities or professional institutes. Young faculty, reaching the level of assistant professor or equivalent, are eligible. Candidates must devote at least thirty percent of their effort in research related to gastrointestinal endoscopy. Five awards are given annually. Contact the address below for further information or websites: http://www.gastro.org; http://www.asge.org; or http://hepar-sfgh.ucsf.edu.

American Digestive Health Foundation
Ms. Irene Kuo
7910 Woodmont Avenue, 7th Floor
Bethesda, MD 20814

1183
Winterthur Museum Fellowships

AMOUNT: $2000–$30000
DEADLINE: January 15
FIELDS/MAJORS: See Listing Below

Fellowships are available for doctoral and postdoctoral research at the Winterthur Museum and Library in African-American history, cultural history, historic preservation, folklore, anthropology, archaeology, art history, decorative arts, material culture, preindustrial technology, women's history, architectural history, and urban studies. Generally, stipends are $1000 to $2000 per month and the fellowships range from one to six months. Must be U.S. citizens to apply. Write to the address below for information.

Winterthur Museum and Library
Advanced Studies Office
Research Fellowship Program
Winterthur, DE 19735

1184
Wolcott Foundation Fellowships

AMOUNT: $1800   DEADLINE: February 1
FIELDS/MAJORS: Business Administration, Public Management, International Affairs

Fellowships for master's degree students at George Washington University. Award is considered a grant if for four years after graduation, recipients work in federal, state, or local government or in select private international business. Some preference given to persons active in Masonic activities (Demolay, Job's Daughters, Rainbow, etc.). Must be a U.S. citizen. Information is available from the address below.

High Twelve International
Wolcott Foundation Fellowships at GWU
402 Beasley Street
Monroe, LA 71203

1185
Women's Auxiliary to Greater Albuquerque Medical Assoc. Scholarship

AMOUNT: None Specified   DEADLINE: March 1
FIELDS/MAJORS: Medicine

Awards are available at the University of New Mexico for medical students with demonstrated merit and qualities of heart and mind that indicate humanitarian principles dedicated to high ideals of medical practice. Write to the address below for more information.

University of New Mexico, Albuquerque
Office of Financial Aid
Albuquerque, NM 87131

1186 Women's Research and Education Institute Congressional Fellowship

AMOUNT: None Specified   DEADLINE: February 15
FIELDS/MAJORS: Women and Public Policy Issues

Annual fellowship program that places women graduate students in congressional offices and on strategic committee staffs. Encouraging more effective participation by women in the formation of policy at all levels. Must be currently enrolled in a graduate degree program. Award is tuition and a living stipend for an academic year. Write to the address below for details and enclose a SASE.

Women's Research and Education Institute
Shari Miles, Director
1750 New York Avenue, NW, # 350
Washington, DC   20006

1187 Women's Studies Research Grants

AMOUNT: $1500   DEADLINE: November 1
FIELDS/MAJORS: Women's Studies

For doctoral candidates in the above fields who will soon complete all doctoral requirements except the dissertation. These grants are to be used for research expenses connected with the dissertation. The purpose is to encourage original and significant research on topics about women. Approximately twenty grants per year. Write to the attention of Women's Studies Department for further information. Application request deadline is October 18.

Woodrow Wilson National Fellowship Foundation
Women's Studies Research Grants
Cn 5281
Princeton, NJ   08543

1188 Woodrow Wilson Fellowships

AMOUNT: $43000   DEADLINE: October 1
FIELDS/MAJORS: Research in Humanities, Social Sciences

Residential fellowships for postdoctoral scholars for advanced research in the fields above. Selection primarily based on scholarly promise, importance, and originality of project proposal, and the likelihood that the work will advance basic understanding of the topic of study. Applicants must hold a doctorate or have equivalent professional accomplishments. Write to the address listed for more information.

Woodrow Wilson International Center
Fellowships Office
1000 Jefferson Drive, SW, SI MRC 022
Washington, DC   20560

1189 Woodrow Wilson Memorial Scholarship

AMOUNT: None Specified   DEADLINE: None Specified
FIELDS/MAJORS: Law

Scholarships for students in the School of Law at the University of Virginia who are direct descendants of worthy confederates. Must be able to prove lineage. Contact the UDC nearest you for details. If the address is unknown, write to the address below for further information and address.

United Daughters of the Confederacy
Scholarship Coordinator
328 North Boulevard
Richmond, VA   23220

1190 Workshops and Coursesto Improve Language Teaching and Pedagogy

AMOUNT: Maximum: $5000   DEADLINE: October 1
FIELDS/MAJORS: Japanese Language

Grants are available for scholars to design workshops or courses to improve the teaching of the Japanese language at the college or pre-college level. Applicants should be prepared to explain the character or rationale of their project and be able to prepare a budget estimate. Write to the address below for more information.

Northeast Asia Council Association for Asian Studies
1 Lane Hall
University of Michigan
Ann Arbor, MI   48109

1191 Wyeth Fellowship

AMOUNT: $16000   DEADLINE: November 15
FIELDS/MAJORS: American Art

Two-year fellowships are available for doctoral scholars researching for the dissertation. One year will be spent on research, and one year will be spent at the National Gallery of Art. Applicants must know two foreign languages related to the topic of the dissertation and be U.S. citizens or legal residents. One fellowship is given annually. Write to the address below for information.

National Gallery of Art
Center for Advanced Study in Visual Arts
Predoctoral Fellowship Program
Washington, DC   20565

1192 Wyeth-Ayerst Scholarships

AMOUNT: $2000   DEADLINE: April 15
FIELDS/MAJORS: Bio/Medical Research and Technology, Pharmaceuticals, Public Health

Scholarships are open to women twenty-five years of age or older who are U.S. citizens studying in one of the fields above. Applicants must be graduating within twelve to twenty-four months from September 1, demonstrate need for financial assistance, and be accepted into an accredited program of course study at a U.S. institution. Student must have a plan to use the training to upgrade skills for career advancement, to train for a new career field, or to enter or re-enter the job market. Write to the address below for details.

Business and Professional Women's Foundation
Scholarships
2012 Massachusetts Avenue, NW
Washington, DC   20036

1193
Y.C. Hsu Memorial Award

AMOUNT: None Specified   DEADLINE: March 1
FIELDS/MAJORS: Mechanical Engineering

Awards are available at the University of New Mexico for students who have received a graduate degree in the field of mechanical engineering in the past twenty-three months. Must have demonstrated excellence in graduate work. Write to the address below for more information.

University of New Mexico, Albuquerque
Office of Financial Aid
Albuquerque, NM   87131

1194
Zeneca Pharmaceuticals Underserved Healthcare Grant

AMOUNT: $5000   DEADLINE: None Specified
FIELDS/MAJORS: Osteopathic Medicine

Grants for third-year students committed to practice in underserved minority populations. Grant is intended to encourage the participation of minority students in this field. Write to the address below for more information. Applications are available from the foundation office after January 1.

National Osteopathic Foundation
5775G Peachtree-Dunwoody Road
Suite 500
Atlanta, GA   30342

1195
Zola N. and Lawrence R. Nell Educational Trust Scholarship Program

AMOUNT: $1500–$3000   DEADLINE: May 1
FIELDS/MAJORS: Medicine, Dentistry, or Related Fields

Applicants must be graduates of a high school in Segdwick County, Kansas (Wichita, Kansas area). Must be qualified students who have been accepted for the study of medicine, dentistry, or other health practitioners programs at the post-baccalaureate level and return to Kansas for practice. Fifteen to twenty awards are offered annually. Write to the address below for more information.

Commerce Bank, N.A.
Attn: Judy Quick, IMG Dept.
PO Box 637
Wichita, KS   67201

Indexes

Major/Career Objective Index

Special Criteria Index

School Index

Major/Career Objective Index

FINE ARTS

HUMANITIES

✚ MEDICINE

⚛ SCIENCE

SOCIAL SCIENCES

VOCATIONAL

Special Criteria Index

School Index